ADOBE® PHOTOSHOP® ELEMENTS 9
CLASSROOM IN A BOOK®

The official training workbook from Adobe Systems

www.adobepress.com

Adobe® Photoshop® Elements 9 Classroom in a Book®

Adobe Press books are published by Peachpit, a division of Pearson Education located in Berkeley, California. For the latest on Adobe Press books, go to www.adobepress.com. To report errors, please send a note to errata@peachpit.com. For information on getting permission for reprints and excerpts, contact permissions@peachpit.com.

Printed and bound in the United States of America

ISBN-13:   978-0-321-74973-4
ISBN-10:   0-321-74973-1

9 8 7 6 5 4 3 2 1

WHAT'S ON THE DISC

Here is an overview of the contents of the Classroom in a Book disc

The *Adobe Photoshop Elements 9 Classroom in a Book* disc includes the lesson files that you'll need to complete the exercises in this book, as well as other content to help you learn more about Adobe Photoshop Elements 9 and use it with greater efficiency and ease. The diagram below represents the contents of the disc, which should help you locate the files you need.

Lesson files

Each lesson has its own folder inside the Lessons folder. You will need to copy these lesson folders to your hard drive before you can begin each lesson.

Adobe Press

ADOBE PRESS

Find information about other Adobe Press titles, covering the full spectrum of Adobe products, in the Online Resources file.

Online resources

Links to Adobe Community Help, product Help and Support pages, Adobe certification programs, Adobe TV, and other useful online resources can be found inside a handy HTML file. Just open it in your Web browser and click on the links, including a special link to this book's product page where you can access updates and bonus material.

CONTENTS

GETTING STARTED   **1**

About Classroom in a Book 1

Prerequisites 1

Requirements on your computer 1

Required skills 2

Installing Adobe Photoshop Elements 9 2

Copying the Classroom in a Book files 2

Copying the Lessons files from the CD 2

Creating a work folder 3

About catalog files 3

Additional resources 4

1   A QUICK TOUR OF PHOTOSHOP ELEMENTS   **6**

How Photoshop Elements works 8

Workflow 8

The library catalog file 9

Creating a new catalog 9

Importing media 10

Getting photos from files and folders 10

The Organizer workspace 12

About keyword tags 14

Reviewing and comparing 15

Comparing photos side-by-side 15

Choosing files 17

Viewing photos at full screen 17

Switching between the Organizer and the Editor 18

The Editor workspace 18

Multitouch support 20

Using panels and the Panel Bin 21

Sharing photos in e-mail 22

Getting photos from a digital camera 24

Using the Adobe Photo Downloader 24

Creating an Adobe ID 26

Signing up from the Welcome screen 26

Signing up from the Organizer or Editor 26

Signing in to your Photoshop.com account 27

Using Windows 7 features 27

Using Help 28

Navigating Help 28

Search tips 28

Links to help in the application 29

Hot-linked tips 29

Additional resources 29

Review questions 30

Review answers 30

2 BASIC ORGANIZING   **32**

Getting started 34

Creating a new catalog 34

Getting photos 35

Dragging photos from Windows Explorer 36

Dragging photos from the Mac OS Finder 37

Importing attached keyword tags 38

Getting photos from a known location 38

Automatically fixing red eyes during import 40

Searching for photos to import 42

Importing from a digital camera. 43

Using watched folders 45

Viewing photo thumbnails in the Organizer 46

Using the Media Browser views 46

Using the Date View 49

Working with star ratings and keyword tags 52

Applying keyword tags and rating photos 53

Using Star ratings and the Hidden tag 54

Creating new categories and sub-categories. 55

Applying and editing category assignments 55

Creating and applying new keyword tags. 56

Converting keyword tags and categories 58

Working with keyword tags in Full Screen mode 60

Creating a keyword tag for your working files. 61

Using keyword tags to find pictures 62

Automatically finding faces for tagging. 64

Using People Recognition. 64

Tagging faces in the Media Browser 65

Tagging faces in the Label People dialog box 66

Review questions 69

Review answers. 69

3   ADVANCED ORGANIZING   70

Getting started 72

Creating a new catalog. 72

Advanced import options 73

Photo Downloader options 73

Acquiring still frames from a video. 78

Importing from a PDF document. 80

Scanning images on Windows. 82

Scanning images on Mac OS 83

Organizing photos. 84

Working with version sets 84

About stacks. 86

Tips for working with stacks 87

Stacking photos automatically 87

Creating albums 90

Working with smart albums 93

Viewing and finding photos 95

Viewing and managing files by folder location 96

Finding photos using details and metadata 98

Metadata support for audio and video files 98

Viewing video files 99

Hiding files 100

Using a text search to find photos 100

Finding photos by visual similarity 102

The Map view 103

Review questions 107

Review answers 107

4 CREATING PROJECTS   108

Getting started 110

Creating a new catalog 110

Importing the lesson files 112

Reconnecting missing files to a catalog 113

Exploring the artwork library 115

Creating a greeting card 118

Choosing a size and theme 118

Replacing the background image 121

Working with photos and frames 121

Adjusting a photo inside a frame 122

Working with backgrounds 123

Adding graphics from the Content library 125

Using layers and layer styles to refine a project 126

Producing a Photo Book 128

Rearranging the order of images in a project 128

Setting up a Photo Book layout. 129

Adding more photos to your Photo Book 133

Refining your Photo Book layout 133

Adding graphics 134

Adding text to your project 135

Assembling a photo collage. 138

Setting up your project page. 139

Adding a background. 141

Adding more images. 142

Working with layers to refine a project. 143

Adding graphics from the Content library. 144

Applying effects 144

Review questions. 146

Review answers. 146

5   PRINTING, SHARING, AND EXPORTING   148

Getting started 150

About printing. 151

Printing a contact sheet. 151

Printing a Picture Package. 154

Printing individual photos. 157

Ordering professionally printed photos online 159

Creating an Adobe ID 161

Signing up from the Welcome screen. 161

Signing up from the Organizer or Editor 161

Signing in to your Photoshop.com account 162

Launching the Inspiration Browser 162

Sharing pictures 163

Using Photo Mail 163

Creating an Online Album. 165

Customizing your Online Album 166

Sharing an existing album online. 168

Using an online sharing service 169

Backing up and synchronizing media files 171

Setting backup and synchronization options 172

Checking backup and synchronization status 173

Synchronizing separate computers 174

About exporting 174

Saving copies of your images for use on the Web 175

Review questions 177

Review answers 177

6   EASY EDITING   178

Getting started 180

Editing photos in the Organizer 180

Editing in Full Screen mode 182

Getting to know the Edit modes 184

Making easy color and lighting adjustments 187

Fixing files automatically in batches 187

Adding the auto-corrected files to the Organizer 188

Using Guided Edit 189

Correcting color in Guided Edit mode 189

Removing a color cast using Guided Edit 190

Adjusting lighting using Guided Edit 191

Creative fun with Guided Edit 192

Using Quick Edit mode 194

Applying automatic adjustments separately 194

Opening an image for Quick Fix editing 195

Using Smart Fix 195

Applying more automatic fixes 196

Using the Smart Brush 197

Applying a Smart Brush adjustment 198

Tweaking a Smart Paint adjustment 200

Applying multiple Smart Paint adjustments 201

Review questions 203

Review answers 203

7 ADJUSTING COLOR IN IMAGES

Getting started 206

Batch-processing the lesson files 206

Adding auto-corrected files to the Organizer. 207

Correcting color problems 208

Comparing methods of fixing color. 208

Creating extra working copies of an image 209

Correcting color automatically 210

Adjusting the results of an automatic fix manually 210

Tweaking the results of an automatic fix 212

Comparing results 214

Adjusting skin tones 215

Using the Touch Up tools 216

Brightening a smile 216

Setting up the Quick Edit workspace .217

Using the Whiten Teeth tool. 217

Adding to and subtracting from an adjustment selection. . .218

Modifying the Touch Up tool adjustment 221

Working with red eye 223

Using the automatic Red Eye Fix. 223

Using the Red Eye Removal tool 224

Making selections 226

Using the Selection Brush tool 228

Editing a saved selection 229

Using the Quick Selection tool 230

Working with selections. 232

Why won't Photoshop Elements do what I tell it to do? 234

Replacing the color of a pictured object 236

Using the Color Replacement tool 236

Replacing a color throughout an image. 238

Replacing a color in a limited area of an image. 240

About printing color pictures. 242

Working with color management. 242

Setting up color management. 242

Review questions 244

Review answers. 244

8   FIXING EXPOSURE PROBLEMS   246

Getting started 248

Batch-processing the lesson files 248

Brightening an underexposed image. 250

Applying Quick Fix adjustments 250

Adjusting exposure in Guided Edit mode 251

Fixing exposure in Full Edit mode. 253

Using blending modes. 253

About adjustment layers 255

Using adjustment layers to correct lighting 255

Correcting parts of an image selectively 256

Creating a selection. 257

Using layers to isolate parts of an image 260

Correcting underexposed areas 261

Adding more intensity 262

Adjusting color curves 264

Improving faded or overexposed images 265

Creating a set of duplicate files 265

Using blending modes to fix a faded image. 266

Adjusting shadows and highlights manually 268

Adjusting brightness and contrast manually 269

Adjusting levels. 269

Comparing results 271

Review questions 273

Review answers. 273

9   REPAIRING, RETOUCHING, AND RECOMPOSING IMAGES   274

Getting started 276

Using the Straighten tool 277

Improving the composition of an image 280

Recomposing a group photo 281

Fixing blemishes. 284

Removing wrinkles and spots 285

Preparing the file for editing 285

Using the Healing Brush tool 286

Refining the Healing Brush results. 288

Removing unwanted objects from images. 290

Using the Content-Aware healing feature. 291

Restoring a damaged photograph 294

Setting up for the exercises 294

Preparing a working copy of the image file 295

Using the Clone Stamp tool to fill in missing areas 296

Using the Selection Brush tool 298

Refining a saved selection. 300

What is a mask?. 300

Creating a layer mask 301

Filtering flaws out of the backdrop area. 303

Adding definition with the Smart Brush. 304

Merging layers. 306

Finishing up the project. 307

Review questions 309

Review answers. 309

10 WORKING WITH TEXT   **310**

Getting started 312

Placing text on an image 312

Using a text search to find a file 313

Working with the image canvas 313

Adding a border to a photo 314

Adding a text layer. 317

Adding a quick border 317

Editing a text layer 319

Saving a work file with layers 321

Overlaying text on an image 322

Distinguishing between pixel-based and vector graphics . .322

Creating a new document for the text .323

Applying a Layer Style to a text layer. .325

Locating the lesson files. 326

Adding the same text to multiple images 326

Working with layer blending modes 328

About type 330

Using Layer styles and distortions 331

Locating the lesson image 331

Adding a layer style 332

Warping text 334

Simplifying layers. 335

Working with simplified text 336

Working around transparency in a layer 338

Hiding, revealing, and deleting layers. 339

Working with paragraph type 340

Creating a type mask 341

Locating the lesson image 341

Working with the Type Mask tool. 341

Adding impact to a type mask. 344

Review questions. 346

Review answers. 346

11 COMBINING MULTIPLE IMAGES   **348**

Getting started 350

Merging photos into a panorama 350

Setting up the Photomerge Panorama options. 351

Photomerge Panorama layout options 352

Creating a Photomerge Panorama interactively 357

Vanishing point. 358

Cropping the merged image 359

Creating a composite group shot. 360

Working with Photomerge Group Shot 360

Removing unwelcome intruders 367

Using the Scene Cleaner 367

Blending differently exposed photos 371

Using the Photomerge Exposure tool. .371

Merging exposures automatically 372

Adjusting the automatically merged image 373

Merging exposures manually. 374

Combining multiple photographs in one file. 375

Arranging the image layers. 375

Creating a gradient layer mask 377

Matching the colors of blended images. 379

Cleaning up selection edges with the Defringe command. . 381

Review questions 384

Review answers. 384

12 ADVANCED EDITING TECHNIQUES   **386**

Getting started 388

Improving a camera raw image. 388

Working with camera raw images 388

Getting to know the Camera Raw window 389

What is a raw image? 390

Workflow overview for raw images 391

Adjusting the white balance 392

Camera Raw white balance settings .395

Working with the Temperature and Tint settings 396

Using the tone controls on a raw image 397

Saving the image 401

About the DNG format 401

About histograms. 402

Using the histogram 402

Understanding highlights and shadows 404

Adjusting levels. 404

About Unsharp Mask. 408

Applying the Unsharp Mask filter 409

Using the filter gallery 410

Creating effects with filters. 411

Experimenting with filters in the gallery 414

Using the Cookie Cutter tool 415

Creating your own cutter. 416

Cookie Cutter Shape Options. 416

Learning more. 418

Review questions 419

Review answers. 419

INDEX   **420**

GETTING STARTED

Adobe® Photoshop® Elements 9 delivers image-editing tools that balance power and versatility with ease of use. Whether you're a home user or hobbyist, a professional photographer or a business user, Photoshop Elements 9 makes it easy to produce good-looking pictures, share your stories in sophisticated creations for both print and web, and manage and safeguard your precious photos.

If you've used an earlier version of Photoshop Elements, you'll find that this Classroom in a Book® will teach you advanced skills and provide an introduction to the many new and improved features in this version. If you're new to Adobe Photoshop Elements, you'll learn the fundamental concepts and techniques that will help you master the application.

About Classroom in a Book

Adobe Photoshop Elements 9 Classroom in a Book is part of the official training series for Adobe graphics and publishing software developed with the support of Adobe product experts. Each lesson in this book is made up of a series of self-paced projects that will give you hands-on experience using Photoshop Elements 9.

The *Adobe Photoshop Elements 9 Classroom in a Book* includes a CD attached to the inside back cover. On the CD you'll find all the image files used for the lessons in this book, together with additional learning resources.

Prerequisites

Before you begin the lessons in this book, make sure that you and your computer are ready by following the tips and instructions on the next few pages.

Requirements on your computer

You'll need about 750 MB of free space on your hard disk—around 200 MB for the lesson files and up to 550 MB for the work files that you'll create as you work through the exercises.

Required skills

Note: In this book, the forward slash character (/) is used to separate equivalent terms and commands for Windows / Mac OS, in the order shown here.

The lessons in this book assume that you have a working knowledge of your computer and its operating system. Make sure that you know how to use the mouse and the standard menus and commands, and also how to open, save, and close files. Can you scroll (vertically and horizontally) within a window to see content that may not be visible in the displayed area? Do you know how to use context menus, which open when you right-click (Windows) / Control-click (Mac OS) items? If you need to review these basic and generic computer skills, see the documentation included with your Microsoft® Windows® or Apple® Mac® OS X software.

Installing Adobe Photoshop Elements 9

You must purchase the Adobe Photoshop Elements 9 software separately and install it on a computer running Windows Vista®, Windows® XP, Windows® 7, or Mac® OS X. For system requirements and complete instructions on installing the software, see the Photoshop Elements 9 Read Me file on the application disc and the accompanying documentation.

Copying the Classroom in a Book files

Note: The files on the CD are practice files, provided for your personal use in these lessons. You are not authorized to use these files commercially, or to publish or distribute them in any form without written permission from Adobe Systems, Inc. and the individual photographers who took the pictures, or other copyright holders.

The CD attached to the inside back cover of this book includes a Lessons folder containing all the digital files you'll need for the lessons. As you work through the exercises, learning to organize and manage these files is an essential part of many of the projects in this book. Keep the lesson files on your computer until you have completed all the exercises.

Copying the Lessons files from the CD

1 Create a new folder named **PSE9CIB** inside the *username/My Documents* (Windows) or *username/Documents* (Mac OS) folder on your computer.

2 Insert the *Adobe Photoshop Elements 9 Classroom in a Book* CD into your CD-ROM drive. For Windows users: if a message appears asking what you want Windows to do, choose Open Folder To View Files Using Windows Explorer, and then click OK. If no message appears, open My Computer and double-click the CD icon to open it.

3 Locate the Lessons folder on the CD and copy it to the PSE9CIB folder you've just created on your computer.

4 When your computer has finished copying the Lessons folder, remove the CD from your CD-ROM drive and put it away.

Creating a work folder

Now you need to create a folder for the work files that you'll produce as you work through the lessons in this book.

1 In Windows Explorer (Windows) / the Finder (Mac OS) open the Lessons folder that you copied to your new PSE9CIB folder on your hard disk.

2 Choose File > New > Folder (Windows) / File > New Folder (Mac OS). A new folder is created inside the Lessons folder. Type **My CIB Work** as the name for the new folder.

About catalog files

Photoshop Elements stores information about your images in a library catalog file, which enables you to conveniently manage the photos on your computer. The catalog file is a central concept in understanding how Photoshop Elements works.

Photoshop Elements doesn't actually "import" your images at all; for each image you import Photoshop Elements simply creates a new entry in the catalog that is linked to the source file, wherever it is stored. Whenever you assign a tag or a rating to a photo, or group images as an album, the catalog file is updated. All the work you put into organizing your growing photo library is recorded in the catalog.

As well as digital photographs, a catalog can include video and audio files, scans, PDF documents, and any presentations and layouts you might create in Photoshop Elements, such as slide shows, photo collages, and CD jacket designs.

The first time you launch Photoshop Elements it automatically creates a default catalog file (named My Catalog) on your hard disk. Although a single catalog can efficiently handle thousands of files, you can also establish separate catalogs for different purposes if that's the way you prefer to work.

For each of the first three lessons in this book—which deal with importing, organizing, sorting, and searching images—you'll create and load a new, dedicated catalog into which you'll import the lesson sample images. In this way, any mistakes you make will be easy to rectify; if you lose track—or simply wish to repeat the exercises—you can clear the catalog and start again without affecting the lessons to follow.

In Lesson 4—once you've worked through the lessons on organizing and have become familiar with the workspace—you'll create one more catalog that you can work with for the rest of the book.

Note: In this book, the forward arrow character (>) is used to denote submenus and commands found in the menu bar at the top of the workspace or in context and options menus; for example, Menu > Submenu > Command. The forward slash character (/) is used to separate equivalent keyboard shortcuts and commands for Windows / Mac OS, in the order shown here.

Additional resources

Adobe Photoshop Elements 9 Classroom in a Book is not meant to replace the documentation that comes with the program, nor to be a comprehensive reference for every feature; only the commands and options used in the lessons are explained in this book. For comprehensive information and tutorials about program features, please refer to these resources:

Adobe Community Help Community Help brings together active Adobe product users, Adobe product team members, authors, and experts to give you the most useful, relevant, and up-to-date information about Adobe products. Whether you're looking for a code sample or an answer to a problem, have a question about the software, or want to share a useful tip or recipe, you'll benefit from Community Help. Search results will show you not only content from Adobe, but also from the community. With Adobe Community Help you can:

- Access up-to-date definitive reference content online and offline
- Find the most relevant content contributed by experts from the Adobe community, on and off Adobe.com
- Comment on, rate, and contribute to content in the Adobe community
- Download Help content directly to your desktop for offline use
- Find related content with dynamic search and navigation tools

To access Community Help The Community Help application downloads when you first install Photoshop Elements 9. To invoke Help, press F1 or choose Help > Elements Organizer Help in the Organizer, or Help > Photoshop Elements Help in the Editor. This companion application lets you search and browse Adobe and community content, and to comment on and rate any article just as you would in the browser.

You can also download Adobe Help and language reference content for use offline, and subscribe to new content updates (which can be downloaded automatically) so that you'll always have the most up-to-date content for your Adobe product. You can download the application from www.adobe.com/support/chc/index.html

Adobe content is updated based on community feedback and contributions. You can contribute in several ways: you can add comments to both content and forums—including links to web content, or publish your own content using Community Publishing. You'll find more information about how to contribute at www.adobe.com/community/publishing/download.html

See http://community.adobe.com/help/profile/faq.html for answers to frequently asked questions about Community Help.

Adobe Photoshop Elements 9 Help and Support Point your browser to www.adobe.com/support/photoshopelements/ where you can find and browse Help and Support content on adobe.com.

Adobe TV http://tv.adobe.com is an online video resource for expert instruction and inspiration about Adobe products, including a How To channel to get you started with your product.

Resources for educators www.adobe.com/education includes three free curriculums that use an integrated approach to teaching Adobe software and can be used to prepare for the Adobe Certified Associate exams.

Also check out these useful links:

Adobe Forums http://forums.adobe.com lets you tap into peer-to-peer discussions, and questions and answers on Adobe products.

Adobe Marketplace & Exchange www.adobe.com/cfusion/exchange is a central resource for finding tools, services, extensions, code samples, and more to supplement and extend your Adobe products.

Adobe Photoshop Elements 9 product home page
http://www.adobe.com/products/photoshopel/

Adobe Labs http://labs.adobe.com gives you access to early builds of cutting-edge technology, as well as forums where you can interact with both the Adobe development teams building that technology and other like-minded members of the community.

1 A QUICK TOUR OF PHOTOSHOP ELEMENTS

Lesson overview

This lesson provides an overview of Adobe Photoshop Elements 9.

The exercises will familiarize you with the Photoshop Elements workspace and with many of the tools and procedures you'll use to capture and edit your digital images.

As you work through the exercises in this lesson you'll be introduced to the following basic skills and concepts:

• Working with the Organizer and the Editor

• Creating and loading Catalogs

• Attaching media

• Reviewing and comparing photos

• Sending photos in e-mail

• Using the Photo Downloader

• Creating an Adobe ID

• Using Photoshop Elements Help

 You'll probably need between one and two hours to complete this lesson.

Welcome to Adobe Photoshop Elements! Take a quick tour and get to know the Photoshop Elements workspace. You'll find all the power and versatility you'd expect from a Photoshop application in an easy-to-use, modular interface that will help you take your digital photography to a new level.

How Photoshop Elements works

Photoshop Elements has two primary workspaces: the Elements Organizer and the Editor. An easy way to understand these two components is to think of the Organizer as a library and browser for your photo collection, and the Editor as a darkroom and workshop.

You'll work in the Organizer to locate, import, manage, and share your photos and media files, and use the Editor to edit and adjust your images and to create presentations to showcase them.

Workflow

A typical Photoshop Elements workflow follows these basic steps:

- Bring images and other media into the Organizer from a digital camera, scanner, digital video camera, or a hard disk.

- Sort and group images and media by a variety of methods, including applying keyword tags and creating albums, in the Organizer.

- Edit, adjust, and correct images and media or add text in the Editor.

- Share your images and media by creating projects and presentations, using e-mail or an online sharing service, or by burning them to CD/DVD-ROM.

- Back up and synchronize your catalog to Photoshop.com and across multiple computers.

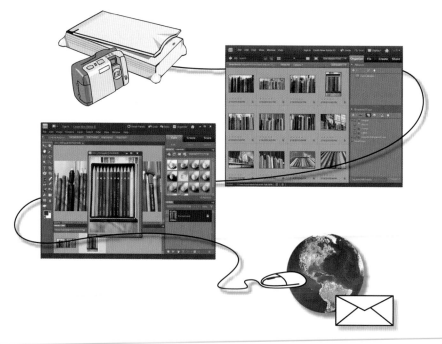

The library catalog file

Photoshop Elements stores information about your images in a library catalog file, which enables you to conveniently manage the photos on your computer from within the Organizer.

Photoshop Elements creates a new entry in the catalog file for each image you import. Whenever you assign a tag or a rating to a photo, or group images as an album, the catalog file is updated. In the Organizer, all your work is recorded in the catalog.

As well as digital photographs, a catalog can include video and audio files, scans, PDF documents, and any presentations and layouts you might create in Photoshop Elements, such as slide shows, photo collages, and CD jacket designs.

Creating a new catalog

The first time you launch Photoshop Elements it automatically creates a default catalog file (named My Catalog) on your hard disk. A single catalog can efficiently handle thousands of files, but you can also establish separate catalogs for different purposes if that's the way you prefer to work.

In this exercise you'll create and load a new catalog specifically to handle the sample files used for this lesson.

1   Start Adobe Photoshop Elements 9. Click the Organize button in the Welcome screen to launch the Elements Organizer module.

Note: Before you start working on this exercise, make sure that you've installed the software on your computer from the application CD (see the Photoshop Elements 9 documentation) and that you have correctly copied the Lessons folder from the CD in the back of this book onto your computer's hard disk (see "Copying the Classroom in a Book files" on page 2).

Note: You don't need to be concerned about the prompt to create an Adobe ID; this topic is covered later in this lesson.

2   When the Organizer has opened, choose File > Catalog.

3 In the Catalog Manager dialog box, click New. Don't change the location setting, which specifies where the Catalog file is stored.

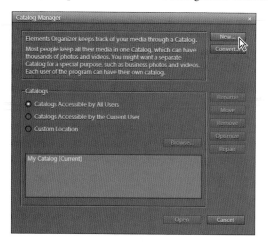

4 In the Enter A Name For The New Catalog dialog box, type **Lesson1** as the new catalog name, disable Import Free Music Into This Catalog, if necessary, and then click OK.

The new Lesson1 catalog is loaded in the Organizer. If you're ever unsure which catalog you're working with, you can always check the name of the currently active catalog in the lower left corner of the Organizer workspace.

Now that you have a special catalog that you'll use just for this lesson, all you need are some pictures to put in it.

Importing media

Before you can view, organize, and edit your photos in Photoshop Elements, you first need to link them to your catalog by importing them into your image library. Bringing your digital files into Photoshop Elements is easy.

Getting photos from files and folders

You can bring photos into Photoshop Elements from a variety of sources and in a number of different ways.

If your image files are already on your computer hard disk, you can either drag them directly into the Organizer workspace from Windows Explorer / the Finder or import them from within Photoshop Elements by using a menu command.

1   Choose File > Get Photos And Videos > From Files And Folders.

2   In the Get Photos And Videos From Files And Folders dialog box, navigate to and open the Lessons folder inside your PSE9CIB folder. Click once to select the Lesson01 folder.

3   Make sure that the option Automatically Fix Red Eyes is disabled. On Windows, you can also disable the Automatically Suggest Photo Stacks option.

4   Click Get Media.

The Getting Media dialog box appears briefly as the photos are imported. Since the imported photos contain keyword metadata, the Import Attached Keyword Tags dialog box appears. You'll learn more about keyword tags in Lessons 2 and 3.

5   In the Import Attached Keyword Tags dialog box, click Select All, and then click OK. Click OK to close any other alert dialog box.

Thumbnails of the imported photos appear in the Organizer's Media Browser pane.

The Organizer workspace

In the Organizer, the main work area is the Media Browser pane. This is where you sort, organize , and search your photos and media files, and preview the presentations that you create to showcase and share them. At the right of the Organizer window is the Task Pane, with tabs for the Organize, Fix, Create, and Share modes.

Note: The Elements Organizer is an integral part of both Adobe Photoshop Elements and Adobe Premiere Elements video editing software. You can import, manage, and view both your photos and video clips in Elements Organizer, which serves as a hub, allowing seamless integration of the two editing applications.

The Media Browser pane can display a single photo or show thumbnails of the files in your catalog arranged in a variety of ways. You can view your images sorted by import batch, folder location, or keywords—or presented in a calendar format in the Date view. The Media Browser makes it easy to browse, preview, organize, and search all the files in your catalog in one comprehensive window.

On the Organize tab of the Task Pane are the panels you'll use to sort, search and manage your photos by applying keyword tags and grouping them in albums.

The Fix tab offers tools for some of the most common editing tasks. For more sophisticated editing, you'll switch to one of the three editing modes in the Editor.

On the Create tab you'll find options and guidance for creating projects and presentations—from greeting cards to slide shows.

The Share tab offers a variety of options for sharing your files with your friends, family, clients, or the world at large by burning a CD or DVD, sending your photos as e-mail attachments or photo mail layouts, or publishing an online album.

1   Experiment with the Thumbnail Size slider above the Media Browser pane. Note that when you reduce the thumbnails to a very small size, the orange tags are no longer visible at the lower right of the image cells; set the thumbnails to a large enough size to see the tags.

2   Move the pointer over the orange tag below any of the images in the Media Browser; a tool tip appears to show that the image has been tagged with the keyword **Lesson 01**. This is the tag that you imported in the last step of the previous exercise.

3   In the Keyword Tags panel to the right of the thumbnail view, click the small triangle to expand the Imported Keyword Tags category; you can see that the newly imported **Lesson 01** tag is nested inside.

4   Double-click any thumbnail in the Media Browser. Use the arrow keys on your keyboard to cycle through the photos in the single photo view. When you're done, double-click the enlarged image to return to the thumbnail grid view.

> **Tip:** To switch to the single photo view, you can also press Ctrl+Shift+S (Windows)/ Command+Shift+S (Mac OS). In single photo view, you can use the controls below the enlarged image to add either a text or audio caption to a photo.

About keyword tags

Keyword tags are personalized labels, such as "Vacation" or "Beach," that you attach to photos, video clips, audio clips and other creations in the Media Browser to make it easier to organize and find them.

When you use keyword tags, there's no need to manually organize your photos in subject-specific folders or rename files with content-specific names.

In fact, both of the latter solutions confine a given photo to a single group. By contrast, you can assign multiple keyword tags to a photo, allowing it to be included in several different groupings. You can then easily retrieve the selection of images you want by clicking the appropriate keyword tag or tags in the Keyword Tags panel.

For example, you could create a "Beach - Normandy" keyword tag and attach it to every photo you took at that location. You can then instantly find all the photos with the Beach - Normandy keyword tag by clicking the Find box next to that tag in the Keyword Tags panel, even if the photos are stored in different folders on your hard disk.

You can create keyword tags to group your images any way you want. For example, you could create keyword tags for individual people, places and events in your life.

You can attach multiple keyword tags to your photos and easily run a search based on a combination of keyword tags to find a particular person at a particular place or event.

For example, you can search for all "Pauline" keyword tags and all "Sophie" keyword tags to find all pictures of Pauline taken together with her sister Sophie.

Or search for all "Pauline" keyword tags and all "Beach - Normandy" keyword tags to find all the pictures of Pauline vacationing at the beach in Normandy.

Use keyword tags to organize and find photos by their content or any other association. You'll learn more about keyword tags in Lessons 2 and 3.

Reviewing and comparing

Photoshop Elements provides several options for quickly and easily reviewing and comparing your images in the Elements Organizer. Use the Full Screen view to assess your photos in detail, or to effortlessly present a selection of images as an instant slideshow. The Side By Side viewing mode lets you keep one image fixed on one side of a split screen while you cycle through a selection of photos on the other—great for comparing composition and detail or for choosing the best of a series of similar shots. In both Full Screen and Side By Side viewing mode you can add keyword tags, add photos to albums, and even perform a range of editing tasks.

Comparing photos side-by-side

The Side By Side View lets you compare photos at any zoom level without the distraction of interface items such as windows, menus and panels.

1 Ctrl+Shift+A / Command+Shift+A to ensure that no images are selected in the Media Browser.

2 Click the Display button (■) near the upper right corner of the Organizer window, and choose Compare Photos Side By Side from the menu.

Because we made no selection in the Media Browser, the Organizer treats all the images visible in the Media Browser as the selection. The Film Strip at the right of the screen displays thumbnails of the photos in the selection.

▶ **Tip:** If you don't see the Film Strip at the right of the screen, press Ctrl+F / Command+F on your keyboard or click the button at the left end of the control bar at the bottom of the screen. If you don't see the control bar at the bottom of the screen, move the pointer; the control bar fades from view after a few seconds of inactivity.

By default, the photo on the left—image #1—is active, as indicated by the blue line surrounding the preview and the highlighted thumbnail in the Film Strip.

3 With the photo on the left—image #1—still active, scroll down the Film Strip at the right of the screen and click another thumbnail. Your new choice becomes the #1 image in the Side By Side view.

4 Click image #2—the photo on the right—to make it active. Click the forward and back navigation buttons in the control bar at the bottom of the screen, or use the arrow keys on your keyboard, to cycle the #2 preview through all the photos in the filmstrip, while the photo on the left of the screen remains fixed.

5 Click either image repeatedly to toggle between fit-to-view and 100% magnification. To compare detail at higher magnification, zoom in and out in the active image using the scroll-wheel on your mouse—or by pressing the Ctrl / Command key together with the plus (+) or minus (-) key. Drag the zoomed photo with the hand cursor to see a different portion of the image.

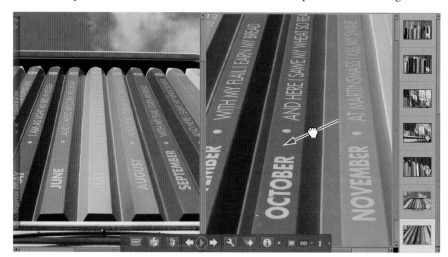

Tip: You can sync panning and zooming in the #1 and #2 photos by clicking the chain-link icon at the right end of the extended control bar. If you don't see the chain-link icon, click the triangle at the right end of the control bar to extend it.

As well as the forward and back navigation buttons, the control bar contains buttons that let you show and hide the Film Strip, the Quick Edit pane and the Quick Organize pane, where you can perform common editing tasks and tag images or group them by adding them to an album.

6 If necessary, click the triangle at the end of the control bar to extend it. Click the triangle next to the Side By Side View button (▣) to switch the split-screen arrangement from Side By Side to Above And Below.

7 Press the Esc key on your keyboard or click the Exit button (x) in the control bar to close the Side By Side view and return to the regular Organizer workspace.

Choosing files

In the Media Browser, there are a number of ways to select images. You can simply drag a selection marquee in the thumbnail view, but for better control, use your mouse together with a modifier key.

1   To select a series of four or five images that are in consecutive order, click the first photo in the series, and then hold down the Shift key as you click the last. All the photos in the range you Shift-clicked are selected.

2   Add three or four non-consecutive photos to the selection by holding down the Ctrl / Command key and clicking the thumbnails you wish to select. Keep your selection active for the next exercise.

Viewing photos at full screen

1   Click the View, Edit, Organize In Full Screen button, beside the Thumbnail Size slider in the bar above the thumbnails view.

2   The Full Screen view opens in slideshow mode, cycling through the images in the Film Strip. Experiment with the three buttons at the left of the control bar to show and hide the Film Strip and the Quick Edit and Quick Organize panels.

> **Tip:** You can also access Full Screen view by choosing from the menu on the Display button, or by clicking the Full Screen View button on the control bar in Side By Side view. You'll learn more about working in Full Screen view in the next lesson.

3   Try the two buttons to the right of the navigation controls to set Full Screen View and slideshow options and to choose a style for the transitions between slides. When you're done, press the Esc key to return to the Organizer.

Switching between the Organizer and the Editor

Although the Fix tab in the Organizer offers one-step tools for some of the most common editing tasks, for more sophisticated editing, you'll switch to the Editor.

1   Select any two photos in the Media Browser.

2   Do one of the following:

•   Choose Edit > Edit With Photoshop Elements.

•   Click the Fix tab in the Task Pane, and then click the Edit Photos button.

•   Right-click / Control-click either of the selected images and choose Edit With Photoshop Elements from the context menu.

Once both the Organizer and the Editor are open, you can move quickly between the two workspaces by using the task bar in Windows or the Dock in Mac OS.

The Editor workspace

The Editor is where you'll edit, adjust and correct your images, and create projects and presentations to showcase them. You can choose between the default Full Edit mode, with a powerful set of tools for color correction, special effects, and image enhancement, the Quick Edit mode, with simple tools and commands for quickly fixing common image problems, and the Guided Edit mode, which provides step-by-step instructions for a range of editing tasks.

In the Editor, the main work area is the Edit pane. This is where you'll work on your photos and the presentations that you create to showcase and share them. Below the Edit pane is the Project Bin, which provides easy access to the images you're working with, no matter how many files you have open. The Edit pane is flanked by the tool bar on the left and the Panel Bin on the right. The Panel Bin has tabs for Edit, Create, and Share modes. At the top of the Edit tab, you'll find buttons for switching between the three editing modes.

If you're new to digital imaging, the Quick Edit and Guided Edit modes make a good starting point for fixing and modifying your photos, and provide a great way to learn as you work. The Full Edit mode provides a more powerful and versatile image editing environment, with commands for correcting exposure and color and tools for making precise selections and fixing image imperfections. The Full Edit tool bar also includes painting and text editing tools. You can arrange the flexible Full Edit workspace to suit the way you prefer to work by floating, hiding, and showing panels or rearranging them in the Panel Bin.

1   In the Project Bin, double-click each of the thumbnails in turn to bring that photo to the front in the Edit pane, making it the active image.

2   Choose Preferences > General from the Edit / Photoshop Elements menu. On the General tab of the Preferences dialog box, click the check box to activate the option Allow Floating Documents In Full Edit Mode. Click OK.

3   Drag the front image by its name tab, away from its docked position to float above the Editor workspace.

Note: Once you've activated the option to allow floating document windows, this becomes the default for any image opened in Full Edit mode. Throughout the rest of this book however, it will be assumed that you are working with tabbed image windows that are docked (consolidated) in the Edit pane, unless otherwise specified. When you complete this exercise you'll disable floating document windows so that it'll be easier for you to follow the exercise steps as written.

Multitouch support

If the hardware and operating system of your computer supports the Touch functionality, you can use touch gestures to scroll, rotate, and zoom in on an image in the Editor. In Photoshop Elements 9, Multitouch is supported in all three Edit modes: Full Edit, Quick Fix, and Guided Edit.

Flicking scrolls the image horizontally or vertically. To scroll an image, touch the screen with one finger (Windows) / trackpad with two fingers (Mac OS) and move left or right, and up or down.

Twisting rotates the image clockwise or counterclockwise by 90 degrees. To rotate an image, touch two spots on the screen / trackpad, and twist the image just as you'd twist a real photo. Move both fingers in opposite directions or pivot one finger around the other.

Pinching in or out zooms in or out of the image. To zoom in, place two fingers on the screen / trackpad, and pinch. Similarly, , to zoom out of the image, place two fingers close together on the screen / trackpad, and then move them apart.

4 Explore the options for arranging image windows that are available from both the Window > Images menu, and from the menu on the Arrange button (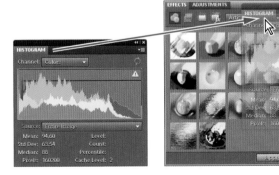) at the top of the Editor workspace to develop a feel for the way you prefer to work with your images. When you're done, Choose Preferences > General from the Edit / Photoshop Elements menu and disable floating documents. Click OK.

Using panels and the Panel Bin

In the Full Edit workspace, the Panel Bin provides a convenient location to organize the panels you use most often. By default, the Effects, Content and Layers panels are docked in the Panel Bin; other panels can be opened from the Window menu. All panels can either be kept docked in the Panel Bin or dragged to float in a convenient position above your image as you work. It's a good idea to familiarize yourself with organizing the Full Edit workspace so that you'll always have the controls you need at your fingertips.

1 Try each of the following tips and techniques:

- To open a panel that you don't see in the workspace, choose its name from the Window menu in the menu bar at the top of the workspace.

- To collapse an open panel so that you see only its header bar, choose its name from the Window menu or double-click its header bar.

- To float a panel above your image in the work area, drag it out of the Panel bin by its header bar. You can also float the Project Bin and the toolbox by dragging them away from their default positions.

- To return a floating panel to the Panel Bin, drag it into the Panel Bin and release the mouse button when you see a blue line indicating the new position. Place the panel between two others, or drag it onto another panel to create a tabbed panel group. Switch between grouped panels by clicking their name tabs. Drag the name tag to move a panel out of a group.

Tip: Floating panels can also be grouped in this manner, or snapped together one above the other.

- To collapse a floating panel to an icon, click the two white triangles at the right of the header bar. You can collapse a group of floating panels that are snapped together in the same manner.

- To expand a single panel in a collapsed group, choose its name from the Window menu.

- To close a panel, drag it out of the Panel Bin and click the close button (x) in its header bar (at the right on Windows, at the left for Mac OS) or click the small menu icon at the right of the header and choose Close from the panel's Options menu.

- To adjust the height of panels in the Panel Bin, drag the separator bars between panels up or down. To adjust the size of a floating panel, drag the panel's lower right corner. (Some panels can not be resized.)

- To return the workspace to the default arrangement, you can either choose Window > Reset Panels or click the Reset Panels button (⟳) at the top of the workspace.

2 Choose File > Close All to close both of the open images. Close the Editor window by clicking the Close button (in the top right corner of the workspace on Windows, at the upper left on Mac OS).

Sharing photos in e-mail

Have you ever had to wait a long time for an incoming e-mail to download, and then found that the e-mail contained photos at an unnecessarily high resolution? You can avoid imposing this inconvenience on others by using the Organizer's e-mail function, which exports images optimized specifically for sending via e-mail.

1 In the Media Browser, select a photo to attach to an e-mail.

Note: The first time you access this feature you may be presented with the E-mail dialog box. Choose your e-mail client (such as Outlook Express or Adobe E-mail Service / Mail or Microsoft Entourage) from the menu, and then click Continue. You can review or change your settings later by choosing Sharing from the Preferences menu.

2 Click the Share tab at the top of the Task Pane; then click the E-mail Attachments button.

3 Drag another photo from the Media Browser to the Items pane to add to your selection.

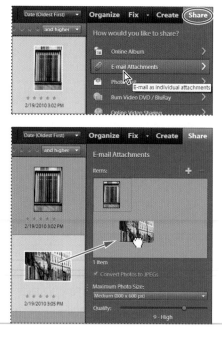

4 Choose Very Small (320 x 240 px) from the Maximum Photo Size menu and adjust the image quality using the Quality slider. The estimated file size and download time for a typical 56 Kbps dial-up modem are displayed for your reference. When you're done, click Next.

▷ **Tip:** The higher the quality setting, the larger the file size and therefore, the longer the download time.

5 Select the example text in the Message box and type a message of your own.

6 Click the Edit Recipients In Contact Book button (▨) above the Select Recipients box to create a new Contact Book entry. In the Contact Book dialog box, click New Contact .

7 In the New Contact dialog box, type in the personal details and e-mail address of the person to whom you wish to e-mail the picture. Click OK to close the New Contact dialog box, and then click OK again to close the Contact Book dialog box.

8 Make sure that there is a check mark beside the new contact in the Select Recipients box, and then click Next.

Photoshop Elements automatically launches your default e-mail application and opens an e-mail message with the images you selected already attached. You can edit the Subject line and the message as you wish. When you're done, either click Send if you want to go ahead and send this example e-mail, or close the message without saving or sending it.

9 Click the Organize tab above the Task Pane to switch back to the standard Elements Organizer workspace.

Getting photos from a digital camera

If you have a digital camera or memory card at hand with your own photos on it, you can step through this exercise using those images. Alternatively, you can simply follow the process in the book without performing the steps yourself, or skip to the next section and return to this exercise when you are prepared.

There are several ways that you can download photos from your camera to your hard disk, and then several ways to get them from your hard disk into Photoshop Elements, but these are two-step processes.

By far the most streamlined option is to download images from your camera or card reader directly into the Elements Organizer using the Adobe Photo Downloader—a one-step process that will save you time and get you started working with your photos sooner.

Using the Adobe Photo Downloader

The Adobe Photo Downloader is a feature of Photoshop Elements that searches for and downloads photos from attached card readers, cameras, or mobile phones, making it easy to import photos from these devices directly into your Photoshop Elements catalog.

On Windows, you can set the Adobe Photo Downloader to import your photos automatically, as soon as you attach your camera to the computer; you can configure the automatic download options in the Camera Or Card Reader section of the Organizer Preferences. Even with automatic detection disabled, you can always access the Adobe Photo Downloader from within the Elements Organizer by choosing File > Get Photos And Videos > From Camera Or Card Reader.

1 Connect your camera or card reader to your computer. For instructions on connecting your device, refer to the manufacturer's documentation.

2 If you're working on Mac OS, skip to step 3. On Windows, the Auto Play dialog box may appear. You could choose the option Organize And Edit Using Adobe Elements Organizer 9, but for the purposes of this lesson, simply click Cancel to dismiss the dialog box. If the Photo Downloader dialog box appears automatically, you can skip to step 4; otherwise, continue to step 3.

3 Choose File > Get Photos And Videos > From Camera Or Card Reader.

4 Under Source at the top of the Photo Downloader dialog box, choose the name of the connected camera or card reader from the Get Photos From menu.

5 Under Import Settings, accept the folder location listed next to Location, or click Browse / Choose to specify a new destination.

6 Next to Create Subfolder(s), choose one of the date formats from the menu if you want the photos to be stored in subfolders named by capture or import date. You can also choose the Custom Name option to create a folder using a name you type in the text box, or choose None if you don't want to create any subfolders at all. Your selection is reflected in the Location pathname.

Note: You'll learn more about customizing import settings and using the advanced features of the Adobe Photo Downloader in Lessons 2 and 3.

7 From the Rename Files menu, choose Do Not Rename Files and from the Delete Options menu choose After Copying, Do Not Delete Originals. On Windows, if the Automatic Download option is activated, click the check box to disable it.

8 Click the Get Media button.

The photos are copied from the camera to the specified folder location.

9 If the Files Successfully Copied dialog box appears, click Yes. The Getting Photos dialog box appears as the photos are imported into Photoshop Elements. Click OK to dismiss the dialog box informing you that the files you just imported are the only ones visible in the Media browser.

10 Click OK to close any other alert dialog box. On Windows, click No if you are asked whether you wish to import files newly detected in a watched folder. Thumbnails of the newly imported photos appear in the Media Browser pane.

Creating an Adobe ID

Note: At this stage, Elements Membership services are available only to users in the United States.

Photoshop Elements users in the U.S. can create an Adobe ID to register their software and sign up for a free Photoshop.com account. Creating an Adobe ID enables Elements Membership services that are integrated with your software, giving you access to the Inspiration Browser as well as Organizer-based backup and sharing and other exciting Adobe-hosted services that extend the capabilities of your Photoshop Elements software.

Basic Elements Membership is free and gives you your own storage space and a personal Photoshop.com URL where you can not only share and showcase your images but access your photos and videos anytime and from anywhere that you can connect to the Internet. You can also use your Photoshop.com account to back up your Photoshop Elements albums and even to synchronize albums on multiple computers. Basic membership includes access to the Inspiration Browser, with integrated tips, tricks and tutorials related to whatever you're currently working on, providing a powerful way to advance your skill set and helping you make the most out of your photos and creations.

You can upgrade to a Plus Membership to get more storage space as well as access to advanced tutorials. With Plus membership you also get regularly updated content such as project templates, themes, backgrounds, frames, and graphics delivered directly to your software to help you keep your projects fresh and appealing.

Signing up from the Welcome screen

1 Start Photoshop Elements or—if Photoshop Elements is already running—click the Welcome Screen button (⌂) at the top right of the workspace.

2 In the Welcome screen, click Create New Adobe ID. Enter your name, e-mail address and a password, type a name for your personal Photoshop.com URL, and then click Create Account. An e-mail message will be sent to you to confirm the creation of your account. Follow the instructions in the e-mail to activate your account. If you are asked whether you wish to activate backup and synchronization, click No; you'll learn about using this feature in Lesson 5.

Signing up from the Organizer or Editor

Tip: You don't have to start from the Welcome screen to create an Adobe ID. Links for registering and signing in are conveniently located throughout the Photoshop Elements workspace.

1 In the Organizer or Editor, click the Create New Adobe ID link in the menu bar.

2 Enter your personal details in the Create Your Adobe ID dialog box, and then click Create Account. Follow the instructions in the e-mail to activate your account. Don't activate backup and synchronization yet.

Signing in to your Photoshop.com account

Once you've created an Adobe ID, you may still need to sign in if you or another user has signed out of your account.

1 Make sure your computer is connected to the Internet, and then start Adobe Photoshop Elements.

2 In the Welcome screen, enter your Adobe ID and password, and click Sign In.

If you didn't sign in at the Welcome screen, you can always click the Sign In link at the top of either the Organizer or Editor workspace.

Using Windows 7 features

Photoshop Elements Editor supports the following Windows 7 features:

Live Taskbar Displays icons for all running and pinned applications. The icons for all running applications are highlighted with a border. Point to an icon to view images of the open files and applications. To work with an application, point to its icon, move over the images to preview in full screen, and click on the full screen image.

Aero Peek Makes all open windows transparent, allowing you to view the desktop. To view a hidden window, point to its taskbar icon.

Aero Shake Enables you to focus on a window by hiding all others. To work in an application, click its pane and shake the mouse. This hides all open windows except the selected window. To display the hidden windows, shake the mouse again.

Aero Snap Allows you to quickly resize and organize windows. To resize a window, drag it to a side of the display and expand vertically or horizontally.

Photoshop Elements Editor supports the following Windows 7 keyboard shortcuts:

Result	Shortcut
Activate Aero Peek	Windows + Spacebar
Activate Aero Shake	Windows + Home
Maximize	Windows + Up Arrow
Restore or minimize	Windows + Down Arrow
Maximize vertically	Windows + Shift + Up Arrow
Zoom in on the desktop	Windows ++
Zoom out of the desktop	Windows +- (minus)
Snap the current window to the side of the display	Windows + Left Arrow or Right Arrow
Move the current window to the left or right display	Windows + Shift + Left Arrow or Right Arrow

Using Help

Help is available in several ways, each one useful in different circumstances:

Note: You do not need to be connected to the Internet to view Help in the application. However, with an active Internet connection you can see a more complete version of the user documentation and also access the latest updates as well as community-contributed content.

Help in the application The complete user documentation for Adobe Photoshop Elements is available from the Help menu, in the form of HTML content that displays in the Adobe Community Help application. This documentation provides quick access to summarized information on common tasks and concepts, and can be especially useful if you are new to Photoshop Elements or when you are not connected to the Internet.

Help on the Web You can also access the most comprehensive and up-to-date documentation on Photoshop Elements via your default browser.

Help PDF Help is also available as a PDF document, optimized for printing; you can download the document by clicking the View Help PDF link in the top right corner of any Help page.

Links in the application Within the Photoshop Elements application there are links to additional help topics, such as the hot-linked tips associated with specific panels and tasks, and the tips and tutorials links that appear below the Task pane in both the Organizer and the Editor.

Navigating Help

Depending on which module you're working with, choose Help > Elements Organizer Help or Help > Photoshop Elements Help, or simply press the F1 key. Even if you are not currently connected to the Internet, the Adobe Community Help application will open to the front page of the respective Help documentation, which was installed on your computer with the Photoshop Elements software. Click a topic heading in the table of contents. Click the plus sign (+) to the left of a topic heading to see its sub-topics. Click a topic or sub-topic to display its content. In Community Help, choose View > Show Search Panel. Type a search term in the Search text box at the top of the Search panel, choose search options, and then press Enter on your keyboard.

Search tips

Community Help searches the entire Help text for topics that contain all the words typed in the Search box. These tips can help you improve your search results:

* If you search using a phrase, such as "shape tool," put quotation marks around the phrase. The search returns only those topics containing that specific phrase.

* Make sure that the search terms are spelled correctly.

* If a search term doesn't yield results, try using a synonym, such as "photo" instead of "picture."

Links to help in the application

You'll find links to additional task-specific help at various places in the Photoshop Elements workspace. Clicking these links will either take you to the corresponding topic in Help or—in the case of the links shown here—open the Elements Inspiration Browser.

Hot-linked tips

Hot-linked tips, marked with a light bulb icon, are scattered throughout Adobe Photoshop Elements. These tips either display information in the form of a typical tip balloon or link you to the appropriate topic in Help.

Additional resources

Adobe Photoshop Elements 9 Classroom in a Book is not meant to replace the documentation that comes with the program, nor to be a comprehensive reference for every feature; only the commands and options used in the lessons are explained in this book.

Additional resources are listed in detail at the end of the Getting Started chapter in this book; please refer to these resources for comprehensive information and tutorials about program features.

You've reached the end of the first lesson. Now that you know how to import photos, understand the concept of the catalog, and are familiar with the essentials of the Photoshop Elements interface, you are ready to start organizing and editing your photos in the next lessons.

Before you move on, take a few moments to read through the review questions and answers on the next page.

Review questions

1 What are the primary workspaces and working modes in Adobe Photoshop Elements?

2 Define the typical Photoshop Elements workflow.

3 What is a catalog?

4 What are keyword tags?

5 How can you select multiple thumbnail images in the Media Browser?

Review answers

1 Photoshop Elements has two primary workspaces: the Elements Organizer and the Editor. You'll work in the Organizer to locate, import, manage, and share your photos, and use the Editor to adjust your images and to create presentations to showcase them.

   The Editor offers three editing modes: Full Edit, Quick Edit, and Guided Edit. Both the Organizer and the Editor provide access to the Create and Share modes.

2 A typical Photoshop Elements workflow follows these basic steps:

   - Bring images and media into the Organizer from a digital camera, scanner, digital video camera, or from your hard disk.

   - Sort and group images in the Organizer by a variety of methods, including applying keyword tags and creating albums.

   - Edit, adjust, and correct images, or add text and effects in the Editor.

   - Share your images and media by creating projects and presentations, using e-mail or an online sharing service, or by burning them to CD/DVD-ROM.

3 Photoshop Elements stores information about your images in a library catalog file, which enables you to conveniently manage the photos on your computer from within the Organizer.

   For each image you import, Photoshop Elements creates a new entry in the catalog file. Whenever you assign a tag or a rating to a photo, or group images as an album, the catalog file is updated. All your work in the Organizer is recorded in the catalog.

As well as digital photographs, a catalog can include video and audio files, scans, PDF documents, and any presentations and layouts you might create in Photoshop Elements such as slide shows, photo collages, and CD jacket designs.

A single catalog can efficiently handle thousands of files, but you can also create separate catalogs for different types of work.

4 Keyword tags are labels with personalized associations that you attach to photos, creations, and video or audio clips in the Media Browser so that you can easily organize and find them.

5 To select more than one photo in the Media Browser, hold down the Ctrl / Command key and click the photos you want to select. Ctrl- / Command-clicking enables you to select multiple non-consecutive files.

To select images that are in consecutive order, click the first photo in the series, and then hold down the Shift key and click the last. All the photos in the range that you Shift-clicked will be selected.

2 BASIC ORGANIZING

Lesson overview

As you capture more and more images with your digital camera, it becomes increasingly important that you have effective ways to organize and manage your pictures on your computer so that those valuable memories are always accessible.

Adobe Photoshop Elements makes it easy to import your photos and other media files from a variety of sources and provides an array of powerful tools for sorting and searching your collection.

This lesson will get you started with the essential skills you'll need to import images and keep track of your growing photo library:

- Opening Adobe Photoshop Elements 9 in Organizer mode

- Creating a catalog for your images

- Importing images from folders on your computer

- Importing photos from a digital camera

- Switching between viewing modes in the Media Browser

- Working in the Date and Folder Location views

- Creating, organizing, and applying keyword tags

- Searching for files by keyword

- Finding and tagging faces in your photos

 You'll probably need between one and two hours to complete this lesson.

Import files to your catalog, and then explore a variety of ways to view and sort them. Learn how tagging and rating your photos can help you find just the pictures you want, just when you want them—easily and quickly. Once they share a keyword tag, a group of related photos can be retrieved with a single click, no matter how big your catalog, or across how many folders those images are scattered.

Getting started

Note: Before you start working on this lesson, make sure that you've installed the software on your computer from the application CD (see the Photoshop Elements 9 documentation) and that you have correctly copied the Lessons folder from the CD in the back of this book onto your computer's hard disk (see "Copying the Classroom in a Book files" on page 2).

For the exercises in this lesson you'll be working in the Elements Organizer component of Adobe Photoshop Elements.

1 Start Photoshop Elements by doing one of the following:

- On Windows, either double-click the shortcut on your desktop, or choose Start > All Programs > Adobe Photoshop Elements 9.

- On Mac OS, either click the Photoshop Elements 9 icon in the Dock, double-click the application icon in the Applications folder, or choose Photoshop Elements 9 from the Apple > Recent Items > Applications menu.

2 In the Welcome screen, click the Organize button at the left.

Creating a new catalog

Photoshop Elements stores information about your images in a library catalog file, which enables you to conveniently manage the photos on your computer from within the Organizer.

A catalog can include digital photographs, video and audio files, PDF documents, scans, and any presentations or layouts you might create in Photoshop Elements.

When you organize your files in Elements Organizer, all your work is recorded in the catalog. A single catalog can efficiently handle thousands of files, but you're free to create as many catalogs as you wish to suit the way that you prefer to work.

To begin this lesson you can create a new catalog so that you won't confuse the practice files for this lesson with files for the other lessons in this book.

1 In the Organizer, choose File > Catalog.

2 In the Catalog Manager dialog box, click New.

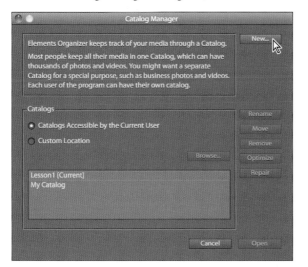

3 In the Enter A Name For The New Catalog dialog box, type **Lesson2**. If necessary, disable Import Free Music Into This Catalog, and then click OK.

The new Lesson2 catalog is loaded in the Organizer. If you're ever unsure of which of your catalogs you're working with, remember that the name of the currently active catalog will appear in a tooltip when you hold the pointer over the Organizer icon (⊞) at the upper left of the workspace window, and is also displayed in the lower left corner of the Organizer workspace.

Getting photos

The Elements Organizer provides a workspace where you can view, sort and organize your media files. Before you print your photos, use them in projects, burn them to CD or DVD-ROM, or share them by e-mail or on the Web, the first step is to assemble them in the Organizer. In the following exercises you'll import the images for this lesson into your new catalog using a variety of different methods.

Perhaps the most direct and intuitive way to bring photographs and other media into the Organizer catalog is to use the familiar drag-and-drop method.

Dragging photos from Windows Explorer

1 Minimize the Organizer by clicking the Minimize button (■) at the right of the Organizer menu bar, or simply click the Organizer application button on the Windows taskbar.

2 Open the My Computer window in Windows Explorer; either double-click a shortcut icon on your desktop, or choose My Computer from the Start menu.

3 Locate and open the Lessons folder that you copied to your hard disk (see "Copying the Classroom in a Book files" on page 2). Open the Lesson02 folder, and then the sub-folder named Import.

4 Inside the Import folder there are three sub-folders: drag the BATCH1 subfolder and hold it over the Organizer application button on the Windows taskbar.

5 Wait until the Organizer becomes the foreground application; then, drag the BATCH1 folder onto the Media Browser pane in the Organizer and release the mouse button. Skip to page 38: Importing attached keyword tags.

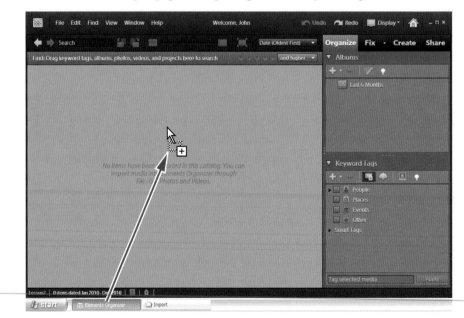

▶ **Tip:** If you can arrange the Windows Explorer window and the Organizer application window on your screen so that you can see both at once, you can simply drag the folder (or individual media files) directly from the Windows Explorer window into the Organizer, rather than going via the Windows taskbar.

Dragging photos from the Mac OS Finder

1 There are several ways to switch to the Finder on Mac OS. For this exercise, we'll use the Application Switcher. Hold down the Command key; then, press and release the Tab key. Continuing to hold down the Command key, click the Finder icon; then, release the Command key

2 In the Finder, press Command+N to open a new Finder window.

3 Navigate to and open the Lessons folder that you copied to your hard disk (see "Copying the Classroom in a Book files" on page 2). Open the Lesson02 folder, and then the sub-folder named Import.

4 Inside the Import folder are three sub-folders: BATCH1, BATCH2, and BATCH3. If necessary, move the finder window enough to see the Elements Organizer workspace behind it; then, drag the BATCH1 subfolder onto the Media Browser pane and release the mouse button.

5 Photoshop Elements briefly displays a dialog box while searching inside the BATCH1 folder for files to import; then, the Import Attached Keyword Tags dialog box opens. Click the Organizer workspace to bring it back to the front.

Importing attached keyword tags

If your files have already been tagged with keywords, the Import Attached Keyword Tags dialog box will appear, whichever method you use to bring your photos into Elements Organizer. The Import Attached Keyword Tags dialog box gives you the opportunity to specify which tags you wish to import with your images.

1 In the Import Attached Keyword Tags dialog box, click Select All; then, click OK.

2 The Getting Media dialog box appears briefly as the Organizer imports the images from your BATCH1 folder. If a message appears telling you that only the newly imported items will be visible in the Media Browser, click OK. Thumbnails of the eight images you imported appear in the Media Browser.

▶ **Tip:** If you don't see the tag icons in the Media Browser, use the Thumbnail Size slider above the Media Browser to increase the size of the thumbnails.

Each thumbnail is displayed with an orange tag icon indicating that the image has keywords attached.

3 Hold the pointer over the tag icon at the lower right of any image cell in the Media Browser to see a tooltip listing attached keywords.

4 In the Keywords panel to the right of the Media Browser, click the small triangle to expand the Imported Keyword Tags category; you can see that the newly imported **Lesson 02** tag is nested inside.

Getting photos from a known location

In this exercise you'll use a menu command to import files to the Organizer from a known folder on your hard disk.

1 Choose File > Get Photos And Videos > From Files And Folders. In the Get Photos And Videos From Files And Folders dialog box, navigate to your Lesson02 folder, open the Import folder, and then the BATCH2 folder.

2 To see preview thumbnails, and information about the files you are about to import, do one of the following:

- On Windows, hold the pointer over an image file in the BATCH2 folder to see a tooltip with detailed information about the photo; select the file to see a thumbnail image in the Preview pane.

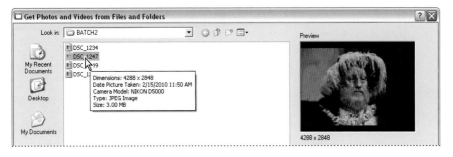

- On Mac OS, click the Column View button (▥) at the top left of the dialog box. Select any of the images in the BATCH2 folder to see a preview together with detailed information about the file.

3 Select all four images and ensure that the Automatically Fix Red Eyes option (Windows and Mac OS) and Automatically Suggest Photo Stacks (Windows only) are disabled, and then click Get Media.

4 Select the keyword "Lesson 02" in the Import Attached Keyword Tags dialog box. An asterisk (*) beside the selected keyword indicates that by default the new batch of images will pick up the existing Lesson 02 keyword tag.

▶ **Tip:** Select a folder in the Get Photos And Videos From Files And Folders dialog box, and then click Get Media to import all items within that folder. Activate the Get Photos From Subfolders option to import files from any subfolders.

5   Click the Advanced button in the lower left of the dialog box. Now you have the option to either use the existing tag of the same name or to type a new one. For now, leave the settings unchanged. Click the Reset To Basic button; then click OK. Click OK to dismiss any other alert dialog box.

Automatically fixing red eyes during import

The term "red eye" refers to the phenomenon common in photos taken with a flash, where the subject's pupils appear red instead of black. This is caused by the flash reflecting off the retina at the back of the eye.

In most cases, Photoshop Elements can successfully remove the red eye effect automatically during the import process, saving you the effort of further editing.

1   If you don't see file names displayed below the thumbnails in the Media Browser, choose View > Show File Names.

2   Double-click the image DSC_1234.jpg to see the enlarged single image view. The red eye effect is very noticeable in the eyes of the young girl in this photo.

3   Double-click the image to return to the thumbnail display in the Media Browser. Make sure that the image DSC_1234.jpg is still selected; then, choose Edit > Delete From Catalog. In the confirmation dialog box, make sure that the option Also Delete Selected Item(s) From The Hard Disk is disabled, and then click OK.

4   Choose File > Get Photos And Videos > From Files And Folders. In the Get Photos And Videos From Files And Folders dialog box, navigate to your Lesson02 folder, open the Import folder, and then the BATCH2 folder.

5   Select the image DSC_1234.jpg, activate the Automatically Fix Red Eyes option, and then click Get Media. Photoshop Elements briefly displays a progress bar in the Getting Media dialog box as the image is processed and imported.

6   In the Import Attached Keyword Tags dialog box, select the Lesson 02 tag, and then click OK. Click OK to dismiss any other alert dialog box.

A thumbnail of the newly imported image appears in the Media Browser. Photoshop Elements has grouped the edited photo with the un-edited original in a Version Set. You can identify a Version Set by the badge in the upper right corner of the thumbnail and the label below the thumbnail. The edited version of the photo is displayed as the top image in the Version Set; the filename has been extended to indicate that the image has been edited.

▶ **Tip:** Click the arrow at the right of the thumbnail once to expand the Version Set, and again to collapse it. You'll learn more about working with Version Sets in Lesson 3.

7   Double-click the top image in the Version Set, DSC_1234_edited-1.jpg, to see the enlarged single image view. Photoshop Elements has successfully removed the red eye effect.

Note: For some images, the automatic red eye fix will not be so effective; more tools and techniques for correcting the effect are discussed in Lesson 7.

8   Click Show All at the top of the Media browser to see all twelve images in your Lesson2 catalog.

Searching for photos to import

This method is useful when you're not sure exactly where on your hard disk you've stashed your photographs and other media files over the years. You might run a search of your entire hard disk or just your My Documents folder. For this exercise, you'll limit the search to just a small branch of your folder hierarchy.

1   In the Organizer, choose File > Get Photos And Videos > By Searching. Under Search Options in the Get Photos And Videos By Searching For Folders dialog box, choose Browse from the Look In menu.

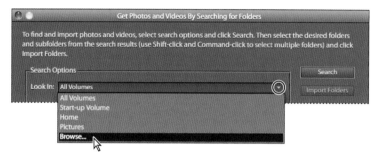

2   In the Browse For Folder / Select Folder For Search dialog box, locate and select your Lessons folder, and then click OK.

3   Under Search Options in the Get Photos And Videos By Searching For Folders dialog box, make sure the Automatically Fix Red Eyes option is disabled; then, click the Search button located at the upper right of the dialog box.

4   The Search Results box lists all folders inside the Lessons folder. The preview pane at the right shows thumbnails of the contents of a selected folder. Select the Lessons/Lesson02/Import/BATCH3 folder and click Import Folders.

5   In the Import Attached Keyword Tags dialog box, click Select All, and then click OK. Click OK to close any other alert dialog box. Click the Show All button above the Media Browser to see all sixteen images in your Lesson2 catalog.

Importing from a digital camera

If you have a digital camera or memory card at hand with your own photos on it, you can step through this exercise using those images. Alternatively, you can simply follow the process in the book without performing the exercise yourself, or skip to the next section of this lesson and return to this exercise when you are prepared.

1 Connect your digital camera or card reader to your computer, following the manufacturer's instructions.

2 If you're working on Mac OS, skip to step 3. On Windows, the Auto Play dialog box may appear. You could choose the option Organize And Edit Using Adobe Elements Organizer 9, but for the purposes of this lesson, simply click Cancel to dismiss the dialog box. If the Photo Downloader dialog box appears automatically, you can skip to step 4; otherwise, continue to step 3.

3 Choose File > Get Photos And Videos > From Camera Or Card Reader.

4 In the Photo Downloader dialog box, choose the name of your connected camera or card reader from the Get Photos From menu.

5 Accept the default target folder listed beside Location, or click Browse / Choose to designate a different destination for the imported files.

6 From the Create Subfolder(s) menu, choose Today's Date (yyyy mm dd) as the folder name format; the Location path reflects your choice.

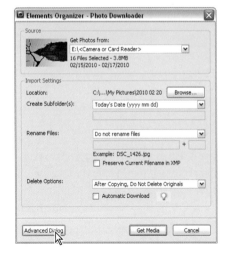

7 Choose Do Not Rename Files from the Rename Files menu. From the Delete Options menu, choose After Copying, Do Not Delete Originals. If you're working on Windows, deactivate the Automatic Download option.

8 Click the Advanced Dialog button.

In advanced mode, the Photo Downloader Dialog displays thumbnail previews of all the photos on your camera's memory card, and also offers options for processing, tagging, and grouping your images during the import process.

9   If there is a photo on your camera that you don't wish to import, click the check box below its thumbnail to remove the check mark. The un-checked photo will be excluded from the selection to be imported.

Note: If you choose one of the Advanced Options that deletes the original images from your camera after copying, only those images selected to be imported will be deleted from the camera; any images that have been excluded from the selection will not be deleted.

10 If you see a photo that needs to be rotated, select its thumbnails and click the appropriate Rotate button in the lower left corner of the dialog box.

11 Under Advanced Options, make sure that the Automatically Fix Red Eyes, Make 'Group Custom Name' A Tag, and Import Into Album options are disabled. On Windows, disable Automatically Suggest Photo Stacks.

12 Click Get Media.

The selected photos are copied from the camera to the specified folder on your hard disk. By default, imports from a camera are copied to your My Pictures / Pictures folder.

13 In the Files Successfully Copied dialog box, click Yes.

14 Photoshop Elements briefly displays a progress bar in the Getting Media dialog box as the photos are imported. Click OK to close any other alert dialog box.

The imported photos appear in the Media Browser, already rotated where specified.

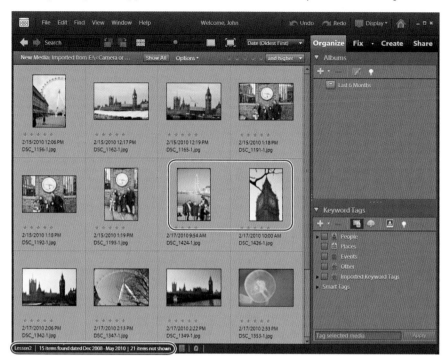

The name of the active catalog is displayed in the lower left corner of the Organizer. You can also see a count of the items currently shown in the Media Browser and an indication of the range of their capture dates. If you apply a search, these details will change to describe the search results.

Using watched folders

Watched folders are not supported for Mac OS; if you're working on Mac OS, you can skip to "Viewing photo thumbnails in the Organizer" on the next page.

On Windows, you can simplify and automate the process of keeping your catalog up to date by using watched folders. Designate any folder on your hard disk as a watched folder and Photoshop Elements will automatically be alerted when a new file is placed in (or saved to) that folder. By default, the My Pictures folder is watched, but you can set up any number of additional watched folders.

You can either choose to have any new files that are detected in a watched folder added to your catalog automatically, or have Photoshop Elements ask you what to do before importing the new media. If you choose the latter option, the message "New files have been found in Watched Folders" will appear whenever new items are detected. Click Yes to add the new files to your catalog or click No to skip them.

In this exercise you'll add a folder to the watched folders list.

1   Choose File > Watch Folders.

2   Under Folders To Watch in the Watch Folders dialog box, click Add, and then browse to your Lesson02 folder.

3 Select the Lesson02 folder and click OK.

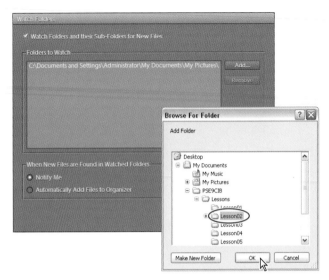

The Lesson02 folder now appears in the Folders To Watch list. To stop a folder from being watched, select it in the list and click Remove.

4 Ensure that the Notify Me option is activated, and then click OK to close the Watch Folders dialog box.

This concludes the portion of this lesson concerned with importing files into your catalog. You'll learn more ways to bring media into Photoshop Elements—together with time-saving techniques for sorting and managing your files even as you import them—in Lesson 3, "Advanced Organizing."

Viewing photo thumbnails in the Organizer

In the Organizer, there are several ways to view the images in your catalog. You can switch between the various viewing modes to suit different stages in your workflow or to make it easier and more efficient to perform specific organizing tasks.

Using the Media Browser views

Up to this point, you've been working in the default Media Browser view: the Thumbnail View, where your images are arranged by capture date and time. You can reverse the display order by choosing either Date (Oldest First) or Date (Newest First) from the menu to the right of the Thumbnail Size slider just above the Media Browser pane.

Let's look at some of the other display options in the Organizer.

1   Click the Show All button if it's visible at the top of the thumbnail view; then, use the Thumbnail Size slider just above the Media Browser pane to reduce the size of the thumbnails so that you can see all the images in your Lesson2 catalog.

2   Click the Display button (⬛)near the upper right corner of the Organizer window, and then choose Import Batch from the menu to see the thumbnails organized by their separate import sessions.

3   In the Import Batch view, a divider bar marked with a film canister icon (🎞) and an import session date separates each group of thumbnails. Click any of the divider bars to select all of the images that were imported in that session.

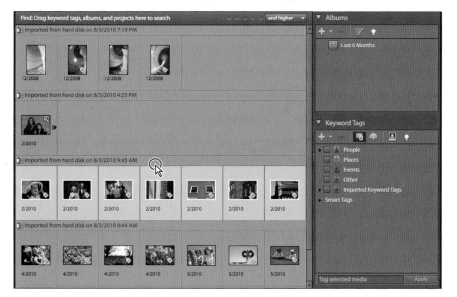

4   Choose Window > Timeline. The timeline shows a series of bars representing the separate import sessions that account for all the images in this catalog.

The varied height of the bars indicates that each import batch contains a different number of images. In this illustration, the timeline represents activity spread across a single day. Your bars may be arranged differently, especially if you've completed the preceding exercises over an hour or less.

5 Choose Edit > Deselect, and then drag the Thumbnail Size slider above the Media Browser to increase the size of the thumbnails until you see only a subset of the images in your Lesson2 catalog.

6 Click each of the bars in the timeline in turn. As you click, the view in the Media Browser jumps to the corresponding import batch; the first image in the batch is surrounded by a green border and its capture date flashes.

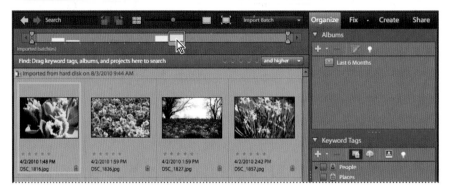

7 Choose Window > Timeline once more to hide the timeline from view.

8 Select any image in the Media Browser; then, click the Display button (▭) near the upper right corner of the Organizer window and choose Folder Location to see the photo's location in the folder hierarchy on your computer. The bar across the top of the Media Browser now displays a Managed Folder icon (▭) and the path-name of the folder containing your selected image.

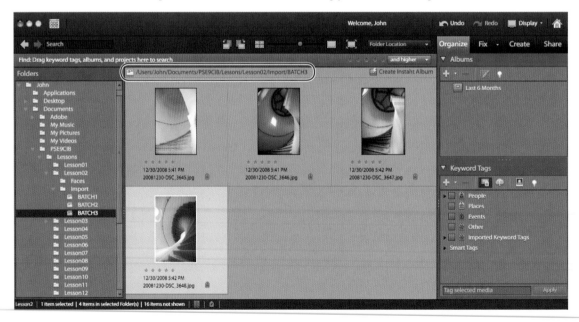

In the Folders panel at the left of the Media Browser, you can see at a glance which folders contain images that have been imported to the Lesson2 catalog; these folders are marked with the Managed Folder icon (). On Windows, you'll also be able to spot your watched folders: look for the Watched Folder icon (▣).

Note: Watched folders are not supported on Mac OS.

The Folder Location view becomes more useful the larger your photo library grows. At this point, you're working with a catalog that contains very few images, so it may not be instantly apparent that a single folder may contain multiple import batches and a single import batch may include files from multiple folders.

9 In the Folders panel, drag the selected image from the Media Browser to the PSE9CIB folder. The Lesson2 catalog is updated to record the new location of the moved photo; in the Folders panel, the PSE9CIB folder is now marked with a Managed Folder icon. Choose Edit > Undo Move.

In the Folders panel, you can move the folders on your hard disk in the same way, making it easy to manage your photo library without leaving the Organizer.

10 Right-click / Control-click any of your managed folders and note the commands available in the context menu.

11 Click the header bar across the top of the Media Browser to select all the photos in the folder you're viewing.

12 Choose Window > Timeline. This time, the bars you see in the timeline represent the three folders containing the images in this catalog. Click each bar in the timeline in turn, the corresponding source folder is highlighted in the Folders panel hierarchy.

13 Choose Window > Timeline once more to hide the timeline from view, and then choose Edit > Deselect. In preparation for the next exercise, click the BATCH1 folder in the Folders panel; then, click the Back To Previous View button (◀) at the upper left of the Organizer window to return to the Thumbnail View.

Using the Date View

The Date View can be a great way to organize and access your images, particularly once you are working with a large collection of photos that span a number of years.

1 Click the Display button (▤) near the upper right corner of the Organizer window and choose Date View from the menu.

2 If the Date View opens to display other than a full year calendar, click the Year view button (▣ Year) below the calendar display.

You can see at a glance that your Lesson2 catalog contains photographs taken on four separate dates during 2010. Dates shown in red are holidays; in the Date View pane of the Organizer preferences you can specify which holidays are marked.

Tip: Photoshop Elements automatically adjusts dates from different time zones; as a result, you may see these four photos placed on May 23.

3 Click May 24, 2010 on the calendar. A thumbnail preview of the first image captured on that date appears at the right of the Organizer window. An image count at the lower left of the preview indicates that there are four files in your catalog that share this creation date.

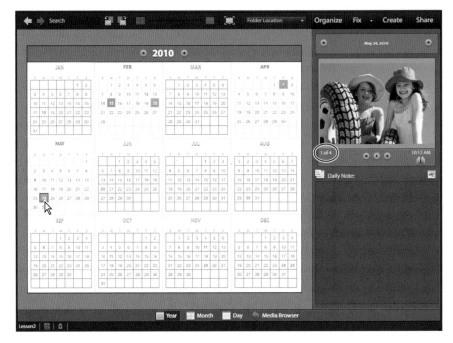

Note: Photoshop Elements automatically adjusts dates from different time zones; as a result, you may see different dates highlighted on your calendar page.

4 Click the Find This Photo In The Media Browser button (📷) below the preview thumbnail to see the currently previewed photo in the Media Browser where it can be selected, ready for action.

5 In the Media Browser, click the Back To Previous View button (◀) near the upper left corner of the Organizer window to return to the Date View.

6 Click the Month view button ( Month) below the calendar; then, click the month name at the head of the calendar page and choose February from the months menu. If you wished to move one month at a time, you could simply click three times on the Previous Month button to the left of the month name.

7 The February page opens with the 15th selected, that being the earliest date in February for which there are photos in your catalog. Click in the Daily Note box at the right of the calendar page and type **A brush with fame!** Click February 15th; a note icon appears on the thumbnail to indicate a note for that day.

> **Tip:** Photoshop Elements automatically adjusts dates from different time zones; as a result, you may see this photo placed on February 14.

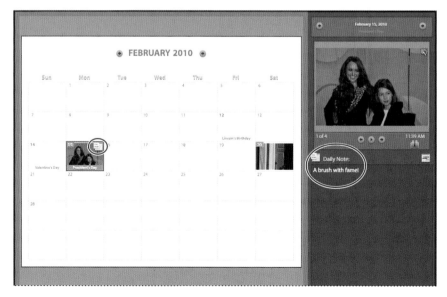

8 Use the Next Item On Selected Day button (●) under the preview image to see the other photographs captured on the same date.

9 Click the Start Automatic Sequencing button (▶) under the preview image to view all the photos taken on the same day as a mini slide show.

Now that you know how to access photos via the calendar you'll be able to return and use the Date View whenever you wish, but for the remainder of this lesson you'll work with the Media Browser in Thumbnail view.

10 Either click the Back To Previous View button (◀) near the upper left corner of the Organizer window or click the Media Browser button below the calendar page. You could also choose Media Browser from the Display menu.

Working with star ratings and keyword tags

Most of us find it challenging to organize our files and folders efficiently. It can be so easy to forget which pictures were stored in what folder—and so tedious when you're forced to examine the contents of numerous folders looking for the files you want. The Elements Organizer offers an array of powerful and versatile tools for organizing, sorting, and searching that make all that frustration a thing of the past.

Earlier in this lesson you learned that even during the import process you can search your computer for the files you want to bring into your catalog. The next set of exercises will demonstrate how just a little time invested in applying ratings and tags to the files you import can streamline the process of locating and sorting your pictures, regardless of how many image files you have or where they are stored.

Applying keyword tags and rating photos

Applying keywords to your photos and grouping those tags in categories can make it quick and easy to find exactly the images you're looking for. With a single click you can rate each photo from one to five stars, adding a simple way to narrow a search. In this exercise, you'll apply a rating to one of the images you imported into your Lesson2 catalog, and then tag it with a keyword from the default set.

1   Make sure that the options Details and Show File Names are activated in the View menu.

2   In the Media Browser, move the pointer slowly from left to right over the stars beneath the thumbnail image of the girl on the sand dune. When you see four yellow stars, as in the illustration below, click to apply that rating.

3   To find images based on the ratings you've assigned, use the stars and the adjacent menu located at the right end of the Find bar above the thumbnail display. For this example set the search criteria at 3 stars and higher. Only the image with the 4-star rating is displayed in the Media Browser.

4   Click the Show All button in the Find bar.

5   In the Keyword Tags panel, click the arrow beside the People category to expand that category so that you can see the two nested sub-categories "Family" and "Friends."

6 Drag the Family keyword tag to the thumbnail of girl in the sand dune.

7 Collapse the People keyword tag category, and then Ctrl-click / Command-click to select the other three images of girls playing at the beach.

8 Click in the text box at the bottom of the Keywords Tags panel and type the letter **f**. As you type a list of the existing keywords starting with **f** appears; choose Family, and then click Apply. The tag is applied to the three images you selected in the Media Browser.

● **Note:** In the Media Browser, the keyword tag icon or icons that you see below the thumbnails will vary in appearance depending on the size at which the thumbnails are displayed. If the thumbnail size is very small, multiple color-coded tags may display as a single generic (beige) tag icon.

9 Rest the pointer for a second or two over a tag icon beneath the thumbnail of any of your newly tagged photos; a tooltip message appears identifying the keyword tags that are attached to that image file.

10 In the Keyword Tags panel, click the triangle to expand the People keyword tags category once more. Click the empty Find box beside the Family sub-category. The Media Browser is immediately updated to display only the four images to which you assigned the Family tag.

11 Click the Find box beside the Family tag again to clear the search. Once more the Media Browser displays all sixteen images in your Lesson2 catalog.

Using Star ratings and the Hidden tag

Star ratings—Use *Star ratings* to rank your photos. You can attach only one star rating value per photo. If you assign 5 stars to a photo that already has 4 stars assigned, the 5 star rating will replace the previous rating.

Hidden—The *Hidden tag* hides photos in the Media Browser, unless you select the Hidden tag as a search criteria. Use the Hidden tag, for example, to hide items that you want to keep, but prefer not to see every time you work in the Organizer.

—From Photoshop Elements Help

Creating new categories and sub-categories

It's easy to add or delete new keyword tag categories and sub-categories in the Keyword Tags panel to help you group and organize your keyword tags.

1   At the top of the Keyword Tags panel, click the Create New Keyword Tag, Sub-category, Or Category button (➕) and choose New Category from the menu.

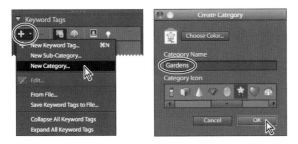

2   In the Create Category dialog box, type **Gardens** as the category name; then scroll the Category Icon menu and select the flower icon. Click OK.

3   In the Keyword Tags panel, expand the People category if necessary; then click to select the Family sub-category. Click the Create New button (➕) and choose New Sub-Category from the menu.

4   In the Create Sub-Category dialog box, type **Kids** as the new Sub-Category name. Ensure that Family is selected in the Parent Category or Sub-Category menu and click OK. Your new keyword tag category and sub-category have become part of this catalog.

Applying and editing category assignments

You can assign keyword categories to (or remove them from) several files at once.

1   In the Media Browser, click any of the six photos featuring children; then hold down the Ctrl / Command key and click to add the other five to the selection.

2   Click in the text box in the header of the Keywords Tags panel and type the letter **k**; choose Kids and click Apply. The tag is applied to the selected images.

3 Leaving the same six images selected, drag the Garden keyword tag to one of the un-selected images of flowers. Selecting the thumbnail or deselecting the other thumbnails is not necessary; the keyword tag is applied to just this picture.

4 Choose Edit > Deselect, and then Ctrl-click / Command-click to select the three un-tagged flower photos. Drag your multiple selection onto the Garden tag in the Keyword Tags panel. The keyword tag Garden is applied to all three images at once.

▶ **Tip:** You can also show and hide the Properties panel by holding down the Alt / Option key on your keyboard, and then pressing Enter / Return.

5 Select the image of the young girl to which you applied a 4-star rating earlier in the lesson. Choose Window > Properties to open the Properties panel, and then click the Keyword Tags tab (🏷) to see which keyword tags are attached to this image.

6 Remove the Family tag from the image by doing one of the following:

- In the Properties panel, right-click / Control-click the listing **Family, Kids**, and then choose Remove Family Sub-Category Keyword Tag.

- In the Media Browser, right-click / Control-click the thumbnail in the Media Browser and choose Remove Keyword Tag > Family from the context menu.

- Right-click / Control-click the tag icon beneath the thumbnail itself, and then choose Remove Family Sub-Category Keyword Tag from the menu.

7 Close the Properties panel by clicking the Close button—in the upper right corner of the panel on Windows, at the upper left on Mac OS—or by choosing Window > Properties again.

Creating and applying new keyword tags

In the last exercise you created new keyword categories and sub-categories. This time you'll create, apply and edit a new keyword tag.

1 In the Keyword Tags panel, click the Create New button (➕) and choose New Keyword Tag from the menu. The Create Keyword Tag dialog box appears.

2 In the Create Keyword Tag dialog box, choose Places as the category and type **Beach** for the tag Name; then, click OK.

3 Drag the picture of the little girl with the 4-star rating to the new Beach tag in the Keyword Tags panel.

The image becomes the default icon for the new tag because it's the first image to have this keyword applied. You'll adjust the tag icon in the next steps, before applying the new keyword tag to additional photos.

4 In the Keyword Tags panel, select the Beach keyword tag; then, click the Create New button (➕) above the list of keyword tags and choose Edit from the menu. You could also right-click / Control-click the Beach keyword tag itself and choose Edit Beach Keyword Tag from the context menu.

5 In the Edit Keyword Tag dialog box, click the Edit Icon button to open the Edit Keyword Tag Icon dialog box.

6 Drag the corners of the bounding box in the preview image so that it surrounds just the little girl. A preview at the top of the dialog box shows you how your edit looks applied to the tag icon.

7 Click OK to close the dialog box; then click OK again to close the Edit Keyword Tag dialog box.

You'll update the keyword tag icon later to an image that works better as an icon for this tag.

8 Ctrl-click / Command-click to select the three images showing two sisters playing at the beach. Drag the Beach keyword tag onto any of the selected photos. The Beach tag is now attached to four images.

9 In the Keyword Tags panel, right-click / Control-click the Beach tag and choose Edit Beach Keyword Tag from the context menu. The Edit Keyword Tag dialog box appears. Click the Edit Icon button to open the Edit Keyword Tag Icon dialog box.

10 In the Edit Keyword Tag Icon dialog box, click the arrow to the right of the Find button beneath the main preview image.

The Find arrows cycle through all photos with the same keyword tag. A small preview at the top of the dialog box shows how each image would look applied as a tag icon.

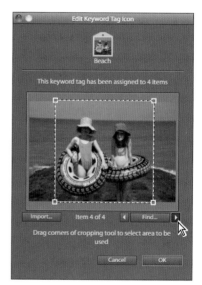

11 Choose a new image for the tag icon; then, drag the bounding box on the main preview (and re-size it, if you wish) until you are satisfied with the way it looks in the small tag preview; then click OK to close the dialog box. Click OK again to close the Edit Keyword Tag dialog box.

Converting keyword tags and categories

Changing the hierarchy of categories and keyword tags in the Keyword Tags panel is easy. Doing this will not remove the rearranged tags or categories from the images to which you've attached them.

1 Click the Find box next to the Kids sub-category. A binoculars icon (📷) appears in the box to remind you that it is now activated. Only the six photos tagged with the Kids keyword are displayed in the Media Browser. Click the Show All button above the Media Browser so that all the images in the catalog are visible.

2 Right-click the Kids sub-category and choose Edit Kids Sub-Category from the context menu. The Edit Sub-Category dialog box appears.

3 From the Parent Category or Sub-Category menu, choose None (Convert To Category) and click OK.

Now Kids is no longer a sub-category under People, Family but a category in its own right. Its new tag, featuring a stylized portrait icon, has been inherited from its former parent category, People.

4 Click the empty Find box beside the Kids category. Notice that the selection of six images tagged with the Kids tag did not change. Move the pointer over the tag icons below any of the images featuring children; note the list of attached keywords. Click the Show All button.

5 In the Keyword Tags panel, drag the Kids category onto the People category.

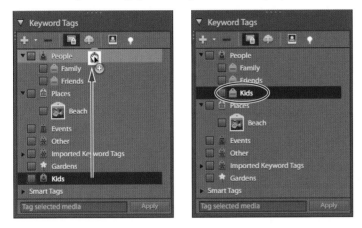

The Kids tag appears as a sub-category once more; this time listed under People. Because it's no longer a category, its tag reverts to the generic sub-category icon.

6 Click the empty Find box beside the Kids category; then, move the pointer over the tag icons below any of the images displayed. Neither the selection of images tagged with the Kids keyword nor the list of attached keywords has changed. Click the Show All button.

7 Under the People category, right-click / Control-click the Family sub-category and choose Change Family Sub-Category To A Keyword Tag from the menu.

8 In the Media Browser, select the image DSC_1251.jpg (a photo from a visit to Madame Tussaud's), in preparation for the next exercise.

Working with keyword tags in Full Screen mode

In Photoshop Elements 9 the Full Screen mode has been improved to give you even more ways to work with keyword tags while reviewing and organizing your photos.

1 Click the View, Edit, Organize In Full Screen button (▢) above the Media Browser, or click the Display button (▢) at the upper right of the Organizer window and choose View, Edit, Organize In Full Screen from the menu.

2 Move the pointer over the full screen image to see the control bar at the bottom of the screen. If necessary, click the Pause button, and then click the Toggle Film Strip button or press Ctrl+F on your keyboard so that you can see a strip of thumbnails at the right of the screen as shown below.

3 Move the pointer to the left edge of the screen, as shown in the illustration below, to show the Quick Organize panel; then, click to deactivate the Auto Hide button at the top of the vertical title bar of the Quick Organize panel so that the panel remains open while you work.

4 Click in the text box at the bottom of the Quick Organize panel and type **Albert**; then click the Apply button (✚) to the right of the text box to attach the new keyword to this image. Move the pointer over the keywords in the Keyword Tags pane of the Quick Organize panel; as you move over each keyword a tooltip message shows that you can click to either apply or remove any of these tags. The keywords already attached to this image are highlighted.

5 Click to activate the Quick Organize panel's Auto Hide button once more; then, move the pointer away; the panel closes after a second or so.

6 Right-click / Control-click the image and choose Show Properties from the menu.

7 In the Properties panel, click the Keyword Tags tab (🏷) to see the keyword tags attached to this image. Right-click / Control-click the tag **Albert** and choose Remove Albert Keyword Tag. You'll explore a better way to tag people later in this chapter. Click the Close button in the header bar to close the Properties panel.

8 Press the Esc key on your keyboard or click the Close button at the right of the control bar to exit Full Screen mode and return to the thumbnail view.

Creating a keyword tag for your working files

You can create a keyword tag to apply to the files that you create and save as you work through the lessons in this book.

1 In the Keyword Tags panel, click the Create New button and choose New Category from the menu.

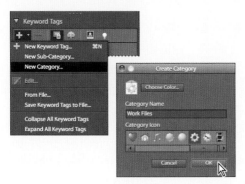

2 In the Create Category dialog box, type **Work Files** and select one of the Category icons. You can scroll to the right to see more icons. Click OK.

3 Apply this keyword tag to all the files you create and save to your My CIB Work folder as you complete the lessons in this book.

Using keyword tags to find pictures

The reason for creating, applying and sorting all these keyword tags is so that you can always find just the picture you want, just when you want it—easily and quickly. Once they share a keyword tag, a group of related photos can be retrieved with a single click; no matter how big your catalog, or across how many folders those images are scattered.

Before you go on to have fun with the People Recognition feature, let's become more familiar with using the Keyword Tags panel to sort and search your files. In the Elements Organizer you now have even more ways to find files by keyword, with enhancements to both the text search feature and the tagging interface.

The most intuitive tool for searching your catalog by keyword is the Keyword Tag Cloud, which displays all the existing tags in your catalog listed in alphabetical order. Varying text sizes indicate the relative number of files tagged with each keyword, which means that those tags that you use most often are the easiest to find at a glance.

> Ansonia Hotel, Asia, Bangkok, Beach, Belgium, Brooklyn Bridge, Elephant, Emma, Empire State Building, Europe, Family, Friends, Giraffe, Hippo, Holidays, Hong Kong, Imagine, Jefferson Market, Kate, Kids, Lilly, New York, Normandy, Ostrich, Patricia, Pauline, Road Trip, San Francisco, Sirani, Sofie, Summer, Tom, Vittorio, Winter, Zebra, Zoo

1 If the Show All button is visible at the top of the Media browser, click it. Click the Keyword Tag Cloud button ( ) at the top of the Keyword Tags panel.

2 In the tag cloud, click **Beach**; then press Ctrl+A / Command+A to select all four images. Type **Vacation** in the text box in the header of the Keyword Tags panel and click Apply to attach the new tag to the four images.

3 Click Show All above the Media Browser. Right-click / Control-click to select the images DSC_1234.jpg, DSC_1247.jpg, DSC_1249.jpg, and DSC_1251.jpg. Drag the tag **Vacation** from the tag cloud to any one of the selected photos.

4 Click the keyword **Vacation** in the tag cloud to see all eight images with this tag displayed in the Media Browser. Click Show All.

You can switch to the hierarchical view of your keyword categories, sub-categories and tags when you want extra organizational control.

5 In the Keyword Tags panel, click the View Keyword Tag Hierarchy button ().

6 In the tag hierarchy, click the empty find box beside the new **Vacation** tag, in the keyword category **Other**; the eight images with this keyword show in the Media Browser.
Leaving the **Vacation** find box active, click the empty find box beside the **Kids** tag; the display is reduced to the six images that have both of these tags attached. Finally, click the find box beside the tag **Beach**.
Only four images are returned by the narrowed search. The Find bar above the thumbnails shows that these images have all three keywords: **Vacation**, **Kids** and **Beach**.

7 From the Options menu in the Find bar above the Media Browser, choose Show Close Match Results.

The thumbnail display is updated to show more photos: images that are tagged with *some*, but not all of the searched keywords. These close matches can be identified by a check mark icon in the upper left corner of their thumbnails.

8 From the Options menu in the Find bar above the Media Browser, choose Hide Close Match Results. Click Show All to display all images. In the Keyword Tags panel, right-click / Control-click the tag **Albert** and choose Delete Albert Keyword Tag from the context menu. Click OK to confirm the deletion.

Automatically finding faces for tagging

Undoubtedly, your growing photo library will include many photos of your family and friends. Photoshop Elements 9 makes it quick and easy to tag your photos of friends and family members with the People Recognition feature, taking most of the work out of sorting and organizing a large portion of your catalog.

The People Recognition feature automatically finds the people in your photos and makes it easy for you to tag them. Once you begin using the feature it learns to recognize the faces you've already tagged and will automatically tag new photos that picture the same faces. The more times a particular person is tagged, the better People Recognition will get at recognizing them.

Using People Recognition

The first experience you'll have of People Recognition will probably be the "Who Is This?" prompt that appears as you move the pointer over a photo in the single-image view in the Elements Organizer. People Recognition displays these hints to help you identify and tag all the people in your photos. You can ignore the hints if you wish, but remember that the more people you identify, the smarter People Recognition gets at tagging faces for you automatically.

The automatic "Who Is This" hints and the People Recognition feature itself can both be disabled. Before continuing with the exercises in this section, you need to make sure that both are activated. You can also import a few more images with faces for People Recognition to find.

1 In the Organizer, choose Preferences > Media-Analysis from the Edit / Adobe Elements 9 Organizer menu. In the Media-Analysis pane of the Preferences dialog box, make sure that the option Analyze Photos For People Automatically is activated. Click OK to save your settings and close the Preferences dialog box.

2 In the View menu, make sure that Show People Recognition is activated.

3 Choose File > Get Photos And Videos > From Files And Folders. In the Get Photos And Videos From Files And Folders dialog box, locate and open your Lesson02 folder; then, click once to select the Faces folder. Disable the option Automatically Fix Red Eyes. On Windows, disable the option Automatically Suggest Photo Stacks.

4   Click Get Media. In the Import Attached Keyword Tags dialog box, click Select
     All, and then click OK. Click OK to close any other alert dialog box. The Media
     browser shows only the eight newly imported images.

5   Above the Media Browser, choose Oldest First for the sorting order.

Tagging faces in the Media Browser

Photoshop Elements helps you with every step of the face tagging process.

1   In the Media Browser, double-click the first photo, **faces_1.jpg**, to see it in the
     enlarged single image view.

2   Move the pointer over the image; white boxes appear over any faces detected in
     the photo. People Recognition has found three of the four faces in this photo.
     Move the pointer over any of the boxes; the "Who is this?" prompt appears.

3   Starting with the girl at the left, click the "Who is this?" text in the black box,
     type the name **Pauline**, and then press Enter / return. Photoshop Elements
     creates a new keyword tag for Pauline. By default, the new tag appears in the
     People category in the Keyword Tags panel. Name the second girl **Sophie** and
     the girl on the right **Lilly**. Be sure to press Enter / return for each tag.

Note: If you type a name that matches a tag you created earlier, Photoshop Elements applies the existing keyword, rather than creating a new tag.

4   Click the Add Missing Person button (⬚) below the lower right corner of the
     enlarged image. Drag the new face tagging box onto the face of the taller girl and
     use the handles around the box to surround her face neatly; then, click the green
     check mark to confirm the position. Type the name **Emma** for this girl; then,
     press Enter / return

5   Click the right arrow key on your keyboard to move on to the next photo.
     This time, People Recognition has detected all of the faces in the photo.

6 Click the "Who is this?" text box for the girl at the right of the photo. You haven't yet tagged enough faces for People Recognition to recognize this girl, but you're offered a choice of possible tags from those available in the People category. Click the name **Sophie**, and then press Enter / return.

7 Click the "Who is this?" text box for the girl at the left. This is the same girl that People Recognition failed to find in the first photo, so it doesn't yet recognize her well enough even to offer the correct choice. Type the name **Emma**, and then press Enter / return. Type the name **Kat** to tag her mother.

8 People Recognition already recognizes the two girls at the center of the photo; click the green check mark to confirm the automatic tagging for **Pauline** and **Lilly**.

9 Double-click the image to return the Media Browser to Thumbnail view.

Tagging faces in the Label People dialog box

Photoshop Elements helps you with every step of the face tagging process.

1 Select the six images with faces you have not yet tagged; click the image **faces_3. jpg**, then Shift-click the image **faces_8.jpg**.

2 Click the Start People Recognition button (▥) in the Keyword Tags panel.

3 In the People Recognition - Label People dialog box, tag as many of the faces as you can. (We'll tell you who *that* is later.) Be sure to press Enter / return whenever you type. When you're done, click Save. A new set of faces appear.

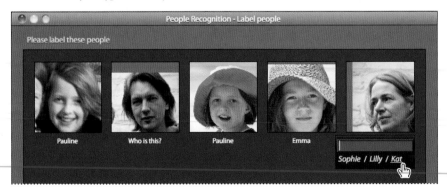

4 Tag the new set of faces. The name of the girls' father is Tom. Click Save.

5 Continue tagging the faces presented in the People Recognition - Label People dialog box and saving each set, until People Recognition displays the image that you see in the illustration at the right.

People Recognition will sometimes incorrectly identify a chance arrangement of light and shadow in an image as a face. When this happens, you'll be asked whether you'd like to label the "person" or not. If you clicked on this image, you would be confirming it as a face that you know; you would then be returned to the Label People dialog box to tag it. If you clicked Save, ignoring this image, People Recognition would no longer see it as a face. For the purposes of this exercise, click Cancel to return to the Media Browser; we'll deal with this case in a different way.

6 In the Media Browser, double-click the photo **faces_6.jpg** to see the image enlarged in the single image view. Move the pointer over the image; you'll see the extraneous tagging box framing the lower half of Lilly's face and her mother's hands.

7 Click the X button at the upper right corner of the tagging box to dismiss it; otherwise People Recognition will register this as a person not yet named. If you see an alert asking you to confirm the exclusion from People Recognition; click Yes.

Note: In the Keywords panel, the newly created tags are listed inside the People category by default, but you can move these tags elsewhere in the hierarchy if you choose; People Recognition will keep track of them.

8 Double-click the photo to return the Media Browser to Thumbnail view. In the keywords panel, activate the Find box beside the each of your new tags in turn, making sure to disable one Find box before clicking the next. Now try activating different combinations and numbers of Find boxes at once. The details of each search are shown in the Find bar above the thumbnail display.

9 Click Show All, if it's visible above the Media Browser. Choose Edit > Select All; then, click the Start People Recognition button (⬛) in the Keyword Tags panel to run the tagging process once more for your entire Lesson2 catalog. People recognition searches the selected images for faces it knows, and presents you with as many as possible arranged in groups in the People Recognition - Confirm Groups Of People dialog box. In this case, all of the grouped faces have been correctly identified, but if you wish to exclude a face, move the pointer over the thumbnail and click the X button in the upper right corner of its bounding box.

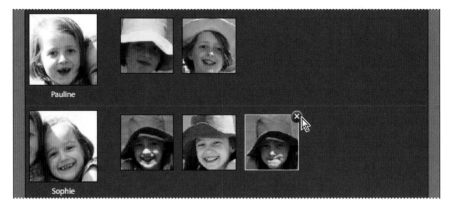

10 Click Save and continue with the process; you still have a few un-tagged friends.

For more information on People Recognition, as well as other aspects of the Auto-Analysis feature including Smart Tags, please refer to Adobe Photoshop Elements Help.

Congratulations, you've finished the lesson! You've imported files into the Elements Organizer using a variety of new techniques and learned several different ways to view and access the images in your catalog. You've also created, edited, and applied keyword tags to individual photographs so that they'll be easy to find in future.

Before you move on, take a few moments to review the concepts and techniques presented in this lesson by working through the following questions and answers.

Review questions

1   How do you open the Elements Organizer component of Adobe Photoshop Elements?

2   Name three ways to import photos from your computer hard disk into your catalog.

3   What is a "watched folder"? (Windows users only.)

4   Summarize the characteristics of the Media Browser and Date views in the Organizer.

Review answers

1   Click the Organize button in the Welcome Screen when you start Photoshop Elements. Alternatively, if the Editor window is already open, click the Organizer button located at the top right of the Editor workspace.

2   This lesson demonstrated three different ways to import photos into Photoshop Elements:

   • Drag-and-drop photographs from a Windows Explorer / Finder window into the Media Browser pane in the Organizer window.

   • In the Organizer, choose File > Get Photos And Videos > From Files And Folders, and then navigate to the folder containing your photos. You can import a whole folder, specify whether to include subfolders, or select just those images you want to add to your catalog.

   • In the Organizer, choose File > Get Photos And Videos > By Searching, and then select the folder on the hard disk that you wish Photoshop Elements to search. This method will locate all images in that folder and its subfolders and offer you the opportunity to select which images to import.

3   If you designate a folder on your computer as watched, Photoshop Elements is automatically alerted when new photos are saved or added to that folder. By default, the My Pictures folder is watched, but you change that, or add any number of watched folders. When new images appear in a watched folder, you can either have Photoshop Elements import them to the Organizer automatically, or ask you what to do.

4   In the default Media Browser view in the Organizer you can browse thumbnail images of your photos. You can choose to see them sorted by chronological order, by folder location, or by import batch. The Date view is organized in the form of a calendar where you can quickly find photos taken on a particular day, month, or year.

3 ADVANCED ORGANIZING

Lesson overview

As your collection grows to hundreds or even thousands of images, keeping track of your photos can be a daunting task. Photoshop Elements 9 delivers sophisticated organizing tools that not only get the job done, but actually make the work quite enjoyable.

In this lesson you'll learn a few new methods of importing images and some of the more advanced techniques for organizing, sorting, and searching your growing photo collection:

- Using advanced Photo Downloader options

- Acquiring still frames from video

- Importing pictures from a PDF document

- Importing pictures from a scanner

- Using Version Sets and Stacks to organize photos

- Grouping photos in Albums and Smart Albums

- Viewing and managing files in the Folder Location view

- Finding photos by similarity, metadata, and text search

- Hiding unwanted files from view

- Sorting photos by location using the Map view

You'll probably need between one and two hours to complete this lesson.

Discover some advanced import options that will make organizing your photos even easier. Have Photoshop Elements apply tags and group images automatically during import so your files will already be organized by the time they arrive in your catalog! Simplify navigating your catalog with Stacks, Version Sets and Albums and learn about a range of powerful search features to help you find exactly the right files.

Getting started

Note: Before you start working on this lesson, make sure that you've installed the software on your computer from the application CD (see the Photoshop Elements 9 documentation) and that you have correctly copied the Lessons folder from the CD in the back of this book onto your computer's hard disk (see "Copying the Classroom in a Book files" on page 2).

In this lesson you'll be working mainly in the Organizer workspace, though you will switch to the Editor in order to capture frames from a video and import images from a PDF document.

1 Start Photoshop Elements by doing one of the following:

- On Windows, either double-click the shortcut on your desktop, or choose Start > All Programs > Adobe Photoshop Elements 9.

- On Mac OS, either click the Photoshop Elements 9 icon in the Dock, double-click the application icon in the Applications folder, or choose Photoshop Elements 9 from the Apple > Recent Items > Applications menu.

2 In the Welcome screen, click the Organize button at the left.

Creating a new catalog

You'll start by creating a new catalog so that you won't confuse the practice files for this lesson with files for the other lessons in this book.

1 In the Organizer, choose File > Catalog.

2 In the Catalog Manager dialog box, click New.

3 In the Enter A Name For The New Catalog dialog box, type **Lesson3** as the catalog name. If necessary, disable the option Import Free Music Into This Catalog, and then click OK.

Now you have a special catalog that you'll use just for this lesson; all you need are some pictures to put in it.

Advanced import options

In Lesson 2 you imported images into the Organizer using a variety of methods, and learned how to apply keyword tags manually as a way of organizing photos once they are in your catalog.

In the following exercise you'll explore some advanced import options that will make organizing your photos even easier.

By having Photoshop Elements apply tags and create groups automatically during the import process, your images will already be organized by the time they arrive in your catalog! You'll also learn about importing photos from some different sources: capturing still frames from a movie, extracting the images embedded in a PDF document, and acquiring an image from a scanner.

Photo Downloader options

If you have a digital camera or memory card at hand with your own photos on it, you can step through this first exercise using those images. To get the best results from this exercise, you should have several batches of pictures taken at different times on the same day.

Alternatively, you can simply follow the process and refer to the illustrations in the book, without actually performing the exercise yourself, and then return to this exercise when you are prepared.

1 Connect your digital camera or card reader to your computer, following the manufacturer's instructions.

2 If you're working on Mac OS, skip to step 3. On Windows, the Auto Play dialog box may appear. You could choose the option Organize And Edit Using Adobe Elements Organizer 9, but for the purposes of this lesson, simply click Cancel to dismiss the dialog box. If the Photo Downloader dialog box appears automatically, you can skip to step 4; otherwise, continue to step 3.

3 Choose File > Get Photos And Videos > From Camera Or Card Reader.

4 If the Photo Downloader dialog box opens in the Advanced mode, click the Standard Dialog button located at the lower left corner of the dialog box.

5 From the Get Photos From menu at the top of the Photo Downloader dialog box, choose the name of the connected camera or card reader.

6 Under Import Settings, accept the default destination folder listed beside Location, or click Browse / Choose to choose a different destination. By default, the image files are saved to your My Pictures folder.

7 Without making any other changes to the settings, click the Advanced Dialog button in the lower left corner of the dialog box.

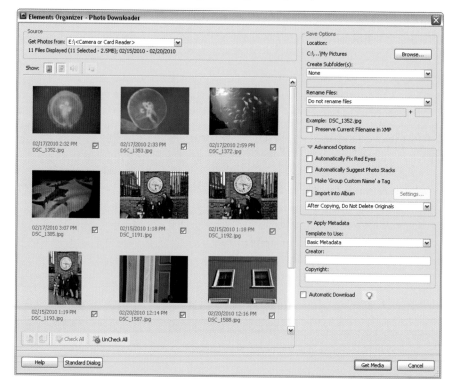

In advanced mode, the Photo Downloader Dialog displays thumbnail previews of all the photos on your camera's memory card, and also offers options for processing, tagging, and grouping your images during the import process.

In the next steps you'll set up the automatic creation of subfolders for the files copied from your camera and apply keyword tags to the images as they are imported.

8 Under Save Options, choose Custom Groups (Advanced) from the Create Subfolder(s) menu. Your selection is reflected in the Location pathname.

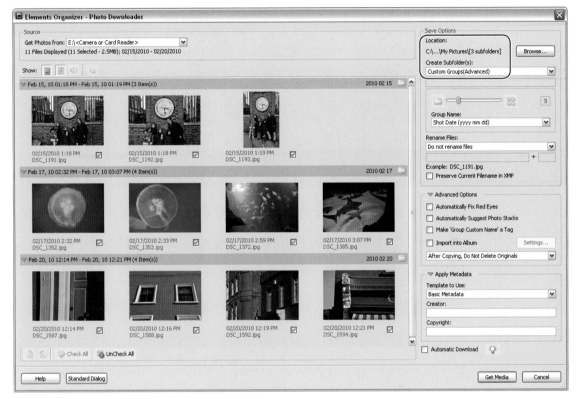

The images have been automatically divided into groups, based on capture time and date. A slider below the Create Subfolder(s) menu enables you to adjust the granularity of the subdivision and the box to the right of the slider shows the resulting number of groups. In our example, the automatic grouping based on capture time has done a good of job separating our subjects, producing three groups.

9 Experiment by moving the slider to the left to generate fewer groups (subfolders) or to the right to generate more. Scroll down the list of thumbnails to review the effect of the slider on the grouping of your photos. Note that the number of groups created is displayed in the box to the right of the slider.

Tip: To increase or decrease the number of groups, you can also press Ctrl / Command together with Shift+M or Shift+L respectively on your keyboard.

10 Next you'll apply custom names to the subfolders for your grouped photos. From the Group Name menu, choose Shot Date (yyyy mm dd) + Custom Name.

11 On the right end of the separator bar above the thumbnails of the first group, click the Custom Name field and type a descriptive name in the text box.

12 Repeat step 9 for the other groups in the list, giving each group a distinct name. In our example, we used the group names: **Greenwich, London Aquarium**, and **Portobello Rd**.

13 Under Advanced Options, activate the Make 'Group Custom Name' A Tag option by clicking the check box. This will automatically create keyword tags corresponding to the group custom names and apply them to your photos as they are imported into the Organizer. If the options Automatically Fix Red Eyes and Import Into Album are currently activated, disable them by clicking their checkboxes. On Windows, disable Automatically Suggest Photo Stacks.

14 Click Get Media. The photos are copied from the camera or memory card reader to the specified group subfolders on your hard disk.

15 If the Files Successfully Copied dialog box appears, click OK.

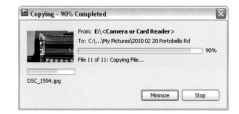

The Getting Media dialog box appears briefly while the photos are being imported into your Lesson3 catalog. The imported images appear in the Media Browser. Photoshop Elements has automatically applied keywords to the images during the import process; the new tags are listed inside the keyword tag category Other.

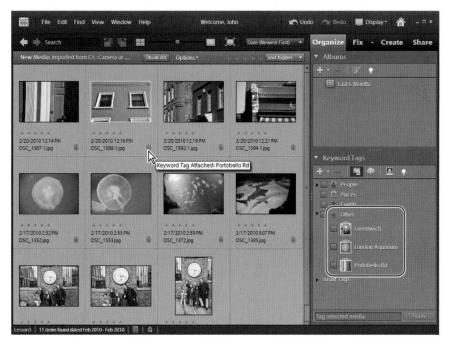

The Advanced Photo Downloader dialog box also offers other options: you can choose to import only a specified selection of the images on your memory card, rotate images as they are imported, fix red eye effects automatically, rename your photos, add a range of metadata, and add images to an Album. On Windows you can choose to have visually similar images automatically grouped into Stacks. The more of these advanced options you take advantage of when importing your photos into the Organizer, the less time and effort you'll need to spend sorting and organizing your files later—and the easier it will be to find that specific photo months or even years after you added it to your catalog.

Later in this lesson you'll learn further techniques for organizing your catalog, but first let's look at some more methods of bringing images into Photoshop Elements.

Acquiring still frames from a video

Note: On Mac OS, WMV video files can be imported, but are not supported for playback.

You can capture frames from digital videos in any of the file formats supported by Photoshop Elements. These include: ASF, AVI, MLV, MOV, MPG, MPEG, and WMV. To capture and import frames from video, you'll need to open the Editor.

1   If you still have any images selected in the Organizer from the previous exercise, choose Edit > Deselect.

2   Click the small arrow on the Fix tab at the top of the Task Pane and choose Full Photo Edit from the menu. When the Editor opens choose File > Import > Frame From Video.

3   In the Frame From Video dialog box, click the Browse button. Navigate to your Lesson03 folder, select the file **Tiger.avi**, and click Open.

Note: Some video formats do not support rewind or fast-forward. When these functions are not available, the Rewind (◀◀) and Fast Forward (▶▶) buttons are dimmed.

4   To start the video, click the Play button (▶). Click the Pause button (⏸) after 3 or 4 seconds, and then use the arrow keys on your keyboard to move forward or backward one frame at a time until you find a frame you want to capture.

5   To capture any frame of the video as a still image, click the Grab Frame button or press your spacebar when the frame you want is visible on the screen.

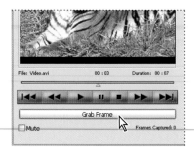

6   Continue to move forward and backward in the video to capture several additional frames. When you have all the frames you want, click Done.

Depending on your video footage and which frames you captured, you might notice artifacts in the still image resulting from the fact that a video picture consists of two interlaced half-pictures. The odd-numbered scanlines of the image, also called odd fields, constitute one half of the picture, and the even-numbered scanlines, or even fields, the other. Since the two halves of the picture were recorded at slightly different times, the captured still image might look distorted.

For the purposes of this exercise, it's worthwhile to deliberately choose a frame with this kind of distortion, which is most easily identified as a 'zigzag' effect and is particularly noticeable on vertical detail, as can be seen in the image on the right.

In Photoshop Elements you can remedy this problem with the De-Interlace filter, which will remove either the odd or even fields in an image captured from video, and then replace the discarded lines either by duplication or by interpolation from the remaining lines, depending on the options you specify.

7   Choose the image you wish to use for this exercise. You can discard the others by clicking the Close button (×) in the name tab of each image window. Click Don't Save in the alert dialogs that ask if you wish to save the images.

8   With the image you've chosen still open in the Editor, switch from Full to Quick Edit mode. Click Quick on the Edit tab at the top of the Panel Bin.

9   From the View menu in the lower left corner of the Editor window, choose Before & After - Vertical.

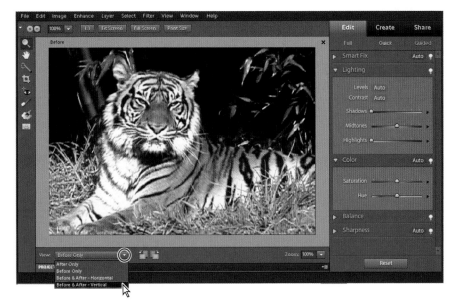

10 Double-click to highlight the number in the Zoom value box in the lower right corner of the image display window, type **300**, and then press Enter. Use the Hand tool to drag the image in either the Before or After pane so that you can see the tiger's eyes. (When you're working with tigers, it's *always* a good idea to watch the eyes!)

11 Choose Filter > Video > De-Interlace. Position the De-Interlace dialog box so that you can see both the Before and After views, and then choose either Odd Fields or Even Fields under Eliminate and either Duplication or Interpolation under Create New Fields By, and then click OK. The combination of options that will produce the best results depends on the image at hand. You can Undo after each trial and repeat this step until you are satisfied with the result.

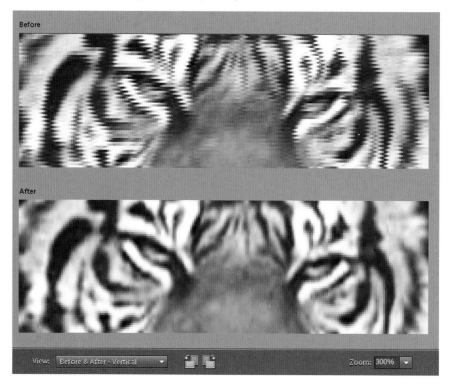

12 Return to the Full Edit mode, save the image (File > Save) in your My CIB Work folder, and then close the image window in the Editor.

Importing from a PDF document

Photoshop Elements enables you to import either whole pages from a PDF document or to select and extract just the images you want.

1 In the Editor, choose File > Open.

2 In the Open dialog box, navigate to your Lesson03 folder, select the file Ansonia.pdf, and then click Open. If you can't see the file Ansonia.pdf in the Open dialog box, click the Files Of Type / Enable menu at the bottom of the dialog box and choose either All Formats / All Readable Documents or Photoshop PDF (*.PDF,*.PDP).

In the Import PDF dialog box, you can choose to import entire pages or just the images from a PDF file. If you choose to import pages from a multiple-page PDF file, you can Ctrl-click / Command-click the page thumbnails to select those pages you wish to import. Pages are rasterized (converted to bit-mapped graphics) according to your choice of image size, resolution, and color mode. The imported result will be an image similar to that acquired by scanning a printed document.

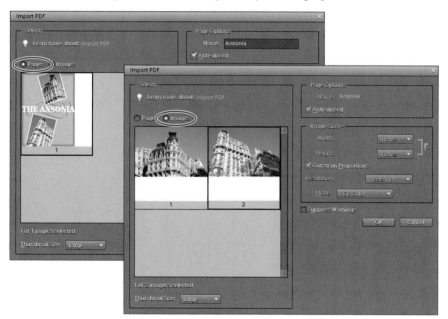

If you choose to import the images embedded in a PDF file rather than full pages, you can use the same method to multiple-select the images you want.

3 Under Select in the Import PDF dialog box, choose Images.

4 From the Thumbnail Size menu, select Fit Page to see the image previews at the largest possible size. Scroll the preview pane to see the last image.

5 Select Large from the Thumbnail Size menu. This enables you to see both of the images in this file. Click to select an image you wish to import. Ctrl-click / Command-click the other image if you would like to add it to the import, and then click OK.

6 If an alert dialogs appear to let you know that the image files use an unsupported color mode, click Convert Mode.

Each image imported from the PDF file opens in its own document window in the Editor, ready for further processing.

7   For each imported image choose File > Save As, navigate to your My CIB Work folder, and save the file with a descriptive name in Photoshop (*.PSD,*.PDD) file format. You could add the files to your catalog by activating the option Include In The Elements Organizer, but for now, leave that option disabled. Click Save.

Scanning images on Windows

This exercise is optional; it requires that you have a scanner available.

Tip: Photoshop Elements 9 also allows you to scan images using a video input source such as a web camera attached to your computer.

1   To prepare for acquiring images from a scanner, first switch to the Organizer. Choose Edit > Preferences > Scanner, and then do the following:

   •   If you have more than one scanner or an additional video input source installed, make sure that the correct device is selected in the Scanner menu.

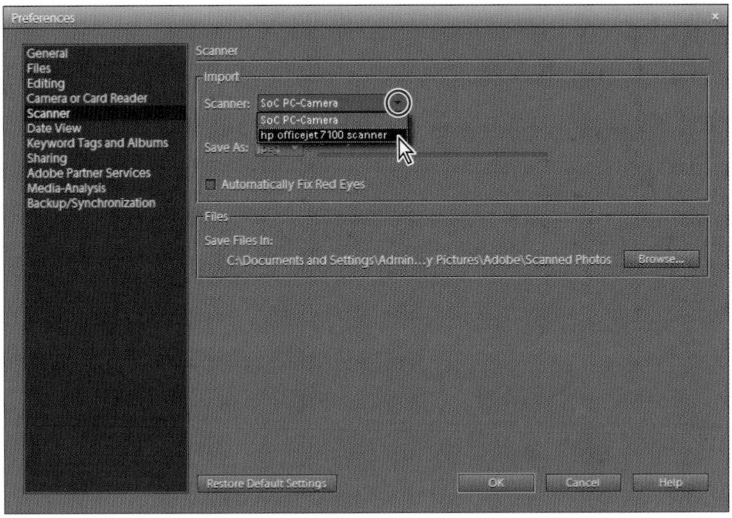

   •   Either accept the default settings for Save As (jpeg), and Quality or, if you prefer different settings, change them now.

   •   Disable the Automatically Fix Red Eyes option. You will learn about fixing red eye in the Organizer in Lesson 7, "Adjusting Color in Images."

   •   If you want to change the location to which the scanned files will be saved, click Browse, and then find and select the folder you want to use.

   •   Click OK to close the Preferences dialog box.

2   Place the picture or document you want to scan on the scanner bed and make sure your scanner is turned on.

3 If the scan dialog box does not appear automatically, go to the Organizer and choose File > Get Photos And Videos > From Scanner.

4 In the Scan dialog box, click the Preview button and examine the result.

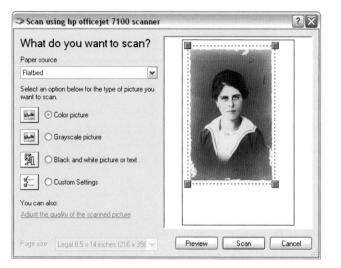

Note: The overall appearance of the dialog box, and the options available for your scanner, may differ from what is shown in this illustration.

Tip: When you scan several photographs at once, Photoshop Elements can crop the scan into individual photos automatically and will also straighten them for you. For information on the Divide Scanned Photos command, see Photoshop Elements Help.

5 If you are not satisfied with the preview, change the scanner settings as preferred.

6 Click Scan. When the scan is complete, the thumbnail of the scanned image appears in the Media Browser pane in the Organizer.

7 Click Show All to see all the images in your catalog.

Scanning images on Mac OS

You can import scanned images directly into Photoshop Elements from any scanner that has a Photoshop Elements-compatible plug-in module.

To use your scanner's plug-in module, see your scanner documentation for instructions on installing the scanner plug-in, and then choose the device name from the File > Import submenu.

Another option is to use the stand-alone software that came with your scanner, or Apple's Image Capture, to scan and save your images to your hard disk. You can then bring the images into Photoshop Elements by choosing File > Get Photos And Videos > From Files And Folders (or From iPhoto) in the Organizer, or by using the File > Open command in the Editor.

When you scan several items at the same time, Photoshop Elements can crop the scan into individual images automatically and will also straighten them for you. For information on the Divide Scanned Photos command, and more about scanning on Mac OS, please see Photoshop Elements Help.

Note: Before you try to import an image to Photoshop Elements from your scanner, read carefully through the manufacturer's documentation and make sure that you've installed any software that came with the device. Make sure also that the scanner is connected properly to your computer.

Organizing photos

Organizing your files and folders efficiently can be challenging. It's easy to forget what pictures are stored in which folder—and being forced to open and examine the content of numerous folders to find files can be both time consuming and extremely frustrating.

The Organizer can make the whole process much simpler and more enjoyable. The next set of exercises will show you how investing a little time in organizing your catalog can streamline the process of sorting through your image files, regardless of where they are stored.

Working with version sets

A version set groups a photo in its original state with any edited copies, so that you can find all the versions of the image stacked behind a single thumbnail in the Media Browser, rather than scattered amongst the rest of the items in your catalog.

Photoshop Elements automatically creates a version set whenever you modify a photo in the Elements Organizer. When you edit an photo from your catalog in the Editor, however, you'll need to choose File > Save As, and then activate the option Save In Version Set With Original.

Grouping your work in this way not only makes it much easier for you to find the version you want, but also enables you to keep your original un-edited photo intact, easy to find and ready for a different treatment whenever you want to re-use it.

To prepare for the following exercises, you'll first clear any images that you've added to your Lesson3 catalog since the beginning of this lesson, and then import the lesson files.

> ▶ **Tip:** The name of the currently active catalog is always displayed in the lower left corner of the Organizer window.

1   In the Organizer make sure your Lesson3 catalog is loaded. If the Show All button is visible above the Media Browser, click it. Choose Edit > Select All, and then choose Edit > Delete (Selected Items) From Catalog. The Confirm Deletion From Catalog dialog box appears; if you see the options Delete All Photos In Collapsed Stacks and Delete All Items In Collapsed Version Sets, activate both options by clicking their checkboxes, and then click OK.

2   Choose File > Get Photos And Videos > From Files And Folders.

3   In the Get Photos And Videos From Files And Folders dialog box, navigate to your Lesson03 folder and select the folder Photos London. Activate the option Get Photos From Subfolders. If the option Automatically Fix Red Eyes is activated, click the check box to disable it. On Windows, disable the Automatically Suggest Photo Stacks option.

4   Click Get Media. The Import Attached Keyword Tags dialog box appears; click Select All, and then click OK. Click OK to close any other alert dialog box.

In the Media Browser, you can see thumbnails of the sixteen images you've just added to your Lesson3 catalog.

5   In the Keyword Tags panel, click the triangle beside the Imported Keyword Tags category to see the newly added tags.

6   If you don't see filenames displayed with the thumbnails in the Media Browser, activate the options Details and Show File Names in the View menu.

7   Select the image DSC_1165.jpg, and then choose Edit > Auto Smart Fix. The Auto Smart Fix command corrects the overall color balance and improves shadow and highlight detail, if needed. The edited copy of the image is automatically grouped in a version set with the original photo, with the edited version topmost. A version set can be identified in the Media Browser by the badge displayed in the upper right corner of the thumbnail.

▶ **Tip:** Remember: if you edit an image in the Editor you need to choose File > Save As, and then activate the option Save In Version Set With Original.

8 Click the expand button to the right of the thumbnail image to see the original and edited images in the version set displayed side by side.

Tip: If you edit a photo that's already in a version set, the edited copy is placed at the top of the existing version set. To specify a different photo as the topmost, select it in the expanded view of the version set, and then choose Edit > Version Set > Set As Top Item.

9 To see only the topmost photo in the version set, click the collapse button to the right of the thumbnail image on the right, or right-click / Control-click either image in the set and choose Version Set > Collapse Items In Version Set from the context menu. Note the other commands available from the same context menu; these commands can also be found in the Edit > Version Set menu.

About stacks

You can create stacks to group a set of related photos in the Media Browser, making them easier to manage. Stack photos that make up a series, or multiple images of the same subject, to help reduce clutter in the Media Browser. For instance, you might create a stack for several photos of your family taken in the same pose, keeping the candidates together until you have a chance to pick the best shot—or for photos taken at a sports event using your camera's burst mode or auto-bracket feature. Generally, when you take photos this way you end up with many variations of what is essentially the same photo, but you only want the best version to appear in the Media Browser. Stacking the photos lets you easily access them all in one place instead of having them scattered across rows of thumbnails.

1 In the Keyword Tags panel, click the empty Find box next to the new Big Ben tag in the Imported Keyword Tags category.

2 Ctrl-click / Command-click to select the four landscape format (horizontal) photos, and then choose Edit > Stack > Stack Selected Photos. The four images are stacked, with the first photo you selected on top. A stack can be identified in the Media Browser by the stacked photos badge in the upper right corner of the image thumbnail. Expand and collapse the stack by clicking the expand or collapse arrows at the right side of the stack frame.

3 Expand the stack, and then right-click / Control click the topmost image in the version set that you created in the previous exercise: DSC_1165_edited-1.jpg. From the context menu, choose Stack > Set As Top Photo.

4 Collapse the stack; the topmost image now displays both the version set and stack badges.

Tips for working with stacks

You should keep these points in mind when you're working with stacks:

- To specify a new image as the topmost, expand the stack, right-click the desired photo, and then choose Stack > Set As Top Photo from the context menu.

- Combining two or more stacks merges them to form one new stack, with the most recent photo on top of the stack. The original groupings are not preserved.

- Many actions applied to a collapsed stack, such as editing, printing, and e-mailing, are applied to the topmost item only. To apply an action to multiple images in a stack, either expand the stack and group-select the images, or un-stack them first.

- If you edit a photo that you've already included in a stack, the photo and its edited copy will be grouped as a version set nested inside the stack.

- If you apply a keyword tag to a collapsed stack, the keyword tag is applied to all items in the stack. When you run a search on the keyword tag, the top photo in the stack appears in the search results marked with the stack icon. If you want to apply a keyword tag to only one photo in a stack, expand the stack first and apply the keyword tag to just that photo.

Tip: To access stack commands, right-click / Control-click any image in a stack and choose from the Stack sub-menu. Alternatively, select a photo in the stack and choose from the Edit > Stack menu.

Stacking photos automatically

Automatic stacking is not supported for Mac OS; if you're working on Mac OS, you can skip to the next section, "Creating albums" on page 90.

On Windows, you can have Photoshop Elements suggest stacks automatically, based on visual similarities between images.

1 In the Find bar above the Media Browser, click the Show All button. In the Keyword Tags panel, click the empty Find boxes beside the imported keyword tags Greenwich and London Aquarium.

2 Ctrl-click / Command-click to select the three photos of the family posing in front of the famous Greenwich Observatory clock, together with the two photos of jellyfish. Choose Edit > Stack > Automatically Suggest Photo Stacks.

The Automatically Suggest Photo Stacks dialog box appears. The three photos of the family at Greenwich have been successfully placed in a group already, but the jellyfish photos will need to be grouped manually; the two shots are too different in color to score high enough on visual similarity. Experiment with your own photos to get a feel for the kind of images that perform best with this feature.

3 In the Automatically Suggest Photo Stacks dialog box, drag either of the jellyfish photos into the same group as the other.

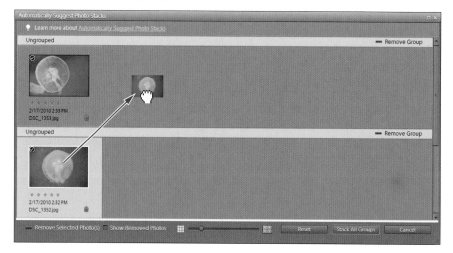

4 Select either of the photos of the jellyfish and click Remove Selected Photo(s) at the lower left of the Automatically Suggest Photo Stacks dialog box.

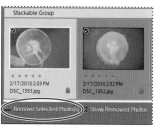

5 Activate Show Removed Photo(s) at the lower left of the Automatically Suggest Photo Stacks dialog box; then, drag the excluded image back into the group to be stacked.

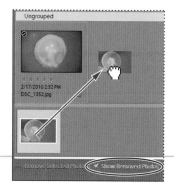

If you wish to exclude a suggested group from being stacked, click the Remove Group button at the right of the divider bar for that group.

6   Click the Stack All Groups button at the lower right of the Automatically Suggest Photo Stacks dialog box.

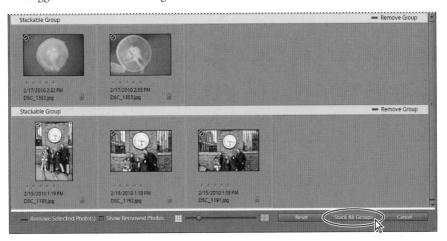

In the Media Browser, the two new stacks can be identified at a glance by the stacked photos badge in the upper right corner of the thumbnails.

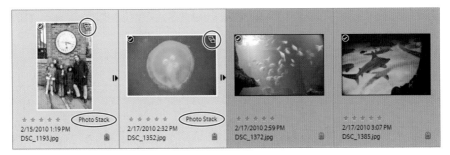

7   Click Show All in the Find bat above the thumbnail view. Your three new stacks have simplified the view in the Media Browser considerably.

Remember, you can access stack commands by right-clicking / Control-clicking any image in a stack and choosing from the Stack submenu. Alternatively, select a stack, or a photo in a stack, and choose from the Edit > Stack menu.

Creating albums

Another way of grouping your photos is to organize them into albums. You might create a new album to group shots from a special occasion such as a wedding or a vacation, or to assemble the images that you intend to use in a project such as a presentation to a client or a slideshow.

An album is like a virtual folder where you can assemble a group of images that may be drawn from any number of folders on your hard disk. The principal difference between grouping photos in an album and grouping them with a shared keyword tag is that in an album you can rearrange the order of the photos as you wish. In the Media Browser, each photo in an album displays a number in the upper left corner, representing its place in the order. You can drag photos to rearrange their order within the album, which will effect the order in which they appear in a slideshow or their placement in a project layout.

A photo can be added to more than one album—the same image might be the first in a New York album and the last in a National Monuments album. You can also group albums; for example, you might group your New York and San Francisco albums inside your Vacations album. Your San Francisco album may also be included in a Road Trips album while the New York album is not.

1   Choose File > Get Photos And Videos > From Files And Folders.

2   In the Get Photos And Videos From Files And Folders dialog box, navigate to your Lesson03 folder and select the Photos New York folder. Activate the option Get Photos From Subfolders and disable the other options.

3   Click Get Media. The Import Attached Keyword Tags dialog box appears; click Select All, and then click OK. Click OK to close any other alert dialog box.

In the Media Browser, you can see thumbnails of the images you've just added to your Lesson3 catalog. In the Keyword Tags panel, the newly added tags are listed in the Imported Keyword Tags category.

4   If the Albums panel is collapsed, click the triangle in the panel's header bar to expand it.

5   To create a new album, click the Create New Album Or Album Category button (✚) at the upper left of the Albums panel and choose New Album from the menu.

6   In the Album Details pane, type **New York** as the name for the new album. For the purposes of this exercise, disable the Backup/Sync option.

7 Ctrl-click / Command-click to select any six of the New York photos in the Media Browser; then, drag the group into the album Content box. Click Done.

Tip: If you add a collapsed version set or stack to an album, only the topmost image in the version set or stack will be visible in the album. To add a picture other than the topmost photo to the album, expand the version set or stack, and select the image you want.

8 To isolate the contents of the new album, click in the Albums panel, or drag the New York album entry onto the Find bar above the Media Browser. Notice the number in the top left corner of each photo, representing its order in the album.

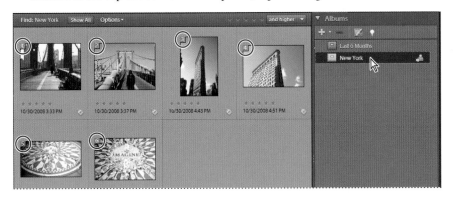

Note: It's not possible to view the contents of more than one album at a time, as images may appear in more than one album and occupy a different position in each.

9 Click the Back To Previous View button (◀) at the left of the Find bar to see all of the imported images in the Media Browser once more. If the thumbnails are set to display at a large enough size, photos that are included in your new album are marked with a green album icon below their thumbnails.

If you don't see the album badges, experiment with the thumbnail size slider above the Media Browser.

Tip: To see which album or albums a photo belongs to, hold the pointer over the album icon associated with the image in the Media Browser.

10 In the Media Browser, select the six New York photos that are not yet part of the new album, and then drag the selection directly onto the New York album entry in the Albums panel. (Alternatively, you can drag the album icon onto any one of the selected photos in the Media Browser.)

▶ **Tip:** In the Albums panel, you can group related albums in an album category, just as you group keyword tags in a category. To change an album's name, icon, or backup-sync settings, click the Edit Album button (🖉) in the Albums panel's header bar.

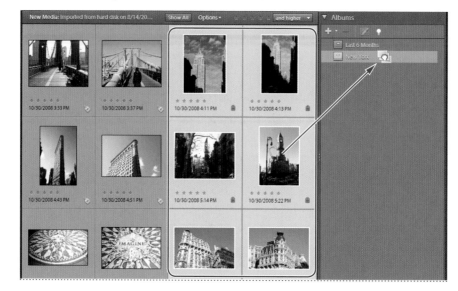

11 All twelve images are now included in your New York album. To change the order of the images in an album, first isolate the images in the New York album by clicking the album's entry in the Albums panel. Select one or more photos in the Media Browser, and then simply drag the selection to the new position. The photos in your album are reordered when you release the mouse button.

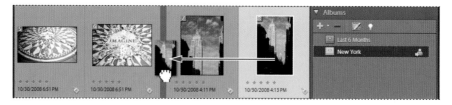

12 To remove a photo from the album, right-click / Control-click the image in the album view, and then choose Remove From Album > New York from the context menu. Choose Edit > Undo Remove Item(s) From Album.

13 Click Show All above the Media Browser.

⬤ **Note:** Deleting an album does not delete the photos in the album from your catalog. Albums store only references to the image files.

14 To delete the album, right-click / Control-click its entry in the Albums panel, and choose Delete New York Album from the context menu. For this exercise, click Cancel in the Confirm Album Deletion dialog box.

Working with smart albums

Rather than manually selecting photos as you do for an ordinary album, you only need to specify search criteria to create a smart album. Once you set the criteria, any photo in a catalog that matches the specified conditions will automatically appear in that smart album. As you add new images to your catalog, any photos that match a smart album's criteria will be added to that album. In other words, Smart Albums keep themselves up-to-date.

1   To create a new smart album, click the Create New Album Or Album Category button ( ) in the Albums panel and choose New Smart Album from the menu.

2   Type **New York Project** as the album name. Under Search Criteria, activate the option All Of The Following Search Criteria [And]. From the first search criteria menu, choose Keyword Tags. From the associated value menu, choose Lesson 03.

3   Click the Add Additional Criteria button (+) to the right of the criteria you just defined. Set the new search criteria to Albums Include New York. Repeat the process and set the third criteria to Rating Is Higher Than 3 Stars. Click OK.

4   Your New York Project album appears in the Albums panel; the blue album icon indicates that this is a smart album. As yet, there are no images in your catalog that match all the criteria, so the Media Browser is empty. Click Show All in the Find bar to see all the files in the Lesson3 catalog.

5   In the Media Browser, Ctrl-click / Command-click to select three or four of the images from New York, and as many from London; then, click the fourth star below any of the selected photos to apply a 4-star rating to the entire selection.

6 Click the New York album; the Media Browser displays only the twelve New York photos. Click the smart album New York Project; the album now contains those photos from the New York album that you rated in step 5.

7 To change the name of your smart album, make sure the smart album is selected in the Albums panel and click the Edit button () at the top of the panel. In the Edit Smart Album dialog box, type **New York Presentation** for the new album name, and then click OK.

8 To change the search criteria for your smart album, first make sure the smart album is selected in the Albums panel; then click Options in the Find bar and choose Modify Search Criteria from the menu.

9 In the Find By Details (Metadata) dialog box, click the Remove This Criteria From This Search button (-) to the right of the Albums Include New York rule.

If you clicked Search now, your changes to the criteria would affect the results of the current search, but would not be saved to the existing smart album.

10 Activate Save This Search Criteria As Smart Album, type **Best Travel Shots** as the name for the new smart album, and then click Search.

The new smart album, containing all the photos that you rated earlier, is added to the Albums panel.

11 Right-click / Control-click the smart album New York Presentation and choose Delete New York Presentation Smart Album from the context menu. Click OK to confirm the deletion. Click the Show All button in the Find bar.

You cannot change the order of photos in a smart album, as you can for other albums. Nor can you add photos to a smart album by dragging them onto the album's icon; a smart album can contain only images that match its criteria.

The content of a smart album may change over time—even if you don't modify the search criteria, add photos to, or remove them from your catalog. For example, a smart album may be set up to filter for photos captured within the last six months from the current date. Photos included in the album today may not fall within that date range tomorrow.

Viewing and finding photos

Photoshop Elements offers a variety of options for sorting and viewing the media in your catalog, and a range of tools to help you quickly find just the files you need. In the Organizer you can search your catalog by media type, filename, date, folder location, star rating, album, keyword tag, text, or a range of other criteria, and then refine, sort and view the search results by album or in chronological order.

*   **The Find bar** You can drag a photo, keyword tag, creation, or album onto the Find bar across the top of the Media Browser to locate similar photos and media files. The Find bar also offers options for sorting the search results.

*   **The Find menu** Use the Find menu commands to search your catalog by date, caption, file name, history, media type, metadata, or—on Windows—by visual similarity. The Find menu also provides options for finding photos and media files that have unknown dates, are un-tagged, or are not included in any album.

*   **Keyword Tags, Albums and Star Ratings** View only those files with a selected keyword tag, or combination of tags, by clicking in the Keyword Tags panel, or files in a particular album by clicking in the Albums panels. Use the Star Ratings filter in the Find bar to see just those photos and media files with a specified rating, or to narrow a search based on any other criteria.

*   **Text Search box** Type in the text box above the Find bar to locate media with matching text—whether it's in the filename, caption, metadata, or album name. The Text Search box also includes a dynamic list of all your existing keywords.

*   **The Timeline** Choose Window > Timeline to display the timeline above the Media Browser. Use the Timeline as a search tool in its own right, or in combination with any of the other tools and views to help you refine a search or navigate the results. You might search for photos with a particular keyword tag, and then use the Timeline to limit the search to a specified date range.

In Thumbnail view, click a month or set a date range in the Timeline to find photos and media files by capture date. The Timeline shows you a breakdown of your catalog by import date in the Import Batch view and an overview of the folder by folder distribution of your media files in Folder Location view. The height of the bars in the timeline indicates the relative number of files in each group. The Timeline becomes particularly useful when your catalog contains a large number of files captured over a period of several years.

Viewing and managing files by folder location

In the Folder Location view you can rename, move, and delete files and folders, add files to your catalog, create instant albums and—on Windows—add folders to, or remove them from, the Watched Folder list.

1   Click the Show All button, if it's visible in the Find bar. In the Media Browser, select any of the photos from New York; then click the Display button () above the Task Pane and choose Folder Location from the menu.

The Folder Location view divides the Media Browser into two parts. On the left, the Folders panel displays the hierarchy of folders on your hard disk. Folders containing *managed* files (files that you've already imported to the current catalog) are indicated by a Managed folder icon ( ). Watched folders (on Windows only) have a Watched folder icon ( ). The viewing pane on the right displays thumbnail images of the contents of any managed folder selected in the Folders panel.

2 Press Ctrl+A / Command+A to select all the photos in the Media Browser; then, drag the selection to the Photos New York folder in the Folders panel. In the Folders panel, the folder from which you moved the photos has lost its Managed folder icon (), while the Photos New York folder has acquired one. You may need to make the Folders panel wider to see the complete folder names.

3 Right-click / Control-click the folder from which you moved the photos and choose Delete Folder from the context menu. Click Yes to confirm the deletion.

4 Right-click / Control-click the Photos New York folder and choose Reveal In Explorer / Reveal In Finder from the context menu. A Windows Explorer / Finder window opens to display the contents of the Photos New York folder. You can see that the files you moved in the Folders panel have actually been moved on your hard disk, and that the folder you deleted no longer exists. Switch back to the Elements Organizer.

5 Right-click / Control-click the Photos New York folder and choose New Folder from the context menu; a new sub-folder is created inside the Photos New York folder. Type a name for the new folder—if you remember it, you can use the name of the folder you deleted.

6 Drag the thumbnails for the photos in the Photos New York folder from the Media Browser into the new sub-folder. The Photos New York folder has lost its Managed folder icon (), while the new sub-folder has acquired one.

7 In the Folders panel, click the Portobello Road folder (inside Photos London); then, click the Create Instant Album button at the right of the header above the image thumbnails. The Portobello Road album appears in the Albums panel.

8 In the folder hierarchy, expand the Lesson02 folder to show its sub-folders by clicking the plus icon (+) / triangle at the left of the folder name. Right-click / Control-click the folder Faces and choose Import To Organizer from the menu. In the Import Attached Keyword Tags dialog box, click Cancel. Click OK to dismiss any other dialog box.

9 With the Faces folder still selected in the Folders panel, click the header bar above the thumbnails to select all six photos. Drag the Lesson 03 tag from the Keyword Tags panel to any of the selected images.

10 Click the Display button (▣) above the Task Pane and choose Thumbnail View from the menu. Click the Show All button in the Find bar.

Finding photos using details and metadata

Searching your catalog by metadata detail is useful when you want to narrow a search by applying multiple criteria.

Some of the metadata that may be attached to an image file is generated automatically by your camera; some is added when you spend time organizing your catalog. Searchable metadata includes file name, size, and type, keyword tags, ratings, albums, version sets, captions, notes, capture date, and a range of camera, lens, and exposure details—to mention just a few!

1 Choose Find > By Details (Metadata).

If you've completed the smart albums exercises, you should already be familiar with setting up a multiple-criteria search in the Find > By Details (Metadata) dialog box. In fact, any search you define in this dialog box can be saved as a new smart album by activating that option below the search rules.

Note: To add a new criteria to your search, click the plus (+) button beside an existing rule; then, specify a category and values using the menus. To remove a criteria, click the minus sign (-) beside the rule. Activate the appropriate option to find files that match any or all of the criteria.

2 Under Search Criteria, click the first menu and scroll down the list, noting the many categories available. Choose a criteria category and experiment with defining the rule by choosing values from the other menu or menus. Click the plus icon (+) to the right of your first rule and define a new criteria. Repeat the process several times, exploring more of the search criteria menu options.

3 Click Cancel to dismiss the Find > By Details (Metadata) dialog box.

Metadata support for audio and video files

Photoshop Elements provides metadata support for audio and video files in the Organizer, making it just as easy to find those files as it is to locate your photos.

1 Choose File > Get Photos And Videos > From files And Folders. Locate and open your Lesson03 folder.

2 Select the audio file Temple of the Moon.wav and the video Tiger.avi. Disable any active automatic processing option, and then click Get Media. Click OK to dismiss any other dialog box.

You can inspect the metadata in these files using the Properties - Metadata panel, where metadata information is categorized into separate audio and video sections. In the Brief view, you'll find information such as pixel aspect ratio for video, while the audio section includes artist, album name, etc, if that information is present in the file. The File Properties section displays the filename, document type, creation and modification dates, and—if you activate the Complete view—the file size for your audio and video files.

3 Right-click / Control-click the file Tiger.avi and choose Show Properties to open the Properties panel. To view all the available metadata, click the Info button (ⓘ) at the top of the panel, and then enable the Complete view option below the Info pane.

4 Keeping the Properties - Metadata panel open, click Temple of the Moon.wav in the Media Browser to see the properties and metadata for this audio file.

Note: You cannot edit the metadata for audio and video files in Photoshop Elements.

5 Close the Properties panel by clicking the close button (×) in the panel's header.

Viewing video files

In Photoshop Elements 9, you can play video files without ever leaving the Organizer. Simply double-click the video file in the Media Browser to open the new integrated playback window, where you can even apply keyword tags. You can now also play videos in the Full Screen mode.

Using a text search to find photos

You can quickly find the photos you want using a text-based search. Type a word in the Text Search box just above the left end of the Find bar, and the Organizer will display images that match the text across a wide range of criteria. Matches can include items such as author, captions, dates, filenames, keyword tags, metadata, notes, album names, album groups, and camera information; Photoshop Elements will look for the search term in *any* text that is associated with the file.

You can use a text search as a convenient shortcut—for example, type the name of a tag, rather than navigating to the Keyword Tags panel. The text search feature has been enhanced to make it even easier and quicker to use; the search box has been augmented with a dynamic list of existing tags. As soon as you type a letter, the search box displays a list of tags starting with that letter; as you type more text the list changes to offer tags that match whatever you type. Click the item you want in the list and the Media Browser displays only the images tagged with that keyword.

Text search also supports the operators **and**, **or**, and **not**, if they are preceded and followed by a space. For example, you could type **vacation and kids** to find only images with both words in their metadata, not just either one. Some words can be processed by Photoshop Elements as special instructions, not as specific search criteria. For example, you may want to search for a file tagged Birthday, but only among your video files. You can use the Media **Type** and **Video** keywords. So, you would type **Type: Video Tag: Birthday**. For a list of supported operators and special tags, please refer to Photoshop Elements Help.

Hiding files

You've already learned how you can simplify the process of working with your growing catalog by creating stacks and version sets to help reduce clutter and repetition in the Media Browser. Stacking related shots and grouping edited versions with their originals effectively reduces the number of images on view; you can choose the most interesting image in a stack or version set as the topmost and keep the other images tucked out of view until you choose to work with them.

In many cases it may be more effective to hide those images from view entirely. Once you've settled on the best of a stack of similar photos, or of several edits in a version set, you can hide the other images from view so that they will no longer appear in search results to distract you when making selections, or need to be taken into consideration when applying commands. Hiding a photo does not delete it from its folder on your hard disk, remove it from your catalog, or even from an album—you can un-hide it at any time if you start a new project where it might be useful or if you find that you could make use of a differently edited version.

1 In the Albums panel, click the album New York. Ctrl-click / Command-click to select both photos of the Empire State Building; then, choose Edit > Auto Smart Fix Selected Photos. Auto Smart Fix is applied to both images and both are automatically grouped in separate version sets with the edited versions topmost.

2 Select both version sets and choose Edit > Version Set > Convert Version Set To Individual Items. There are now four images of the Empire State Building in the Media Browser: two originals and two edited copies.

3 If necessary, activate the option Show All Files in the Edit > Visibility menu.

4 Select both of the original photos of the Empire State Building, and then add any other image to the selection. Choose Edit > Visibility > Mark As Hidden. The Hidden File icon appears in the lower left corner of all three thumbnails.

5 Ctrl-click / Command-click to de-select the two images of the Empire State Building, leaving only the third photo selected in the Media Browser. Choose Edit > Visibility > Mark As Visible. The selected photo loses its Hidden File icon.

6 Choose Edit > Visibility > Hide Hidden Files. The two un-edited photos of the Empire State Building are removed from the Media Browser view.

7 In the Keyword Tags panel, expand the Imported Keyword Tags category if necessary; then, click the empty Find box beside the Empire State Building tag. The two hidden files do not appear in the search results. Click Show All.

8 Choose Edit > Visibility > Show Only Hidden Files. Select both images and choose Edit > Delete Selected Items From Catalog. In the Confirm Deletion From Catalog dialog box, activate the option Also Delete Selected Items From The Hard Disk, and then click OK. Choose Edit > Visibility > Hide Hidden Files.

This concludes the advanced organizing lesson for Mac OS users. The remainder of this lesson covers the Map view and finding photos by visual similarity: features not supported in Photoshop Elements 9 for Mac OS.

If you're working on Mac OS, you can skip to the lesson review on page 107.

Finding photos by visual similarity

On Windows, you can search for photos by visual similarity; Photoshop Elements finds and ranks images by similarity in shapes, colors, patterns or composition.

1 Click Show All, if it's visible in the Find bar. Select the photo stack containing images of London's Big Ben. Choose Edit > Stack > Unstack Photos; then, drag the collapsed version set DSC_1165_edited-1.jpg to the Find bar.

The images in the Media Browser are displayed in descending order of visual similarity to the photo you dragged to the Find bar. A marker displaying the calculated percentage of visual similarity for each image appears in the bottom left corner of its thumbnail. Photoshop Elements has done well to find all the other shots of the same subject—including the close-up of the clock tower in vertical orientation.

2 Click the Show All button to clear this search.

The Map view

On Windows, you can arrange and search for your photos by geographic location in the Map view. You can link an image to a location either by typing an address or by simply dragging its thumbnail from the Media Browser directly onto the map.

Note: You must have an active Internet connection to use this feature.

1   In the Albums panel, click the album New York. In the Media Browser, right-click the first thumbnail of the Empire State Building and choose Place On Map from the context menu.

2   In the Photo Location On Map dialog box, type **Empire State Building** in the text box, and then click Find.

3   In the Look Up Address dialog box, click OK to confirm the address: Empire State Building, New York, NY. 10001 US.

The Map view opens. The red pin indicates the location for your photo. Below the map are the Zoom, Hand, and Move tools. You can zoom the view in or out, use the Hand tool to drag the map, or reposition the pin with the Move tool. Use the menu at the lower right to switch between the Map, Hybrid and Satellite modes.

4 Drag the second image of the Empire State Building to the pin you've already placed on the map. The pin is highlighted to show you when the new photo is in position; release the mouse button to locate the photo with its partner.

5 Choose Hybrid from the pop-up menu in the lower right corner of the Map panel, below the Share button.

6 Select the Zoom Out tool ( ) and click on the map twice, south of the pin for the Empire State Building.

7 Use the Hand tool to drag the map a little upwards and to the right so that you can see the Brooklyn Bridge, while keeping the pin for the Empire State Building in view.

8 If you still have an image selected in the Media Browser, choose Edit > Deselect. Drag the Brooklyn Bridge tag from the Keyword Tags panel onto the map and release the mouse button when the tag is positioned over the Brooklyn Bridge.

9 Click on the new pin you just placed on the Brooklyn Bridge to display a preview of the photos you've assigned to that location.

10 Click the Limit Search To Map Area check box in the lower left corner of the Map View. Only photos mapped to the currently visible map area are displayed in the Media Browser.

11 Right-click the Imagine tag and choose Place On Map from the context menu; then, type **Central Park New York, NY** in the Photo Location On Map dialog box and click Find. Click OK in the Look Up Address dialog box to confirm the address.

12 Once you have a pin in Central Park, use the map's Move Tool to drag the pin a little inside the entrance at West 72nd St. (The Imagine mosaic is part of the John Lennon Memorial there.)

13 (Optional) Place the other New York photos on the map, varying your method. The Ansonia Hotel is at 2109 Broadway New York, NY 10023. The Flatiron Building is at 175 Fifth Ave New York, NY 10011. The Jefferson Market branch of the New York Public Library is at 425 Sixth Avenue New York, NY 10011.

14 Click the Close button (■) in the upper right corner of the Map panel to close it; then, click the Show All button in the Find bar.

15 Right-click either of the Imagine photos in the Media Browser and choose Show On Map from the context menu. The Map view opens, showing the location to which the photo was mapped.

16 Close the Map view.

Congratulations—you've reached the end of Lesson 3! In this lesson, you've learned about the advanced import options in the Photo Downloader, how to acquire still frames from a video, and how to import images from a PDF file or acquire them from a scanner. You've organized images into version sets, stacks and albums, placed photos on a map, and learned some advanced techniques for finding and managing the files in your catalog.

Before you move on, take a moment to review what you've learned, and test your command of the concepts and techniques presented in this lesson by working through the following questions and answers.

Review questions

1 How can you automatically create and apply keyword tags to images while importing them from a digital camera or card reader?

2 What does the Photoshop Elements De-Interlace filter do?

3 What does the Auto Smart Fix command do?

4 What are Version Sets and Stacks?

5 What is the main difference between grouping files using shared keyword tags and grouping them in an album?

Review answers

1 In the Advanced Photo Downloader dialog box, choose Custom Groups (Advanced) from the Create Subfolder(s) menu. Next, choose an option including Custom Name from the Group Name menu, and then enter a Group Name in the Custom Name field on the separator bar above each group of thumbnails. Finally, activate the option Make 'Group Custom Name' A Tag before clicking Get Photos.

2 The Photoshop Elements De-Interlace filter can improve the appearance of a still frame acquired from a video by removing the artifacts caused by the fact that a video picture consists of two interlaced half-pictures taken at slightly different times. The De-Interlace filter removes either the odd or even fields in a still image from video and replaces the discarded lines by duplication or interpolation from the remaining lines.

3 The Auto Smart Fix command corrects the overall color balance and improves shadow and highlight detail, if necessary. The Auto Smart Fix command automatically groups the edited copy of the photo with the original in a version set.

4 A version set groups an original photo and its edited versions. Stacks are used to group a set of similar photos, such as multiple shots of the same subject or photos taken using your camera's burst mode or auto-bracket feature. A version set can be nested inside a stack: if you edit a photo that's already in a stack, the photo and its edited copy are put in a version set that is nested inside the original stack.

5 The main difference between grouping files in an album, rather than with a shared keyword tag, is that in an album you can rearrange the order of the files.

4 CREATING PROJECTS

Lesson Overview

Photoshop Elements makes it simple to create stylish, professional-looking projects to showcase your photos. Choose from the preset themes and layouts—or create your own designs from scratch—as you put together a range of creations from greeting cards and Photo Books to animated slide shows and online albums.

Use your own images in personalized CD or DVD jackets and labels, calendars, collages, and digital flip-books. Combine images, text, animation and even music and narration, to produce unique multimedia creations.

Whether you're designing your own coffee table book, sharing your photos online, or creating personalized gifts for family and friends, Photoshop Elements will help unleash your creativity.

This lesson will familiarize you with the Create mode by stepping you through some basic techniques and simple projects:

- Creating a personalized greeting card
- Producing a stylish Photo Book
- Telling a story with a Photo Collage
- Using the Content library
- Working with layers

 You'll probably need around two hours to complete this lesson.

Photoshop elements offers a huge library of design themes, layout templates, and clip graphics that make it easy to produce eye-catching projects using your own photos. Show loved ones how much you care with stylish personalized greeting cards; preserve and share your precious memories in a sophisticated Photo Book or combine pictures and mementos to tell an evocative story in an artistic Photo Collage.

Getting started

Before you start working on the exercises in this lesson, make sure that you have installed the software on your computer from the application CD (see the Photoshop Elements 9 documentation) and that you have correctly copied the Lessons folder from the CD in the back of this book onto your computer's hard disk. (See "Copying the Classroom in a Book files" on page 2.)

You'll start this lesson by setting up a new catalog in the Elements Organizer, and then move to the Editor, where you'll get to know the Create mode.

1   Start Photoshop Elements by doing one of the following:

- On Windows, either double-click the shortcut on your desktop, or choose Start > All Programs > Adobe Photoshop Elements 9.

- On Mac OS, either click the Photoshop Elements 9 icon in the Dock, double-click the application icon in the Applications folder, or choose Photoshop Elements 9 from the Apple > Recent Items > Applications menu.

2   In the Welcome screen, click the Organize button at the left.

Creating a new catalog

In each of the first three lessons in this book, you created a new catalog intended to manage the media files, keywords, stacks, and albums for just a single lesson.

Photoshop Elements enables you to create and manage as many special-purpose catalogs as you wish to suit the way that you prefer to work, but remember that a single catalog can efficiently handle thousands of files. You may prefer the convenience of using just one catalog to manage your entire image library from a single location, making use of tags and albums to organize the media for specific projects rather than creating more and more catalogs.

Now that you've learned how to import images and video and become familiar with a variety of techniques for organizing, managing, and searching your images you can set up a single catalog that you'll use for the rest of the lessons in this book.

1 In the Organizer, choose File > Catalog.

2 In the Catalog Manager dialog box, click New.

3 In the Enter A Name For The New Catalog dialog box, type **CIB Catalog**. If necessary, disable Import Free Music Into This Catalog, and then click OK.

The new CIB Catalog is loaded. If you're ever unsure of which catalog you're working with, remember that the name of the currently active catalog will appear in a tooltip when you hold the pointer over the Organizer icon (⊞) at the upper left of the workspace window, and is also displayed in the lower left corner of the Organizer workspace.

At the start of each the remaining lessons in this book, you'll import the lesson files to your new CIB (Classroom in a Book) Catalog.

Importing the lesson files

When you have a little free time, we recommend that you repeat the first three lessons to increase your familiarity with the Photoshop Elements workspace and the various viewing and working modes, and to reinforce your organizing skills.

To this end, you can import the files for Lessons 1, 2, and 3 to your CIB Catalog, together with the sample photos for this lesson, That way, when you've finished all the lessons in this book, you'll have a single catalog to which you can refer, complete with all your tags, stacks, albums, working files, and projects.

1   Choose File > Get Photos And Videos > From files and Folders. In the Get Photos And Videos From files and Folders dialog box, navigate to and open your Lessons folder, inside the PSE9CIB folder that you created at the beginning of this book.

2   Control-click / Command-click to group-select the folders Lesson01, Lesson02, Lesson03, and Lesson04. Make sure that Media Files (Photos, Video, Audio) is selected in the Enable menu, that the option Get Photos From Subfolders is activated, and that Automatically Fix Red Eyes is disabled. On Windows, disable Automatically Suggest Photo Stacks.

3   Click Get Media. The Getting Media dialog box displays a progress bar as the files in the selected folders are imported.

The Import Attached Keyword Tags dialog box appears, listing all the keywords that have been assigned to the files you're importing.

4   In the Import Attached Keyword Tags dialog box, click Select All below the list of keyword tags; then, click OK. A progress bar is displayed as the new keyword tags are added to the catalog. Click OK to dismiss the dialog box alerting you that the only images visible in the Media Browser are those you just imported.

Reconnecting missing files to a catalog

When you bring a photo or video clip into Photoshop Elements, the name and location of the file is recorded in the catalog. If you wish to move, rename, or delete a file that has already been imported into your catalog, its best if you do it from within the Elements Organizer.

If you move, rename, or delete a file in the Windows Explorer / Mac OS Finder after it has been added to the catalog, Photoshop Elements may no longer be able to find it. If a file cannot be located, the missing file icon ( ) appears in the upper left corner of its thumbnail in the Photo Browser to alert you that the link between the file and your catalog has been broken.

Photoshop Elements searches your computer for missing files automatically, and will usually do a great job finding them—even when the files have been renamed; however, you need to know what to do if the automatic search fails.

1   Switch to the Windows Explorer / Mac OS Finder by doing one of the following:

*   On Windows, minimize the Elements Organizer by clicking the Minimize button ( ) at the right of the menu bar, or simply click the Elements Organizer application button on the Windows taskbar.

*   On Mac OS, click the Finder icon in the Application Switcher (hold down Command; then press and release tab) or the Dock.

> ▶ **Tip:** To avoid the problem of missing files in your catalog, use the File > Move, File > Rename, and Edit > Delete From Catalog commands to move, rename, or delete files in Photoshop Elements, rather than doing so outside the application.

2   Open an Explorer / Finder window—if there's not one already available—and navigate to your Lesson04 folder. Drag the folder Photobook out of your Lesson04 folder and drop it in the Recycle Bin / Trash. Do not empty the Recycle Bin / Trash.

3   Switch back to the Elements Organizer and choose File > Reconnect > All Missing Files. Photoshop displays a message to let you know it's busy searching for the missing files. We don't expect the files to be found in the Recycle Bin / Trash, so you can stop the automatic search by clicking the Browse button.

The Reconnect Missing Files dialog box opens, just as it would had you let the search run its course, and Photoshop Elements could not locate the missing files.

4   For this exercise, you won't follow this process through to completion, but you should inspect the dialog box thoroughly. At the upper left is a list of missing files. Below that, a preview thumbnail displays the file selected in the list. To the right, you can browse the contents of your computer. When you select a file on the Browse tab, you'll see a preview thumbnail adjacent to the missing file preview, enabling you to verify the photo visually, even if its name has changed.

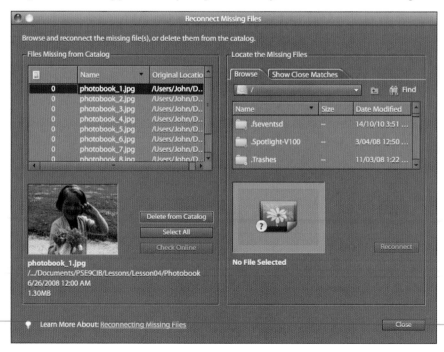

5 Once you've verified a file or files to be reconnected, you can click the Reconnect button. For now, click Close to cancel the operation.

6 Switch back to the Explorer / Finder; then, drag the Photobook folder out of the Recycle Bin / Trash and return it to your Lesson04 folder.

7 Switch back to the Elements Organizer and choose File > Reconnect > All Missing Files. Photoshop displays a message to let you know that there are no missing files to reconnect. Click OK to dismiss the message.

Exploring the artwork library

Photoshop Elements makes it quick and easy to create distinctive photo projects by providing an extensive collection of themes, backgrounds, frames, text styles, clip-art shapes and graphics in the Content library. Although this content is also available in the Create mode, we'll start by exploring the Content panel.

1 In the Organizer, choose Edit > Deselect to make sure you have no images selected in the Media Browser. Click the arrow on the Fix tab above the Task Pane and choose Full Photo Edit from the menu.

2 In Full Edit mode, choose Window > Reset Panels or click the Reset Panels button (⟳) at the top of the workspace. By default, the Effects, Content, and Layers panels are open in the Panel Bin. Choose Window > Favorites to open the Favorites panel as well.

3 Drag the Content panel by its name tab out of the Panels Bin, onto the header of the Project Bin. Release the mouse button when you see a blue highlight around the Project Bin. Enlarge the Content panel by dragging the top border of its header bar upwards. In the Panels Bin, collapse the Layers and Effects panels by double-clicking their headers. The Favorites panel expands to fill the Panels Bin.

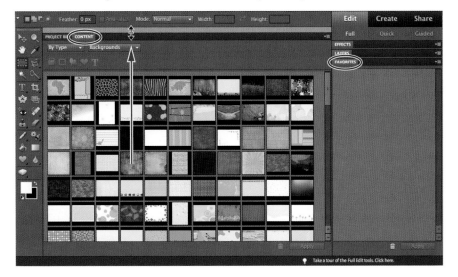

What you see displayed in the Content panel depends on the options set with the sorting menus and filter buttons above the sample swatches.

4 In the Content panel, By Type is selected in the sorting menu at the upper left of the panel. With this setting, the contents of the library are sorted by functional category. The second sorting menu, to the right, lists the categories Backgrounds, Frames, Graphics, Shapes, Text, and Show All. Choose each option in turn and scroll down the Content panel see the options available.

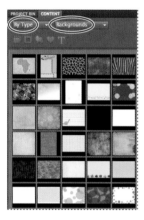 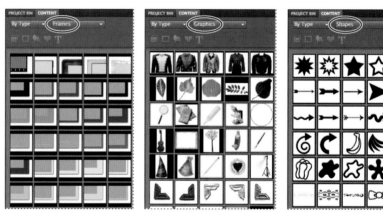

5 Choose By Word from the sorting menu; then, type **beach** in the search box and click Find. Make sure that all of the filter buttons below the sorting menu are activated, as shown in the illustration below. Drag the first swatch, "Beach With Seashells," into the Favorites panel and release the mouse button when you see a blue line highlighting the panel. Add the "Sea Shell" and "Star Fish" graphics to the Favorites panel. You'll use these items later in this lesson.

Tip: Hover the pointer over a swatch to see the name of the artwork item displayed in a tooltip.

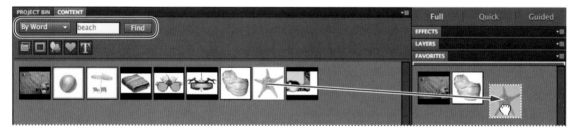

Tip: Hover the pointer over each content filter button to see the name of the filter displayed in a tooltip.

6 Swipe over the word "beach" in the search box and type **handmade**. Click to disable the Text Effects, Shapes, Graphics, and Frames filters below the sorting menu, leaving only the Backgrounds filter active; then, click Find. Drag the backgrounds "Handmade Paper 03" and "Scrapbook 08" into the Favorites panel.

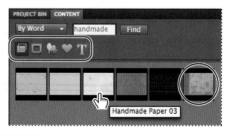

7 In the Content panel, disable the Backgrounds filter and activate the Graphics filter. Swipe over the word "handmade" in the search box and type **travel**; then, click Find. Drag the graphics "Plane Stamp" and "Travel Compass" into the Favorites panel.

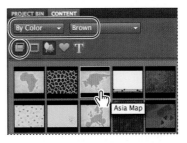

8 Activate the Backgrounds filter once more. From the sorting menu, choose By Color; then choose Brown from the colors menu. Add the Background "Asia Map" to your collection in the Favorites panel.

9 Disable the Backgrounds filter, leaving only the Graphics filter active. From the sorting menu, choose By Object and select Flower from the objects menu. Add the two purple petals and both of the yellow-centered white daisies to the Favorites panel as shown in the illustration.

10 To make just one more addition to your artwork favorites, disable the Graphics filter in the Content panel and activate the Frames filter. From the sorting menu, choose By Style. From the styles menu, choose Scrapbook. Locate the frame "Scrapbook 03" and drag it into the Favorites panel.

As you've seen, the Content library includes a great many backgrounds, frames, graphics, shapes and text styles. At first, the number of choices may seem overwhelming, but a little practice with the sorting and filtering controls will make it quick and easy to locate the artwork items you need. The search and filter functions in the Content panel are not available on the Artwork tab in Create mode, so it can save you time to do a little advance planning and assemble the items you want for a project in Full Edit mode, using the Content and Favorites panels in tandem as you've just done.

11 Click the Reset Panels button (⟳) at the top of the workspace; then, click the Organizer button (▦) at the top right to return to the Organizer.

Creating a greeting card

Personalized greeting cards based on your own photos make a great way to show friends and family how much you care—a really attractive card can spend months on a loved one's mantelpiece and may even be framed and displayed with pride.

You can include one or more images on each page of a greeting card and either print it on your home printer, order prints online, or save it to your hard disk, and then send it via e-mail. Once you've begun your greeting card, the Create tab offers controls for navigating between pages and easy access to layout templates, artwork, and effects to help you to create sophisticated designs quickly and easily.

Choosing a size and theme

For this project you'll use a vacation photo as the basis for a greeting card.

▶ **Tip:** If you don't see file names displayed below the thumbnail images in the Media Browser, ensure that the Details check box in the bar above the browser pane is activated and choose View > Show File Names.

1   In the Organizer, click Show All in the Find bar above the Media Browser. In the Keyword Tags panel, expand the Imported Keyword Tags category, and click the find box beside the Lesson 04 tag to isolate the images for this lesson.

2   In the Media Browser, select the image card.jpg.

3   Click the Create tab above the Task Pane. On the Create tab, click the Greeting Card button. The Greeting Card window opens.

4   At the left, the Sizes pane lists size options suitable for various online services; choose the first listing under Kodak Gallery: 5.00 x 7.00 inches (Flat, Portrait). From the options in the Themes pane, choose Family. You can either use a card theme "as is" or as a template that you can customize, as you'll do for this project. Make sure Autofill With Selected Images is activated; then, click OK.

Note: Although the Sizes pane lists options compatible with various online services, any greeting card can also be printed from your home printer. The choice of online services depends on your location and your operating system.

Photoshop Elements takes a few moments to generate a preview, create the appropriate number of pages for the type of card you specified, and place the selected image in the template. The card design appears in the Edit window and the Create tab presents the Pages navigator. For this flat card design, the Pages tab displays only a single thumbnail for the front of the card. A thumbnail for your as yet untitled project appears in the Project Bin.

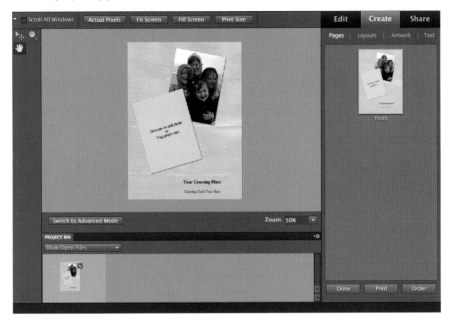

5 At the top of the Create tab, click Layouts to see some basic templates for the card theme you selected. Double-click the first layout thumbnail in the second row, "2 Tilted Text," and then double-click the thumbnail at the upper left, "2 Tilted Brown Text" to return to the default layout.

6 Click Artwork at the top of the Create tab. The thumbnail menu displays a small subset of the artwork from the Content library, with choices most likely to be appropriate for the theme you selected. Click the triangle beside Backgrounds to Collapse the category, and then scroll down in the menu, if necessary, to see the all ten options in the Frames menu.

7 Click the Switch To Advanced Mode button at the left below the Edit pane. Scroll through the Frames menu again; the menu now contains all the frames from the Content library. Note that the sort and filter functions you used in the Content panel in Full Edit mode are not available for the Artwork menus in Create Mode.

8 On the Create tab, scroll about one-third of the way down the Frames menu to locate the frame "Basic White Frame 40px." Check that the photo of the girls is selected in the project preview; it should be surrounded by a bounding box with control handles. If the photo is not selected, click in the preview to select it now. Double-click the frame "Basic White Frame 40px" to apply it to the selected image.

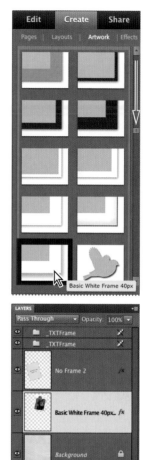

9 If you can't see all of the contents of the Layers panel, drag the divider between the Artwork menu and the Layers panel upwards.

The Layers panel displays a separate layer for each element in this card design. Starting from the bottom, the Background layer contains a background graphic from the Content library, marked with a Smart Object icon in the lower right corner. A Smart Object is resolution independent; it can be scaled or rotated repeatedly without any degradation of the image. For each transformation, the image data is re-drawn from a source file that always remains in its original state.

Above the Background is the layer with the currently selected photo, together with the frame you applied. Next in the stacking order is the placeholder for a second photo. Both this layer and the layer with the framed photo are marked with the *fx* icon, indicating that these layers both have layer styles—in this case a drop-shadow effect to lift the images against the background. The top two layers are live text layers, each marked with an icon indicating a non-editable text style.

10 In the project preview, click the empty image placeholder and press the Backspace / Delete key; then, confirm the deletion. The corresponding layer disappears from the Layers panel. Click the top text layer; the larger text is selected in the project preview. Press the Backspace / Delete key; then, confirm the deletion. Repeat the process to delete the second text object; you won't be using text in this design. Your card now has just two layers: a background image and a framed photo with its own drop shadow effect.

Replacing the background image

Each theme consists of a different combination of background artwork, image frame, graphics, layer effects and text styles. In some cases you may be happy with the un-edited result once your image has been placed in the layout but in other instances you may wish to treat the theme as a starting point or template and go on to customize the design. All the design elements can be moved, replaced, or deleted. Images (with or without frames) can also be duplicated, which is one way to add more photos to the layout if you wish.

1   Double-click the Hand tool to fit your view of the card to the Edit window.

2   Choose Window > Favorites to open the Favorites panel. If the Favorites panel opens in an inconvenient position, drag it into the Panels Bin by its header bar or position it where it won't obstruct your view of the card or the Layers panel.

3   Select the Background layer in the Layers panel, and then double-click the swatch for the background image "Beach With Seashells" in the Favorites panel. Wait a few moments while Photoshop Elements replaces the background image.

Working with photos and frames

The design theme you chose as a first step in creating your greeting card did not include frames, but each design differs. You already assigned a frame from the Artwork menu to the photo in this design. You would follow exactly the same steps if you wanted to replace it with another. For now, you can work on the placement of the framed photo and its positioning within the frame.

1   Select the Move tool ( ) in the tool bar. Drag the framed image to center it in the layout, and then right-click / Control-click inside the bounding box of the photo and frame. Choose Fit Frame To Photo from the context menu. The frame is re-sized so that its outside border conforms to the edge of the image.

2   Click one of the corner handles of the bounding box around the framed photo. In the tool options bar above the Edit pane, type **–10.5** in the Set Rotation box, just to the right of the Constrain Proportions option; then, click the Commit button (✔) at the lower right of the bounding box to commit the change.

3   Move the pointer over one of the corner handles on the bounding box around the framed image. When the diagonal double-arrow cursor appears, hold down the Alt / Option key on your keyboard to scale the image from the center as you drag the handle outwards, enlarging the image together with its frame. Release the mouse button when the distance between the outside of the white frame and the edge the image is roughly equivalent to the width of the frame.

4   Move the pointer close to one of the corner handles, keeping it just outside the bounding box. When the curved double-arrow cursor appears, drag to rotate the image clockwise. Hold down the Shift key as you drag to constrain the rotation to 15° increments, releasing the mouse button when you've rotated the image by 15°. Click inside the bounding box and drag the photo upwards, holding down the Shift key to constrain the movement to the vertical axis. Position the photo as shown in the illustration at the right, and then click the Commit button (✔) to commit the changes.

Adjusting a photo inside a frame

As you noticed when you examined the layers for this design after switching to advanced mode, the photo frame and the image it surrounds occupy the same layer—even though the frame appears to be overlaid on the photo. In fact, by default the layer even takes its name from the frame.

When you scale, rotate, or move the photo, the frame is transformed or moved with it. To move or transform the image independently within its frame, you first need to right-click / Control-click the image and choose Position Photo In Frame from the context menu—or alternatively, isolate the image by double-clicking the photo inside the frame with the Move tool (➤).

Whichever of these actions you take to isolate the image, a control bar appears above the photo, with a scaling slider and buttons to re-orient the image or replace it with another.

- To rotate the photo inside the frame, move the pointer close to any handle; when the pointer becomes a curved double-arrow cursor, drag the handle in either direction.

- To re-size the image, either drag the slider or the handles on the bounding box, if you can see them.

- To reposition the image within the frame, simply drag it in any direction.

Working with backgrounds

You've already replaced the default background graphic in this theme template. It's also possible to move, rotate, scale, or delete the preset background.

Unlike the framed photo however, you can't simply select and drag the background image. Being the basis for the file, the locked Background layer is a special case. For some operations, a Background layer will first need to be "simplified"—unlocked and converted to bit-mapped data—before it can be edited as can other layers.

For simple transformations such as moving, scaling, and rotating, all you need to do is to isolate the Content library image on the background layer, much as you need to isolate a photo before you can move it within a frame.

1 If you can't see the entire page, choose View > Zoom Out. Alternatively, press the Ctrl key (Windows) / Command key (Mac OS) together with the minus (–) key, or double-click the Hand tool to fit the view to the Edit pane.

2   Right-click / Control-click the background and choose Move Background from the context menu. The Background layer becomes active in the Layers panel and a bounding box appears around the background image, though most if it is out of view; the background image is much larger than your 5 x 7 inch page.

3   In order to rotate the background, you could drag the image until one of the control handles was visible, but for our project it will be much more convenient to use the controls in the tool options bar. Type **90** in the Set Rotation text box to the right of the Constrain Proportions option. The background image is rotated 90° clockwise. Don't click the Commit button just yet.

4   Click anywhere inside the bounding box, and then drag to move the background picture upwards and to the left until the lower right corner of the image snaps to the lower right corner of the card design. Click the Commit button (✔) to commit the changes.

Adding graphics from the Content library

Now you can use some artwork items that you collected from the Content library earlier to add a little dimension to the design and help make the photo look like it really belongs in our little beach scene.

1 Click the small menu icon at the right of the Favorites panel's header bar to open the panel Options menu. Choose Large Thumbnail View.

2 Drag the yellow starfish from the Favorites panel onto the top right corner of your card design, and then place the broken seashell a little to the right of the other shells. You'll use these items to stop the photo blowing away.

3 Use the bounding box handles to scale and rotate the new objects; then drag to position them as shown below. When you're satisfied with the placement of each item, click the Commit button ( ) to commit the changes.

> **Tip:** When the Move tool is active, you can use the arrow keys on your keyboard to move the project elements in small steps instead of dragging them.

Using layers and layer styles to refine a project

Now that all the elements of the design are in place, you can add a little polish to your project with a few quick touches.

1 In the Layers panel, right-click / Control-click the layer "Star Fish" and choose Simplify Layer from the context menu; then, repeat the process for the seashell.

2 Select each of the simplified layers in turn and choose Enhance > Adjust Lighting > Brightness/Contrast. For the starfish, use the sliders or type in the text boxes in the Brightness/Contrast dialog box to increase both values to **10**, and then click OK. For the seashell, set the Brightness to **−20** and the Contrast to **50**; then, click OK.

3 In the Layers panel, click to select the layer "Basic White Frame 40px 1" (the framed image), and then double-click the *fx* icon to the right of the layer name.

4 In the Style Settings dialog box, note that the Drop Shadow effect is already activated for this layer. Use the Lighting Angle wheel or type in the text box to set the lighting angle to **25°**. In the Drop Shadow settings, set the values for both Size and Distance to **50** px and the Opacity to **80**%.

5 Click the Drop Shadow Color box (currently black) to the right of the Size value. As you move the pointer over the image it becomes an eyedropper cursor; click with the eyedropper to sample the darkest shadow between the two seashells in the lower left corner. Click OK to close the Select Shadow Color dialog box, and then click OK to close the Style Settings dialog box.

6 In the Layers panel, select the layer "Sea Shell."

7 If you can't see the Pages, Layouts, Artwork, and Effects tabs at the top of the Task pane, choose Window > Reset Panels or click the Reset Panels button (). Click the Effects tab. Click the arrow beside Filters to collapse that category; then, scroll about two-thirds of the way down the Layer Styles thumbnail menu and double-click the Soft Edge style to apply a drop shadow to the seashell.

8 In the Layers panel, double-click the *fx* icon on the layer "Sea Shell." In the Style Settings dialog box, set the lighting angle to **25°**. In the Drop Shadow settings, set the Size to **20** px, Distance to **10** px and Opacity to **60**%. Repeat step 5 to change the color of the drop shadow; then, click OK to close the Style Settings dialog box. Keep the layer selected.

9 Choose Layer > Layer Style > Copy Layer Style. Right-click / Control-click the layer "Star Fish" and choose Paste Layer Style from the context menu. Click the background image to deselect the starfish.

10 Click Done at the bottom of the Task pane. In the confirmation dialog box, click Save. Name the file GreetingCard_1 and save it to your My CIB Work folder in the default format, which will keep the greeting card editable as a project. Be sure to activate the option Include In The Elements Organizer. Click Save.

Congratulations; you've completed your first photo project!

Producing a Photo Book

A Photo Book is a multi-page digital project that offers an attractive way to present and share your memories and makes the perfect personalized gift for a loved one.

You can either have your completed Photo Book commercially printed and bound by ordering through an online service—great for a sophisticated gift—or print it yourself on your home printer. However, unless you have high-quality, double-sided paper in a large enough size you may have to make some design compromises and possibly scale your layout in the printer dialog box to fit standard paper sizes.

Rearranging the order of images in a project

When you create a photo book—or any other photo project—Photoshop Elements places your photos in the layout template in the order in which they appear in the Project Bin.

For a multiple-page project such as a photo book, you can save a lot of time and effort by arranging your photos before you begin. The quickest way to do this is to open the images for your project in Full Edit mode, rearrange their order, and then initiate the photo book from the Editor—rather than from the Organizer.

1 Check that you still have the images for this lesson visible in the Organizer. If you do, you can skip this step; if not, click Show All (if it's visible) in the Find bar above the Media Browser. In the Keyword Tags panel, click the find box beside the Lesson 04 tag to isolate the images for this lesson.

2 In the Media Browser, select the image photobook_1.jpg; then Shift-click the image photobook_9.jpg to select all nine images for this exercise.

3 Right-click / Control-click any of the selected thumbnails and choose Edit With Photoshop Elements from the context menu.

4 If your photos open in the Editor in separate floating image windows choose Window > Images > Consolidate All To Tabs.

5 If you don't see all nine images in the Project Bin, drag the top edge of the header bar upwards to increase the depth of the panel.

6 Right-click / Control-click any of the thumbnails in the Project Bin and choose Show Filenames from the context menu.

7 Reverse the order of the last two photos in the series by dragging the image photobook_9.jpg to a new position to the left of the image photobook_8.jpg.

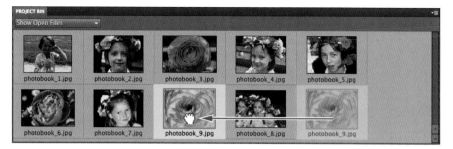

It's that easy! You can move multiple selections of images in the same way. If you find you can't drag an thumbnail to a new position, you probably have all of the images in the Project Bin selected.

Setting up a Photo Book layout

You can either use a Photo Book theme or layout "as is" or treat it as a starting point and go on to customize your own design.

1 Click the Create tab above the Panel Bin, and then click the Photo Book button.

2 Under Print Locally, in the Sizes pane at the left of the Photo Book dialog box, choose 11.00 x 8.50 inches. From the Themes menu, choose Colorful. Make sure the Autofill With Selected Images option is activated and that the number of pages for the photo book is set to 2; then, click OK.

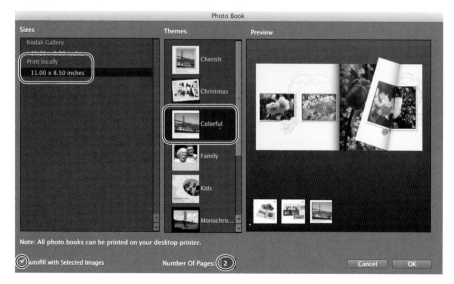

Note: Although the Sizes pane lists options compatible with various online services, any of the photo book formats can also be printed from your home printer.

You'll see a progress bar while Photoshop Elements generates previews, creates pages, and places your images in the template. The title page of the photo book appears in the Edit window and thumbnail previews for the title page and a single two-page are displayed on the Pages tab.

You can see that four of our nine images have already been placed, in the order in which they appear in the Project Bin. You'll need more than two pages, but you'll have more control over the layout of additional pages if you add them yourself. When you have Photoshop Elements generate pages automatically, each page is randomly assigned a different layout.

3 Click the thumbnail preview for the first spread, pages 1 and 2. When the spread has appeared in the Edit pane, click Layouts at the top of the Create tab. On the Layouts tab, click the triangle to collapse the Different Layouts category.

4 Scroll down the thumbnail menu of One Photo layouts. Drag the last layout, "Photobook Landscape" onto page 2, the page at the right of the spread. The page is updated with the new layout.

5 Rearrange the layout of the spread as shown in the illustration below:

- Click the photo on page 2. Drag the lower left bounding box handle upwards and to the right. Keep an eye on the W (width) and H (height) values in the tool options bar; stop when you've scaled the image to approximately 75%. Drag the image a little closer to the top right corner of the page and click the Commit button (✔) to accept the changes.

- Drag the flower photo from page 1 to page 2. Use the bounding box handles to scale the photo to 80% and rotate it −20°; then, drag to position it as shown and click the Commit button.

- Scale the remaining photo on page 1 to around 160% and drag to center it on the page; then, click the Commit button.

▶ **Tip:** You can use the arrow keys on your keyboard to fine tune the positioning of a selected element in the layout by nudging it in small increments, rather than dragging it with the mouse.

6 Select each of the two text objects on page 2 in turn and press Backspace / Delete to remove them. Click Yes to confirm each deletion, and then click the Switch To Advanced Mode button below the Edit pane.

7 Select any of the three images in the spread. Scroll about two-thirds of the way down the Frames menu on the Artwork tab to locate the "Paper Frame." Double-click the swatch to apply the new frame to the selected photo, and then repeat the process for the other two images in the spread.

8 Choose Window > Favorites to open the Favorites panel; then, drag the panel by its name tab onto the header bar of the Layers panel. In the favorites panel, double-click the background graphic "Handmade Paper 03." The spread is updated with the new background.

9 Collapse the grouped Layers and Favorites panels by double-clicking the header bar, and then click Pages at the top of the Create tab. Click the New Pages button (➕) at the top of the Pages tab twice to create two new spreads with the same layout that you just fine-tuned for the page 1/2 spread.

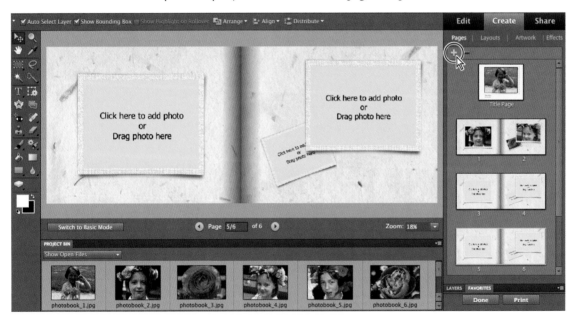

10 Select the small angled frame on page 6 and press Backspace / Delete; then, click Yes to confirm the deletion. Move the remaining frame on page 6 towards the lower left of the page; then, scale, rotate, and drag the frame on page 5 to position it as shown in the illustration at the left.

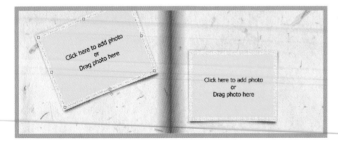

Adding more photos to your Photo Book

Now that you have your layout and pages set up, you can fill all those empty frames.

1   Scroll down in the Project Bin, if necessary, so that you can see the last two photos. Drag the image of the flower to the angled frame on page 5, and the photo of the three girls to the frame on page 6.

2   Below the Edit pane, click the blue button with the left-facing arrow to move to pages 3 and 4. The page counter between the blue navigation buttons lets you know at a glance where you are in the photo book—handy when the Pages tab is not visible.

3   From left to right, fill the frames on pages 3 and 4 with the images photobook_5, photobook_6, and photobook_7. Right-click / Control-click the photo of the pink flower in the small angled frame and choose Bring Forward from the context menu.

4   Drag the angled photo upwards and the larger image downwards to change the layout for page 4 as shown in the illustration at the right. Hold down the Shift key as you drag to constrain the movement to the vertical axis.

Refining your Photo Book layout

In this exercise you'll polish your Photo Book design and refresh some of the skills you picked up in the greeting card project. You can start by giving the title page a different look from the inside pages of your project.

1   On the Pages tab, you can see your entire book layout at a glance. Click the thumbnail preview for the title page. Expand the Favorites panel by double-clicking its header; then, double-click the swatch for the background image "Scrapbook 08." The new background image is applied to the page in the Edit pane. Drag the frame "Scrapbook 03" out of the Favorites panel onto the title page photo. The new background and the frame give the title page a completely different look that is complementary to the home-made, family feel of the inside pages.

Tip: When the Move tool is active, you can use the arrow keys on your keyboard to move a selected project element in small steps instead of dragging them with the mouse.

2 Drag the handle at the lower left corner of the photo's bounding box to resize the image, and then drag to position it as shown in the illustration at the right. When you're done, click the Commit button (✓).

3 Right-click / Control-click the new background and choose Move Background from the context menu. Drag the image a little to the right to align its left edge with the left edge of the page, and then click the Commit button. The darker strip on the left side of the page is now wider.

4 Click the blue forward arrow below the Edit pane to advance to the first spread. A blue border highlights the active spread in the Pages tab preview.

Tip: If your photos do not automatically fill their frames, right-click / Control-click each photo and choose Fit Frame To Photo, and then resize the frame and photo together using the handles on the bounding box. Alternatively, double-click the photo and resize it within its frame by using the slider, as discussed in "Adjusting a photo inside a frame" on page 122.

5 The frame around the larger photo on page 2 is cutting off too much if the girl's face. Double-click the photo. You can see that the photo is march larger than the frame. We don't want to change the size of the frame, so the photo will have to be reduced. Use the scaling slider to reduce the image so that its edges are just hidden by the frame, and then commit the changes.

6 Advance to the final spread, pages 5 and 6. The image of three girls on page 6 also needs to be better positioned within its frame. Right-click / Control-click the photo and choose Position Photo In Frame from the context menu. Use the scaling slider to reduce the image very slightly and the arrow keys on your keyboard to nudge it upwards and to the right inside the frame; then, commit the changes.

Adding graphics

The Photo Book is almost complete. Before adding text, you can liven up the design with a judicious use of graphics from the content library.

1 Use the navigation buttons below the Edit pane, or click in the Pages preview, to move to the page 1 and 2 spread.

2 Expand the Favorites panel if necessary. Drag just one or two of the petals or flowers onto the spread, scaling and rotating them as you wish. To alter an element's position in the layer stacking order, right-click / Control-click the item and choose from the context menu.

3 Repeat the process for the remaining pages, but remember—be sparing; when it comes to design, less is more!

4 With the page 5 and 6 spread open, click Artwork at the top of the Create tab, Scroll down the artwork menu, almost to the bottom of the Graphics category. Drag the graphic "Speech Bubble 10" onto page 6; then, use the bounding box handles to scale the shape. Position it as shown below; then, commit the change.

Adding text to your project

In this exercise you'll personalize the Photo Book as a gift by adding some text.

1 Select the Horizontal Type tool; then choose a font from the font menu in the Tool Options bar across the top of the Edit pane. On Windows, we chose Zapfino Linotype One (LTZapfino One)—Zapfino on Mac OS—but any other calligraphic or script font such as Monotype Corsiva will suit the design. From the font size menu, we chose 72 pt (the largest size available) as a starting point.

2 Ensure that the Anti-aliased button is activated so that the edges of the letters are smoothed, and then choose Center Text from the text alignment menu.

3 Click the Text Color swatch in the tool options bar. Drag the Select Color dialog box away from the image on page 6 by its header bar; then, move the pointer onto the image and sample a deep grape color from one of the flowers in the photo. Click OK to close the dialog box.

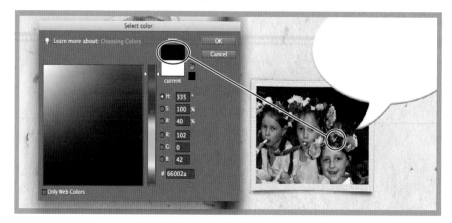

4 With the Type tool, click on the background below the image on page 5 and type **Happy Birthday Mom**. The text is placed on a layer above the background but below the framed photo. (If the text appears on top of the photograph, or too large, you can change the layer order and scale and position the text a little later.) Click the Confirm button in the tool options bar to deactivate the text.

5 With the Move tool, select the speech bubble graphic on page 6. Select the Type tool again and choose Right Align Text from the text alignment menu. In the Leading text box—to the left of the text color swatch—type **60** pt for Linotype Zapfino One on Windows / **80** pt for Zapfino on Mac OS. With the Type tool, click a point in the upper right of the speech bubble and type **from your**. Press Enter / Return and type **darling blossoms**; then, click the Confirm button. Scale and position the text on both pages as shown in the illustration below.

6 Click the title page thumbnail in the Pages preview, or navigate to the title page using buttons below the edit pane. Select and delete each of the preset text objects on this page, clicking Yes to confirm each deletion. Select the Type tool and choose Center Text from the alignment menu; then, click on the background in the center of the title page and type **for you.**; then, click the Confirm button in the tool options bar. Use the Move tool to reposition and scale the text as shown here. Tweak the size and position of the photo if necessary.

7 As a final touch, you can soften the title page text by reducing its opacity. Use the Move tool to select the text. In the Panel Bin, expand the Layers panel, if necessary, by clicking its name tab. Make sure the text layer "for you" is active; then, reduce the layer opacity to 50%. Repeat this adjustment for the two text layers on the page 5 and 6 spread.

8 The Photo Book is complete; choose File > Save. In the Save As dialog box, name the file **PhotoBook_1** and navigate to your My CIB Work folder. By default your project will be saved in Photo Project Format (PSE), a multi-page document format that preserves text and layers so that they can be edited later. You could also choose to save the project as a PDF file that can be shared as an e-mail attachment. Make sure that your project will be included in the Organizer.

9 Click Save, and then choose File > Close All.
Congratulations—you've completed another project!

Assembling a photo collage

In the next few exercises you'll create another project—this time, a Photo Collage. You can print your collage on your home printer, order prints on-line, save it to your hard drive to send by e-mail, or import it into another digital document.

Start by locating the images for this project.

1 Check that you still have the images for this lesson visible in the Organizer. If you do, you can skip this step; if not, click Show All (if it's visible) in the Find bar above the Media Browser. In the Keyword Tags panel, click the find box beside the Lesson 04 tag to isolate the images for this lesson.

2 In the Media Browser, select the image ChinaCalendar.jpg; then, Shift-click the image ChinaScan4.jpg to select all six images for this project. For this exercise, the order of our images won't be an issue, so you can initiate your collage project from the Organizer.

3 Click the Create tab at the top of the Task pane; then, click the Photo Collage button. Under Print Locally in the Photo Collage dialog box, make sure that the default size, 8.50 x 11.00 inches is selected, together with the default Basic theme. For this project, disable Autofill With Selected Images; you'll build up your collage gradually, bringing in the photos as you need them. Click OK.

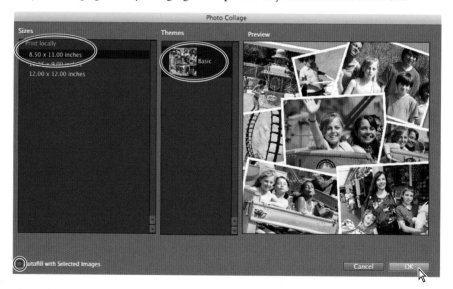

Photoshop Elements generates a single page containing only empty frames. The Pages tab displays a single layout thumbnail, and the Project Bin is in Show Files Selected In Organizer mode.

4 If you don't see file names below the thumbnails in the Project Bin, right-click / Control-click any of the thumbnails and choose Show Filenames from the context menu. If necessary, scroll in the Project Bin to see all six thumbnails.

As you can see, none of the images for this project are actually digital photographs as such. They are all scans of mementos from a trip to China: a cheaply printed calendar page, a much-used map and four paper photographs printed in sepia tone, complete with thumb-tack holes. Most of us like to keep little reminders like these—an old concert ticket, a pressed flower, or the stamps on a torn envelope can hold as many memories as any photograph. A Photo Collage is a perfect way to preserve and present such evocative mementos.

Tip: You can even scan or photograph three-dimensional keepsakes; a handful of seashells or colored pebbles on the scanner bed can make a great background image.

Setting up your project page

In any Photoshop Elements project each image or object occupies its own layer. If you had activated the Autofill With Selected Images option, the position of the images in the "stacking order" of the layers would correspond to their order in the Project Bin. The first image in the Project bin would be placed on the lowest layer—immediately above any preset background from the content library, which is assigned to the bottom layer by default. Each image, graphic or text object added subsequently will be placed above the last. Unoccupied space on a layer is transparent, enabling you to see through it to the layers below.

1   Click Switch To Advanced Mode in the bar below the Edit pane. Drag the Layers panel out of the Panels Bin by its name tab. Enlarge the panel enough to see four or five of the layers that make up the automatically generated page. Scroll to the bottom of the Layers panel; the Background layer for this Basic template contains only a patterned graphic from the Content library. For now, position the Layers panel where it won't block your view of the Create tab.

2   Click Layouts at the top of the Create tab. Click the small triangles beside the category names to collapse the first three categories in the menu: Different Layouts, One Photo, and Three Photos. Double-click the first layout in the Two Photos group, "2 Portrait Vertical."

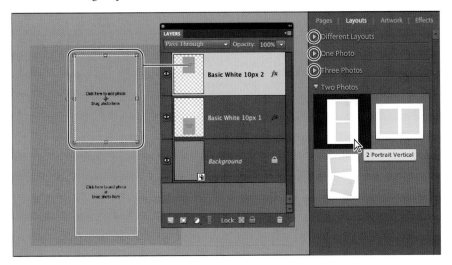

The new layout appears in the Edit pane and the Layers panel now contains only three layers. The most recently created layer, on the top of the stack, is already selected and active, as is the corresponding object in the Edit pane.

3 Collapse the Two Photos layout category and click the Reset Panels button (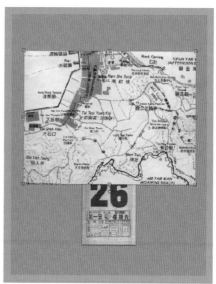) at the top of the workspace to return the Layers panel to the Panels Bin. Drag the divider between the Layers panel and the Create tab upwards so that the Layers panel is as deep as you can make it. Choose View > Fit On Screen.

4 Double-click the fx icon on the top layer to examine the preset layer style. The Style settings dialog box shows that this layer has a low drop shadow effect and a white, 10 pixel wide stroke frame around the photo placeholder. Leave the drop shadow as it is, but disable the Stroke settings for the frame. Click OK.

5 Right-click / Control-click the top layer and choose Copy Layer Style from the context menu; then, right-click / Control-click the middle layer and choose Paste Layer Style.

6 Drag the thumbnail of the map onto the photo placeholder at the top of the page and the calendar page onto the lower one. In the Layers panel, the layer thumbnails are updated to show the newly placed images. Right-click / Control-click each image in the Edit pane and choose Fit Frame To Photo from the context menu. Select each image in turn, click a corner handle of the bounding box, and then type **200%** in the W (width) box in the tool options bar. Commit each change. Drag the map downwards so that it overlaps the calendar page slightly.

7 In both the Edit window and the Layers panel you can see that the map is on a layer above—or in front of—the calendar. Right-click / Control-click the calendar page and watch the Layer panel as you choose Bring To Front; the stacking order for your two image layers is reversed.

Adding a background

You've already chosen an appropriate background for this design from the Content library and stored it in your Favorites panel.

1   Choose Window > Favorites to open the Favorites panel. Double-click the first swatch "Asia Map." This image came from the Backgrounds library, so it's automatically placed on the bottom layer—the Background layer—replacing the preset background. Double-click the black bar at the top of the Favorites panel to minimize it, and then drag it where it won't get in your way.

2   In the layers panel, click the eye icon beside each of the upper layers to hide the scanned map and the calendar page. Right-click / Control-click the background image in the Edit pane and choose Move Background from the context menu. Type **175**% in either the W (width) or H (height) box in the tool options bar; by default the image is scaled proportionally.

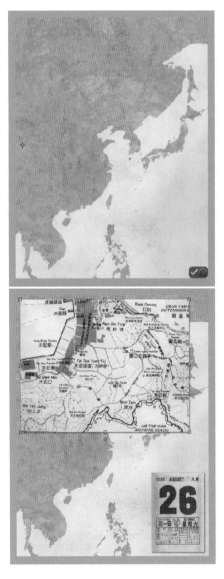

3   Drag the background image to position it so that the East Asian coastline makes a rough diagonal across the page, as shown in the illustration at the right. When you're done, click the Commit button (✓) at the bottom of the page preview to commit the changes.

4   Make both the upper layers visible again by clicking the boxes beside the layer thumbnails in the Layers panel, reinstating the eye icons.

5   Drag the scanned map to the upper left of the page and the calendar to the lower right. Don't worry about precise placement at the moment; you'll work more with these elements later.

6   Click the scanned map to make the middle layer active in preparation for the next exercise.

Adding more images

In this exercise you'll add the rest of the images in the Project Bin to your collage. Pre-selecting the scanned map ensures that the next image added will be placed on the layer immediately above the map—and therefore, below the calendar page.

Tip: If you don't see the images for your collage in the Project Bin, make sure the Project Bin's display menu is set to Show Files Selected In Organizer, and not Show Open Files.

1   Drag the image ChinaScan1.jpg from the Project Bin onto the page and place it below and slightly overlapping the scanned map. Don't drop it inside the bounding box surrounding the map or it will replace that image.

2   Leaving the new item selected, drag the image ChinaScan3.jpg from the Project Bin onto the page and place it a little below and overlapping the first image you added, being careful to place it outside the active bounding box.

3   Repeat the process with ChinaScan4.jpg. Position the photos as much as possible as shown in the illustration at the left, below.

4   Click to select the calendar page. Drag the final image ChinaScan2.jpg from the Project Bin and place it a little outside the calendar's bounding box, and overlapping ChinaScan4.jpg.

5   Select any one of the four sepia-toned photos, and then shift-click to add the other three to the selection.

6   Click any of the corner handles on the single bounding box that now surrounds the four selected images. In the tool options bar, type **175**% in either the W (width) or H (height) box; then, commit the change.

All four images are scaled proportionally and the spatial relationship between them is preserved. In the Edit pane, you can now see the layering order of all the elements in your collage quite clearly.

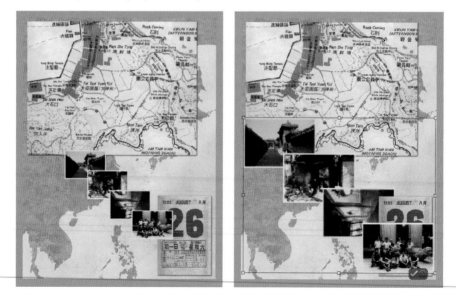

Working with layers to refine a project

Remember that each element in your collage occupies its own layer, with the background at the bottom and the other images overlaid in successive layers in the order in which they were added to the project. The only *apparent* exception is a frame applied to an image, which may appear to be overlaid and may even throw a drop shadow on the photo it surrounds, but is nevertheless in the same layer.

Layers are like transparent overlays on which you can paint or place photos, artwork, or vector graphics. The checkerboard areas in layer thumbnails represent transparency through which you can see lower layers. As well as photos and artwork from the content library, layers can contain text, fills, masks, and gradients.

You can apply filters or special effects to any layer and specify the way those effects will affect other layers in the project. You can change a layer's opacity and blending mode and add adjustment layers, which do not themselves contain images but allow you to tune the appearance of the layer or layers below.

1   In the Layers panel, click the eye icons to hide each of the sepia photographs.

2   Click in the Layers panel to select the layer containing the scanned map. Use the handles on the bounding box to scale and rotate the image as shown at the left below, and then click the Commit button.

3   Use the Opacity slider at the top of the Layers panel to set the opacity of the map image to **50**%.

4   Click in the Layers panel to select the second layer from the top—the scanned calendar page. Use a corner handle to enlarge the image; then drag to position it as shown in the illustration at the right; then, click the Commit button.

> **Note:** Background artwork chosen from the Content library will always appear on the bottom layer, even when they are added to the layout after the photographs—as was the case in this project.

> **Tip:** If you'd prefer to scale and rotate the image numerically, the values are **95**% and **25**°.

> **Tip:** If you'd prefer to scale the image by entering a numeric value, type **150**%.

5 In the Layers panel, click the eye icon beside the thumbnail for each of the ChinaScan layers to make the photos visible again. Reverse the layer order of the images ChinaScan1, 3, and 4 by dragging the respective layers in the Layers panel.

Tip: When the Move tool is active, you can use the arrow keys on your keyboard to move the project elements in small increments instead of dragging them with the mouse.

6 Use the Move tool to select each of the four images in turn, moving and rotating them to arrange them in the collage as you see in this illustration. Hint: all four images have been enlarged again to a value of **105**%. Select the top layer in preparation for the next steps.

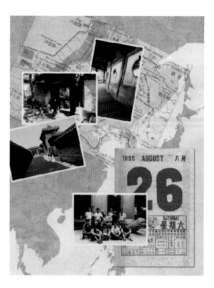

Adding graphics from the Content library

The design is almost complete, but it all looks a little two-dimensional. You can use your travel-related favorites from the Content library to set it off.

1 Expand the Favorites panel by double-clicking its header. Enlarge the panel or scroll down through the artwork swatches.

2 Drag the graphics "Travel Compass" and "Plane Stamp" onto your Photo Collage page, and then scale and rotate them as shown in the illustration.

3 In the Layers panel, set the opacity of the Plane Stamp layer to **70**%.

Applying effects

Note: For more detailed information about applying effects and working with layer styles, refer to Photoshop Elements Help.

As a finishing touch you can apply a drop shadow effect to the compass and the four sepia photographs to give them greater presence and lift them from the flatness of the background elements; this will add contrast and increase visual impact.

1 Right-click / Control-click the image of the compass and choose Edit Layer Style from the context menu. In the Style Settings dialog box, click the check box to activate the Drop Shadow option. Set the Lighting Angle to **135**° and the Size, Distance, and Opacity values to **20**, **25**, and **50** respectively; then click OK.

2 With the compass still selected, choose Layer > Layer Style > Copy Layer Style, and then deselect the compass.

3 Shift-click to select all four sepia photographs and choose Layer > Layer Style > Paste Layer Style. Click the background to deselect the photos.

4 The collage design is complete. Save it to your My CIB Work folder as **Collage_1.psd**. Activate the Layers option so that the file is saved with its layers intact and editable. Activate the option Include In The Elements Organizer. Click Save; then, click Done. Choose File > Close All.

A Photo Collage not only makes a great way to preserve and present fading mementos but, by combining a group of images and objects, can actually tell a story. The title of this particular picture-story is "Leaving Cheung Chau."

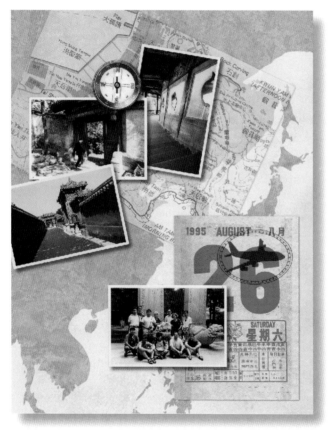

Congratulations! You've completed the last project in this lesson. You've learned about using the preset Theme and Layout templates, explored the content library, and become familiar with a variety of methods for locating the content you need. You've also learned the basics of working with layers and applying layer styles. Before you move on to the next lesson, "Printing, Sharing, and Exporting," take a moment to refresh your new skills by reading through the review on the next page.

Review questions

1 How do you begin a new project such as a greeting card, Photo Book or collage?

2 How do you scale and reposition a photo in a photo project?

3 How do you change the order of the pictures in a photo book?

4 How can you find the items you want amongst all the choices in the Content library?

5 What are layers, how do they work, and how do you work with them?

6 What is a Smart Object, and how does it affect your editing workflow?

Review answers

1 To create a project, select a project option on the Create tab in the Panel Bin by clicking one of the project buttons or choosing from the More Options menu. The Create tab presents page previews and navigation controls, and provides access to layout templates, backgrounds, frames, graphics and effects.

2 Once you've selected and applied a theme and a layout, an edit window opens with a bounding box around the photo. You can scale or rotate the photo by dragging the bounding box handles and move it on the page by dragging the image itself. To scale, rotate, or move a photo within its frame you need to double-click the image before using the same techniques, so that the changes affect the photo independently and are not applied to the photo and its frame together.

3 You can change the order of images in a photo book by dragging them to new positions in the Project Bin below the Edit pane.

4 You can sort and search the items in the Content library by using the menus and buttons at the top of the Content panel. From the first menu you can choose options to sort the content by type, activity, mood, season, color, keywords and other attributes. Once you have set up the first menu, you use the other menu to narrow the search—to specify which type, color, or mood you want. Use the content filter buttons to filter the search results to display only backgrounds, frames, graphics, shapes, text styles, or themes with the attributes you've specified. Use the favorites panel to assemble a collection of the items you're most likely to use, rather than looking through the entire library every time you want to add a library item to a project.

5 Layers are like transparent overlays on which you can paint or place photos, artwork, or text. Each element in a photo project occupies its own layer—the background is at the bottom and the other elements are overlaid in the order in which they are added to the project. Photos from the Project Bin are placed in the order of their capture date, so that the oldest is on the lowest layer. You can drag the thumbnails in the Project Bin to change that order. You work with layers in the Layers Panel, where you can toggle their visibility, change their order and add layer styles and effects. The checkerboard grid areas in the layer thumbnails represent the transparent parts of the layers through which you can see the layers below.

6 Layers that contain graphics from the content library are marked with a Smart Object icon in the lower right corner. A Smart Object is resolution independent; it can be scaled or rotated repeatedly without any degradation of the image, because the data is always drawn from the source file which remains in its original un-edited state. If you wish to further edit a Smart Object layer, you must first "simplify" the layer, making it a normal bit-mapped image and breaking its connection with the source file. Always scale and rotate the image first; then when you're ready for further editing, select the layer and choose Layer > Simplify Layer. You can also access this command in the Layers panel Options menu.

5 PRINTING, SHARING, AND EXPORTING

Lesson overview

In previous lessons you've imported images from a range of sources, explored a variety of ways to organize and find your files, and created projects and presentations to showcase your photos.

In this lesson, you'll learn how you can output your images and creations to share them with family, friends, or the world at large:

- Printing at home and ordering prints online
- Fine-tuning the composition of an image in the print preview
- Sharing photos by e-mail and Photo Mail
- Signing up for an Adobe ID and a Photoshop.com account
- Backing up and synchronizing your files
- Synchronizing multiple computers
- Creating your own Online Album or Web Gallery
- Using an online sharing service
- Burning your photos and projects to CD or DVD
- Exporting images for use on the Web

 You'll probably need between one and two hours to complete this lesson.

Now that you've learned how to find your way around the Photoshop Elements workspace, how to organize and find the photos and other media in your growing collection, and how to create photo projects and digital presentations, you're ready to share your images and creations with the world as printed output, by e-mail, or online.

Getting started

Before you start working on the exercises in this lesson, make sure that you have installed the software on your computer from the application CD (see the Photoshop Elements 9 documentation) and that you have correctly copied the Lessons folder from the CD in the back of this book onto your computer's hard disk. (See "Copying the Classroom in a Book files" on page 2.)

To start, you'll import the sample images for this lesson to the CIB Catalog that you created at the beginning of Lesson 4.

1 Start Photoshop Elements and click Organize in the Welcome Screen.

2 The name of the active catalog is always shown in the lower left corner of the Organizer window. If your CIB Catalog is already loaded, you can skip step to step 4. If another catalog is currently loaded, continue with step 3.

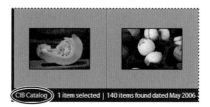

3 Choose File > Catalog. In the Catalog Manager dialog box, click to select your CIB Catalog in the Catalogs list, and then click Open. If you don't see the CIB Catalog listed, review "Creating a new catalog" at the beginning of Lesson 4.

4 Choose File > Get Photos And Video > From Files And Folders. In the Get Photos And Videos From Files And Folders dialog box, locate and open your Lesson05 folder. Select the folder Printing. Activate the option Get Photos From Subfolders and disable the automatic processing options; then, click Get Media.

5 In the Import Attached Keyword Tags dialog box, click Select All, and then click OK. Click OK to close any other alert dialog box.

In the Media Browser, you can see thumbnails of the images you've just imported to your CIB catalog. In the Keyword Tags panel, the newly added tags have been listed in the category Imported Keyword Tags.

About printing

Whether you wish to use your home printer or order professional prints from an online service, Photoshop Elements offers a range of options for printing your photographs and Photo Projects such as photo books, greeting cards, and collages.

You can print your photos individually or in picture packages with one or more photos repeated at a variety of sizes on the same page, preview a multiple selection of photos printed as thumbnail images arranged on a contact sheet, or produce your own photo labels using commercially available label paper.

Printing a contact sheet

A contact sheets is a great way to preview and assess a multiple selection of images by printing them at thumbnail size, arranged on a single page in a grid layout.

To learn how to set up a contact sheet on Mac OS, skip ahead to page 153.

Printing a contact sheet on Windows

1   Click the Show All button in the Find bar above the Media Browser.

2   Click the empty Find box beside the keyword tag To Print (in the Imported Keyword Tags category), and then press Ctrl+A to select all the images tagged with the keyword To Print.

3   Choose File > Print.

The Prints dialog box opens. The column on the left displays thumbnails of all the photos you selected for this print job. At center stage is the print preview.

▶ **Tip:** You can also open the Prints dialog box in contact sheet mode from the Create tab in the Task pane. Click Photo Prints, and then click the Print Contact Sheet button.

4 Set up the options in the Prints dialog box as shown in the illustration below. Choose a printer from the Select Printer menu. For the purposes of this demonstration choose Letter from the Select Paper Size menu. From the Select Type Of Print menu, choose Contact Sheet, and then disable the Crop To Fit option.

▶ **Tip:** To remove a photo from the contact sheet, select its thumbnail in the image menu column and click the Remove button (▬) below the menu pane.

The contact sheet layout includes all the images in the thumbnail menu column at the left. With a four-column layout, all twenty photos fit neatly on a single page; the page count below the print preview indicates that you are viewing page 1 of 1.

5 Under Select A Layout, click the down arrow button beside the Columns number or type **3** in the text box: With only three columns the images are larger, but only nine photos will fit on a single page at this paper size; the page count below the print preview now indicates that you are viewing page 1 of 3. Use the Next Page and Previous page buttons on either side of the page count to navigate between the pages.

6 Change the number of columns to nine. You can see that a single letter page can accommodate many photos at this setting. Return the layout to four columns.

7 Click to select any photo in the print preview; then, use the slider below the print preview to zoom in. Drag the photo to reposition it within the frame of its image cell. Select another image, and then use the Rotate buttons to the left of the zoom slider to change the photo's orientation.

● **Note:** Some words in the text label may be truncated, depending on the page setup and column layout.

8 To print image information labels below each image on the contact sheet, first click to activate Show Print Options (just below the Columns setting), and then activate any or all of the Text Label options. Activate Date to print the capture date extracted from the images' metadata, Caption to print any caption text, Filename to print the filename beneath each photo, or Page Numbers to print a page number on each page of a multiple-page contact sheet.

9 Click Print or Cancel and skip to "Printing a Picture Package" on page 154.

Printing a contact sheet on Mac OS

On Mac OS, you need to initiate a contact sheet print from the Editor. For this demonstration, in which we'll use all the photos in a single folder, it will be quicker to open the Editor without first making a selection in the Organizer. If you want to print a contact sheet with photos drawn from multiple folders, you'll need to select the images in the Media Browser—where you can Command-click to select non-consecutive images—and then switch to the Editor as described in step 2:

1 Press Shift+Command+A to deselect any images that are currently selected in the Media Browser.

2 Click the small arrow on the Fix tab at the top of the Task Pane and choose Full Photo Edit from the menu.

3 When the Editor opens choose File > Contact Sheet II. Set up the Contact Sheet dialog box as shown in the illustration at the right. Choose Folder from the Use menu under Source Images. Click Choose and locate the Printing folder inside your Lesson05 folder. Under Document, specify a size for your contact sheet. Under Thumbnails, specify the order in which the images will be placed. Activate Use Auto-Spacing; then, type **4** and **5** in the Columns and

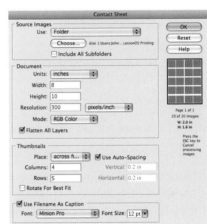

> **Tip:** The alternative option in the Use menu under Source Images fills your contact sheet with whatever images are already open in the Editor. This is the setting you would use if you had made a selection of images in the Media Browser before switching to the Editor.

Rows text boxes respectively. Your Columns and Rows settings are reflected in the layout preview at the right. Disable Rotate For Best Fit, and activate Use Filename As Caption.

4 Click OK, and then wait while Photoshop Elements places the image thumbnails.

In our example, all twenty images fit onto a single page. When the number of images selected for printing exceeds the capacity of a single page at the layout settings specified, Photoshop Elements generates more pages to accommodate them.

5 Select the contact sheet page(s) in the Project Bin. Choose File > Print if you wish to print the contact sheet. If not, choose File > Close; then, click Don't Save.

> **Tip:** You can also open the Contact Sheet dialog box from the Create tab in the Task pane. Click Photo Prints, and then click the Print Contact Sheet button. If you do this from the Organizer, you'll see a message asking if you'd like to open the Editor to initiate printing.

Printing a Picture Package

A Picture Package layout lets you print a photo repeated at a choice of sizes on the same page, much as professional portrait studios do. You can choose from a variety of layout options and range of image sizes to customize your picture package print.

To learn how to set up a picture package on Mac OS, skip ahead to page 156.

Printing a Picture Package on Windows

1 Select two or more pictures in the Media Browser, and then choose File > Print.

2 In the Prints dialog box, choose a printer from the Select Printer menu and a paper size from the Select Paper Size menu. Which layout options are available for your picture package depends on your choice of paper size; for the purposes of this exercise, choose Letter.

3 Choose Picture Package from the Select Type Of Print menu. If a Printing Warning dialog box cautioning against enlarging pictures appears, click OK; for this exercise you'll print multiple images at smaller sizes.

> ▶ **Tip:** You can also open the Prints dialog box in picture package mode from the Create tab in the Task pane. Click Photo Prints, and then click the Print Picture Package button.

4 Choose a layout from the Select A Layout menu, and then activate the option Fill Page With First Photo. This will result in a page with a single photo repeated at a variety of sizes, according to the layout you have chosen. If you selected more than one photo in the Media browser, a separate Print Package page will be generated for each photo selected; you can see the print preview for each page by clicking the page navigation buttons below the preview pane.

The layout options available for a Picture Package depend on the paper size specified in the Prints dialog box, the page setup, and the printer preferences. To change the paper size, choose from the Select Paper Size menu or click either the Page Setup button at the lower left of the Prints dialog box or the Change Settings button under Printer Settings. Depending on your printer, you may need to look for the paper size options in the Advanced preferences settings.

5 Try a few of the options in the Select A Frame menu. For this demonstration, we chose Color Swirl, the last frame style in the menu. You can select only one style per picture package print; it will be applied to every picture in the layout.

6 Toggle the Crop To Fit option and assess the result; the Crop To Fit option may fit the multiple images more closely to the layout to better fill the printable area, especially when your photo is of non-standard proportions.

Note: The images in a Picture Package layout are automatically oriented to make the best use of the printable paper area for the layout you have chosen. You cannot manually rotate the image cells (or print wells) in a picture package layout; however, you can still zoom or rotate each image within its print well using the zoom slider and orientation buttons below the preview. Drag any image in the picture package to adjust its position within its print well.

7 Click the Add button (➕) below the thumbnails menu at the left. In the Add Photos dialog box, you can add images to your print job by choosing from those photos currently visible in the Media Browser, from your entire catalog, or from the images included in a specific album or tagged with a particular keyword. Choose one or more photos from any of these sets, and then click Done; the selected images are added to the thumbnails column in the Prints dialog box.

8 Drag the thumbnail of one of your newly acquired photos from the thumbnails column onto any image cell in the print preview; the original image is replaced.

9 Click Print or Cancel and skip to "Printing individual photos" in 157.

Printing a Picture Package on Mac OS

1 If necessary, switch to the Organizer, leaving the Editor open. Select two or more photos in the Media Browser.

2 Click the small arrow on the Fix tab at the top of the Task Pane and choose Full Photo Edit from the menu.

3 When the Editor opens, double-click whichever image in the Project Bin that you'd like to print first. Choose File > Picture Package.

4 Under Document in the Picture Package dialog box, make a selection from the Page Size and Layout menus, and then click the Edit Layout button below the Layout preview box.

5 In the Picture Package Edit Layout dialog box, click to select an image in the layout preview, and then click the Delete Zone button in the Image Zones options. Select another image in the preview and drag it to a new position on the page preview. Drag the handles on the image's bounding box to scale it or change its orientation.

> **Tip:** You can open the Picture Package dialog box from the Create tab in the Task pane. Click Photo Prints, and then click the Print Picture Package button. If you do this from the Organizer, you'll see a message asking if you'd like to open the Editor to initiate printing.

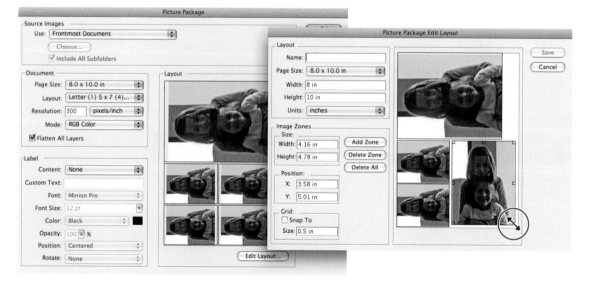

6 Option-click an image in the Edit Layout preview and try out some of the menu choices; then experiment with the other settings and buttons in the Image Zones options. For now, click Cancel; clicking Save would overwrite the settings for the selected layout preset.

7 Click OK in the Picture Package dialog box, and then wait while Photoshop Elements creates a new document and places the images for your Picture Package. If you wish to see the Picture Package printed choose File > Print; otherwise choose File > Close All, and then click Don't Save.

Printing individual photos

The Photoshop Elements Prints dialog box presents all your printing options in one convenient place and now also enables you to fine-tune the placement of each image within its own print well (its frame in the print preview). You can zoom or rotate an image with the controls beneath the preview and drag to reposition it, enabling you to get the image placed just right for printing without first editing it.

1   In the Organizer, Ctrl-click / Command-click to select eight or more images.

2   Choose File > Print. Alternatively, click the Create tab in the Task pane, click Photo Prints, and then click the Print With Local Printer button. On Mac OS, click Yes to continue to the Editor, where printing will be initiated.

3   In the Prints / Print dialog box, select a printer, paper size and print size from the menus at the right. On Windows, choose Individual Prints from the Select Type Of Print menu. If you see a print resolution alert, click OK to dismiss it.

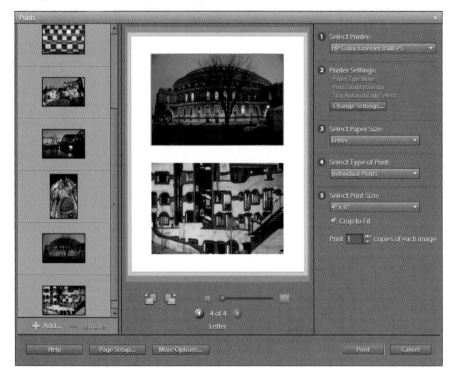

Note: On Mac OS, the options in the Print dialog box differ from those illustrated here. For more detailed information on printing on Mac OS, please refer to Photoshop Elements Help and search other online resources in Community Help.

4   Experiment with the controls below the Print preview. Click to select an image in the preview and zoom in and out inside the image cell using the zoom slider. Use the Rotate Left and Rotate Right buttons beside the zoom slider to change the orientation of the image within its print well frame. Drag the selected image to reposition it within the frame. Toggle the Crop To Fit option below the Select Print Size menu and observe the effect in the print preview.

5   Select any image thumbnail in the menu column on the left side of the dialog box and click the Remove Selected Photo(s) button (—).

● **Note:** You can add images to the selection to be printed only if they are part of the currently active catalog.

6   Click the Add Photos button (✚) below the thumbnails menu. In the Add Media dialog box, choose a source option under Add Media From; select from photos currently visible in the Media Browser, from your entire catalog, or from the images included in a specific album or tagged with a particular keyword.

Choose one or more photos from any of these sets, and then click Add Selected Media. The selected images are added to the thumbnails column in the Print dialog box, and the Add Media dialog box remains open. Choose a different source option, select one or more photos; then, click Done to add the photos to your print job and dismiss the Add Media dialog box.

If you've selected more pictures than will fit on one page at the image dimensions you specified, Photoshop Elements automatically generates extra pages.

7   Check the page count below the Print Preview. If your print job has more than one page, preview the other pages by clicking the arrow buttons at either side of the page count.

8   Click the More Options button at the bottom of the dialog box and explore the settings available in the More Options dialog box. In the Printing Choices section, you can choose to print text details with your images, add image borders or a background color, and print crop marks to help you trim your images. The More Options dialog box also offers Custom Print Size and Color Management settings. Click Cancel to close the More Options dialog box.

9   In the Prints / Print dialog box, click Print if you wish to see these images printed; otherwise, click Cancel to save your ink and paper for your own prints. On Mac OS, choose File > Close All, but stay in the Editor for the next exercise.

Ordering professionally printed photos online

If you want high quality prints of your photos and photo projects—for yourself or to share with others—you can order professional prints from an online service.

Note: You need an active Internet connection to order prints online.

Photoshop Elements provides integrated links to online printing partners that you can conveniently access from anywhere in the workspace. In this exercise you'll learn how to order individual prints from the Organizer.

1   In the Organizer, select one or more photos in the Media Browser, and then do one of the following:

   • Choose File > Order Prints > Order Shutterfly Prints.

   • Click the Create tab at the top of the Task pane. On the Create tab, click the Photo Prints button, and then click Order Prints From Shutterfly.

2   In the Order Shutterfly Prints dialog box, do one of the following:

   • If you are already a Shutterfly member, click the "Already a member? Sign in." link, enter e-mail address and password and click Sign In.

   • If you are not already a Shutterfly member, create a new account by entering your name, e-mail address, and a password of at least six characters. If you accept the Shutterfly Terms and Conditions, click the check box below the personal details fields, and then click Join Now / Next.

Whether you choose to order prints from Shutterfly or Kodak, the experience is similar. Both services lead you through the ordering process in easy-to-follow steps.

3 In the first step—Size/Qty for Shutterfly, Customize for Kodak—you can customize your order by specifying print sizes and quantities for the photos in your order. Click Remove under a thumbnail image in the list on the left side of the dialog box to remove that photo from your order.

Alert icons beside the thumbnails let you know if your selected photos have a high enough resolution for high-quality prints at the sizes you've selected.

4 When you're done reviewing your order, click Next.

5 As you proceed with your order, you'll add the names and delivery addresses of recipients, review your order—making changes if necessary, provide your credit card details in the Payment / Billing dialog box, upload your images and confirm your order. For this exercise, click Cancel. A dialog box appears to ask if you want to stop using this service. Click OK.

Creating an Adobe ID

Photoshop Elements users in the U.S. can create an Adobe ID and sign up for a free Photoshop.com account. You can register and sign in from within the application.

Creating an Adobe ID enables Elements Membership services that are integrated with your the Elements Organizer application, giving you access to the Inspiration Browser as well as backup and sharing, and other exciting Adobe-hosted services that extend the capabilities of your Photoshop Elements software.

Basic Elements Membership is free and gives you your own storage space and a personal Photoshop.com URL where you can not only share and showcase your images but also access your photos and videos anytime and from anywhere that you can connect to the Internet. You can also use your Photoshop.com account to back up your Photoshop Elements albums and even to synchronize albums on multiple computers. Basic membership also gives you access to the Inspiration Browser, with integrated tips, tricks and tutorials related to whatever you're cur-rently working on, providing a powerful way to advance your skill set and helping you make the most out of your photos and creations.

You can upgrade to a Plus Membership to get more storage space as well as access to advanced tutorials. With Plus membership you also get regularly updated con-tent such as project templates, themes, backgrounds, frames, and graphics deliv-ered directly to your software to help you keep your projects fresh and appealing.

Note: At this stage, Elements Membership services are available only to users in the United States.

Signing up from the Welcome screen

1 Start Photoshop Elements. If Photoshop Elements is already running, click the Welcome Screen button (🏠) in the upper right corner of the workspace.

2 In the Welcome screen, click Create New Adobe ID. Enter your personal details, your e-mail address and a password, type a name for your personal Photoshop.com URL, and then click Create Account.

3 An e-mail message will be sent to you to confirm the creation of your account. Follow the instructions in the e-mail to activate your account.

Signing up from the Organizer or Editor

1 In the Organizer or Editor, click the Create New Adobe ID link in the menu bar.

2 Enter out your personal details in the Create Your Adobe ID dialog box, and then click Create Account.

Tip: You don't have to use the link in the Welcome screen to create an Adobe ID. Links for registering and signing in are conveniently located throughout the Photoshop Elements workspace.

Signing in to your Photoshop.com account

1 Make sure, your computer is connected to the Internet, and then start Adobe Photoshop Elements.

2 In the Welcome screen, enter your Adobe ID and password, and click Sign In.

If you didn't sign in at the Welcome screen, you can always click the Sign In link at the top of either the Organizer or Editor workspace.

Launching the Inspiration Browser

Once you've created an Adobe ID, you can access tips and tutorials in the Elements Inspiration Browser, which are regularly updated to help you expand your skills and to get the most out of Photoshop Elements, whatever your level of experience.

1 Click one of the tips that appear in the status bar across the bottom of the workspace window, or choose Help > Elements Inspiration Browser.

2 In the Inspiration Browser home screen, you can browse the available content using the Tutorial Type and Tutorial Category menus and the scrolling menu at the right, flip through the most popular content across the bottom of the screen, or use the search fields at the left to search the Inspiration browser or the Web.

Sharing pictures

In Lesson 1 you learned how to use the E-mail Attachments feature to create copies of your photos optimized as e-mail attachments. In this section we'll look at other ways to share your pictures with friends, family, clients, or the world at large.

Photo Mail is not supported on Mac OS; if you're working on Mac OS, you can skip ahead to "Creating an Online Album" on page 165.

Using Photo Mail

On Windows, another way to share your images by e-mail is to use the Photo Mail feature, which embeds photos in the body of an e-mail, within a customized layout.

1 In the Organizer, select one or more photos in the Media Browser, and then click the Photo Mail button in the Share panel.

Tip: If this is the first time you've accessed an e-mail feature in Photoshop Elements, you'll be presented with the E-mail dialog box. Choose your e-mail client, enter your name and e-mail address, and then click Continue. You can change these settings on the Sharing tab in the Elements Organizer Preferences.

2 Activate the Include Captions option beside Items, and then click Next.

3 In the Message text box, delete the default text and type a message of your own.

4 Select a recipient for your Photo Mail from the list in the Select Recipients pane. If your recipient list is still empty, click the Edit Recipients In Contact Book button (🧑) and create a new entry in the Contact Book dialog box.

5 Click Next. In the Stationery & Layouts Wizard dialog box, click each category in the list at the left in turn to see the range of designs available. Choose a stationery style appropriate to your selected photos; then, click Next Step.

6 Customize the layout by choosing a Photo Size and Layout option. Choose a font; then click the color swatch beside the font menu and choose a text color. To edit the message or caption, first click the text to make it active. Click Next.

Photoshop Elements opens your default e-mail application, creates an e-mail, and embeds your layout in the body of the message.

7 Switch back to the Elements Organizer.

Creating an Online Album

A great way to share and showcase your photos is by creating an Online Album. You can choose from a variety of interactive layout templates that are optimized for viewing photos on the Web. Photoshop Elements guides you through the process of adding and arranging photos, applying templates, and sharing your files.

1   In the Organizer, choose File > Get Photos And Video > From Files And Folders. In the Get Photos And Videos From Files And Folders dialog box, locate and open your Lesson05 folder. Select the folder Wedding. Activate the option Get Photos From Subfolders, if necessary, and disable the automatic processing options; then, click Get Media.

2   In the Import Attached Keyword Tags dialog box, click Select All, and then click OK. Click OK to close any other alert dialog box.

3   In the Media Browser, select the first ten wedding images.

4   Click the Share tab at the top of the Task pane; then click the Online Album button. The Share panel presents you with a choice of options. Activate the option Create New Album; from the Share To options, select Photoshop.com.

5   Click Next; the selected photos are added to the new album and their thumbnails are displayed in the Content pane on the Share tab.

6   Under Album Details, type **Annie & Jim's Big Day** in the Album Name text box.

Note: You can only share your album to Photoshop.com if you are a U.S. resident and have already signed up to Photoshop.com. For information on the other album sharing options, refer to Help.

Tip: If you find that you can't activate the Photoshop.com option, make sure that you are signed in with your Adobe ID. If the option is still unavailable, activate the Backup/Sync Is On option on the Backup/ Synchronization tab of the Elements Organizer preferences.

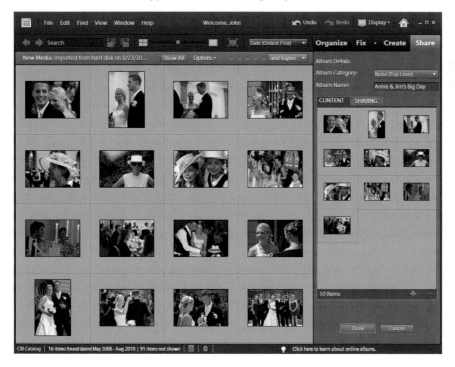

Customizing your Online Album

1   In the Media Browser, select half of the photos that have not yet been added to the album; then, click the Add Items Selected In Media browser button (➕) below the Content pane. The selected photos are added to the album and now appear in the Content pane.

2   Drag the remaining images from the Media Browser directly into the Content pane. All sixteen photos should now be included in the album.

▶ **Tip:** If you're not happy with the order of the photos once you've finished creating your album, you can return to rearrange them later—even once the album is shared online.

3   To rearrange the order in which the photos will appear in your album, select two or more thumbnails in the Content pane and drag them to a new position. Move more photos singly.

4   Click the Sharing tab at the top of the Content pane. A progress bar appears while Photoshop Elements builds an album preview based on the default template. A filmstrip-style menu across the top of the preview pane shows thumbnails for the available album templates. Hold the pointer over a thumbnail to see the name of the template and a brief description.

5   Double-click the Classic template in the filmstrip menu (*see illustration below*). The album preview is updated to reflect your choice. A semi-transparent Slideshow Settings panel floats in front of the preview. The Slideshow Settings panel becomes opaque when you move the pointer over it.

6 In the Sharing pane at the right, activate the option Share To Photoshop.com. Activate Display In My Gallery if you wish to share your album publicly. Leave this option disabled if you wish to share your album only with those friends (or clients) to whom you choose to send an invitation.

7 Type a message to be e-mailed with your invitation in the Message text box. Under Send E-mail To, click the checkbox beside the name of any contact in the list to send an automatically generated e-mail invitation to view your new Online Album. To add more recipients, click the Edit Recipients In Contact Book button (![icon]) and create new entries in the Contact Book dialog box.

8 Specify whether you wish to allow viewers to download photos or order prints.

9 Scroll to the right in the templates menu above the album preview to locate and double-click the Photo Book template. To hide the Slideshow Settings panel, click the Show/Hide Slideshow Settings button (![icon]) above the templates menu. Turn the pages of the photo book by dragging the page corners.

> **Note:** The View Online button in the Sharing pane will not become active until online sharing has been initiated and the upload is complete.

10 Below the Sharing options, click Done. Click the Organize tab above the Task Pane. In the Albums palette, the new album is marked with an Online Album icon (![icon]). You may see an icon with a pair of green arrows to the left of the Online Album icon; this indicates that Photoshop Elements has not yet completed uploading the album to Photoshop.com. Wait a minute or so until the green arrows disappear, and then right-click / Control-click the new shared album and choose View Annie & Jim's Big Day Album Online. Your default web browser opens to show the album in your Photoshop.com gallery.

11 Switch back to the Elements Organizer and click the entry for your new album in the Albums panel. In the Media browser, a number in the upper left corner of each photo indicates its place in the album.

Tip: If you don't see the badges below the thumbnails, as in this illustration, try increasing the size of the thumbnails; if the badges are still not visible, activate Details in the View menu.

Below each thumbnail there is now an Album badge (⌨) to show that the photo is part of an album and a Backup/Synchronization Complete icon (⌨) indicting that the image has been uploaded to Photoshop.com.

12 (Optional) Click the Stop Sharing button (⌨) to the right of the album name to stop sharing it to Photoshop.com. Click the Share button (⌨) to edit the album or send more e-mail invitations.

Sharing an existing album online

If you have a Photoshop.com account it's easy to convert any Photoshop Elements album into an Online Album.

1 Click Show All in the Find bar above the Media Browser; then type **print** in the text search box just above the Find bar. The Media Browser displays the search results: twenty photos tagged with the keyword "To Print." Select the eight images that don't feature children.

2 Click the Create New Album Or Album Category button (➕) in the Albums panel and choose New Album from the menu. Under Album Details, type **Vacation 2010** to name the new album, and then click Done.

3 An entry for your new album appears in the Albums panel; click the new album entry to isolate the eight vacation photos in the Media Browser.

At this stage you could simply click the Share button (⌨) to the right of the album's name to open the Online Album options, but for this exercise we'll use a different method to convert the album.

4 Click the Share tab, and then the Online Album button. In the Online Album sharing options, make sure the Vacation 2010 album is selected in the Albums list and the options Share Existing Album and Share To Photoshop.com are activated. Click Next; then set up a template and sharing options as you did in steps 5 to 9 of the previous exercise.

5 When you're done, click the Organize tab and check the Albums panel; the Vacation 2010 album is now marked with the Online Album icon (⌨).

Using an online sharing service

From within Photoshop Elements you can use Adobe Photoshop Services to upload your images and creations to social networking and photo sharing web sites. You can also use these services to download photos.

1 In the Organizer, select the photos you wish to share in the Media Browser.

2 Click the Share tab above the Task Pane. Click either the Share To Flickr, or Share To Facebook button. For both of these operations, the first step is to authorize Elements Organizer to upload images. Click Authorize.

Your default web browser opens. You'll be stepped through the process of signing in to or creating a Flickr or Facebook account, and then authorizing upload from Photoshop Elements.

3 Return to the Organizer. On the Share tab, click the Send to SmugMug Gallery button. Either log in to your SmugMug account, click Try It for a free trial offer.

4 Return to the Organizer. On the Share tab, click the white arrow to open the More Options menu and choose Share With Kodak Easyshare Gallery.

5   If the Welcome to Adobe Photoshop Services dialog box appears, do one of the following:

- If you are already an Ofoto or EasyShare Gallery member, click Sign In, and then use the e-mail address and password associated with your existing online account to sign in.

- Create a new account by entering your first name, e-mail address, and a password of at least six characters. If you agree with the Terms of Service, select the respective check box under Create Account, and then click Next.

6   In the Share With Kodak Easyshare Gallery dialog box, the first step is to specify recipients for an e-mail invitation to view your pictures on Kodak Easyshare. Select existing contacts from the Address Book list, or click Add New Address.

7   In the Add Address dialog box, complete the address information for the person with whom you wish to share your photos, and then click Next.

8   In the Share With Kodak Easyshare Gallery dialog box, click the check box beside the newly added address. Under Message, type **Photos** in the subject field and **Enjoy!** in the message field; then, click Next and Photoshop Elements will begin uploading your photos.

9   In the Confirmation screen, click Done. Alternatively, if you wish to purchase prints of your photos click Order Prints, and then follow the on-screen instructions.

An e-mail will be sent to the recipient or recipients you specified in step 6, including a Web link to the photos which can be viewed as an online slide show.

Backing up and synchronizing media files

If you've signed up for Elements Membership and activated your Photoshop.com account, you can choose to synchronize the files in your Photoshop Elements catalog with your Photoshop.com account, making your photos and videos available to you from any web browser through Photoshop.com and Photoshop Express.

You can manage your media from any web browser: add, delete, edit, or re-organize items at home or on the road. Any changes you make online will be synchronized back to Photoshop Elements on your desktop. Don't worry; the Synchronization feature will not overwrite anything on your base computer—Photoshop Elements creates a Version Set on your computer, so you'll still have the original file. If you delete something online, a copy is kept on your computer unless you confirm that you really do want it deleted from your Photoshop Elements Catalog.

In previous versions of Photoshop Elements only Albums could be backed up and synchronized in this way, but in Photoshop Elements 9 you can choose to back up your entire catalog, making it even easier to protect your precious files.

Another exciting feature in Photoshop Elements 9 is Multi Machine Sync. If you have separate installations of Photoshop Elements on more than one computer—perhaps on desktop computers at home and at the office, as well as the laptop you use when you travel—you can now synchronize them all to your Photoshop.com account. Any changes you make in your Photoshop Elements catalog on one computer, such as adding, deleting, editing or reorganizing images or albums, will be replicated on your other computers.

In Photoshop Elements 9 it's easier than ever to manage and monitor backup and synchronization—simply click the Backup/Synchronization Agent icon (), either at the bottom of the Organizer workspace or in the Windows System Tray (XP), in the Notification Area (Vista), or at the right of the menu bar on Mac OS.

Note: This feature is currently only available to Photoshop Elements users in the U.S. who have signed up for Elements Membership and a Photoshop.com account.

Setting backup and synchronization options

1 In the Organizer, click the Backup/Synchronization Agent icon (![]) at the
   bottom of the Organizer workspace and choose Open Backup/Synchronization
   Preferences. In the Backup/Synchronization Preferences dialog box, click the
   triangle beside Advanced Backup/Sync Options.

2 Examine the Backup/Synchronization settings, where you can find out everything there is to know about the current Backup and Synchronization status:

   • Backup and Synchronization is activated. The status bar shows how much of
      your online storage space is being used and how much free space you have.

   • New albums are set to backup and synchronize by default, and by default
      you will be asked for confirmation before files deleted online are deleted
      from your computer. Conflicts between the data in your catalog and your
      backed-up data online will not be resolved without a decision on your part,
      and there is currently no restriction on backup for large files.

   • All media file types supported for import are enabled for synchronization.
      By default, creations built in Photoshop Elements will not be backed up.

   • In the table below the preferences settings, you can see that synchronization
      is not enabled for media that is not included in any album, and that both of
      the albums you created in this lesson are enabled for backup and synchroni-
      zation. The Online Album icon (![]) indicates that these albums are currently
      being shared and the dimmed check-mark in the Sync column reflects the
      fact that backup and synchronization cannot be disabled while an album is
      being shared.

In the Backup/Synchronization Preferences dialog box you'll also find a button for upgrading your account to Plus membership (which increases your online storage space at Photoshop.com), a setting for specifying a downloads folder, and a button to enable backup and synchronization for your entire catalog.

3 Click OK to close the Backup/Synchronization Preferences dialog box.

You'll also find a status bar indicating online space usage—together with a link to manage your Backup/Synchronization Preferences—in the Welcome Screen.

Checking backup and synchronization status

The Backup/Synchronization Agent (🔲) at the bottom of the Organizer workspace (and in the System Tray on Windows XP or the Windows Vista Notification Area) makes it easy to check on backup and synchronization status for your files without needing to open the preferences dialog box. It also offers additional commands that can be accessed without interrupting your workflow.

1 In the Organizer, click Show All if it's visible above the Media Browser.

2 Click the Backup/Synchronization Agent icon (🔲) at the bottom of the Organizer workspace and choose View Backed Up/Synchronized Files. The media Browser displays the photos in the two albums you created in this lesson.

3 Click the Backup/Synchronization Agent icon in the Organizer just once more and choose View Backup/Synchronization Status. The Elements Backup/Synchronization Status dialog box shows that (within the parameters set in the preferences) your catalog is currently in sync with your online account.

When backup and synchronization is in progress the Backup/Synchronization Status dialog box shows the real-time transfer of data from your desktop Photoshop Elements catalog to your storage space at Photoshop.com.

4 On Windows, right-click the Backup/Synchroniz-ation Agent (🔲) in the Windows System Tray (XP) or the Notification Area (Vista). On Mac OS, click the Backup/Synchronization Agent in the menu bar. Here you'll find some commands that can't be accessed from the agent in the Organizer, such as Backup/Sync Only When Idle and the Stop Backup/Synchronization command.

Synchronizing separate computers

To synchronize your Photoshop Elements catalog across multiple computers, you first need to connect the machines to be synchronized to the same Photoshop.com account by signing in from your Photoshop Elements installation on each machine. It's not necessary that you do this at the same time.

On each computer, turn on Backup/Sync and enable Backup/Sync for your entire catalog in the Backup/Synchronization area of the Elements Organizer Preferences. Once one or two synchronization cycles have run, all your computers should have identical catalogs, with exactly the same Albums, keyword tags, image captions, and so on.

Don't attempt to aid the process; for example, by deliberately recreating a new album on your laptop to match the one you created on your desktop computer. In fact, Photoshop Elements would consider these to be two different files and you would end up with multiple copies on each machine. Simply make your changes on whichever computer you're working on and Photoshop Elements will update the other copies of your catalog.

The exception to this rule is that Photoshop Elements will not synchronize Stacks and Version Sets across multiple computers. The images inside your Stacks will be synchronised, but you'll need to recreate the stacking on each machine. For Version Sets, only the top-most version—your edited version—will be synchronized.

If you're working on one computer and wish to make sure that the changes you make are synchronized to your other machines before you need to work with them, click the Backup/Synchronization Agent and choose View Backup/Synchronization Status. In the Elements Backup/Synchronization Status dialog box, click Sync Now; then, do the same when you get to the next machine.

About exporting

Even though Photoshop Elements offers a variety of ways to share your photos and creations, there may be situations where you wish to export copies of your files to send to a friend or client on physical media, or for use in another application.

You can copy selected files to a CD or DVD, and copy or move selected files to an external hard disk by simply choosing File > Copy/Move To Removable Drive.

You can also export photos in a different file format than your source files. In the next exercise we'll look at exporting images optimized for use in a web page design application.

Saving copies of your images for use on the Web

As a final exercise in this lesson you'll convert a file to JPEG format and optimize it for use on the Web. The JPEG file format reduces the file size and can be displayed by web browsers such as Internet Explorer. If your file contains multiple layers, the conversion to the JPEG file format will flatten them into one layer.

For this operation you'll use the Save For Web feature, which enables you to tweak the export settings while comparing the original image file with the proposed web-ready version of the image.

1 In the Media Browser, select a photo you want to export for use on the Web.

2 Click the small arrow on the Fix tab at the top of the Task Pane and choose any of the three Edit modes—the Save For Web command is available from anywhere in the Editor.

3 In the Editor, choose File > Save For Web.

4 In the Save For Web dialog box, choose Fit On Screen from the Zoom menu in the lower left corner of the dialog box.

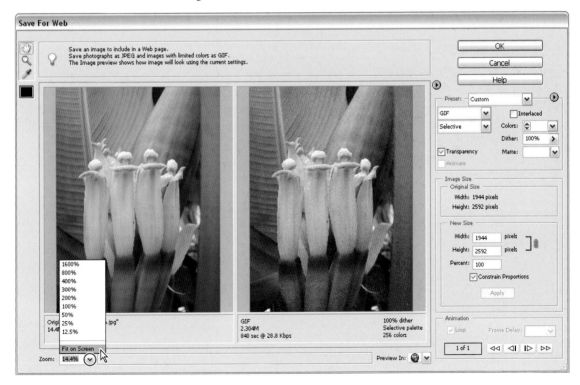

5 Notice the file-size information under each view of the image. The view on the left displays the file size of the original document.

While you're previewing photos in the Save For Web dialog box, you can magnify an image by clicking it with the Zoom tool (🔍) from the toolbox in the upper left corner of the dialog box. Alt-click / Option-click the image with the Zoom tool to zoom out. While you're zoomed in, you can drag either of the images with the Hand tool (✋); the images move in unison so that you see the same part of the photo in both views.

Note: If you need to further reduce the file size, choose the JPEG Low setting, which reduces the file size by discarding more image data and further compressing the image. You can specify intermediate levels between these options by tweaking the Quality setting, either by typing a new value or by clicking the arrow and dragging the slider.

6 On the right side of the dialog box, select JPEG Medium from the Preset menu. Notice the change in file size for the JPEG image on the right.

7 Under New Size, select Constrain Proportions and type **300** in the Width field. The Height is adjusted automatically to retain the image's original proportions. Click the Apply button. Once again, notice the change in the file size displayed beneath the JPEG view of the image. If necessary, choose Fit On Screen from the Zoom menu.

8 Click OK. Navigate to the My CIB Work folder in the Save Optimized As dialog box, add _**Work** to the end of the file name, and then click Save.

The JPEG format reduces the file size by using JPEG compression, which discards some of the data. The amount of data lost, and the resulting image quality, will vary depending on the image you're working with and the settings you choose.

9 In the Editor, choose File > Close, without saving changes.

Congratulations! You've completed this lesson and should now have a working understanding of the basics of printing, sharing, and exporting. You've learned how to set up single or multiple images for printing at home, how to order professional prints online and how to share photos in Photo Mail or to an online sharing service. You've created on Online Album and exported photos for use on the Web. Before you move on to the next lesson, take a few moments to work through the following review.

Review questions

1 What is Photo Mail? (Windows)

2 What is a Picture Package?

3 How can you fine-tune the composition of a photo for printing?

4 What are the advantages of backing up and synchronizing your catalog to your Photoshop.com account?

5 Is the Save For Web command available only in Full Edit mode?

Review answers

1 The Photo Mail feature embeds selected photos in the body of an e-mail within a colorful custom layout. You can tweak the layout and image size, choose backgrounds, frames, and effects, and add text messages and captions. You can send Photo Mail through Outlook Express, Outlook, or Adobe E-mail Service.

2 A Picture Package lets you print a photo repeated at a choice of sizes on the same page. You can choose from a variety of layout options with a range of image sizes to customize your picture package print.

3 You can now fine-tune the placement of each image within its own print well frame in the print preview, enabling you to get the image placed just right for printing without first editing it. Zoom or rotate an image with the controls beneath the print preview and drag to reposition it in the frame.

4 Backing up and synchronizing your catalog to your Photoshop.com account means that you can manage your media from any web browser—and any changes made to your catalog online will be synchronized back to Photoshop Elements on your desktop. Furthermore, with Multi Machine Sync you can now even synchronize your files across separate computers. Any changes you make to your catalog on one computer, such as adding, deleting, editing or reorganizing images or albums, will be replicated on your other machines. The capability to backup and synchronize your entire catalog now makes it even easier to manage and protect your precious files.

5 The Save For Web command is available in all three Edit modes: Full Edit, Quick Edit and Guided Edit.

6 EASY EDITING

Lesson overview

Photoshop Elements offers a suite of easy-to-use tools and a choice of three editing modes that make it easy to achieve impressive results, whatever your level of experience. The Guided Edit mode helps digital imaging novices to learn as they work, Quick Edit presents an array of one-touch controls for correcting some of the most common image problems, and Full Edit mode delivers all the power and sophistication experienced users expect from a Photoshop application.

This lesson takes you on a test drive of the three editing modes, and then introduces you to a range of quick and easy techniques to help you get more from your photos in just a few clicks:

- Making quick and easy edits in the Organizer
- Batch-processing photos
- Using automatic options to improve images
- Working in Guided Edit mode
- Making Quick Edit adjustments
- Using adjustment previews to modify settings
- Applying editing presets with the Smart Brush
- Correcting an image using Smart Fix

 You'll probably need about one and a half hours to complete this lesson.

Explore the many powerful and versatile tools and options that make it easy to get more from your photos in Photoshop Elements—even if you're a beginner. Start with a few of the easy-to-use, one-step image correction features, and then experiment with a few more advanced techniques, such as layering preset adjustments with the Smart Brush.

Getting started

Before you start working on the exercises in this lesson, make sure that you have installed the software on your computer from the application CD (see the Photoshop Elements 9 documentation) and that you have correctly copied the Lessons folder from the CD in the back of this book onto your computer's hard disk. (See "Copying the Classroom in a Book files" on page 2.)

To start, you'll import the sample images for this lesson to the CIB Catalog that you created at the beginning of Lesson 4:

1   Start Photoshop Elements and click Organize in the Welcome Screen.

2   The name of the active catalog is always shown in the lower left corner of the Organizer window. If your CIB Catalog is already loaded, you can skip step to step 4. If another catalog is currently loaded, continue with step 3.

3   Choose File > Catalog. In the Catalog Manager dialog box, click to select your CIB Catalog in the Catalogs list, and then click Open. If you don't see the CIB Catalog listed, review "Creating a new catalog" at the beginning of Lesson 4.

4   Choose File > Get Photos And Video > From Files And Folders. In the Get Photos And Videos From Files And Folders dialog box, locate and open your Lessons folder. Select the Lesson06 folder, disable any automatic processing option that is currently active, and then click Get Media.

5   In the Import Attached Keyword Tags dialog box, click Select All, and then click OK. Click OK to close any other alert dialog box.

In the Media Browser, you can see thumbnails of the images you've just imported to your CIB catalog. In the Keyword Tags panel, the newly added Lesson 06 tag has been listed under Imported Keyword Tags.

Editing photos in the Organizer

Some of the easiest and most convenient ways to quickly fix many of the most common image problems are at your fingertips, without even leaving the Organizer.

1   In the Keyword Tags panel, click the empty Find box beside the Lesson 06 tag to ensure that the photos for the following exercises are isolated in the Media Browser. Make sure that the Details and Show File Names options are activated in the View menu. In the Media Browser, select the image DSC_2076.jpg.

2   Click the Fix tab at the top of the Task pane. On the Fix tab, click the Auto Smart Fix button. The edited file is grouped with the original in a Version Set. In the media browser, the edited version appears as the top image in the collapsed (or closed) Version Set. Click the arrow at the right of the image frame to expand the Version Set.

When you edit a photo in the Organizer, a Version Set is created automatically. If you want to preserve your original image and group versions modified in the Editor, rather than the Organizer, you'll need to choose File > Save As, and then activate the options Include In Organizer and Save In Version Set With Original.

3 In the expanded Version Set, select the image on the right—the original photo, DSC_2076.jpg, in its un-edited state.

4 On the Fix tab, click the Auto Color button. The newly edited version is added to the Version Set. In the Media browser the new version appears at the left of the expanded Version Set; if the set was collapsed, this would be the top image.

5 Select the original, un-edited image again and repeat the process for the Auto Levels button, and again for the Auto Contrast button. You should now have a Version Set grouping five images.

6 Double-click the original version of the image to see it enlarged in the Media Browser's single image view. Use the left arrow key on your keyboard to compare the un-edited photo with the results of the four single-click adjustments you applied in steps 2–5.

7 Double-click the image in the enlarged single image view to return the Media Browser to the thumbnail view. Ctrl-click / Command-click to select all four edited versions of the image; then, right-click / Control-click any of the selected thumbnails and choose Delete Selected Items From catalog.

8 In the Confirm Deletion From Catalog dialog box, click to activate the option Also Delete Selected Item(s) From The Hard Disk; then, click OK. Click the Organize tab above the Task pane.

Editing in Full Screen mode

Full Screen mode in the Elements Organizer not only offers a fun way to view your images as an instant slideshow, but also provides access to the same automatic editing commands you'll find on the Fix tab. The controls in the Full Screen mode Quick Edit panel enable you to make substantial improvements to an image with just a click or two and assess the results at a conveniently high zoom level.

1   In the Media Browser, select the image DSC_3583.jpg. Click the View, Edit, Organize In Full Screen button (▣) above the Media Browser, or click the Display button (▣) at the upper right of the Organizer window and choose View, Edit, Organize In Full Screen from the menu.

2   Move the pointer over the full screen image to see the control bar at the bottom of the screen. If necessary, click the Pause button, and then click the Toggle Film Strip button at the left of the control bar, or press Ctrl+F on your keyboard, so that you can see a strip of thumbnails at the right of the screen as shown below.

3   Move the pointer to the upper left edge of the screen to show the Quick Edit panel; then, click to deactivate the Auto Hide button at the top of the vertical title bar of the Quick Edit panel so that the panel remains open while you work.

You can also access the Quick Edit panel by clicking the Toggle Quick Edit Panel button—right beside the Toggle Film Strip button in the control bar.

4 In the Quick Edit panel, hold the pointer over each button in turn to see a tooltip describing the effect it will have on the photo. Click the Auto Levels button, and then click the Auto Red Eye Fix button. Click OK to accept the creation of a new Version Set.

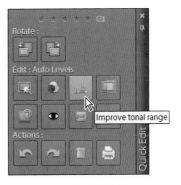

5 Click to re-activate the Quick Edit panel's Auto Hide button, and then move the pointer away; the Quick Edit panel closes after a second or so.

You've improved this photo dramatically with just two clicks—and without leaving the organizer; you can click the play button in the Full Screen view control bar to restart the slideshow, and go right back to reviewing and organizing your images.

6 Press the Esc key on your keyboard or click the Close button (x) in the control bar to exit Full Screen mode and return to the Media Browser.

7 Expand the Version Set that you just created; then, right-click / Command-click the edited version of the image and choose Delete From Catalog from the menu. In the Confirm Deletion From Catalog dialog box, activate the Also Delete Selected Item(s) From The Hard Disk option; then, click OK.

You'll be using a different technique to fix this photo later in the lesson.

Getting to know the Edit modes

For some photos, applying one-click fixes in the Organizer will be enough, but when you want more control—and access to the full power of Photoshop Elements editing, adjustment and correction tools—you'll work in the Editor. In the rest of this lesson you'll improve images in each of the three Editor modes: Full Edit, Quick Edit, and Guided Edit. Before you continue with the exercises, you can take a few minutes to familiarize yourself with switching between the three working modes, and to get an overview of the different editing workspaces.

Full Edit mode

1 Select two or three images in the Media Browser; then, click the small arrow on the Fix tab at the top of the Task Pane and choose Full Photo Edit from the menu.

2 In Full Edit mode, choose Window > Reset Panels or click the Reset Panels button ( ) at the top of the workspace. By default, the Effects, Content, and Layers panels are open in the Panel Bin.

The Full Edit mode is Photoshop Elements' most powerful and versatile image editing environment, with commands for correcting exposure and color and tools for making precise selections and fixing image imperfections. The Full Edit tool bar even includes painting and text editing tools. You can arrange the flexible Full Edit workspace to suit the way you prefer to work by floating, hiding, and showing panels.

The Project Bin below the Edit pane displays thumbnails of the photos you opened for editing. In the Project Bin menu, you can also choose to display files currently selected in the Organizer, or show the contents of any of your albums.

3 Click a thumbnail in the Project Bin to select an image. Double-click a thumbnail to bring that image to the front. At the top of the Edit pane, the name tab of the foremost image is highlighted. Click another name tab to bring that photo to the front.

4 Drag any panel out of the Panel Bin by its header bar, to float the panel wherever you like in the workspace. Click the Close button (x) in the header bar of the floating panel to close it.

5 Choose the name of the panel you just closed from the Window menu. Checkmarks are displayed beside the names of panels that are currently open. Drag the re-opened floating panel back into the Panel Bin. You can dock the panel as part of a tabbed panel group by dragging it to the header of another panel, or drop it between the frames of other panels. Whichever way you choose, release the mouse button when a blue line appears to highlight the targeted position.

6 Experiment with dragging the Toolbox and Project Bin to float over the Edit pane, and then re-docking them. When you're done exploring, click the Reset Panels button (⟳), and then click the Quick Edit tab above the Panel Bin.

Note: In this lesson you will not be working with floating image windows. If your images open in floating windows, choose Images > Consolidate All To Tabs from the Window menu.

▶ *Tip:* You can review the techniques for working with panels in "Using panels and the Panel Bin" on page 21.

Quick Edit mode

Each Edit mode offers a different set of tools, controls and views. In Quick Edit mode, the Panel Bin is occupied by the Quick Fix panel, with separate panes for Smart Fix, Lighting, Color, Balance, and Sharpness controls.

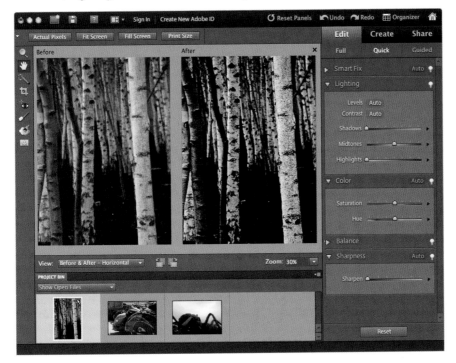

▶ *Tip:* In Quick Edit mode you cannot add, remove or float panels. To clear extra screen space, collapse the Project Bin by double-clicking its header bar and hide the Toolbox by un-checking Tools in the Window menu.

1 Choose a Before & After view option from the View menu below the Edit pane.

2 Collapse and expand any of the control panes in the Quick Fix panel by clicking the triangle at the left of the header of that pane.

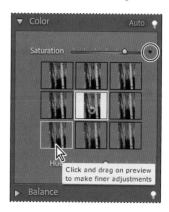

3 Click the small black arrow to the right of any control slider. A grid of preview thumbnails is displayed, showing the full range of variation possible with that control. A white frame highlights the current setting. Move the pointer slowly over each preview thumbnail in the grid to see that level of adjustment applied temporarily to your image in the After view.

4 Click the Reset button at the bottom of the Quick Fix panel to discard any changes you've made. Click the Reset Panels button (), and then click the Guided Edit tab at the top of the Panel Bin.

Guided Edit mode

▶ **Tip:** If you're new to digital imaging, the Guided Edit mode enables you to learn as you work, making it a great starting point for fixing and modifying your photos.

In Guided Edit mode the Panel Bin displays the Guided Edit panel, with grouped listings for a wide range of common—and not-so-common—image editing tasks.

1 Click any listing to find simple step-by-step instructions and any tools or controls that you'll need for that task. Try several of the guided procedures.

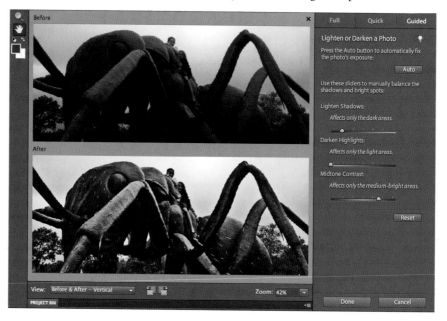

▶ **Tip:** In Guided Edit mode you can't add, remove or float panels or image windows as you would in Full Edit mode. To clear extra screen space, you can collapse the Project Bin by double-clicking its header bar.

2 When you're done experimenting, choose File > Close All. Click Don't Save to discard any changes you made, keeping the images intact for the next exercise.

Making easy color and lighting adjustments

Many of the photographs used for the lessons in this book were chosen to illustrate common image faults—the kind of challenges that people face every day as they try to make the most of their photographs. Artificial light sources, unusual shooting conditions, and incorrect camera exposure settings can all result in tonal imbalances and unwelcome color casts in an image. In the following exercises we'll look at some quick and easy ways to correct such problems in Photoshop Elements.

You can make adjustments using the simple controls in Quick Edit mode, let the Guided Edit mode step you through a wide range of editing tasks, perform sophisticated edits selectively in Full Edit mode—or even have Photoshop Elements batch-process your photos, applying your choice of automatic corrections.

Fixing files automatically in batches

Photoshop Elements enables you to fix multiple photographs with a single command by processing them as a batch. In this exercise, you'll apply automatic fixes to all the image files used in this lesson. You'll save the auto-adjusted files as copies so that at the end of each project you can compare these automatic results to the edits you've made to the original files using various other techniques.

1 Make sure you're in Full Edit mode; then choose File > Process Multiple Files.

2 From the Process Files From menu in the Process Multiple Files dialog box, choose Folder; then, set the source and destination folders as follows:

- Under Source, click the Browse button. Find and select the Lesson06 folder in your Lessons folder. Click OK / Choose to close the Browse For Folder / Choose A Folder For Processing Multiple Files dialog box.

- Under Destination, click Browse; then, find and select the My CIB Work folder that you created at the start of the book. Click OK / Choose to close the Browse For Folder / Choose A Destination Folder dialog box.

3 Under Quick Fix on the right side of the dialog box, click the checkboxes to activate all four options: Auto Levels, Auto Contrast, Auto Color, and Sharpen.

4　Under File Naming, activate Rename Files. Choose Document Name from the menu on the left and type _**Autofix** in the second field. This adds the appendix "_Autofix" to the existing document name as the files are saved.

5　Review the settings in the dialog box. Make sure that the Resize Images and Convert Files options are disabled, and then click OK.

● **Note:** For Windows users; if an error message appears after you click OK in the Process Multiple Files dialog box warning that some files couldn't be processed, you can ignore it. This error is often caused by a hidden file that is not an image, so it has no effect on the success of your project.

Photoshop Elements goes to work, automatically opening and closing image windows. All you need to do is sit back and wait for the process to finish. The newly copied files are automatically tagged with the same keywords as the source files.

Adding the auto-corrected files to the Organizer

For most files modified in the Editor, the Include In Organizer option is activated in the Save, Save As, and Save Optimized As dialog boxes by default. However, when you batch-edit files with the Process Multiple Files feature, this option isn't part of the process—you must add the edited files to the Organizer manually.

1　Switch to the Organizer; then, choose File > Get Photos And Videos > From Files And Folders.

2　In the Get Photos From Files And Folders dialog box, locate and open your My CIB Work folder, and then Ctrl-click / Command-click or marquee-select all eight files with the suffix "_Autofix."

3　Activate Automatically Fix Red Eyes and disable any other automatic processing option that is currently active; then, click Get Media. If the Auto Red Eye Fix Complete dialog box appears, click OK to accept the creation of a Version Set.

4　In the Import Attached Keyword Tags dialog box, click Select All, and then click OK. Click OK to dismiss any other dialog box.

The files are imported to your CIB Catalog and the Organizer displays thumbnails of the newly added images in the Media Browser.

Using Guided Edit

If you're a newcomer to digital image editing, the Guided Edit mode is a great place to start. By letting Photoshop Elements step you through the process of improving your photos you'll not only achieve impressive results quickly, but also learn a lot about image problems and solutions as you work.

Click any of the wide range of editing tasks listed in the Guided Edit panel and Guided Edit will provide easy-to-follow steps and instructions, conveniently presented alongside any tools and controls you'll need for that procedure.

Even more experienced users will enjoy the ease and simplicity of performing editing tasks in Guided Edit mode—and may just pick up some new tricks on the way!

Note: As you try more advanced tasks in Photoshop Elements 9, you may find that you need more information to solve any problems you encounter. For help with some common problems you might have while working through the lessons in this book, see the section "Why won't Photoshop Elements do what I tell it to do?" in Lesson 7.

Correcting color in Guided Edit mode

One of the images in the Lesson06 folder, a photo featuring some old perfume bottles, has an obvious color cast as a result of inadequate artificial lighting. In this exercise, you'll correct this common image problem in Guided Edit mode.

1   If you're not already in the Organizer, switch to it now by clicking the Organizer button (⊞) at the top right of the Editor workspace.

2   In the Keyword Tags panel, click the Find box beside the Lesson 06 tag to find and isolate all the Lesson 6 images. The Image Browser should now display the eight original photos from the Lesson06 folder, eight automatically edited copies from your My CIB Work folder, and a single automatic red eye fix grouped in a version set with its _Autofix original.

3   This last image is the only file shown in the Image Browser that is not tagged with the Lesson 06 keyword. Drag the Lesson 06 tag to the un-tagged image, and then collapse the Version Set.

4   Select the original photo of the perfume bottles, DSC_2474.jpg, making sure not to confuse the original file with the _Autofix copy.

5   Click the small arrow on the Fix tab at the top of the Task Pane and choose Guided Photo Edit from the menu.

Removing a color cast using Guided Edit

Unwelcome color casts are a very common problem in digital images. Fortunately, in Guided Edit you can correct the color in just one step!

1 If necessary, click the triangle beside the Color Correction header in the Guided Edit panel so that you can see the nested options in that group, and then click Remove A Color Cast.

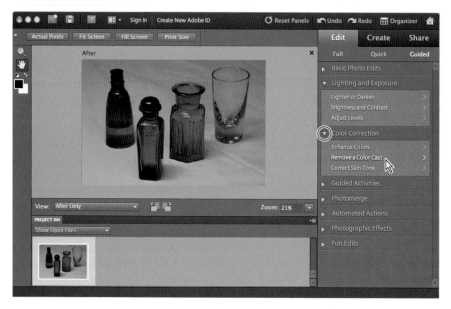

2 From the View menu at the left of the bar below the Edit pane, choose the Before & After - Horizontal view.

3 Read the instructions under Correct Color Cast. Then, using the Color Cast Eyedropper tool, click the bright area in the lower left corner of the Before image to remove the color cast. Notice the change in the After image.

4 If you're not satisfied with the result, click the Reset button in the Guided Edit panel, and then click a different point in the Before image with the Color Cast Eyedropper tool. Although the color cast is removed, the image is still quite dull; you'll fix that in the next exercise

5 When you're satisfied with what you see in the After image, click Done.

Adjusting lighting using Guided Edit

As is often the case with poorly exposed photos, this image has more than just one problem. After the color cast has been removed, it's obvious that the image would benefit from some lighting adjustments.

1 If necessary, click the triangle beside the Lighting And Exposure header in the Guided Edit panel so that you can see the options in that group, and then click Lighten Or Darken.

2 In the Guided Edit panel's Lighten Or Darken A Photo controls, click the Auto button. Notice the substantial improvement in the appearance of the image.

3 Use the Lighten Shadows, Darken Highlights, and Midtone Contrast sliders to fine-tune the lighting for this image. We set a value of 50 for Lighten Shadows, left the Darken Highlights slider at 0, and set Midtone Contrast to a value of 70. Your choices may differ, depending on the results of your color correction in the previous exercise and your preferences for the look of the final image.

4   When you're satisfied with the results of your lighting adjustment as displayed in the After image, click Done.

5   In the Guided Edit panel, click Sharpen Photo in the Basic Photo Edits group. Click the Auto button near the top of the Sharpen Photo panel. Use the slider to fine-tune the sharpening to your liking, and then click Done.

6   Choose File > Save As. In the Save As dialog box, navigate to and open your My CIB Work folder. Leaving the JPEG file format selected, name the file **DSC_2474_Guided**. Activate Include In The Elements Organizer and disable Save In Version Set With Original.

7   Click Save. In the JPEG Options dialog box, choose High from the Quality menu, and then click OK.

8   Choose File > Close, and then switch back to the Organizer.

With just a few clicks you've improved the appearance of the photo dramatically. You don't need to have prior experience using an image editor to get good results in Guided Edit mode.

Try the Guided Activities—Touch Up Scratches And Blemishes, Guide For Editing A Photo, and Fix Keystone Distortion—with some of your own photos. Each of these procedures will step you through several image editing tasks in the order recommended to achieve professional-looking results.

Creative fun with Guided Edit

The Guided Edit panel includes a lot more than just correction, adjustment, and retouching tasks. The Photomerge pane includes procedures for combining multiple photos (you'll learn about those in Lesson 11), and the Photographic Effects and Fun Edits panes let you experiment with a range of striking and unusual creative treatments for your photos.

1   If necessary, click the Find box beside the Lesson 06 tag In the Keyword Tags panel, to find and isolate all the Lesson 6 images. Select the original image of the girls on unicycles, making sure not to confuse it with the _Autofix copy.

2   Click the small arrow on the Fix tab at the top of the Task Pane and choose Guided Photo Edit from the menu.

3   In the Guided Edit panel, expand the Fun Edits pane and click Out Of Bounds.

4   Hide the Project Bin; then click the Fit Screen button above the Edit pane.

5   Follow the instructions in the Guided Edit panel. Start by clicking Add A Frame, and then let Guided Edit step you through the process of setting up the frame as you see in the illustration below. When you're happy with the frame, click the green Commit button (✔) at the lower right corner.

6   Continue with the guided steps until you can replicate something similar to what you see in the illustration below; then, click Done. Don't be discouraged if you need a few attempts—with a little practice you'll get great results.

▶ **Tip:** Remember these pointers when you're using the Quick Selection tool in step 3 of this guided edit:
• Use Ctrl / Command+[to decrease the brush size, Ctrl / Command+] to increase it.
• Hold down the Alt / Option key to subtract from the selection.
• Difficult selections can be made much easier using the Auto-Enhance and Refine Edge options in the tool options bar above the Edit pane.

7   Choose File > Save As. Name the file, check Include In The Elements Organizer, disable Save In Version Set With Original, and save to your My CIB Work folder.

Experiment with the other guided edits in the Photographic Effects and Fun Edits groups. Apply these effects as they come, use them as inspiration, or treat them as a starting point for further editing. Illustrated here are examples of the Reflection, Old Fashioned Photo, Pop Art, Lomo Camera Effect, and Line Drawing edits.

Using Quick Edit mode

In the exercise to follow, you'll move on to the next level of editing: working in the Quick Edit mode, where Photoshop Elements conveniently presents many of the basic photo fixing tools so that they're all at your fingertips in the Quick Fix panel.

If you find that one control doesn't work for your image, click the Reset button and try another. Whether or not you've used the Quick Fix panel before, the intuitive slider controls make adjusting your image easy.

Applying automatic adjustments separately

When you apply a combination of automatic fixes to a set of images using the Process Multiple Files feature, the process happens too fast for you to see the changes made to each image at each stage of processing.

In this exercise, you'll apply some of the same automatic fix options one at a time. This will enable you to see how each editing step affects an image and give you the opportunity to fine-tune the default settings for the best results.

Opening an image for Quick Fix editing

Once again, you can use the Lesson 06 Keyword Tags to find the sample image you want, and then open it in Quick Edit mode.

1 If you are already in the Organizer with the Lesson 06 files still isolated in the Media Browser from the last exercise, skip to step 3.

2 Switch to the Organizer and click the Find box beside the Lesson 06 tag in the Keyword Tags panel.

3 Select the original photo of the perfume bottles, DSC_2474.jpg, making sure not to confuse the original file with the edited copies.

4 Click the small arrow on the Fix tab at the top of the Task Pane and choose Quick Photo Edit. Wait while the image opens in the Editor.

Using Smart Fix

In the Quick Edit workspace the Quick Fix panel at the right contains five adjustment panes—Smart Fix, Lighting, Color, Balance, and Sharpness. The Smart Fix feature is actually a combination of several adjustments applied at once; it corrects overall color balance and improves shadow and highlight detail in your image. As with the other editing options in Quick Edit mode, you can either click the Auto button to apply the correction automatically or use the slider controls to fine-tune the adjustment. You can also combine these methods, as you will in this exercise.

1 Choose Before & After - Horizontal from the View menu in the bar below the Edit pane. Alternatively, if you prefer the before and after images one above the other rather than side-by-side, choose the Before & After - Vertical view.

2 In the Quick Fix panel, click the Smart Fix Auto button in the Smart Fix pane. Notice the immediate effect on the image.

3 Now, move the Smart Fix Amount slider to change the color balance and the highlight and shadow settings for your image. Experiment to find the setting you prefer. We set the Smart Fix Amount to a value of 70.

4 Click the Commit button () in the header of the Smart Fix pane to commit the changes.

Remember that whenever you change a setting in the Quick Fix panel, you need to click the Commit or Cancel button in the header of the relevant task pane to accept or discard the changes.

Applying more automatic fixes

Four more automatic Quick Fix adjustments are available in the Lighting, Color, and Sharpness panes. (There is no Auto Balance adjustment.)

1 In the Lighting pane, click the Auto Levels and Auto Contrast buttons.

You may or may not see a significant shift in the tonal balance of this image, depending on the adjustment you made with the Smart Fix edit.

2 Click the Auto Color and Auto Sharpen buttons, noting the effects of each of these adjustments in the After view.

3 In the Quick Fix Color pane, click the small black arrow to the right of the Saturation slider.

A grid of nine preview thumbnails is displayed, showing the full range of variation possible with the Saturation slider. A white frame highlights the central thumbnail—the preview that represents the current saturation setting.

4 Move the pointer slowly over each preview thumbnail in the grid to see that level of saturation applied temporarily to your image.

Clicking any of the thumbnails will apply the respective level of adjustment; click a thumbnail and drag left or right to fine-tune the adjustment. The Quick Fix previews not only provide a intuitive editing interface but also make a great way to learn about the effects of the various adjustment controls as you work with them.

5   Experiment with the slider controls and Quick Fix preview grids in each pane of the Quick Fix panel. When you're satisfied with an adjustment, click the Commit button (✔) in the title bar of that pane to accept the changes.

6   If you wish to undo your modifications and start again with the original version of the image, click the Reset button at the bottom of the Quick Fix panel.

7   When you've achieved the results you want, choose File > Save As. In the Save As dialog box, navigate to and open your My CIB Work folder, rename the file **DSC_2474_Quick** and select the JPEG format. Activate Include In The Organizer and disable Save In Version Set With Original.

8   Click Save. When the JPEG Options dialog box appears, choose High from the Quality menu, and then click OK. Choose File > Close.

Using the Smart Brush

The Whiten Teeth, Blue Sky, and Black And White - High Contrast tools in the Quick Fix mode toolbox are all variants of the Smart Brush tool in Full Edit mode.

The Smart Brush is both a selection tool and an image adjustment tool—it creates a selection based on similarities in color and texture, through which your choice of editing preset is applied.

While the selection is active, you can add to or subtract from it, without needing to re-applying the adjustment. Each Smart Brush edit is made on its own adjustment layer, so it doesn't permanently alter the original photo. The Smart Brush edit remains active on its adjustment layer; you can return at any time to edit the selection area or change the way the adjustment is being applied—or even to delete the adjustment layer entirely—without degrading your original image.

1. If you're not already in the Organizer with the Lesson 6 files isolated in the Media Browser, switch to the Organizer now and click the Find box beside the Lesson 06 tag In the Keyword Tags panel.

2. In the Media Browser, select the image DSC_1830.jpg, a photo of a very unusual building—making sure not to confuse the original file with the _Autofix copy.

3. Click the small arrow on the Fix tab at the top of the Task Pane and choose Full Photo Edit from the menu.

Applying a Smart Brush adjustment

In the final two exercises for this lesson you'll use the Smart Brush to liven up defined areas of a photograph selectively.

1. In Full Edit mode, click the Reset Panels button (⟳) at the top of the workspace. Hide the grouped Effects and Content panels, and the Project Bin, by double-clicking their header bars, and then choose View > Fit On Screen.

2. Select the Smart Brush ( ) from the toolbox; then, drag the Smart Brush adjustment presets picker from the tool options bar to a position where it won't obstruct your view of the photo while you work.

3 Click the categories menu at the top of the floating Smart Brush presets picker and choose the category Nature. Scroll down through the options in the Nature category and select the Greenery preset.

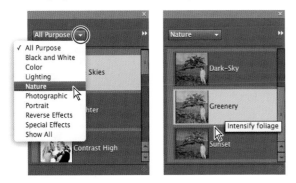

4 Click the Close button (x) in the header of the Smart Brush presets picker. In the tool options bar, open the Brush Picker and set the brush diameter to 20 px (pixels). To close the Brush Picker, click elsewhere in the tool options bar, or use the Esc key on your keyboard. Drag half-way across the dull-looking lawn in the foreground as shown in the illustration below; then, release the mouse button.

Don't be concerned if your selection expands to include the road and shrubs. If you wish to subtract from the selection, hold down the Alt / Option key as you paint.

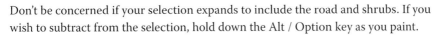

Tweaking a Smart Paint adjustment

The Greenery brush has not made a very effective difference to the image. Let's try some methods for modifying the adjustment to boost the effect.

1 The adjustment you applied shows a "pin"—a colored marker that identifies a Smart Brush edit when the Smart Brush tool is active—at the point that you first clicked with the Smart Brush. Right-click / Control-click the pin and choose Change Adjustment Settings from the context menu.

Note: Invoking the Change Adjustment Settings command will call up a different set of controls for each Smart Brush preset, depending on the combination of adjustments that make up that preset.

2 The Adjustments panel opens in the Panel Bin. Experiment with the three sliders, noting the changes in the image. When you're done experimenting, click the Reset button at the bottom of the Adjustments panel to return the settings to the defaults for the Greenery preset; you'll be looking at another way to modify the effects of this Smart Brush adjustment yet.

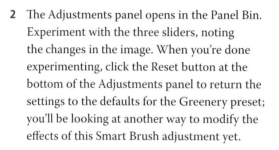

3 Collapse the Adjustments panel by double-clicking its header bar. If necessary, use the same method to expand the Layers panel.

4 In the Layers panel, the new adjustment layer, Greenery 1, is the active layer. Set the Opacity value for the new layer to 50% and the Blending Mode to Screen.

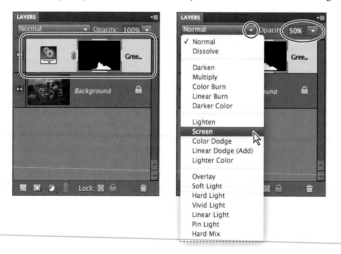

For this particular photo, this setting is far more effective, intensifying the colors in the lawn area and giving the scene as a whole a much sunnier look.

Original image   Greenery preset, Normal blend, 100%   Greenery preset, Screen blend, 50%

5 Paint over the rest of the lawn with the modified Greenery adjustment settings. Leave the road selected if you wish, but try to exclude the walls and towers. Hold down the Alt / Option key as you paint to subtract from the selection. Press the left bracket key ([) to decrease the brush size, and the right bracket (]) to increase it. While you're fine-tuning the selection, use a small brush and slow, short strokes. When you're satisfied, choose Select > Deselect Layers.

Applying multiple Smart Paint adjustments

You can use the Smart Brush on the same area as many times as you wish. If you re-apply the same adjustment preset the effects are usually cumulative, though the results will depend on the layer blending mode for that preset. You can also apply different Smart Brush presets to the same image area, combining their effects.

1 With the Smart Brush tool still selected in the toolbox, click the thumbnail in the tool options bar to open the Smart Brush adjustment presets picker once more. Drag the presets picker to a convenient position clear of the image.

2 In the presets picker, choose the Nature category; then select the Blue Skies preset. Drag across the sky from the upper left corner. It will be impossible to deal with the bare trees other than to deliberately include them in the selection. In the Layers panel, change the Blending mode for the new layer Blue Skies 1 from the preset Color Burn to Overlay and decrease the Opacity value from 75% to 50%. Choose Select > Deselect Layers to deactivate the new adjustment.

3 In the presets picker, select Cloud Contrast; then drag left across the sky from the upper right, just clear of the tree branches. There are now three Smart Brush pins on the image. Change the Blending mode for the new layer Cloud

Contrast 1 from Normal to Soft Light and reduce the Opacity value to 40%. Choose Select > Deselect Layers to make the new adjustment inactive.

4   Choose the Dark Sky preset and drag across the sky from the lower left, just above the trees. Change the layer Opacity to 100% and the Blending mode to Luminosity. In the Layers panel, select the layer Greenery 1. You can see that there are now three Smart Brush pins on the sky, and three corresponding new layers in the Layers panel. Use the eye icon at the left of each layer to toggle its visibility so you can compare the different treatments you applied to the sky.

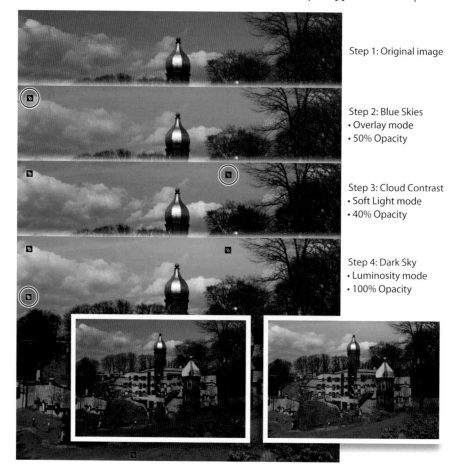

Step 1: Original image

Step 2: Blue Skies
• Overlay mode
• 50% Opacity

Step 3: Cloud Contrast
• Soft Light mode
• 40% Opacity

Step 4: Dark Sky
• Luminosity mode
• 100% Opacity

▶ **Tip:** After you save the file, experiment more with the opacity and blending of the layers. Right-click / Control-click each pin to explore the settings. If you wish, you can discard your changes by clicking Don't Save when you close the file.

5   Chose File > Save As. Name the file **DSC_1830_SmartBrush** and save it to your My CIB Work folder in Photoshop (.PSD, .PDD) format with Layers activated. Activate the Include In The Organizer option and disable Save In Version Set With Original.

Congratulations, you've completed this lesson. You've gained a lot of experience with all three Edit modes and discovered many of the fast and easy options for improving your photos. Take a few moments now to review what you've learned.

Review questions

1 What are the key differences between adjusting images in Full Edit mode, Quick Edit mode and Guided Edit mode?

2 Can you apply automatic fixes when you are in Full Edit mode?

3 What is the purpose of the Project Bin?

4 Can you float panels and other interface elements in any Edit mode?

5 What is the Smart Brush tool?

Review answers

1 Full Edit provides the most flexible and powerful image correction environment. Full Edit offers lighting and color correction commands and tools for fixing image defects, making selections, adding text, and painting on your images. Quick Fix provides easy access to a range of basic image editing controls for quickly making common adjustments and corrections. If you're new to digital photography, Guided Edit is the best place to start—stepping you through each procedure to help you get professional-looking results.

2 Yes; the Enhance menu contains commands that are equivalent to the Auto buttons in the Quick Fix panel: Auto Smart Fix, Auto Levels, Auto Contrast, Auto Color Correction, as well as Auto Red Eye Fix. The Enhance menu also provides an Adjust Smart Fix command, which opens a dialog box in which you can specify settings for automatic adjustments.

3 The Project Bin provides easy access to the photos you want to work with, without needing to leave the Editor workspace. You can set the Project Bin to display all the photos that are currently selected in the Media Browser, just those images that are open in the Editor (helpful when some of the open images are hidden behind the front window), or the entire contents of any album in your catalog.

4 No; you can rearrange the workspace only in Full Edit mode.

5 The Smart Brush is both a selection tool and an image adjustment tool—it creates a selection based on similarities in color and texture, through which your choice of editing preset is applied. You can choose from close to seventy Smart Brush presets, each of which can be customized, applied repeatedly for a cumulative effect, or layered with other adjustment presets to produce an almost infinite variety of results.

7 ADJUSTING COLOR IN IMAGES

Lesson overview

Photoshop Elements delivers a broad range of tools and options for working with color. Whether you want to make corrections for unusual lighting conditions, remove red eye effects, or brighten a smile, you'll find a range of solutions from one-click Auto Fixes to options that give you precise control of the adjustments you apply.

This lesson introduces you to a variety of tools and techniques for fixing color problems in your photos:

- Using automatic options to correct color
- Tweaking automatic color adjustments
- Using Color Variations to correct color balance
- Adjusting skin tones
- Whitening yellowed teeth
- Removing red eye effects
- Using the selection tools and saving selections
- Changing the color of a pictured object
- Replacing a color throughout an image
- Working with color management

 You'll probably need about two hours to complete this lesson.

Explore the many powerful and versatile tools and options available in Photoshop Elements for correcting color problems in your photos. Start with a few of the easy-to-use, one-step image correction features, and then experiment with some of the more advanced photo editing features and techniques that can be mastered easily.

Getting started

Before you start working on the exercises in this lesson, make sure that you have installed the software on your computer from the application CD (see the Photoshop Elements 9 documentation) and that you have correctly copied the Lessons folder from the CD in the back of this book onto your computer's hard disk. (See "Copying the Classroom in a Book files" on page 2.)

To start, you'll import the sample images for this lesson to the CIB Catalog that you created at the beginning of Lesson 4:

1   Start Photoshop Elements and click Organize in the Welcome Screen.

2   Check the name of the active catalog in the lower left corner of the Organizer window. If your CIB Catalog is already loaded, you can skip step to step 4. If another catalog is currently loaded, continue with step 3.

3   Choose File > Catalog. In the Catalog Manager dialog box, click to select your CIB Catalog in the Catalogs list, and then click Open. If you don't see the CIB Catalog listed, review "Creating a new catalog" at the beginning of Lesson 4.

4   Choose File > Get Photos And Video > From Files And Folders. In the Get Photos And Videos From Files And Folders dialog box, locate and open your Lessons folder. Select the Lesson07 folder, disable any automatic processing option that is currently active, and then click Get Media.

5   In the Import Attached Keyword Tags dialog box, click Select All, and then click OK. Click OK to close any other alert dialog box.

Batch-processing the lesson files

As you discovered in Lesson 6, the batch-processing command lets you apply a choice of automatic adjustments to an entire folder of image files at once.

Before you start this lesson, you can set up automatic processing for the photos you'll use in the exercises.

You can save the auto-adjusted files as copies so that at the end of each project you can compare the automatic fixes to the results you achieve using various other techniques.

1   Make sure that you have no images selected in the Media Browser; then, click the small arrow on the Fix tab at the top of the Task Pane and choose Full Photo Edit from the menu.

2   In the Editor, choose File > Process Multiple Files.

3   From the Process Files From menu in the Process Multiple Files dialog box, choose Folder. Under Source, click the Browse button to locate and select

the Lesson07 folder in your Lessons folder. Click OK / Choose to close the Browse For Folder / Choose A Folder For Processing Multiple Files dialog box. Under Destination, click Browse; then, find and select the My CIB Work folder that you created at the start of the book. Click OK / Choose to close the Browse For Folder / Choose A Destination Folder dialog box.

4   Under File Naming, activate the Rename Files option. Choose Document Name from the menu on the left and type **_Autofix** in the second field. This will add the appendix "_Autofix" to the existing document name as the files are saved.

5   Under Quick Fix on the right side of the dialog box, click the checkboxes to activate all four options: Auto Levels, Auto Contrast, Auto Color, and Sharpen.

6   Review the settings in the dialog box. Make sure that the Resize Images and Convert Files options are disabled, and then click OK.

Note: For Windows users; if an error message appears after you click OK in the Process Multiple Files dialog box warning that some files couldn't be processed, you can ignore it. This error is often caused by a hidden file that is not an image, so it has no effect on the success of your project.

Photoshop Elements goes to work, automatically opening and closing image windows; all you need to do is sit back and wait for the process to finish. The newly copied files are automatically tagged with the same keywords as the source files.

Adding auto-corrected files to the Organizer

For most files modified in the Editor, the Include In Organizer option is activated in the Save, Save As, and Save Optimized As dialog boxes by default. However, when you batch-edit files with the Process Multiple Files feature, this option isn't part of the process—you must add the edited files to the Organizer yourself.

1 Switch to the Organizer; then, choose File > Get Photos And Videos > From Files And Folders.

2 In the Get Photos And Videos From Files And Folders dialog box, locate and open your My CIB Work folder, and then Ctrl-click / Command-click or marquee-select all the files with the prefix "07_" and the suffix "_Autofix."

3 Activate Automatically Fix Red Eyes and disable any other automatic processing option that is currently active; then, click Get Media. If the Auto Red Eye Fix Complete dialog box appears, click OK to accept the creation of a Version Set.

4 In the Import Attached Keyword Tags dialog box, click Select All, and then click OK. Click OK to dismiss any other dialog box.

The files are imported to your CIB Catalog and the Organizer displays thumbnails of the newly added images in the Media Browser.

Correcting color problems

Artificial light sources, unusual shooting conditions, and incorrect camera exposure settings can all result in the most common image problems: unwelcome color casts and tonal imbalances in your photos.

For some images your color problem may be more specific, such as red eyes in a photo taken with a flash, or a portrait spoiled by yellow-looking teeth. Even when a photo is technically perfect, you may still wish to adjust the color—either across the entire image, or just for a particular area or object—in order to create an effect.

You'll begin this lesson by revisiting, and comparing, some of the tools and techniques for making quick and easy adjustments using the simple controls in the Quick Edit mode and the step-by-step editing tasks in Guided Edit mode.

Later in the lesson you'll explore methods for dealing with red eyes and yellow teeth, and learn how to use the selection tools—an essential skill for performing sophisticated, localized edits in Full Edit mode.

Comparing methods of fixing color

The automatic correction features in Photoshop Elements do an excellent job of bringing out the best in most photographs, but each image—and each image problem—is unique. Some photographs don't respond well to automatic fixes and require a more hands-on approach to color correction.

Photoshop Elements offers many ways to deal with color correction. The more techniques you master, the more likely you'll be able meet the challenge of fixing a difficult photograph. In this section, you'll study different methods for correcting a color problem, and then compare the results.

Creating extra working copies of an image

In the next exercises you'll compare three different approaches to correcting the same color problem, so you'll need three copies of the original photograph.

1　In the Organizer, use the Lesson 07 keyword tag to locate the image 07_01.jpg: a poorly exposed photo of three Thai dancers.

2　Select the image 07_01.jpg in the Media Browser, taking care not to confuse the original file with the Autofix copy; then, click the small arrow on the Fix tab at the top of the Task Pane, and choose Quick Photo Edit.

3　Click the Reset Panels button (🔄) at the top of the Quick Edit workspace, and then double-click the Hand tool in the toolbox or choose View > Fit On Screen.

4　Right-click / Control-click the thumbnail in the Project Bin and choose Duplicate from the context menu. In the Duplicate Image dialog box, click OK to accept the default name 07_01 copy.jpg. Repeat the process to create two more duplicates, 07_01 copy 2.jpg and 07_01 copy 3.jpg.

Although you can view only one image at a time in the Edit pane while you're in Quick Edit mode, you can easily see which files are open by checking the Project Bin. The name of each image in the Project Bin appears as a tooltip when you hold the pointer over the thumbnail. Alternatively, right-click / Control-click anywhere inside the Project Bin and choose Show File Names from the context menu.

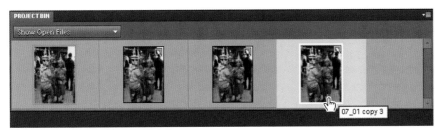

A highlighted frame surrounds the front, or active, image—the photo that is currently visible in the Edit pane.

5　Double click the original image 07_01.jpg—the thumbnail at the left—to make it the active photo. Close the file by choosing File > Close, or clicking the Close button (x) in the upper right corner of the Edit pane.

Correcting color automatically

When you processed the sample files as a batch at the start of this lesson, you applied all four automatic Quick Fix options to all of the images in the Lesson07 folder. In this exercise, you'll apply the Quick Fix color adjustment on its own, so that you can assess the result unaffected by other settings.

1 In the Project Bin, double-click the thumbnail at the left—07_01 copy.jpg—to make it the active file.

2 Choose Before & After - Horizontal from the View menu below the Edit pane.

3 In the Quick Fix panel, click the Auto button in the Color pane to auto-correct just the color. Compare the Before and After views.

There is a marked improvement in the image; the Auto Color fix has corrected most of the blue-green color cast resulting from fluorescent lighting. The skin tones are somewhat warmer, but the contrast has suffered and the tonal range is still flat.

4 Choose File > Save. Save the file to your My CIB Work folder in JPEG format, changing the name to **07_01_AutoColor**. Make sure that Include In The Elements Organizer is activated and the Save In Version Set With Original option is disabled. Click Save; then, click OK in the JPEG Options dialog box.

Adjusting the results of an automatic fix manually

An automatic fix can serve as a good starting point for some manual fine-tuning.

1 In the Project Bin, double-click the image 07_01 copy 2.jpg to make it active.

2 In the Quick Fix panel, click the Auto button in the Color pane.

3   The image still has a slight blue-green cast. This can be seen clearly in the white wall showing at the top right of the frame. In the Balance pane, increase the Temperature and Tint values to 53 and 3 respectively to make the color warmer.

4   In the Lighting pane, click the Auto Contrast button; then set the Lighten Shadows value to 5 and the Midtone Contrast value to 15. Click the Commit button () at the top of the Lighting pane.

▶ **Tip:** When you're making multiple Quick Fix adjustments it's not necessary to click the Commit button for each edit. The current adjustment is automatically committed as soon as you move on to change any other setting in the Quick Fix panel.

The contrast has improved, the color is intensified and the skin tones have lost the greyish look caused by the fluorescent lighting, but the image is still under-exposed. Once again, this is quite evident in the tone of the white wall in the background.

5   Choose Enhance > Adjust Lighting > Levels. In the Levels dialog, move the white slider—the highlights slider—to the left to a value of 200; then click OK.

6   Choose File > Save. Save the file to your My CIB Work folder in JPEG format, changing the name to **07_01_ColorBalanceLighting**. Make sure that Include In The Elements Organizer is activated and the Save In Version Set With Original option is disabled. Click Save; then, click OK in the JPEG Options dialog box.

Tweaking the results of an automatic fix

The top five commands in the Enhance menu apply the same image adjustments as the various Auto buttons in the Quick Fix panel. Enhance menu commands are available in both the Quick Fix and Full Edit modes, but not in Guided Edit.

Both the Quick Fix and Full Edit modes also offer other methods of enhancing color that give you greater control over the results. These are the commands in the lower half of the Enhance menu. In this exercise, you'll use one of these options to tweak the adjustments applied by the Auto Color fix button.

1   In the Project bin, double-click the image 07_01 copy 3 to make it the active file.

2   In the Color pane, click Auto to apply the Quick Fix color correction; then, choose Enhance > Adjust Color > Color Variations to open the Color Variations dialog box.

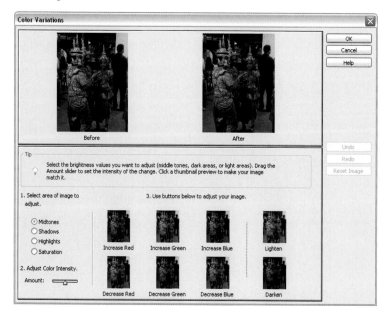

3   In the lower left area of the Color Variations dialog box, make sure that Midtones is selected, and then move the Amount slider down three stops to the minimum position. Click the Increase Red thumbnail twice.

4 Change the settings from Midtones to Highlights and move the Amount slider up to the half-way position. Click the Decrease Green thumbnail twice, Decrease Blue three times, and Lighten five times; then click OK.

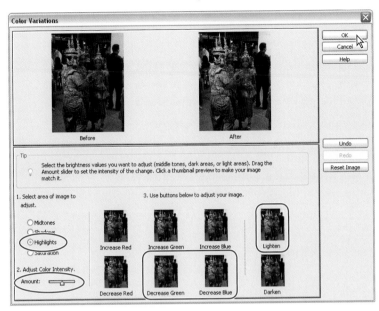

The Color Variations adjustments have made the colors warmer and more vivid, reduced the blue-green color cast, and improved the tonal range. If you wish to try again, click Reset at the bottom of the Quick Fix panel and start from Step 3.

5 Choose File > Save As, and navigate to your My CIB Work folder. Rename the file **07_01_ColorVariations**, select the JPEG format, and set the options to include the saved file in the Organizer, but not in a Version Set. Click Save.

Comparing results

In the Project bin, you can see that all three of your saved work files are still open in the Editor. Let's compare them to the batch-processed Autofix file.

1 Choose File > Open. Locate and open your My CIB Work folder. Select the file 07_01_Autofix, and then click Open. At the top of the Edit tab in the Task pane, click Full to switch to Full edit mode.

Note: Once you've activated the option to allow floating document windows, this becomes the default for any image opened in Full Edit mode. Throughout the rest of this book however, it will be assumed that you are working with tabbed image windows that are docked (consolidated) in the Edit pane, unless otherwise specified. When you complete this exercise you'll disable floating document windows so that it'll be easier for you to follow the exercise steps as written.

2 Choose Preferences > General from the Edit / Photoshop Elements menu. Activate Allow Floating Documents In Full Edit Mode, and then click OK.

3 Hide the Project Bin by double-clicking its header bar; then, choose Window > Images > Tile. Use the Zoom and Hand tools to see an area of interest in one of the images, and then choose Window > Images > Match Zoom and Window > Images > Match Location. These commands are also accessible by clicking the Arrange button (⊞) at the top of the workspace and choosing from the menu.

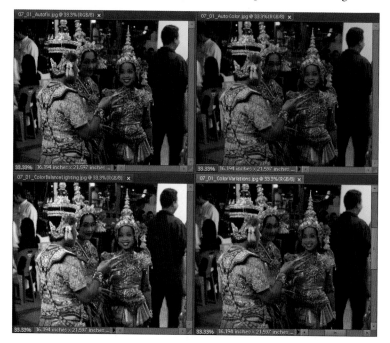

Tip: At any given time there is only one active image window. Look at the text in the title bars of the open image windows; the file name and image details are dimmed in the title bars of all but the active image window.

4 In the toolbox, select the Hand tool. In the tool options bar, activate the Scroll All Windows option. Drag in the active window to see different areas of the image. Compare the four images and decide which looks best. Make your choice the active window and choose Window > Images > Float In Window.

5 Choose View > Fit On Screen to enlarge the image so it fits in the window. You can cycle through all open windows by pressing Ctrl-Tab or Ctrl-Shift-Tab.

6 Choose File > Close All. From the Edit / Photoshop Elements menu, choose Preferences > General and disable the floating documents option. Click OK.

Adjusting skin tones

Photoshop Elements offers another unique solution to color cast problems that is available in both the Full Edit and Quick Fix modes.

1 Choose File > Open. Navigate to and open your Lesson07 folder; then select the image 07_01.jpg and click Open. Use the Zoom and hand tools to position the image so that you can focus on the faces and hands of the three dancers.

2 Choose Enhance > Adjust Color > Adjust Color For Skin Tone. In the Adjust Color For Skin Tone dialog box, make sure the Preview option is activated.

Consider the peculiarities of the image at hand. Be aware of strongly colored lighting or other factors apart from the color cast that might produce unrealistic skin tones. In this case, the dancers' faces are heavily made-up for a stage performance.

3 As you move the pointer over the image, the cursor changes to an eyedropper tool. Look for the lightest part of the raised hand of the dancer on the left—just above the wrist— and click with the eyedropper tool. The color balance for the entire photo is adjusted using the sampled skin tone as a reference.

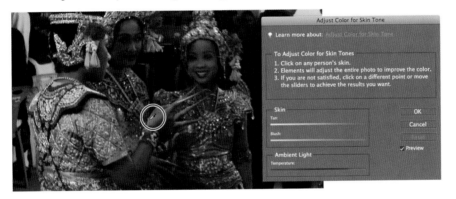

▶ **Tip:** Even while the Adjust Color For Skin Tone dialog box is open, you can still use keyboard commands to change the zoom level. or press the space bar to call up the Hand tool and move the image if you wish to focus on a different area.

4 Move the Tan, Blush, and Temperature sliders to achieve the skin tones you want, and then click OK. Choose File > Save As. Name the file 07_01_Skin and save it to your My CIB Work folder with the usual options. Choose File > Close.

Using the Touch Up tools

If you're familiar with an earlier version of Photoshop Elements, you may expect to find the Touch Up pane in the Quick Fix panel. In Photoshop Elements 9, the familiar Touch Up tools are located in the toolbox at the left of the workspace.

All four Quick Edit Touch Up tools enable you to apply corrections and adjustments selectively to a delineated part of an image:

Note: The Whiten Teeth, Blue Sky, and Black And White - High Contrast tools in Quick Edit mode are all variants on the Smart Brush tool in Full Edit mode. For more information on the Smart Brush, see "Using the Smart Brush tool" in Lesson 6.

- The Red Eye Removal tool removes red eye effects in flash photos of people, and green or white eye effects in flash photos of pets.

- The Whiten Teeth tool brightens smiles.

- The Blue Sky tool can bring new life to a dull image.

- The Black And White - High Contrast tool simulates the high-contrast image effects that black and white film photographers produce by placing a red filter over the camera lens.

Except for Red Eye Removal, all Touch Up tool adjustments are applied on separate adjustment layers; they do not make any permanent change to information on the image layer. The adjustments remain "live"; you can return and modify the settings or the area to which they are applied, without degrading the original image.

Brightening a smile

We'll be looking closely at the Red Eye Removal feature in a later exercise. For now, let's try the Whiten Teeth tool.

1 If you already have the Lesson 7 files isolated in the Organizer from the last exercise, switch to the Organizer now, and then skip to step 4.

2 Start Photoshop Elements if it's not already running and open the Organizer. Check the lower left corner of the workspace to make sure that your CIB Catalog is loaded; if not, choose File > Catalog and load the CIB Catalog now.

3 In the Organizer, click the Find box beside the Lesson07 tag, listed under Imported Keyword Tags in the Keyword Tags panel.

4 In the Media Browser, select the image 07_02.jpg, a photo of a woman's face—making sure not to confuse the original file with the Autofix copy.

5 Click the small arrow on the Fix tab at the top of the Task Pane and choose Quick Photo Edit from the menu. Wait while the image opens in the Editor.

Setting up the Quick Edit workspace

You can prepare for the exercise by customizing the Quick Edit workspace.

1 Hide the Project Bin by double-clicking its header bar.

2 From the View menu below the Edit pane, choose Before & After - Vertical.

3 Use both the Hand tool and the Zoom slider below the After image to position the photo so that you have the closest possible view of the woman's mouth. You can drag either the Before or After view with the Hand tool—the two images will move in unison.

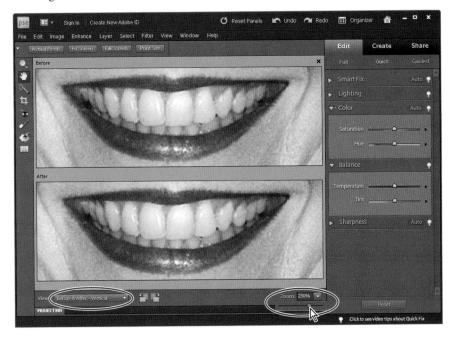

Using the Whiten Teeth tool

Now it's time for a little Photoshop Elements dental magic. With the Whiten Teeth tool, as with the other Touch Up tools, you'll work directly into the After image; these tools have no effect on the Before image.

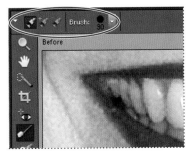

1 Click to select the Whiten Teeth tool ( ) in the toolbox.

2 Notice that once the Whiten Teeth tool is active, settings and variants for the tool become available in the tool options bar, right above the toolbox.

3 In the Whiten Teeth tool settings, click the triangle to open the Brush picker. As the image you're using for this exercise is of a fairly low resolution, you'll need a small brush; set the Diameter to 5 px. Set the Hardness value to 50%, and then click the triangle again or press the Esc key on your keyboard to close the Brush picker.

4 Move the pointer over the After image. A small cross-hair cursor indicates the brush size set for the Whiten Teeth tool: Notice that in the tool settings at the top left of the Editor window, the brush icon on the left is highlighted to indicate that the tool is in New Selection mode. Drag the cross-hair across half of the upper teeth as shown below, and then release the mouse button.

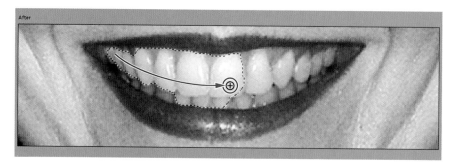

Adding to and subtracting from an adjustment selection

The Whiten Teeth tool, like the Blue Sky and Black And White Touch Up tools, is both a selection tool and an image adjustment tool. You have just used the tool to create a selection through which the tooth whitening adjustment is applied once. While this selection is active, you can still add to it or subtract from it, without re-applying the adjustment.

The Whiten Teeth selection and adjustment is being made on a new layer separate from the original image in the background layer. The edit remains active on its own adjustment layer—so you can return to alter the selection area or the way the adjustment is being applied at any time without degrading the original image.

1 Notice that in the tool options bar, the brush icon in the center is now highlighted. Now that there is already an active selection, the brush has switched from the default New Selection mode to the Add To Selection mode automatically.

2 To add the rest of the upper teeth to the selection, drag with the Add To Selection brush as shown below, and then release the mouse button. You don't need to drag all the way to the last tooth on the right; the selection will expand automatically. Don't worry if the gums and parts of the lips are also selected—you'll deal with that in step 4.

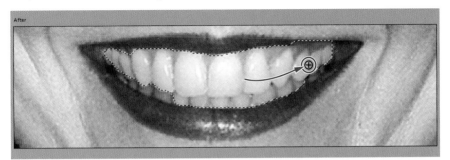

3 Carefully add the shaded lower teeth at both sides of the mouth to the selection by making two short, slow strokes as shown below—overlapping the cross-hairs cursor on the flashing border of the existing selection. If your selection expands too far, press Ctrl+Z / Command+Z to undo the last action and try again.

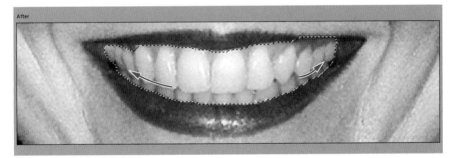

4 Hold down the Alt / Option key. The cursor changes to that of the Subtract From Selection brush—the cross-hairs become a minus sign. Notice that in the tool options bar the brush icon on the right is now highlighted. Holding down the Alt / Option key, carefully drag with the Subtract From Selection brush to remove the lip and gum areas from the adjustment selection as shown below.

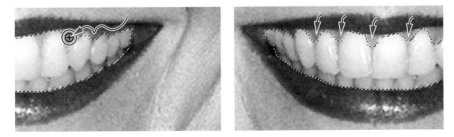

▶ **Tip:** Use very short strokes, slowly working the cursor towards the line you want. If you're not happy with the results that you're seeing, try altering the direction of your strokes, or even just clicking rather than dragging.

5 Release the Alt / Option key. The brush returns to Add To Selection mode. Look for any areas that still need to be added to the selection or that you may have removed from the selection by mistake in the last step. Drag very short strokes or simply click with the Add To Selection brush to pick up these areas.

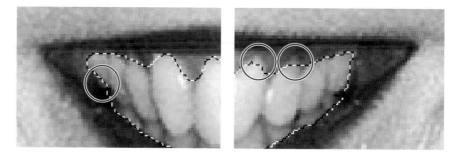

The selection is complete. The Whiten Teeth adjustment has been applied to the selected area on its own adjustment layer separate from the original image. Although the adjustment has had a noticeable effect, you can improve the image further by using the Whiten Teeth tool again.

6 Keeping the Whiten Teeth tool active, choose Select > Deselect to deselect the current adjustment. Using the Whiten Teeth tool again now, with no selection active, will create a new selection on a new adjustment layer—applying a second instance of the Whiten Teeth adjustment.

7 Use the brush picker to change the Hardness of the brush to 10%. Alternate between the Add To Selection and Subtract From Selection brushes to create a deliberately irregular selection area including only the brighter areas of the smile as shown in the illustration below. Avoid the most shadowed teeth—the whitening will look unnatural if applied too evenly. Teeth near the edges of the selection, and the naturally shaded lower teeth should only be partially selected.

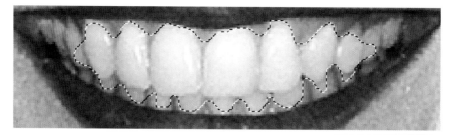

The Whiten Teeth adjustment is applied a second time through the new selection. Both the irregular selection and the softer brush setting help to create a more natural effect than re-applying the adjustment to the entire smile. You'll add some finishing touches to your dental work in the next exercise by tweaking the adjustments that you've already applied with the Whiten Teeth tool.

8 Choose Select > Deselect to deselect your last adjustment.

Modifying the Touch Up tool adjustment

Each time you applied The Whiten Teeth tool a separate adjustment layer was created in the image. Each edit remains active on its adjustment layer—you can still alter both the selection area and the way the adjustment is applied for each layer.

1 Click Full at the top of the Edit tab to switch to Full Edit mode.

2 In Full Edit mode, click the Reset Panels button (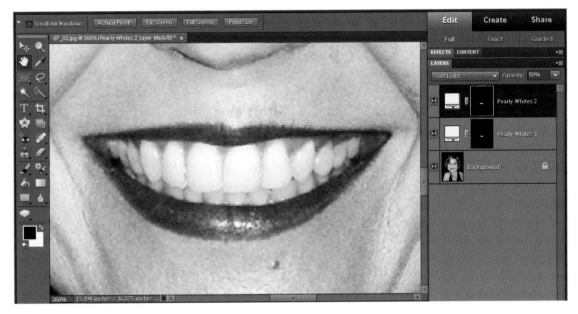) at the top of the workspace. Hide the Project Bin and the grouped Effects and Content panels in the Panel Bin by double-clicking their header bars.

3 Notice that in the Layers panel there are two adjustment layers stacked above the original image in the Background layer. The layer Pearly Whites 2 with your most recent adjustment is highlighted, indicating that it's the active layer.

4 Choose View > Actual Pixels or double-click the Zoom tool in the toolbox to see more of the woman's face.

5 Toggle the visibility for each of the adjustment layers in turn by clicking the eye icon beside each layer's name. Watch the image to judge how effective your adjustments have been.

6 For the Whiten Teeth tool, Soft Light is the preset blending mode and the default opacity for each layer is 50%. Use the menu and slider at the top of the Layers panel to experiment with the Blending Mode and the Opacity value for each layer.

7 When you're done experimenting, reset the Blending Mode for both adjustment layers to Soft Light. Increase the Opacity value for the layer Pearly Whites 1 to 80% and for the layer Pearly Whites 2 to 60%.

8 Double-click the colored layer thumbnail for the layer Pearly Whites 2 to open the color picker.

The Whiten Teeth tool applies a fill of an "ivory" color. You can brighten the effect, while still maintaining realism, by reducing the Saturation (S) value for that color.

9 Type in the text box to reduce the Saturation value from 20 to 10, and then click OK.

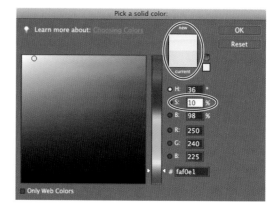

10 Repeat step 9 for the other adjustment layer, Pearly Whites 1.

11 Choose File > Save As. Save the edited file to your My CIB Work folder in Photoshop format, to be included in the Organizer, but not in a Version Set. Name the file **07_02_Dental**; then, click Save and close the file.

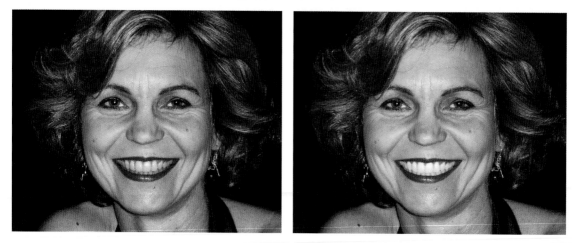

For many photographs, you'll probably find that you can achieve satisfactory results with the Whiten Teeth tool in fewer steps, but the concepts and techniques you've learned in this lesson are equally applicable to working with any of the other Touch Up tools, or with the Smart Brush itself.

Working with red eye

The red eye effect occurs when a camera flash is reflected off the retina at the back of the eye so that the dark pupil looks bright red.

If you wish, you can activate the Automatically Fix Red Eyes option when you're importing photos and have Photoshop Elements apply the automatic red eye fix before your images reach the Organizer (see *"Automatically fixing red eyes during import"* in Lesson 2). You can also apply the automatic red eye correction with a single menu command in both Full Edit and Quick Edit mode.

However, as you'll discover in the next exercise, the automatic fix is not effective for every photo. In the exercises to follow, you'll learn more techniques for dealing with the problem.

Using the automatic Red Eye Fix

1   In the Organizer, use the Lesson 07 keyword tag to locate the file 07_03.jpg. Select the file in the Media Browser, taking care not to confuse the original file with the Autofix copy; then, click the small arrow on the Fix tab above the Task Pane and choose Quick Photo Edit.

2   Hide the Project Bin by double-clicking its header bar. From the View menu below the Edit pane, choose Before & After - Horizontal. Use the Zoom and Hand tools to focus on the face of the girl in the middle.

3   Choose Enhance > Auto Red Eye Fix.

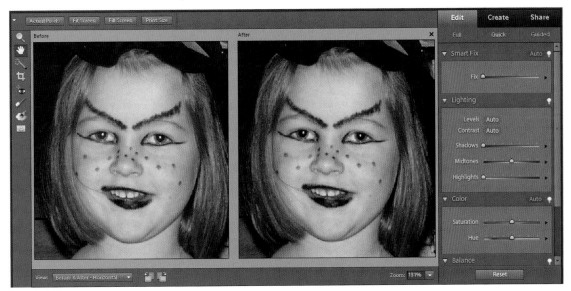

As you can see, the automatic red eye correction does a great job for this little girl. Unfortunately, it hasn't worked for her sisters.

4 Use the Zoom and Hand tools to check the eyes of the other two girls.

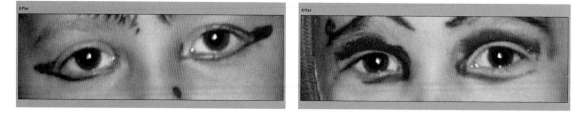

The adjustment had no discernible effect for the girls at either side of the photo. Admittedly, the red eye effect is less pronounced in both cases, but it's also more difficult to remove. The pupils of the girl in the center are crisply defined against her blue irises while there is less contrast in the hazel irises of the other girls.

5 Click the Reset button at the bottom of the Quick Fix panel to clear the Auto Red Eye Fix.

The automatic red eye removal feature works well for most images, but when you want more control you need to use the Red Eye Removal tool.

Using the Red Eye Removal tool

For stubborn red eye problems that don't respond well to the automatic fix, the Red Eye Removal tool (⬛), which can be found in both the Full Edit and Quick Edit toolbox, is an easy-to-use and efficient solution.

In this exercise you'll now learn how to customize the Red Eye Removal tool to deal with difficult cases.

1 If the image 07_03.jpg is not already open in Quick Edit mode—and reverted to its original state—from the last exercise, open it now in Quick Edit mode.

2 From the View menu below the Edit pane, choose Before And After - Vertical.

3 Zoom and position the image so that you can focus on the eyes of the girl on the left of the photo.

4 Select the Red Eye Removal tool (⬛) from the toolbox.

5 In the Red Eye Removal tool settings in the tool options bar, change the Pupil Size to 20% and the Darken Amount to 70%. You can either use the slider controls, type the new values in the text fields, or simply drag left or right over the Pupil Size and Darken Amount text.

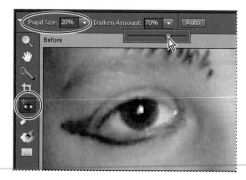

6 In the After image, click once in the reddest part of each pupil with the Red Eye Removal tool. If there is little effect, undo and click a slightly different spot.

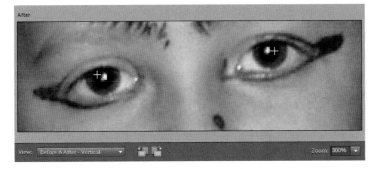

The red is removed from both eyes. The adjustment has also darkened the less defined parts of the irises, but we'll accept that for now.

7 Use the Zoom and Hand tools to position the image so that you can focus on the eyes of the girl on the right of the photo.

8 In the Red Eye Removal tool settings in the tool options bar, change the Pupil Size value to 100% and the Darken Amount to 80%.

9 With the Red Eye Removal tool still selected, drag a marquee rectangle around each eye in turn.

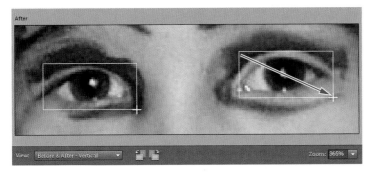

You may need to experiment with the size and positioning of the rectangle you drag around an eye to get the best results. If you're not satisfied, just undo and try again.

10 Finally, you can re-instate the Auto Red Eye Fix for the little girl in the middle. Zoom out just enough so that you can see all three faces, and then choose Enhance > Auto Red Eye Fix.

11 Choose File > Save As and navigate to the My CIB Work folder. Rename the file **07_03_WitchHunt** and select the JPEG format, to be included in the Organizer, but not in a Version Set.

12 Click Save, leaving all other options in the Save and JPEG Options dialog boxes unchanged, and then choose File > Close

Making selections

By default, the entire area of an image or image layer is active—any adjustments you make are applied across the whole photo. If you want to make changes to a specific area or object within an image, you first need to make a selection. Once you've made a selection it becomes the only active area of the image; the rest of the image layer is protected or masked from the effects of your edits.

Typically, the boundaries of a selection are indicated by a selection marquee—a flashing border of dashed black and white lines, sometimes likened to marching ants. Selections can be geometric in shape or free form, and they can have crisp or soft edges. They can be created manually with the pointer, or calculated automatically by Photoshop Elements, based on areas of similarity in color and texture within the image.

You can save a selection, and then re-use it or edit it later, which can be a terrific time-saver when you're building up a complicated selection, or when you need to use the same selection more than once.

In the course of the lessons in this book you'll gain experience with several different selection tools. Perhaps the simplest, most effective way to create a selection is to paint it onto your image. This exercise focuses on the use of two selection tools in Photoshop Elements that let you do just that: the Selection Brush and the Quick Selection tool.

1 In the Organizer, use the Lesson 07 keyword tag to locate the file 07_04.psd. Select the file in the Media Browser, taking care not to confuse the original file with the Autofix copy; then, click the small arrow on the Fix tab above the Task pane and choose Full Photo Edit.

2 Hide the Panel Bin by choosing its name from the Window menu; then, hide the Project Bin by double-clicking its header bar. Double-click the Hand tool or choose View > Fit On Screen.

Notice that this file has been saved in Photoshop format and not as a JPEG file. The Photoshop file format can store additional information along with the image data. In this case, a portion of the flower has been selected previously, and that selection has been saved with the file.

3 Choose Select > Load Selection. In the Load Selection dialog box, choose the saved selection "petals" from the Source menu. In the Operation settings, activate the New Selection option, and then click OK.

The saved selection is loaded. Most of the flower is now surrounded by a flashing selection marquee, indicating that it has become the active portion of the image.

The petals at the lower left need to be added to make the selection complete. In the next exercise, you'll modify the saved selection to include the missing petals.

4   Choose Select > Deselect to clear the current selection.

5   In the toolbox, the Selection Brush is grouped with the Quick Selection tool. Click the Quick Selection tool and hold the mouse button down to choose the Selection Brush from the tool variants menu.

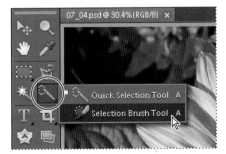

Using the Selection Brush tool

The Selection Brush tool makes selections in either of two ways. In Selection mode, you simply paint over the area you want to select. In Mask mode you paint a semi-opaque overlay over the areas you don't want selected.

1 In the tool options bar, set the Selection Brush controls to match the illustration below. If it's not already activated, click the Add To Selection button at the far left; then set the brush Size to 60 px (pixels), choose Selection from the Mode menu, and set the brush Hardness value to 100%.

2 Drag with the Selection Brush to paint a live selection over the interior of the petals in the lower left quadrant of the flower, as in the illustration below. Don't try to paint all the way to the edges; you'll do that in the next step. Release the mouse button every second or two so that you don't have to repeat too much work if you need to undo a stroke.

Now you need to reduce your brush size to paint around the edges of the petals, adding to your selection. You could move the Size slider to change your brush size, but while you're working it's far more convenient to press the open bracket key ([) to reduce the brush size in increments and the close bracket key (]) to enlarge it.

3 Press the left bracket key ([) to reduce the Selection Brush size to 15 pixels.

4 Paint the selection to the edges of the petals. Use the bracket keys to change the brush size as needed, until the selection outline completely surrounds the petals, as shown below. Try not to select any of the tiny flower parts around the base of the petals.

Tip: When you need to make a difficult or detailed selection, use the Zoom tool to magnify the area of interest. To remove an area from the selection, hold down the Alt / Option key as you paint.

If you found it tedious using the Selection Brush tool, you'll appreciate learning about the Quick Selection tool later in this lesson. You'll also learn that both tools have their uses. But first, you'll make use of your hard work and save the results.

Editing a saved selection

In this exercise you'll add your live selection to the "petals" selection that was saved with the file. You can modify a saved selection by either replacing it, adding to it, or subtracting from it.

1 With your new selection still active, choose Select > Load Selection.

2 In the Load Selection dialog box, choose the saved selection "petals" as the Source Selection. Under Operation, activate the option Add To Selection; this setting will combine your current selection with the saved selection of the rest of the flower. Click OK.

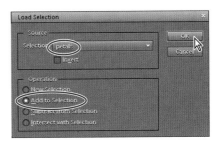

Note: The New Selection setting replaces the saved selection with the current selection. The Subtract from Selection setting subtracts the current selection from the saved selection. Intersect with Selection replaces the saved selection with the intersection between the current selection and the saved selection.

You should now see a selection border entirely surrounding the sunflower's petals.

▶ **Tip:** Once you've loaded a saved selection you can add to it or subtract from it by Shift-dragging or Alt- / Option-dragging with any of the selection tools in the Toolbox.

If you've missed a spot, simply paint it in with the Selection Brush tool. If you've selected too much, set an appropriate brush size, switch to Subtract From Selection mode in the tool options bar, or hold Alt / Option, and paint out your mistakes.

3   Choose Select > Save Selection. In the Save Selection dialog box, choose petals as the Selection name, activate Replace Selection in the Operation options, and then click OK.

4   Choose Select > Deselect.

Using the Quick Selection tool

The Quick Selection tool enables you to select an area in the image by simply drawing, scribbling, or clicking on the area you want to select. You don't need to be precise, because while you're drawing, Photoshop Elements automatically expands the selection border based on similarities in color and texture.

In this exercise, you'll use the Quick Selection tool to select everything but the sunflower, and then switch the selected and un-selected areas in the photo to establish the selection you want. This technique can be a real time-saver in situations where it proves difficult to select a complex object directly.

1   In the toolbox, select the Quick Selection tool (). The Quick Selection tool is grouped in the toolbox with the Selection Brush you used earlier.

2 In the tool options bar, make sure the New Selection mode button on the far left is activated. Set a brush diameter in the Brush picker. For the purposes of this exercise, you can use the default brush diameter of 30 px (pixels).

3 Scribble over the area at the right if the flower, making sure to draw through lighter and darker greens, as well as black areas, as shown in the illustration below. Release the pointer to see the result. As you draw, Photoshop elements automatically expands the selection based on similarities in color and texture.

▶ **Tip:** If you want to simply scribble-select an area in the image, you can use a larger brush. If you need more control to achieve a more precise outline, choose a smaller brush.

4 With an active selection already in place, the Quick Selection tool defaults to Add To Selection mode. Scribble over, or click into, un-selected areas around the sunflower until everything is selected but the flower itself.

5 Finally, turn the selection inside out by choosing Select > Inverse, thereby masking the background and selecting the flower—ready for the next exercise.

Working with selections

Now that you have an active selection outline around the sunflower, you can apply any adjustment you like and only the flower will be affected.

1 Choose Enhance > Adjust Color > Adjust Hue/Saturation.

2 In the Hue/Saturation dialog box, drag the Hue and Saturation sliders to change the color of the sunflower.

3 Hold down the Alt / Option key; the Cancel button changes to the Reset button. Click Reset to clear your changes.

4 Experiment with applying changes to the Master channel, as well as to the Reds and Yellows channels separately.

Notice that the flower changes color, but the background does not. Only the pixels inside a live selection are affected by edits or adjustments.

5 Click Cancel in the Hue/Saturation dialog box to discard your changes.

By inverting the selection, you could apply changes to the background of the photo instead of the sunflower.

6 With the sunflower still selected, choose Select > Inverse.

7 Choose Enhance > Convert To Black And White.

8 Under Select A Style in the Convert To Black And White dialog box, experiment with the different styles to see the effects on the image. Use the Adjustment Intensity sliders to vary the amount of change for red, green, blue, and contrast.

Click Undo if you make an adjustments you don't like. Click Reset to discard all your adjustments and start again

9   When you're done, click Cancel to discard your changes and dismiss the Convert To Black And White dialog box.

10 Choose Select > Inverse to select the flower once more. Hold down the Alt / Option key and try to remove the all of the center parts of the flower from the selection with the Quick Selection tool, leaving only the petals selected.

You can see that it's very difficult to control the results in this situation—especially when it comes to the tiny yellow flower parts which are not only very close to the petals but are also exactly the same color. This is precisely the kind of situation where the Selection Brush comes into its own.

11 Swap the Quick Selection tool for its toolbox partner, the Selection Brush. Work at high magnification while you use the Selection Brush together with the Alt / Option key to remove the central disc—and its ring of yellow florets—from the selection. When you're satisfied, choose Select > Save Selection. Name the new selection **petals quick select**, activate the New Selection option under Operation, and then click OK.

12 Choose File > Save As and save the file to your My CIB Work folder, in Photoshop format. Make sure that the image will be included in the Organizer, but not in a Version Set. Name the file **07_04_SavedSelections**, click Save, and then choose File > Close.

Why won't Photoshop Elements do what I tell it to do?

In some situations, the changes you try to apply to an image may not seem to work. You may hear a beep, indicating that you're trying to do something that's not allowed. The following list offers explanations and solutions for common issues that might be blocking your progress.

Commit is required

Several tools, including the Type tool require you to click the Commit button before you can move on to another task. The same is true when you crop with the Crop tool or resize a layer or selection with the Move tool.

Cancel is required

The Undo command isn't available while you have uncommitted changes made with some tools—for example, the Type tool, Move tool, and Crop tool. If you want to undo these edits, click the Cancel button instead of using the Undo command or shortcut.

Edits are restricted by an active selection

When you create a selection (using a marquee tool, the Quick Selection tool, or the Selection Brush tool, for example), you limit the active area of the image. Any edits you make will apply only within the selected area. If you try to make changes to an area outside the selection, nothing happens. Edits are restricted by an active selection. If you want to deactivate a selection, choose Select > Deselect, and then you can work on any area of the image.

Move tool is required

If you drag a selection, the selection marquee moves, not the image within the selection marquee. If you want to move a selected part of the image or an entire layer, use the Move tool .

Why won't Photoshop Elements do what I tell it to do? *(continued)*

Background layer is selected

Many changes cannot be applied to the Background layer. For example, you can't erase, delete, change the opacity, or drag the Background layer to a higher level in the layer stack. If you need to apply changes to the Background layer, double-click it and rename it (or accept the default name, Layer 0).

Active layer is hidden

In most cases, the edits you make apply to only the currently selected layer—the one highlighted in the Layers palette. If an eye icon does not appear beside that layer in the Layers palette, then the layer is hidden and you cannot edit it. Or, if the image on the selected layer is not visible because it is blocked by opacity on an upper layer, you will actually be changing that layer, but you won't see the changes in the image window.

The active layer is hidden, the view is blocked by opacity on an upper layer, or the active layer is locked.

Active layer is locked

If you lock a layer by selecting the layer and then clicking the Lock in the Layers palette, the lock prevents the layer from changing. To unlock a layer, select the layer, and then click the Lock at the bottom of the Layers palette to remove the Lock.

Wrong layer is selected (for editing text)

If you want to make changes to a text layer, be sure that layer is selected in the Layers palette before you start. If a non-text layer is selected when you click the Type tool in the image window, Photoshop Elements creates a new text layer instead of placing the cursor in the existing text layer.

Replacing the color of a pictured object

Photoshop Elements offers two methods for switching colors in a photo: the Color Replacement tool and the Replace Color dialog box.

As with the Selection Brush and the Quick Selection tool, the color replacement method that will be most effective depends on the characteristics of the image you're working with and the extent of the change you wish to make.

Using the Color Replacement tool

The Color Replacement tool enables you to replace specific colors in your image by painting over a targeted color with another. You can use the Color Replacement tool either for creative effects, or for localized color correction.

1 In the Organizer, use the Lesson 07 keyword tag to isolate the images for this lesson. In the Media Browser, right-click / Control-click the image 07_05.jpg (not to be confused with the Autofix copy), and choose Edit With Photoshop Elements from the context menu.

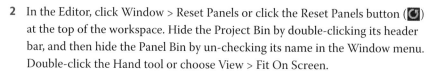

2 In the Editor, click Window > Reset Panels or click the Reset Panels button () at the top of the workspace. Hide the Project Bin by double-clicking its header bar, and then hide the Panel Bin by un-checking its name in the Window menu. Double-click the Hand tool or choose View > Fit On Screen.

3 Click the foreground color swatch below the tools in the Toolbar to open the Color Picker. In the Color Picker, type new values of **40**, **100**, and **100** in the text boxes for Hue (H), Saturation (S), and Brightness (B), respectively. Click OK to close the Color Picker.

4 Select the Color Replacement tool ( ), which is grouped in the toolbox with the Brush tool, the Impressionist Brush tool, and the Pencil tool.

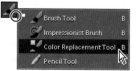

5 Click the small white arrow at the far left of the tool options bar and choose Reset Tool; then, use the Brush Picker to set the brush Diameter to 150 px. You can leave all the other options for this tool at the default settings.

You'll use the yellow foreground color to liven up the gray the wall behind the girls, but before you do, you need to understand how the Color Replacement tool works.

The cursor for the Color Replacement tool consists of cross-hairs at the center of a circle indicating the brush size.

When you drag in the image, the color under the cross-hairs is sampled continuously and the foreground color is applied to any pixel inside the circle that matches the sampled color, within the tolerance value specified in the tool options bar.

What this means is that you can be very relaxed as you paint; as long as you keep the cross-hairs inside the area of color that you wish to replace, the circle can overlap the neighboring area without changing the color, making it easy to paint right up to the edge. Only pixels inside the circle that match the sampled color under the cross-hairs are affected.

6 Paint over the wall, moving slowly around the edges of the girls and always keeping the cross-hairs over the gray shingles. Stop every few seconds so you can undo a mistake without losing a lot of work. Take extra care with the tight angles circled in the illustration at the right; work very carefully, sometimes simply clicking rather than stroking, or reduce the brush size as you work by pressing the left bracket key ([ ). You may need to paint over some areas twice to apply the color evenly.

7 Click the foreground color swatch again. In the Color Picker, type new values of **300**, **90**, and **100** for the Hue (H), Saturation (S), and Brightness (B), respectively.

8 Paint over the raincoat of the girl on the left. Take extra care, or reduce the size of your brush, as you paint the narrow area to the right of the face. Don't forget—even a large brush can overlap the neighboring area as you paint, as long as you keep the cross-hairs inside the area you wish to re-color.

Well, you've done your best; the photo certainly looks more cheerful, but sadly Photoshop Elements does not have a tool that will brighten the girls' expressions.

9 Choose Save As. Name the file **07_05_ReplaceColor** and save it to your My CIB Work folder in JPEG format. Make sure that the image will be included in the Organizer, but not grouped in a Version Set. Click Save, click Ok to accept the JPEG options, and then close the file.

Replacing a color throughout an image

Using the Replace Color dialog box is usually faster than painting with the Color Replacement tool, but it's more effective for some images than for others. However, even for a difficult case, where the color of the object you want to change is present in other areas of the image, you can usually achieve a good result by using the Replace Color dialog box in conjunction with a selection.

Though it's quick and easy to apply, the Replace Color feature can produce quite spectacular results. In the following exercises, you'll repaint a red toy car, making your changes on a duplicate of the Background layer, which will make it easy to compare the finished project to the original picture.

First, you'll work on the entire image area, which will give you an indication of where and how much the color change will affect the rest of the image. For the second part of the project, you'll use a selection to restrict the changes to just the car.

1   In the Organizer, use the Lesson 07 keyword tag to isolate the images for this lesson. In the Media Browser, right-click / Control-click the image 07_06.jpg, taking care not to confuse the original with the Autofix copy, and then choose Edit With Photoshop Elements from the context menu.

2   In the Editor, click Window > Reset Panels or click the Reset Panels button () at the top of the workspace. Hide the Project Bin and the grouped Effects and Content panels by double-clicking their header bars; then, double-click the Hand tool or choose View > Fit On Screen.

3   In the Editor, choose Layer > Duplicate Layer and accept the default name. Alternatively, you can drag the Background layer to the New Layer button ( ) at the bottom of the Layers panel. By duplicating the layer, you'll have an original to fall back on should you need it.

4   With the Background copy layer still selected in the Layers panel, choose Enhance > Adjust Color > Replace Color.

5   In the Replace Color dialog box, make sure that the Eyedropper tool—the left-most of the three eyedropper buttons—is activated, and that Fuzziness is set to the default value of 40. Activate the Image option below the preview thumbnail, and make sure that the Preview option is activated so that you'll be able to see the results of your adjustments in the Edit pane as you work.

6   Move the pointer over the thumbnail preview in the Replace Color dialog box and click once with the eyedropper on the sunlit side of the toy car. Change the preview option from Image to Selection, so that you can see the extent of the color selection you just made indicated as white areas on a black background.

7   Below the selection preview, either use the sliders or type in the text boxes to set the Hue, Saturation, and Lightness values to **−160**, **+50**, and **+5** respectively.

8   To adjust the area of selected color—or color-application area—start by clicking the second of the three eyedropper buttons to switch the Eyedropper tool to Add To Sample mode, and then click in the main image window in a few areas where the paint on the car still appears red.

9   Use the Add To Sample eyedropper again, if necessary, and drag the Fuzziness slider left and right and until you have full coverage on the car. You can see—in both the Edit pane and the black and white selection preview—that it's not possible to change the color of the car using this technique without affecting much of the background, and even the girl's skin.

10 Click Cancel to close the Replace Color dialog box.

Replacing a color in a limited area of an image

In this exercise you'll repeat the previous procedure, but this time you'll limit the color change to a selected area of the photograph.

▶ **Tip:** In the toolbox, the Rectangular Marquee tool is nested with the Elliptical Marquee tool. To switch from one selection tool to another, click the tool currently showing in the toolbox and hold the mouse button until the tool variants menu appears; then, choose the tool you want from the menu.

1 Make sure the Background copy layer is still selected in the Layers panel. In the toolbox, select the Rectangular Marquee tool and drag a rectangular selection marquee just big enough to surround the car.

2 In the toolbox, switch to the Quick Selection tool (🖌). In the tool options bar, click the tool variant at the right to set the Quick Selection tool to Subtract From Selection mode. In the Brush picker, set the brush diameter to 50 pixels.

3 Use the Quick Selection tool to subtract the girl's clothing and leg from the rectangular selection. Trim away the red chair legs in the upper left corner and as much of the sunlit grass around the car as possible. Subtract the portion of the girl's foot that's visible beneath the car. If you go to far and need to add areas back into the selection, simply hold down the Shift key as you work to switch the Quick Selection tool temporarily to Add To Selection mode.

Don't be too concerned about the small amount of grass overlapping the car's wheels; within the limits if our exercise, there's not a lot we can do about it.

4   Choose Enhance > Adjust Color > Replace Color. Using the same techniques and settings you used in steps 5 to 9 of the previous exercise, make adjustments in the Replace Color dialog box to change the color of the car. Be sure to follow the steps in order; you need to sample the red of the car before setting the hue, saturation, and brightness to define the replacement color.

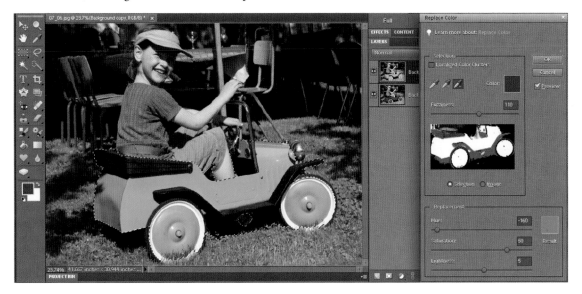

5   When you're satisfied with the results, click OK to close the Replace Color dialog box; then choose Select > Deselect, or press Ctrl+D / Command+D.

6   To compare the edited image with the original, toggle the visibility of the Background copy layer by clicking the eye icon beside the layer thumbnail. When you're done, be sure to leave the visibility for the new layer switched on.

7   Right-click / Control-click the Background copy layer and choose Flatten Image from the context menu. Alternately, you could choose the Flatten Image command from the Layers panel Options menu at the right of the panel's header bar. The image is flattened to a single layer; the layer you edited replaces the original background layer

8   Choose File > Save As. Name the file **07_06_ReplaceColor** and save it to your My CIB Work folder in JPEG format. Make sure that the image will be included in the Organizer, but not grouped in a Version Set. Click Save, accept the JPEG Options settings, and then close the file.

About printing color pictures

Color problems in your photos can result from a variety of causes, such as incorrect exposure, the quality of the camera, artificial lighting, or even weather conditions.

If an image is flawed, you can usually improve it by editing it with Photoshop Elements, as you did with the images in this lesson. Sometimes, however, pictures that looks great on your computer don't turn out so well when you print them; fortunately, there are things you can do to make sure that what you get from the printer is closer to what you see on screen.

Firstly, it's important that you calibrate your monitor regularly so that it's set to display the range of color in your photographs as accurately as possible. Even with a correctly calibrated display, your prints may still look disappointing if your printer interprets color information differently from your computer. You can correct this problem by activating the appropriate type of color management.

Working with color management

Moving a photo from your camera to your monitor and from there to a printer can cause an apparent shift in the colors in the image. This shift occurs because every device has a different *color gamut* or *color space*—the range of colors that the device is capable of interpreting and reproducing.

To achieve consistent color between digital cameras, scanners, computer monitors, and printers, you need to use color management. Color management software acts as a color interpreter, translating the image colors so that each device can reproduce them in the same way. This software knows how each device and program understands color, and adjusts colors so that those you see on your monitor are similar to the colors in your printed image. It should be noted, however, that not all colors may match exactly.

Color management is achieved through the use of device-specific color profiles: mathematical descriptions of each device's color space. If these profiles are compliant with the standards of the ICC (International Color Consortium), they will help you maintain consistent color. When you save a file, activate Embed Color Profile in the Save As dialog box. In Photoshop Elements, you can access the color management controls from the Edit menu in both the Organizer and the Editor.

Setting up color management

1   Choose Edit > Color Settings; then, select one of these color management options in the Color Settings dialog box:

- **No Color Management** uses your monitor profile as the working color space. It removes any embedded profiles when opening images, and does not apply a profile when saving.

- **Always Optimize Colors For Computer Screens** uses sRGB as the working color space, preserves embedded profiles, and assigns sRGB when opening untagged files.

- **Always Optimize For Printing** uses Adobe RGB as the working color space, preserves embedded profiles, and assigns Adobe RGB when opening untagged files.

- **Allow Me To Choose** lets you choose whether to assign sRGB (the default) or Adobe RGB when opening untagged files.

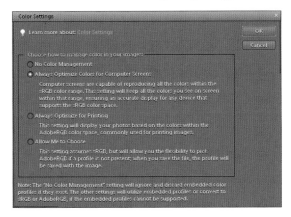

2   Click OK to close the Color Settings dialog box.

Further information on color management, including monitor calibration, can be found in a series of topics in Help. To access this information, choose Help > Photoshop Elements Help and search for these subjects.

Congratulations, you've completed another exercise. You've learned a wide variety of techniques for working with color in your photos—from tweaking automatic corrections to switching the color of a pictured object. You've gained a lot of experience in all three Edit modes and honed your selection skills—essential for many sophisticated and creative color edits. Now, take a minute to refresh your knowledge by reading through the review questions and answers on the following pages.

Review questions

1 How does the Color Variations command help you correct color problems in a photo?

2 What tools can you use to fix the red-eye phenomenon created by some flash cameras?

3 What makes selections so important for adjusting color?

4 Name at least two selection tools and describe how they work.

5 How does the Color Replacement tool work?

Review answers

1 The Color Variations command provides a very visual and intuitive approach to color correction—making it especially useful when you know that you don't like the color in your photo, but are unsure of what you need to do to correct it. The Color Variations dialog box includes not only a good-sized before and after preview, but also an array of image thumbnails that show you how just your image will look if you tweak one color component or another. You can set the dialog box to deal with color saturation, or imbalances in shadows, midtones, or highlights.

2 In both the Full Edit and Quick Edit mode you can fix red eye effects automatically by choosing Enhance > Auto Red Eye Fix. The Red Eye Removal tool located in the toolbox enables you to specify the tool settings to deal with difficult cases. You can also fix red eye automatically during the process of importing photos or choose Edit > Auto Red Eye Fix after the photos have been imported to the Organizer.

3 You use a selection to define an area as the only part of a layer that can be altered. The areas outside the selection are protected from change for as long as the selection is active. This aids greatly in image correction, as it enables you make adjustments selectively, targeting specific areas or objects in an image.

4 The first tool you used in this lesson to make selections is the Selection Brush tool, which works like a paintbrush. The Quick Selection tool is similar to the Selection Brush tool, but is in most cases a faster, more flexible option. There are more selection tools than are discussed in this lesson: The Magic Wand tool selects all the areas with the same color as the color on which you click.

(continued on next page)

The Rectangular Marquee tool and the Elliptical Marquee tool make selections of a fixed geometric shape. The Lasso tool lets you draw free-form selections, and the Magnetic Lasso tool helps to draw complicated selections around even irregular object edges. The Polygonal Lasso tool constrains drawing to straight lines, making it the tool of choice for selecting straight-sided objects.

5   The Color Replacement tool samples the color under the pointer and replaces it with any color that you choose.

The cursor for the Color Replacement tool consists of cross-hairs at the center of a circle indicating the brush size. When you drag in the image, the color under the cross-hairs is sampled continuously and the foreground color is applied to any pixel inside the circle that matches the sampled color, within the tolerance value specified in the tool options bar.

What this means is that you can be very relaxed as you paint; as long as you keep the cross-hairs inside the area of color that you wish to replace, you can overlap the adjacent area without changing the color, making it easy to paint right up to the edge.

8 FIXING EXPOSURE PROBLEMS

Lesson overview

Photoshop Elements makes it easy to fix images that are too dark or too light and rescue photos that are dull, flat, or simply fading away.

Start with Quick Fix and Guided Edit and work up to Full Edit as you learn how to make the most of poorly exposed images, retrieve detail from photos that are too dark and liven up images that look flat and washed-out. Photoshop elements delivers powerful, easy-to-use tools for correcting exposure and lighting problems in all three Edit modes.

In this lesson you'll be introduced to a variety of techniques for dealing with a range of common exposure problems:

- Brightening underexposed photographs
- Correcting parts of an image selectively
- Saving selection shapes to reuse in later sessions
- Working with adjustment layers
- Choosing layer blending modes
- Using layer opacity settings
- Adjusting lighting controls manually
- Enhancing overexposed and faded photographs

You'll probably need about one and a half hours to complete this lesson.

Learn how to make the most of images that were captured in unusual lighting conditions, retrieving detail from overly dark photos and putting the spark back into images that look dull or washed-out. Find out how Photoshop Elements can help you save those faded memories—no matter what your level of experience—with a suite of powerful, easy-to-use tools and the versatility of three Edit modes.

247

Getting started

Before you start working on the exercises in this lesson, make sure that you have installed the software on your computer from the application CD (see the Photoshop Elements 9 documentation) and that you have correctly copied the Lessons folder from the CD in the back of this book onto your computer's hard disk. (See "Copying the Classroom in a Book files" on page 2.)

This lesson builds on the skills and concepts covered in the earlier chapters and assumes that you are already familiar with the main features of the Photoshop Elements workspace. Should you need to brush up on the basic concepts see Lesson 1, "A Quick Tour of Photoshop Elements" and Photoshop Elements Help.

To start, you'll import the sample images for this lesson to the CIB Catalog that you created at the beginning of Lesson 4:

1   Start Photoshop Elements and click Organize in the Welcome Screen.

2   Check the name of the active catalog in the lower left corner of the Organizer window. If your CIB Catalog is already loaded, you can skip step to step 4. If another catalog is currently loaded, continue with step 3.

3   Choose File > Catalog. In the Catalog Manager dialog box, click to select your CIB Catalog in the Catalogs list, and then click Open. If you don't see the CIB Catalog listed, review "Creating a new catalog" at the beginning of Lesson 4.

4   Choose File > Get Photos And Video > From Files And Folders. In the Get Photos And Videos From Files And Folders dialog box, locate and open your Lessons folder. Select the Lesson08 folder, disable any automatic processing option that is currently active, and then click Get Media.

5   In the Import Attached Keyword Tags dialog box, click Select All, and then click OK. Click OK to close any other alert dialog box.

Batch-processing the lesson files

Before you start this lesson, you can set up automatic processing for the photos you'll use in the exercises, as you did for the last two lessons. You can save the auto-adjusted files as copies so that at the end of each project you can compare the automatic fixes to the results you achieve using various other techniques.

1   Make sure that you have no images selected in the Media Browser; then, click the small arrow on the Fix tab at the top of the Task Pane and choose Full Photo Edit from the menu.

2   In Full Edit mode, choose File > Process Multiple Files. From the Process Files From menu in the Process Multiple Files dialog box, choose Folder. Under Source, click the Browse button to locate and select the Lesson08 folder in your

Lessons folder. Click OK / Choose to close the Browse For Folder / Choose A Folder For Processing Multiple Files dialog box. Under Destination, click Browse; then, find and select the My CIB Work folder that you created at the start of the book. Click OK / Choose.

3   Under Quick Fix on the right side of the dialog box, click the checkboxes to activate all four options: Auto Levels, Auto Contrast, Auto Color, and Sharpen.

4   Under File Naming, activate the Rename Files option. Choose Document Name from the menu on the left and type **_Autofix** in the second field. This will add the appendix "_Autofix" to the existing document name as the files are saved.

5   Review the settings in the dialog box. Make sure that the Resize Images and Convert Files options are disabled, and then click OK.

Note: On Windows, an error message may appear after you click OK in the Process Multiple Files dialog box, warning you that some files could not be processed. You can safely ignore this alert; the error is often caused by a hidden system file that will have no effect on the success of your project.

When you batch-edit files in this way, the edited copies are not automatically added to your catalog—you need to bring the files into the Organizer yourself.

6   Switch to the Organizer; then, choose File > Get Photos And Videos > From Files And Folders.

7   In the Get Photos And Videos From Files And Folders dialog box, locate and open your My CIB Work folder, and then Ctrl-click / Command-click to select the two files frida_and _mina_Autofix.jpg and kat_and_kind_Autofix.jpg.

8   Disable any other automatic processing option that is currently active, and then click Get Media.

9   In the Import Attached Keyword Tags dialog box, click Select All; then, click OK. Click OK to dismiss any other dialog box.

At the end of this lesson, you can compare the results of these basic, automatic fixes with the results you achieve by applying the manual techniques you'll learn as you work through the exercises. In some cases, the automatic method of fixing images may be sufficient to meet your needs.

Brightening an underexposed image

Underexposed photographs tend to look dull and flat, or too dark. While the lighting auto-fix feature does a good job with most images, this exercise will teach you techniques that give you more control for correcting exposure in problem photos.

Applying Quick Fix adjustments

The first technique you'll learn makes use of the Quick Edit mode.

▶ **Tip:** Use the View menu below the Edit pane to switch between the After Only view and the Before & After views to help you assess the results of your adjustments as you work.

1   In the Keyword tags panel, click the find box beside the Lesson 08 tag. In the Media Browser, select the file kat_and_kind.jpg; then, click the small arrow on the Fix tab at the top of the Task Pane and choose Quick Photo Edit.

2   Click the Smart Fix Auto button at the top of the Quick Fix panel. The photo becomes a little brighter overall, but the skin tones remain quite dark. Drag both the Shadows and Midtones sliders to set values of 27 and 25 respectively.

You've improved the image substantially with just a few clicks. However, although the skin tones have been lightened, they are still a little cool.

3 In the Color and Balance panes, drag both the Hue and Temperature sliders just fractionally to the right. Take care not to make the sky too pink or overly yellow; we set Hue and Temperature values of 4 and 52 respectively.

4 Commit the changes by clicking the Commit button (✓) in the header bar of the pane in which you made your most recent adjustment.

Original image   Auto Smart Fix and Lighting sliders   Temperature and Hue tweaked

5 Choose File > Save. Name the file **kat_and_kind_Quick** and save it to your My CIB Work folder in JPEG format. Make sure that Include In The Elements Organizer is activated and Save In Version Set With Original is disabled.

6 Click Save. In the JPEG Options dialog box, choose High from the Quality menu, and then click OK. Choose File > Close, or click the Close button (x) in the upper right corner of the Edit pane.

Without much effort, you've improved the image significantly. Let's try some other methods to adjust the lighting in the image, and you can compare the results later.

Adjusting exposure in Guided Edit mode

In Guided Edit mode, you can improve your photos quickly, at the same time as learning concepts and techniques that you can apply even in Full Edit mode.

When you're not sure exactly what adjustments a poorly exposed image needs, the Guided Edit mode offers a choice of three procedures for correcting lighting and exposure—each with easy-to-follow prompts and instructions that make it easy for even a novice to get great results.

1 In the media browser, select the image kat_and_kind.jpg again; then click the small arrow on the Fix tab at the top of the Task Pane and choose Guided Photo Edit from the menu.

2   In the guided tasks menu, click the triangle beside Lighting and Exposure, if necessary, so that you can see the nested options; then, click Lighten Or Darken.

3   Click the Auto button at the upper right of the Lighten Or Darken A Photo pane. For this image, the result is not quite as good as we might wish, resulting in a noticeable color cast. Click the Reset button below the slider controls, or choose Edit > Undo Auto Levels to revert the image to its original state.

4   Whether you use the Auto button or not, you can adjust the lighting controls manually. Drag the sliders to set Lighten Shadows to a value of 50 and Midtone Contrast to 20; then click Done to close the Lighten Or Darken A Photo pane.

5   Choose File > Save As. Navigate to and open your My CIB Work folder, name the new file **kat_and_kind_Guided** and choose the JPEG format. Make sure the file will be included in the Organizer, but not saved in a Version Set.

6   Click Save, and then click OK to dismiss the JPEG Options dialog box. Choose File > Close or click the Close button (x) at the upper right of the Edit pane.

Again, the adjusted image looks considerably better than the original; however, it would be ideal if we could treat the mother and child in the foreground separately from the background of sea and sky, which still looks a little flat.

Fixing exposure in Full Edit mode

Underexposure problems are often caused by your camera automatically cutting down exposure to compensate for backlighting. In the case of our example image, the large area of relatively bright sea and sky may contribute to the problem in this way, compounded by the fact that the lighting on our subjects is low and indirect. It's also possible that the camera's exposure settings were incorrect.

If your photo is a particularly difficult case, more elaborate methods than those you've used in the Quick Fix and Guided Edit modes might be necessary to achieve the best results.

In the Full Edit mode you can work with multiple layers and blending modes, and also make selections to isolate specific parts of an image for special treatment.

Using blending modes

In an image file with multiple layers, each layer has its own blending mode that defines the way it will interact with the layer or layers below it in the stacking order.

By default, a newly created layer has a Normal blending mode: it will not blend with the layer below except where it contains transparency or when the opacity for the layer is set to less than 100%. The Darken and Lighten blending modes will blend a layer with the layers below it only where the result will darken or lighten the lower layers. Other blending modes produce more complex results. If a photo is too dark, duplicating the background layer and applying the Screen blending mode to the new layer may correct the problem. If this technique produces too strong an affect, you can use the layer opacity setting to tone it down. Inversely, if your photo is overexposed—too light—duplicating the background layer and applying the Multiply blending mode may be a solution.

Tip: For information on the effects produced by the different layer blending modes, please refer to Photoshop Elements Help.

1 In the Media Browser, right-click / Control-click the image kat_and_kind.jpg, taking care not to confuse the original file with the edited copies, and choose Edit With Photoshop Elements from the context menu.

2 In Full Edit mode, choose Window > Reset Panels or click the Reset Panels button (⟳) at the top of the workspace. Hide the Project Bin and the grouped Effects and Content panels by double-clicking their header bars. Double-click the Hand tool in the toolbox, or choose View > Fit On Screen.

3 In the Layers panel you can see that the image has only one layer: the Background. Duplicate the Background layer by dragging it onto the New Layer button (▨) at the lower left corner of the Layers panel.

Tip: You can also duplicate a selected layer by choosing Duplicate Layer, either from the Layer menu or from the selected layer's context menu.

The new Background copy layer is highlighted in the Layers panel, indicating that it's currently the selected—or active—layer.

▶ **Tip:** If the layer blending mode menu is disabled, make sure that you have the copy layer—not the original Background—selected in the Layers panel.

4   With the Background copy layer selected in the Layers panel, choose Screen from the layer blending mode menu. Notice that the image becomes brighter.

5   Choose File > Save As. Choose Photoshop (PSD) from the Format menu and make sure the Layers option is activated. Save the file to your My CIB Work folder, to be included in the Organizer, but not in a Version Set. Name the new file **kat_and_kind_Screen**, and then click Save. If the Format Options dialog box appears, activate Maximize Compatibility and click OK.

6   To quickly compare the adjusted image to the original, toggle the visibility of the Background Copy layer by clicking the eye icon beside the layer thumbnail. When you're done, close the file without saving.

In this exercise you've seen how using a blending mode can brighten up a dull image. For many photos, however, you should be careful about applying a blending mode over the entire image, as it can sometimes adversely affect parts of the photos that were OK to begin with. In this example, the sky is now overexposed and some subtle color detail has been lost across the entire background.

About adjustment layers

An adjustment layer is like an overlay or lens filter over the underlying layers, perhaps darkening the photo, perhaps making it appear pale and faded or intensifying its hues—but remaining separate from the image itself. Effects applied on an adjustment layer can be easily revised, or even removed, because the pixels of the image layers are not permanently modified. You can even copy an adjustment layer from one photo and paste it on top of the image layers in another—a real time-saver when you wish to apply the same treatment to several images.

Using adjustment layers to correct lighting

In this exercise you'll work with the same underexposed photo that you used for the last few exercises, but this time you'll open the image from the Editor.

1   In Full Edit mode, choose File > Open Recently Edited File and choose the file kat_and_kind.jpg from the menu.

2   Click the Create New Fill Or Adjustment Layer button ( ) at the bottom of the Layers panel and choose Brightness/Contrast from the menu. The Adjustments panel opens automatically to give you easy access to the Brightness and Contrast controls.

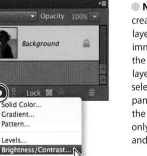

Note: A newly created adjustment layer will always appear immediately above the active layer—the layer that is currently selected in the Layers panel. In this example, the Background is the only layer—it's selected and active by default.

3   In the Adjustments panel, drag the sliders or type in the text boxes to set Brightness and Contrast values of 80 and 25 respectively.

4   Click the Create New Fill Or Adjustment Layer button again, this time choosing Levels from the menu. Notice the new Levels 1 adjustment layer in the Layers panel. The Adjustments panel is updated to present the Levels controls.

5   In the Levels controls, drag the black, gray, and white arrows under the tonal distribution graph to adjust shadows, mid-tones, and highlights, respectively, until the tonal balance looks right to you. We set values of 11, 1.2, and 250.

Tip: The Levels controls provide a very effective and versatile method for adjusting tonal deficiencies, and will also help to correct color imbalances.

6   Choose File > Save As. Choose Photoshop (PSD) from the Format menu, and make sure the Layers option is activated. Save the file to your My CIB Work folder, to be included in the Organizer, but not in a Version Set. Name the new file **kat_and_kind_Adjustment**, and then click Save. If the Format Options dialog box appears, activate Maximize Compatibility and click OK.

7   To quickly assess the effect of the adjustment layers, toggle the visibility of each layer by clicking the eye icon beside its thumbnail in the Layers panel. When you're done, close the file without saving.

The beauty of adjustment layers is that you can always return to adjust your settings, even in future work sessions, as long as you have saved the file in the Photoshop (PSD) format, preserving the layers (the default).

If you reopen the file that you just closed and click the Brightness/Contrast layer, the Adjustments panel will show the Brightness and Contrast values set just as you left them: at 80 and 25. The adjustment is still live and can be refined; if necessary, you could even revert to the original, uncorrected image by either hiding or deleting the adjustment layers.

Correcting parts of an image selectively

Although the adjustment layers did a lot to help bring out the color and image detail from our dark original photo, the background is now overexposed. So far in this lesson, all the corrections you've made to the photo have been applied to the image as a whole. In the next exercise you'll apply adjustments selectively to just part of the image.

Creating a selection

In this exercise you'll divide the image into two parts, separating the background of sea and sky and our subjects in the foreground. You'll start by selecting the silhouette of the mother and child and saving the selection.

There are a variety ways of making a selection—you've already explored some of them in Lesson 7. The choice of selection tool depends largely on the picture. For this exercise, we'll start with the Quick Selection tool, which makes a selection based on similarities in color and texture; just scribble inside a pictured object and the Quick Selection tool automatically determines the selection borders for you.

1   Open the original image file kat_and_kind.jpg once again.

2   In the toolbox, select the Quick Selection tool (🖌), which is grouped with the Selection Brush tool.

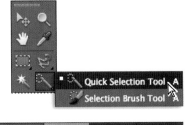

3   In the tool options bar, make sure that the New Selection mode is activated for the Quick Selection tool. Set a brush diameter of between 20 and 30 px (pixels).

4   Place the cursor at the lower right corner of the woman and slowly drag a line to the top of her head and then down across the child's face and body. Notice that the active selection automatically expands to create a border around the silhouette of our subjects. Not bad at all for a quick first pass.

Next you need to refine the border a little to capture the silhouette as closely as possible. You'll need to deselect the small area of background between the child's shoulder and her mother's chin and pay attention to hair and highlight areas. To refine your selection, you'll alternate between the Quick Selection tool's Add To Selection () and Subtract From Selection () modes. Buttons for these modes are located beside the New Selection mode button in the tool options bar.

▶ **Tip:** You can also use the Shift key and the Alt / Option key to switch between the Add To Selection and Subtract From Selection modes. You can use the left and right bracket keys ([,]) to reduce or increase the brush size as you work—without stopping to open the Brush Picker.

5   Choose the Subtract From Selection () mode for the Quick Selection tool from the tool options bar. Reduce the brush size if you wish.

6   With the Subtract From Selection tool, click in the space between the girl's shoulder and her mother's chin. The selection contracts to exclude this background area.

7   Keeping the Quick Selection tool active, press Ctrl+= (equal sign) to zoom in to the image, and hold the spacebar for the Hand tool to pan the image as required. Press the left bracket key '[' on your keyboard repeatedly to reduce the brush size for the Quick Selection tool. Alternate between the Add To Selection () and Subtract From Selection () modes and use a combination of clicks and very short strokes to modify the selection border around the area you deselected in step 6, paying attention to the hair and the small spaces in-between.

8 Without being overly fussy, continue to refine the selection around the subjects' heads using the same technique. Your work will be much simpler if you use the keyboard shortcuts to navigate in the image and for the tool settings. Press Ctrl+= (equal) and Ctrl+− (minus) to zoom in and out. Hold the spacebar for the hand tool to move the image in the preview window. Increase and decrease the brush size by pressing the right and left bracket keys: ']' and '['. With the Quick Selection tool in New Selection mode, you can switch temporarily to Add To Selection mode by holding the Shift key, and to Subtract From Selection mode by holding the Alt / Option key.

9 Finally, pay attention to the brightly highlighted area that runs from the little girl's right cheek down her arm and includes a portion of her mother's fingers. You should end up with a tight flashing selection outline around the silhouettes of both of the subjects.

10 To soften the hard edges of the selection, you can smooth and feather the outline. Click Refine Edge in the tool options bar.

11 In the Refine Edge dialog box, use the sliders or type a value of **2** for Smooth and **1** px (pixel) for Feather.

These settings are quite low, but should be appropriate for our lesson image, which has a relatively low resolution. Notice that the Refine Edge dialog box has its own Zoom and Hand tools to help you get a better view of the details of your selection. Click OK.

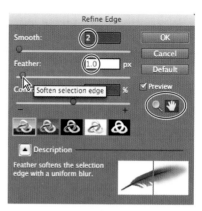

12 Choose Select > Save Selection. In the Save Selection dialog box, choose New from the Selection menu, type **Mother and Child** for the selection name, and then click OK. Once a selection is saved, you can always re-use it later—after assessing your adjustments you can reload the selection to modify them.

Using layers to isolate parts of an image

Now that you've created a selection that includes only the figures in the foreground of the photo, you can adjust the exposure and color for the subjects and the background independently. You can bring out the shaded detail in the faces without overexposing the sky, and accentuate the blues in the background without making the skin tones too cold. The next step in this process is to use your selection to isolate the foreground and background areas on separate layers. To make the job easier, let's make sure that the layer thumbnails are of a satisfactory size.

1 Click the menu icon at the right of the Layers panel to open the Layers panel Options menu; then, choose Panel Options.

2 In the Layers Panel Options dialog box, select either the large or medium thumbnail option. Any thumbnail size will work, just as long as you don't choose None—seeing the layer thumbnails can help you visualize the layers you're working with. Click OK.

3 If necessary, choose View > Fit On Screen or, if the Zoom tool is active, click the Fit Screen button in the tool options bar so that you can see the entire image.

4 If the selection that you made in the previous exercise is still active, choose Select > Inverse, and then go on to Step 5. If the selection is not still active, choose Select > Load Selection. Choose Mother And Child from the Source

Selection menu, click the check box to activate the Invert option and choose New Selection under Operation; then click OK.

5   Choose Edit > Copy to copy the selected area, and then choose Edit > Paste. The copied area is pasted onto a new layer, named **Layer 1** by default. In the Layers panel, the new layer is already selected. The selection is no longer active in the image window.

6   In the Layers panel, select the Background layer once again, and then choose Select > Load Selection. Under Source, choose Mother And Child from the Selection menu, but this time disable the Invert option. Click OK.

7   Choose Edit > Copy, and then, keeping the Background layer selected, choose Edit > Paste.

Note: A new layer will always appear just above the layer that was selected (active) when you created it. The checker-board pattern you see in layers 1 and 2 represents transparent areas.

You now have three layers: Layer 1 with only the sea and sky, Layer 2 with just the figures from the foreground, and the Background layer with the entire image.

8   You'll find it much easier to deal with layers—especially when you're working with many of them—if you give your layers descriptive names in the Layers panel. Double-click the name text of Layer 2 and type **Figures** as the new name for the layer. Change the name of Layer 1 to **Sea & Sky**.

Correcting underexposed areas

We can now apply the most effective technique from the earlier exercises to the subjects of our photo selectively, and then fine-tune the result.

1   In the Layers panel, select the Figures layer and choose Screen from the blending menu. The figures are brighter and clearer, while the Sea & Sky layer remains unchanged.

2   Choose Adjust Color For Skin Tone from the Enhance > Adjust Color menu. The pointer becomes an eyedropper. Sample a neutral skin tone from an area such as the center of the child's forehead, and then click OK.

Adding more intensity

Now that the figures in the foreground look so much better, the sea and sky behind them need to be adjusted to appear less dull and murky.

1   In the Layers panel, select the Sea & Sky layer.

2   Choose Enhance > Auto Levels. The sea and sky look blue again—and far more vibrant—and we have also recovered a lot of textural detail in the background. However, the effect is just a little too strong to sit well with the subdued late-afternoon light on our subjects. Drag the Opacity slider or type in the text box to reduce the opacity of the Sea & Sky layer to 70%.

With these few adjustments to the separate layers, the photograph now looks far more lively.

There are still possibilities that you could play around with to improve different areas of the image; for example you could separate the sky onto a new layer and intensify the cloud contrast. There is also more you could do with blending modes and layer opacity—you'll learn more about those techniques later in this lesson and as you work further through this book.

3   Choose File > Save As. Choose Photoshop (PSD) from the Format menu, and make sure the Layers option is activated. Save the file to your My CIB Work folder, to be included in the Organizer, but not in a Version Set. Name the new file **kat_and_kind_Layers**, and then click Save. If the Format Options dialog box appears, activate Maximize Compatibility and click OK.

4   Close the file.

In Lesson 7 you learned how you can tile the image windows to best compare the results of your different methods for adjusting an image. It's a good idea to make use of that technique now to compare the six adjusted and saved versions of this photograph before moving on to the next exercise.

Adjusting color curves

Using the Adjust Color Curves command is a great way to fix common exposure problems, from photos that are too dark as a result of backlighting to images that appear washed-out due to overly harsh lighting. You can improve color tones by adjusting the highlights, mid-tones, and shadows components of the curve separately or choose one of the preset adjustment styles—either as a solution in itself, or use it as a helpful starting point for making manual adjustments.

Experiment with color curve adjustments on a duplicate layer to preserve your original. In the Adjust Color Curves dialog box, you can see the results of each preset in the before and after preview, and then use the sliders to fine-tune the adjustment.

Choose Enhance > Adjust Color > Adjust Color Curves to open the Adjust Color Curves dialog box. To adjust only a specific area of the image, first select it with one of the selection tools before you open the Color Curves dialog box.

For the example shown below, the Lighten Shadows adjustment preset made a good starting-point for some manual fine-tuning of the shadows and mid-tones.

Improving faded or overexposed images

In this exercise, you'll work with the scan of an old photograph that has faded badly and is in danger of being lost forever—a photo of a beloved grandmother and her twin sister as babies. Such a photo may not be an award-winning image, but it could represent a valuable and treasured record of personal history, well worth preserving for future generations.

The automatic fixes you applied to a copy of this image at the beginning of this lesson (see "Batch-processing the lesson files") improved the photograph markedly. In this project, you'll try to do even better using other techniques.

1 If you're in the Organizer, switch to Full Edit mode in the Editor by clicking the arrow on the Fix tab and choosing Full Photo Edit from the menu.

2 Choose Preferences > General from the Edit / Photoshop Elements menu. Activate Allow Floating Documents In Full Edit Mode, and then click OK.

3 Choose File > Open. Navigate to and open your Lesson08 folder, select the image frida_and_mina.jpg, and then click Open.

Creating a set of duplicate files

You'll compare a variety of editing techniques during the course of this series of exercises. You can begin by creating a separate file to test each method and naming each new file for the technique it will demonstrate.

1 Click the Reset Panels button (⟳) at the top of the Quick Edit workspace, and then double-click the Hand tool in the toolbox or choose View > Fit On Screen. Hide the grouped Effects and Content panels by double-clicking the header bar. If you don't see the filename beneath the photo's thumbnail in the Project Bin, right-click / Control-click the thumbnail and choose Show Filenames.

2 Right-click / Control-click the thumbnail image in the Project Bin again and choose Duplicate from the context menu. In the Duplicate Image dialog box, name the new file **frida_and_mina_Shad_High**, and then click OK.

3 Perform step 2 twice more, naming the duplicates **frida_and_mina_Bright_Con** and **frida_and_mina_Levels**.

4 In the Project Bin, double-click the thumbnail frida_and_mina.jpg to make that image active. If you can't see the whole of a filename under a thumbnail in the Project Bin, hold the pointer over the thumbnail; the name of the file is displayed as a Tooltip.

5 Choose File > Save As. Select your My CIB Work folder as the destination for the new file, then activate Include In The Elements Organizer and disable the option Save In Version Set With Original. Type **frida_and_mina_Blend_Mode** as the new filename and select Photoshop (PSD) from the Format menu.

6 Click Save. Click OK to accept the default settings in any dialog boxes or messages that appear. Leave all four images open for the rest of this project.

7 Choose Window > Images > Consolidate All To Tabs.

While you're working in the Editor, you can always tell which images you have open—even when a single active photo fills the edit window—by looking in the Project Bin. When you can see more than one photo in the edit window, you can identify the active image by the un-dimmed text in its title bar or name tab, and the highlighted frame surrounding its thumbnail in the Project Bin.

8 Choose Window > Images > Tile.

9 Make sure that frida_and_mina_Blend_Mode.psd is the active image, and then choose Window > Images > Match Zoom. Click the Arrange button ( ) at the top of the workspace and choose Match Location.

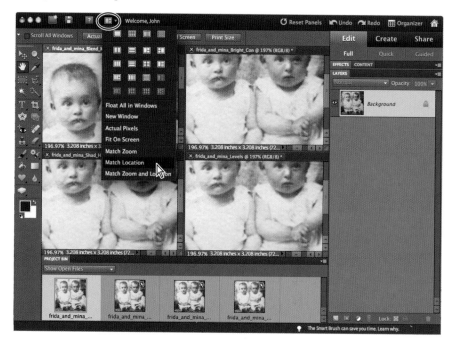

Using blending modes to fix a faded image

A layer's blending mode can cause it to interact with the layers beneath it in a variety of ways. The Multiply mode intensifies or darkens pixels in an image. The Overlay mode tends to brighten the image while preserving its tonal range.

For this exercise, you'll use the Overlay mode to add clarity and brilliance without negating the darkening effect of the Multiply blending mode you'll use on the underlying layers.

1　Make sure that frida_and_mina_Blend_Mode.psd is still the active image. If necessary, double-click its thumbnail in the Project Bin to make it active. In the Layers panel right-click / Control-click the Background layer and choose Duplicate Layer from the context menu. Click OK in the Duplicate Layer dialog box, accepting the default name "Background copy."

2　In the Layers panel, choose Multiply from the layer blending mode menu. Note the effect in the image window.

3　Drag the Background copy layer with its Multiply blend mode onto the New Layer button (⬜) at the bottom of the Layers panel to create a copy of the Background copy layer. Keep the default name, Background copy 2.

4　In the Layers panel, change the blending mode for the layer Background copy 2 from Multiply to Overlay, watching the effect of the new blending mode on the image. Set the layer's Opacity value to 50%, either by dragging the Opacity slider or by typing the new value in the text field.

▶ **Tip:** The stacking order of the layers makes a difference to how their blending modes will affect the image. In our example, if you drag the layer with the Multiply blending mode above the layer with the Overlay mode, you'll see slightly different results.

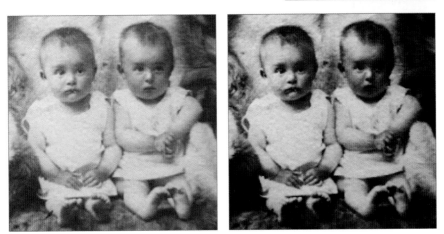

Adding a layer with the Multiply blending mode made the image bolder and the third layer in Overlay mode brightened it considerably. Taken together, our changes have made the detail in the photo clearer, but the contrast is still unimpressive.

5　Choose File > Save to save the file in your My CIB Work folder, leaving the file open. If a message appears about maximizing compatibility, click OK to close it, or follow the instructions in the message to prevent it from appearing again.

Adjusting shadows and highlights manually

Although both the Auto-fix and the technique using blending modes do a good job of correcting many fading images, some of your own photos may be more challenging. You'll try three more techniques in the exercises to follow.

The first method involves making manual adjustments to the Shadows, Highlights, and Midtone Contrast of the image.

Tip: If you can't see the whole of the filename in the Project Bin, hold the pointer over the thumbnail; the name of the file is displayed as a Tooltip.

1 In the Project Bin, double-click the thumbnail frida_and_mina_Shad_High to make it the active window. Choose Window > Images > Float In Window; then double-click the Hand tool or choose View > Fit On Screen.

2 Choose Enhance > Adjust Lighting > Shadows/Highlights.

3 Activate the Preview option in the Shadows/Highlights dialog box if it is not already active. If necessary, move the dialog box so that you can also see most of the frida_and_mina_Shad_High image window.

By default, the Lighten Shadows setting is 25%. You can see the effect on the image by toggling the Preview option on and off in the Shadows/Highlights dialog box.

4 In the Shadows/Highlights dialog box, set the Lighten Shadows value to 30%, the Darken Highlights value to 15%, and the Midtone Contrast value to +20%.

Tip: The controls you are using to make the adjustments for this technique are also available in the Lighting panel in Quick Fix mode.

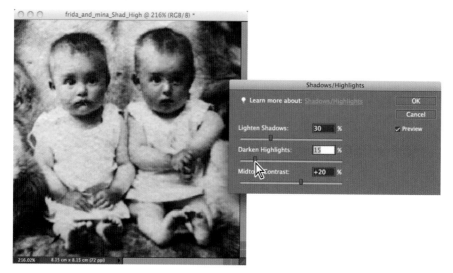

5 Adjust the three settings as needed until you think the image is as good as it can be. When you're done, click OK to close the Shadows/Highlights dialog box.

6 Choose File > Save and save the file as **frida_and_mina_Shad_High** to your My CIB Work folder, in JPEG format. Make sure that the image will be included in the Organizer, but not in a Version Set. Click OK in the JPEG Options dialog box and leave the file open. Choose Window > Images > Tile.

Adjusting brightness and contrast manually

The next approach you'll take to fixing an exposure problem makes use of another option from the Enhance > Adjust Lighting menu.

1 In the Project Bin, double-click the image frida_and_mina_Bright_Con to make it active. Choose Window > Images > Float In Window; then click the Arrange button (⊞) at the top of the workspace and choose Fit On Screen.

2 Choose Enhance > Adjust Lighting > Brightness/Contrast.

3 In the Brightness/Contrast dialog box, click the checkbox to activate Preview, if it is not already active. If necessary, drag the Brightness/Contrast dialog box aside so that you can see most of the frida_and_mina_Bright_Con image window.

4 Drag the Brightness slider to –20, or type **–20** in the text field, being careful to include the minus sign when you type. Set the Contrast to 60.

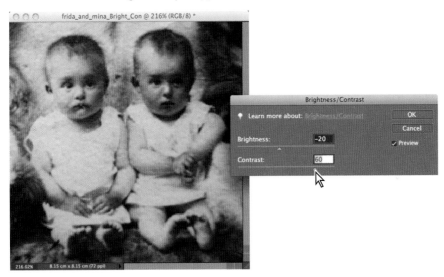

5 Adjust the Brightness and Contrast settings until you are happy with the look of the image. Click OK to close the Brightness/Contrast dialog box.

6 Choose File > Save and save the file as **frida_and_mina_Bright_Con** to your My CIB Work folder, in JPEG format. Make sure that the image will be included in the Organizer, but not in a Version Set; then, click Save. Click OK in the JPEG Options dialog box, but keep the file open. Choose Window > Images > Tile.

Adjusting levels

The Levels controls (again, available from the Enhance > Adjust Lighting menu) affect the range of tonal values in an image—the degree of darkness or lightness, regardless of color. In this exercise, you'll enhance the photograph by shifting the reference points that define the spread of those tonal values.

1 In the Project Bin, double-click the image frida_and_mina_Levels to make it active. Choose Window > Images > Float In Window; then click the Arrange button (⬚) at the top of the workspace and choose Fit On Screen.

2 Choose Enhance > Adjust Lighting > Levels. Activate the Preview option in the Levels dialog box, if it is not already active. If necessary, drag the Levels dialog box aside so that you can also see most of the image window.

The Levels graph represents the distribution of tonal values across all the pixels in the image, from darkest at the left to lightest at the right. A trough (or gap) in the curve indicates that there are few (or no) pixels mapped to that part of the range; a peak shows the opposite.

As you can see from the graph, this image has no truly black pixels or completely white pixels. By dragging the end sliders inward to where the pixels start to register in the graph, you redefine which levels are calculated as black or white. This will enhance the contrast between the lightest and darkest tones in the image.

3 In the Levels dialog box, drag the black triangle below the left end of the graph to the right and position it under the point where the graphed curve begins to climb. The value in the first Input Levels box should be approximately 42.

4 Drag the white triangle from the right side of the graph until it reaches the end of the steepest part of the graphed curve. The value in the third Input Levels box should be approximately 225.

5 Drag the gray triangle below the center of the graph toward the right to set the mid-tone value to approximately 0.90. Click OK to close the Levels dialog box.

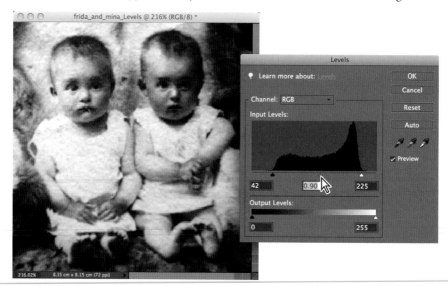

6 Choose File > Save and save the file to your My CIB Work folder in JPEG format as frida_and_mina_Levels. Make sure that the image will be included in the Organizer, but not in a Version Set. Click Save; then, click OK in the JPEG Options dialog box and leave the file open. Choose Window > Images > Tile.

Comparing results

You can now compare the six versions of the image: the original file, the four files you created in this set of exercises, and the image that was fixed automatically as part of a batch process at the beginning of this lesson.

1 Choose File > Open. Locate and open the file frida_and_mina_Autofix.jpg in the My CIB Work folder. If you don't see the file in the Open dialog box, make sure that All Formats / All Readable Documents is the active selection in the Files Of Type / Enable menu. Click Open; then, repeat the process for the original file frida_and_mina.jpg in your Lesson08 folder.

2 Check the Project Bin to make sure that all of the six files for this project are open: the original image, frida_and_mina.jpg and five others with the appendixes _Blend_Mode.psd, _Shad_High.jpg, _Bright_Con.jpg, _Levels.jpg, and _Autofix.jpg. If you can't see the entire file name of an image, hold the pointer over the thumbnail in the Project Bin to see the file name in a Tooltip.

3 Hide the Panel Bin by un-checking its name in the Window menu; then, choose Window > Images > Tile.

4 Now you'll set the zoom level for all the open windows. Select the Zoom tool; then, in the tool options bar, click the Zoom Out button and activate Zoom All Windows. Click in any of the image windows so that you can see enough of the photo to enable you to compare the different results. Zoom in to focus on details. Select an area of interest in any of the six windows, and then choose Window > Images > Match Zoom and Window > Images > Match Location.

> **Tip:** You can also access The Match Zoom and Match Location commands by clicking the Arrange button (⊞) at the upper left of the workspace.

5 Compare the results and pick your favorite. The best method for fixing a file depends on the type of problem being addressed, the areas of the image that are affected, and how you intend to use the adjusted image. For example, the requirements for an image to be used as a background behind text will be very different from those for a featured graphic.

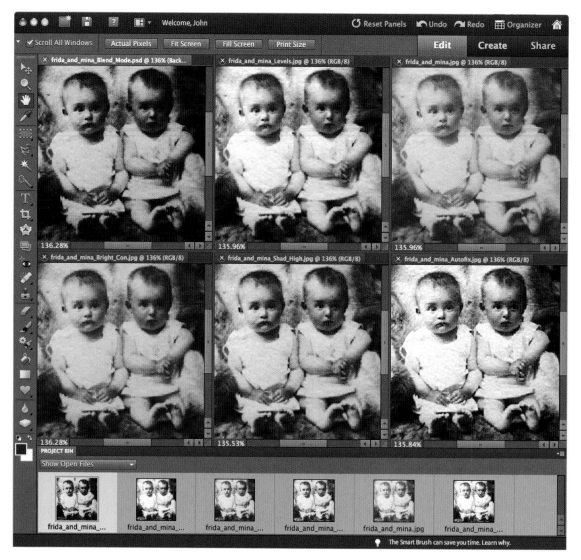

6   Choose Preferences > General from the Edit / Photoshop Elements menu. Disable the floating documents option, and then click OK. Choose File > Close All. Save any changes to your CIB Work folder if you're prompted to do so.

Congratulations! You've finished another lesson. In the exercises in this lesson you used a variety of both automatic and manual techniques for correcting exposure problems. You've tried auto-fixes, layer blending modes, and lighting adjustment controls. You've learned how to apply these different methods both separately and in combination to layers and selected areas to get the most from a problem image.

Before you move on to the next lesson, "Repairing, Retouching, and Recomposing Images," take a few moments to review what you've learned by reading through the questions and answers on the next page.

Review questions

1 How can you create an exact copy of an existing layer?

2 Where can you find the controls for adjusting the lighting in a photograph?

3 How do you change the arrangement of image windows in the work area?

4 What is an adjustment layer and what are its unique advantages?

Review answers

1 You must be in Full Edit mode to copy a layer. Select a layer in the Layers panel and choose Layer > Duplicate Layer. You can access the same command in the Layers panel Options menu or by right-clicking / Control-clicking the layer in the Layers panel. Alternatively, drag the layer to the New Layer button. Whichever method you use, you get two layers identical in all but their names, stacked one above the other.

2 You can adjust the lighting for a photo in Full Edit, Guided Edit, and Quick Edit mode. In Full Edit, you can use the Enhance > Adjust Lighting menu to open various dialog boxes that contain the controls. Alternatively, you can choose Enhance > Auto Levels, Enhance > Auto Contrast, or Enhance > Adjust Color > Adjust Color Curves. In Guided Edit mode, choose operations from the Lighting and Exposure pane. In Quick Edit mode, you can use the Lighting pane in the Quick Fix panel.

3 You cannot rearrange image windows in Quick Edit and Guided Edit modes, which display only one photograph at a time. In the Full Edit workspace, there are several ways you can arrange them. Choose Window > Images, and select one of the choices listed there—you can access the same options and more by clicking the Arrange button (⊞). Another method is to drag the image window title bar to move an image window, and drag a corner to resize it (provided Maximize mode is not active).

4 An adjustment layer does not contain an image; instead, it modifies some quality of all the layers below it in the Layer panel. For example, a Brightness/Contrast layer will alter the brightness and contrast of any underlying layers. One advantage of using an adjustment layer instead of adjusting an existing layer directly is that adjustment layers can be easily modified or even removed. Toggle the eye icon for the adjustment layer to remove or restore the edit instantly. You can change a setting in an adjustment layer at any time—even after the file has been saved. An adjustment layer can also be copied and pasted into another image to apply the same settings there.

9 REPAIRING, RETOUCHING, AND RECOMPOSING IMAGES

Lesson overview

For some images you'll need to deal with flaws other than color or exposure problems. A picture that was taken hurriedly might be spoiled by being tilted or poorly composed. Perhaps you have an antique photograph that is creased and worn or a scanned image marked by dust and scratches.

Sometimes the problem has nothing to do with the photograph itself, such as an extraneous object that clutters an otherwise striking composition or even just spots and blemishes on a portrait subject's skin.

In this lesson, you'll learn a range of techniques for restoring, retouching and rearranging the composition of such flawed images:

- Using the Straighten tool
- Improving the composition of an image with the Recompose tool
- Removing unwanted objects with content-aware healing
- Retouching skin with the Healing Brush tool
- Repairing creases with the Clone Stamp tool
- Working with opacity and blending modes in layers
- Using the Selection Brush tool
- Working with layer masks

 You'll probably need about one and a half hours to complete this lesson.

Not every image problem is a result of incorrect camera settings. Learn how to straighten a tilted photo, rearrange an image's composition, and retouch spots and blemishes on your subject's skin. The same tools, techniques and tricks used to remove spots or repair creases and tears when you're restoring a treasured keepsake can also be used creatively to manipulate reality and produce exactly the image you want.

Getting started

Before you start working on the exercises in this lesson, make sure that you have installed the software on your computer from the application CD (see the Photoshop Elements 9 documentation) and that you have correctly copied the Lessons folder from the CD in the back of this book onto your computer's hard disk. (See "Copying the Classroom in a Book files" on page 2.)

This lesson includes five independent exercises—you can either work straight through or complete them in separate sessions. The first four projects vary only slightly in length and complexity, while the forth is a little more involved.

While you're working on the projects in this lesson, you'll use sample images from the CIB Catalog that you created in the "Getting Started" section at the beginning of this book. To open your CIB Catalog, follow these steps:

To start, you'll import the sample images for this lesson to the CIB Catalog that you created at the beginning of Lesson 4:

1   Start Photoshop Elements and click Organize in the Welcome Screen.

2   Check the name of the active catalog in the lower left corner of the Organizer window. If your CIB Catalog is already loaded, you can skip step to step 4.
    If another catalog is currently loaded, continue with step 3.

3   Choose File > Catalog. In the Catalog Manager dialog box, click to select your CIB Catalog in the Catalogs list, and then click Open. If you don't see the CIB Catalog listed, review "Creating a new catalog" at the beginning of Lesson 4.

4   Choose File > Get Photos And Video > From Files And Folders. In the Get Photos And Videos From Files And Folders dialog box, locate and open your Lessons folder. Select the Lesson09 folder, disable any automatic processing option that is currently active, and then click Get Media.

5   In the Import Attached Keyword Tags dialog box, click Select All, and then click OK. Click OK to close any other alert dialog box.

In the Media Browser, you can see thumbnails of the images you've just imported to your CIB catalog. In the Keyword Tags panel, the newly added Lesson 09 tag has been listed under Imported Keyword Tags.

6   If you don't see filenames below the thumbnails in the Media Browser, choose View > Show File Names.

7   Select the file 09_01.jpg in the Media Browser; then, click the small arrow on the Fix tab above the Task Pane and choose Full Photo Edit. Alternately, you could select the file and choose Edit > Edit With Photoshop Elements.

8 Click the Reset Panels button () at the top of the Editor workspace. Hide the Project Bin by double-clicking its header bar or by un-checking its name in the Window menu. Hide the Panel bin by un-checking its name in the Window menu, and then double-click the Hand tool or choose View > Fit On Screen.

Using the Straighten tool

The picture for this exercise was taken by a child unused to handling the camera, but it can be easy for any of us to be distracted by our live subjects or rushed by awkward shooting conditions, and the result is often an image that would be just fine—if only it were straight! With the Straighten tool you can manually designate a line in your tilted image to be used as either a horizontal or vertical reference in relation to which the photo will be rotated.

1 Select the Straighten tool (). In the tool options bar across the top of the Edit pane, make sure that Canvas Options is set to Grow Or Shrink Canvas To Fit. As there are no truly straight lines in the sculpture in the foreground, our best reference for a true level in this photo is the old building in the background. Drag a line along the ledge between the first and second stories.

2 When you release the mouse button, Photoshop Elements straightens the image relative to the line you've just drawn. Choose Fit On Screen from the View menu or the menu on the Arrange button ( ) so that you can see all of the newly enlarged canvas surrounding the rotated image.

Tip: For this image we chose the Straighten tool option Grow Or Shrink Canvas To Fit because we wish to have manual control over cropping. When this is not an issue, try the options Crop To Remove Background and Crop To Original Size, which are also available from the Canvas Options menu in the tool options for the Straighten tool.

3 In the toolbox, select the Crop tool ( ). From the Aspect Ratio menu in the tool options bar, choose Use Photo Ratio; this will constrain the cropping rectangle to the original proportions. Drag a cropping rectangle inside the image, which is now displayed at an angle—being careful not to include any of the blank area around the photo. When you're satisfied with the crop, click the green Commit button in the lower right corner of the cropping rectangle. The straightened and cropped image is much more comfortable to look at than the tilted original.

4 Choose File > Save As. Make sure the new file will be included in the Organizer, but not in a Version Set. Name the file **09_01_Straight.jpg** to be saved to your My CIB Work folder in JPEG format. Click Save; then, click OK to dismiss the JPEG Options dialog box. Choose File > Close to close the file.

5 Staying in the Editor, choose File > Open; then, navigate to and open your Lesson09 folder, select the file 09_02.jpg, and click Open.

In this photo, the horizon is hidden, the river bank is irregular, and the horizontal lines of the building in the background are angled by perspective—so your best option is to use one of the vertical lines in the large apartment building. By default, the Straighten tool is set for a horizontal reference; to designate a vertical reference you need to use the tool together with the Ctrl / Command key.

6 Select the Straighten tool (). In the tool options bar, make sure that Canvas Options is set to Grow Or Shrink Canvas To Fit. Click and hold down the mouse button on a point at the top of a vertical lines in the apartment building; then, press the Ctrl / Command key and drag a line down your vertical reference. Release the mouse button, and then the Ctrl / Command key.

7 Select the Crop tool (⊞). In the tool options bar, set the cropping aspect ratio to No Restriction. Drag a rectangle inside the rotated photo, retaining as much of the image as possible without including any of the blank canvas surrounding it. When you're satisfied with your crop, click the Commit button in the lower right corner of the cropping rectangle.

> **Tip:** In some cases, you can achieve good results by choosing either Straighten Image, or Straighten And Crop Image from the Image > Rotate > menu. Both of these commands perform straightening functions automatically.

8 Choose File > Save As. Make sure the new file will be included in the Organizer, but not in a Version Set. Name the file **09_02_Straight.jpg**, to be saved to your My CIB Work folder in JPEG format. Click Save; then, click OK to close the JPEG Options dialog box. Choose File > Close to close the file.

Improving the composition of an image

Have you ever wished you could convert a photo from landscape to portrait format without cropping off content at the sides? Do you have a group shot where you wish the group had stood a little closer together? Or a photo where a walk-on extra draws attention away from the stars and the main story? With the new Recompose tool you can fix these and other image composition problems in a few easy steps.

Essentially, the Recompose tool enables you to crop your photo from the *inside*, rather than at the edges. Whether you want to bring people closer together, fit a horizontal image to a vertical space, remove extraneous elements that spoil the composition, or increase the drama in an action shot, the Recompose tool puts image editing magic at your fingertips.

As with the Healing brushes and the Clone Stamp tool that are covered later in this chapter—and the Photomerge tools you'll explore in Lesson 11—the Recompose tool is also a lot of fun to use creatively, making it possible to manipulate reality to produce exactly the image you want.

1 If you're still in the Editor from the previous exercise, switch to the Organizer now by clicking the Organizer button (⊞) at the top right of the Editor workspace. In the Keyword Tags panel, click the Find box beside the Lesson 09 tag, if necessary, to isolate the images for this lesson.

2 In the Media Browser, right-click / Control-click the image 09_03.jpg and choose Edit With Photoshop Elements from the context menu.

Recomposing a group photo

In this exercise, you'll use the Recompose tool to tighten the arrangement of this group portrait—creating a square composition.

1 If you don't already see some gray space around the edge of the photo in the image window, press Ctrl / Command together with the minus sign key (–) to zoom out a little.

2 In the toolbox, click the Crop tool () and hold the mouse button down until the tool variants menu appears. Select the Recompose tool ( ). A message appears with quick instructions on using the Recompose tool, including a link to a video tutorial. For now, click OK to dismiss the message.

The image is now surrounded by a live bounding box, with control handles at the corners and at the mid-point of each side. For simple recomposing operations, all you need to do is drag the handles; the Recompose tool makes use of content-aware scaling technology that distinguishes people and other featured objects and attempts to prevent them being distorted as the background is compressed around them. For this exercise, however, we'll use the special Recompose brushes instead. For more complex images, this generally produce better results.

3 In the Tool options bar immediately above the toolbox, select the green Mark For Protection brush. Either type in the brush size text box or use the slider to increase the brush size to 80 px.

As its name suggests, you can use this brush to define those areas in the image that you want protected from any scaling operation.

4 Paint roughly over the three figures on the left side of the photograph. Cover a little extra space to the left of the girl in the blue T-shirt, and also mark the windows and the white shutter for protection. If you find that you've over-painted, use the green eraser (right beside the protection brush in the tool options bar) to modify your strokes. Use the left and right bracket keys ([,]) to decrease or increase the brush size as you work.

5 Right-click / Control-click the image. In the context menu, change the mode for the brush from the default Use Normal Highlight to Use Quick Highlight.

In the default mode, you need to paint over the entire area you wish to protect. The Quick Highlight mode enables you to quickly mark an area for protection by simply drawing a line to surround it.

6 Set the brush size to 20 px; then, draw a rough outline around the two girls at the right. Release the mouse button; the area you outlined is marked for protection automatically. Right-click / Control-click the image again. Switch back to Normal Highlight mode and paint over the two windows behind the girls.

7 In the tool options bar, select the red Mark For Removal brush.

You can use this brush to define any areas that you wish the Recompose tool to remove from the image. In this photo there is no extraneous object that we need to get rid of, but you can mark parts of the stone wall, as shown in the illustration below, and the Recompose tool will remove those areas before compressing others. This will help to retain the plants against the wall and lessen distortion elsewhere.

8 Alternate between the red Mark For Removal brush and its associated eraser, using the bracket keys to re-size the brush if necessary as you work.

9 Now for the fun part! Move the pointer over the handle on the right side of the bounding box and when the double-arrow cursor appears, drag the handle slowly in towards the center of the photo. Watch the photo as you drag; some areas of the image are removed while others are compressed and merged with their surroundings. As the proportions of the image become closer to a square, keep an eye on the width (W) and height (H) values in the Tool options bar; stop dragging and release the mouse button when the two values are equal.

As this was a rather extreme operation, performed on an image of relatively low resolution, you may find some seam artifacts, especially near the edges of areas that were removed or protected. If these are noticeable enough to worry you, a few strokes with the Clone Stamp tool or the Healing Brush tool will fix the problem. You'll learn about using those tools later in this lesson. Use the Zoom tool to inspect the area between the shutter, which was protected and the leaves on the wall, which were compressed. Experiment with recomposing the original image in different ways; try removing a slice of the image through the climbing roses, instead of down the stone wall, and compare the results.

10 Click the green Commit button at the lower right of the recomposed photo or press Enter / Return to accept and render the new composition.

11 Choose Image > Crop. A cropping box appears on the image; drag the handles to crop the file to the new square format, trimming away the transparent area. The edges of the cropping box snap to the edges of the image to make the operation very easy. Click the green Commit button or press Enter / Return.

12 Choose File > Save As. Make sure the new file will be included in the Organizer, but not in a Version Set. Name the new image **09_03_Recompose.jpg**, to be saved to your My CIB Work folder in JPEG format.

13 Click Save; then click OK to accept the default JPEG Options settings.

14 Choose File > Close to close the file.

The Recompose tool is as easy to use as it is powerful—with creative possibilities that are virtually limitless. Play with as many pictures as you can; you'll learn how content-aware scaling works and what to expect from different types of image as you have fun finding creative new ways to make the most of your photos.

Fixing blemishes

There are three main tools in Photoshop Elements for fixing flaws in your photos:

The Spot Healing Brush tool

The Spot Healing Brush is the easiest way to remove wrinkles in skin and other small imperfections in your photos. Either click once on a blemish or click and drag to smooth it away. By blending the information of the surrounding area into the problem spot, imperfections are made indistinguishable.

The Healing Brush tool

The Healing Brush can fix larger imperfections with ease. You can define one part of your photo as a source to be sampled and blended into another area. The Healing Brush is so flexible you can even remove large objects from a uniform background—such as a person in a wheat field.

The Clone Stamp tool

Rather than blending the source and target areas, the Clone Stamp tool paints directly with a sample of an image. You can use the Clone Stamp tool to remove or duplicate objects in your photo. This tool is great for getting rid of garbage, power lines, or a signpost that may be spoiling a view.

Removing wrinkles and spots

In this exercise, you'll explore several techniques for retouching skin flaws and blemishes to improve a portrait photograph. Retouching skin can be a real art, but luckily Photoshop Elements provides several tools that make it easy to smooth out lines and wrinkles, remove blemishes, and blend skin tones.

1   If you're still in the Editor from the previous exercise, switch to the Organizer now by clicking the Organizer button (⊞) at the top right of the Editor workspace. In the Keyword Tags panel, click the Find box beside the Lesson 09 tag, if necessary, to isolate the images for this lesson.

2   Right-click / Control-click the image 09_04.jpg and choose Edit With Photoshop Elements from the context menu.

If you've already completed Lesson 7, you'll recognise this photo from the teeth whitening exercise. The copy you'll be working with in the following set of exercises has already visited the dentist; this time you get to play beauty therapist.

Preparing the file for editing

Before you start retouching, you'll need to add two extra layers to the image. You can also set up the workspace for working at high magnification.

1   In the Editor, click the Reset Panels button (↺) at the top of the workspace. Drag the Layers panel out of the Panel Bin by its header bar, and then hide the Panel Bin and the Project Bin by un-checking their names in the Window menu.

2   Drag the Background layer to the New Layer button (▨) at the bottom of the Layers panel to create another layer, named "Background copy" by default.

3   Drag the Background copy layer to the New Layer button to create a third layer.

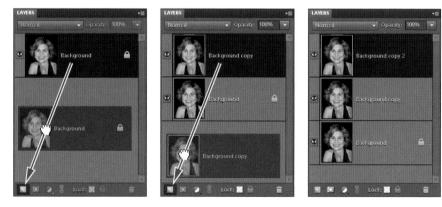

4   If necessary, resize the Layers panel by dragging its lower right corner. You only need the panel to be just big enough to show your three layers.

Using the Healing Brush tool

1   Use the Zoom tool to zoom in on the upper half of the photo, as you'll be retouching the skin around the woman's eyes first.

This photo is quite a challenging candidate for retouching; the harsh flash lighting has caused strong reflections on the skin that only serve to accentuate the wrinkles. You'll begin the retouching process using the Healing Brush tool in botox mode.

2   Make sure that the top layer, Background copy 2, is still active, and then select the Healing Brush tool (✐) which is grouped together with the Spot Healing Brush tool in the toolbox.

3   In the tool options bar, click the small arrow to open the Brush Picker. and set the Diameter to 20 px. Set the brush Mode to Normal and Source to Sampled. Make sure that the options Aligned and Sample All Layers are disabled.

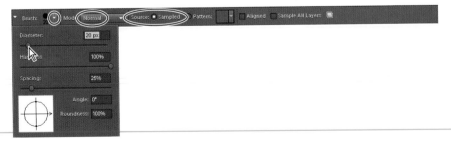

4 Alt-click / Option-click a smooth area on the woman's right cheek to define the area sampled as a reference texture. Note that if you switch to another tool and then back to the Healing Brush, you'll need to repeat this step.

5 Draw a short horizontal stroke under the left eye. As you drag, it may look as if you're creating a strange effect, but when you release the mouse button, the color will be blended and natural skin tones will fill the area.

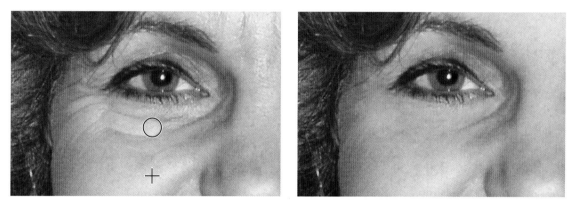

6 Continue to smooth the skin on the face and neck with the Healing Brush. Avoid the areas very close to the eyes, shadowed areas, and the hair-line. You can also reduce the worst of the shine caused by the harsh flash. As you work, re-establish the reference area occasionally by Alt-clicking / Option-clicking in new areas of the face to sample appropriate skin tone and texture. Press the left and right bracket keys ([,]) to decrease or increase the brush size as you work. Be sure to remove the moles om the woman's right cheek and the spots on the left cheek and just below the lower lip

Be careful to keep your brush strokes short. Try just clicking rather than dragging, but take care to overlap your clicks to avoid creating a spotty effect. Longer strokes may produce unacceptable results—especially near shaded areas where the darker tones may spread. If that happens, choose Edit > Undo Healing Brush. If you're still seeing results you don't like, make sure that the Aligned option is not activated in the tool options bar. Try setting the brush to a smaller size or reversing the direction of your strokes. If the problem is related to the shadowed areas beside the nose or at the sides of the face, try stroking towards the shadows rather than away from them, or temporarily changing the mode for the Healing Brush tool from Normal to Lighten in the tool options bar.

7 Choose Window > Undo History. You can use the Undo History panel to quickly undo a series of steps. Every action you perform is recorded in chronological order from the earliest at the top to the most recent at the bottom of the panel. To restore the file to an earlier state, simply select an earlier (higher) action in the Undo History list.

You can still return the image to a more recent state by selecting a step lower in the list—as long as you have not made any further changes to the file. Once you've used the Undo History panel to restore a photo to an earlier state, any change you make to the image will replace all the actions in the more recent history.

The Healing Brush tool copies *texture* from the source area, not color. It samples the colors in the target area—the area you're brushing—and arranges those colors according to the texture of the reference area. Consequently, the Healing Brush tool appears to be smoothing the skin. So far however, the results are not convincingly realistic; you'll work to improve that in the next exercise.

Refining the Healing Brush results

In this exercise, you'll make your retouching work look a little more natural by altering the opacity of the layer you've been working on, and then use another of the texture tools to refine the resulting blend.

1 Choose Window > Navigator. In the Navigator panel, use the zoom slider and drag the red frame in the Navigator preview to focus the view in the image window on the area around the woman's eyes and mouth.

Extensive retouching can leave skin looking artificially smooth, looking a little like molded plastic. Reducing the opacity of the retouched layer will give the skin a more realistic look by allowing some of the wrinkles on the un-edited Background layer to show through slightly.

2 In the Layers panel, change the Opacity of the layer "Background copy 2" to about 50%, using your own judgment to set the exact percentage.

We opted for quite a low setting, wishing a fairly natural look for this photo of a friend, but the opacity value you set will depend on the extent of your retouching and the purpose for which the edited image is intended.

The opacity change restores some realism, but three noticeable blemishes have also made a reappearance—one on each cheek and one just below the lower lip.

3   Select the layer "Background copy" to make it the active layer.

4   Set the brush size for the Healing Brush tool to 20 px and click once or twice on each blemish. Gone!

5   In the toolbox, select the Blur tool ( ). In the tool options bar, set the brush diameter to approximately 13 px and set the Blur tool's Strength to 50%.

6   With the layer "Background copy" still active, drag the Blur tool over some of the deeper lines around the eyes and brow. Use the Navigator panel to change the zoom level and shift the focus as needed. Reduce the Blur tool brush diameter to 7 px and smooth the lips a little, avoiding the edges.

Tip: To remove spots and small blemishes in your photo, try the Spot Healing Brush in Proximity Match mode as an alternative to the Healing Brush. With the Spot Healing Brush, you can either click or drag to smooth away imperfections without needing to set a reference point.

Compare your results to those below—the original, the version retouched with the Healing Brush, and final refined version. Toggle the visibility of your retouched layers to compare the original image in your Background layer with the edited results.

| Original | Healing Brush 100% Opacity | Healing Brush 50% Opacity over Blur tool |

7   Choose File > Save As. Make sure that the new file will be included in the Organizer, but not in a Version Set. Name the edited image **09_04_Retouch**, to be saved to your My CIB Work folder in Photoshop (PSD) format.

8   Make sure that the Layers option is activated, and then click Save.

9   Choose File > Close.

Tip: For a quick and easy solution to portrait retouching, try the new Perfect Portrait procedure listed under Fun Edits in the Guided Edit mode, where you'll be stepped through smoothing skin, removing spots, fixing red eye, increasing definition in facial features, whitening teeth, and even slimming your subject!

In this exercise, you've learned how to set an appropriate source for the Healing Brush tool, and to sample the texture of the source area to repair flaws in another part of the photograph. You also used the Blur tool to smooth textures, and an opacity change to achieve a more realistic look. You've also gained a little experience in working with both the Undo History and Navigator panels.

Removing unwanted objects from images

The impact of a photo can easily be spoiled by an unwanted object in the frame. In the modern world, it's often impossible to photograph even a rural landscape without including a fence, or power lines, television aerials and satellite dishes, or litter—mundane clutter that can reduce the drama of an otherwise perfect shot.

Photoshop Elements offers several tools to help you improve an image by getting rid of extraneous detail. One method is to use the Recompose tool, which—as you've already seen—lets you mark areas to be removed as you scale a photo. In this set of exercises you'll use the Spot Healing Brush tool to remove an object from an image without altering the overall composition.

1   If you're still in the Editor from the previous exercise, switch to the Organizer now by clicking the Organizer button (⊞) at the top right of the Editor work-space. In the Keyword Tags panel, click the Find box beside the Lesson 09 tag, if necessary, to isolate the images for this lesson.

2   In the Media Browser, Ctrl-click / Command-click to select the two images 09_05.jpg and 09_06.jpg; then, right-click / Control-click either selected thumbnail and choose Edit With Photoshop Elements from the context menu.

3   In the Editor, either choose Window > Reset Panels or click the Reset Panels button (◔) at the top of the workspace.

4   In the Project Bin, double-click the photo of the two girls to make it the active image and bring its image window to the front in the Edit pane.

5   Press Shift+Tab on your keyboard to hide everything but the image window and the toolbox.

6   Select the Zoom tool; then, check the tool settings right above the toolbox to make sure that the Zoom In Mode is activated. In the Edit pane, drag a marquee with the Zoom tool to closely surround the lower half of the photo.

Using the Content-Aware healing feature

In the last project, you may have used the Spot Healing Brush in Proximity Match mode to help smooth skin blemishes in a portrait photo. In this exercise you'll set the Spot Healing Brush to Content-Aware mode—new in Photoshop Elements 9.

With the Content-Aware option activated, the Spot Healing Brush tool compares nearby image content to seamlessly fill the area under the pointer, realistically maintaining details such as shadows, object edges, and even perspective, as shown in the illustration above.

1   Select the Spot Healing Brush tool (🖌), which is grouped together in the toolbox with the Healing Brush tool.

2   In the tool options bar, make sure that the Content-Aware option is activated. Type in the text box to set a brush diameter of 330 pixels.

3   Position the circular cursor so that it completely surrounds the yellow plastic package and its shadow; then click once.

4   If you notice any image artefacts such as blurring or obvious repetition of detail, reduce the brush size to 50 pixels and click a few points to break up the effect.

5   Choose File > Save As. Make sure that the new file will be included in the Organizer, but not in a Version Set Name the new file **09_05_Remove**, to be saved to your My CIB Work folder in JPEG format, and then click Save. Click OK to accept the JPEG Options settings; then, close the file.

Now that you've seen how content-aware healing works, you can take on something a little more complex. A little practice will produce impressive results.

6 Use the Zoom tool to focus your view on the length of power line between the left edge of the photo and the sunlit wall at the left of the old church.

7 Select the Spot Healing Brush. In the tool options bar, set the brush diameter to 15 pixels, and check that the Content-Aware option is still activated.

8 Drag from right to left along the power line, starting just to the left of the tree as shown in the illustration below. Keep dragging until you've moved outside the left edge of the photo, and then release the mouse button.

9 With the power line removed from the left edge of the photo, you can now work from left to right across the rest of the image. Press the space bar on your keyboard to switch temporarily to the Hand tool. Drag the image to the left to focus on the next length of power line.

10 Work along the line in short, overlapping strokes, releasing the mouse button after each. If a stroke produces an
unwelcome artefact, press Ctrl+Z /
Command+Z to undo, and then try
again; try reversing the direction or
changing the angle of the stroke.

11 If an area proves to be particularly difficult, try clicking instead of dragging, or drag over the same area two or three times, being careful not to over-work the area. Reduce the brush size as needed. You'll need to take extra care as you cross the roof-line and other mechanical edges. Don't drag through too many textures with the one stroke; move across one border, and then stop.

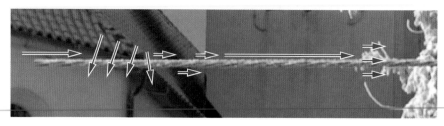

If you find that you can't deal with a problem area effectively, or you can't avoid creating an unnatural-looking artefact, switch temporarily to the Clone Stamp tool, for which you can designate a precise source as you did with the Healing Brush in the portrait retouching exercise.

Although the Clone Stamp offers this extra level of control, the Spot Healing Brush in content-aware mode can help you get the job done much faster; once you've gained some experience, you'll appreciate the fact that you don't need to stop repeatedly to sample a new source. Try a combination of content-aware healing and cloning on some of your own images; practice makes perfect.

12 When you've removed the last of the power line, choose View > Fit On Screen to admire your work.

The photo is vastly improved now that it's wire-less. However, there are still three unsightly spots in the sky caused by dirt or water droplets on the camera lens.

13 Set the brush size for the Spot Healing Brush to 60 px, and then click once or twice on each of the three spots. Done!

14 Choose File > Save As. Make sure that the file will be included in the Organizer, but not in a Version Set. Name the new file **09_06_Remove**, to be saved to your My CIB Work folder in JPEG format; then, click Save.

15 Click OK to accept the JPEG Options settings, and then close the file.

Before

After

Restoring a damaged photograph

All sorts of nasty things can happen to precious old photographs—or precious new photographs, for that matter—and it is often impossible to locate the negative. For this series of exercises you'll work with an uncropped version of one of the photos you adjusted in the previous chapter.

The scanned image of an antique photograph that you'll use in this project is a challenging restoration job, because of large creases in the original print, among other flaws.

Unfortunately, there's no way to fix such significant damage in just one or two keystrokes but to rescue an important heirloom photograph like this one, a little effort is worthwhile and the results can be dramatic.

Photoshop Elements provides the tools you'll need to restore this picture convincingly to an approximation of its original condition. You'll repair creases, replace parts of the image that are actually missing, fix frayed edges and remove dust and scratches. You may be surprised to discover how easy it is to achieve impressive results.

Setting up for the exercises

1 If you're still in the Editor from the previous exercise, switch back to the Organizer now by clicking the Organizer button (⊞) at the top right of the Editor workspace.

2 In the Keyword Tags panel, click the Find box beside the Lesson 09 tag, if necessary, to isolate the images for this lesson.

3 In the Media Browser, right-click / Control-click the image 09_07.psd, a scanned antique photo of twin babies, and choose Edit With Photoshop Elements from the context menu.

4 In the Editor, either choose Window > Reset Panels or click the Reset Panels button (🔘) at the top of the workspace. Hide the Project Bin by double-clicking its header bar.

5 Drag the grouped Effects and Content panels out of the Panel Bin by the header bar—not by the name tabs. Dragging the name tabs will float a single panel, separating the group. Click the menu icon at the right end of the group's header bar and choose Close Tab Group from the panel Options menu.

Preparing a working copy of the image file

You can begin your restoration work by setting up a work file with a duplicate layer.

1 Choose File > Save As. Make sure that the file will be included in the Organizer, but not in a Version Set. Name the new image **09_07_Repair**, to be saved to your My CIB Work folder in Photoshop (PSD) format, and then click Save.

2 Make a duplicate of the Background layer by doing one of the following:

- Choose Layer > Duplicate Layer.
- Click the menu icon at the right end of the Layers panel's header bar and choose Duplicate Layer from the panel Options menu.
- Right-click / Control-click the Background layer in the Layers panel and choose Duplicate Layer from the context menu.

3 In the Duplicate Layer dialog box, click OK to accept the default name: Background copy.

4 Choose Window > Navigator, and then arrange your workspace as shown in the illustration below. In the Panel Bin, drag the divider bar between the Navigator and Layers panels upwards to make the Navigator preview as large as possible without losing sight of the two layers in the Layers panel.

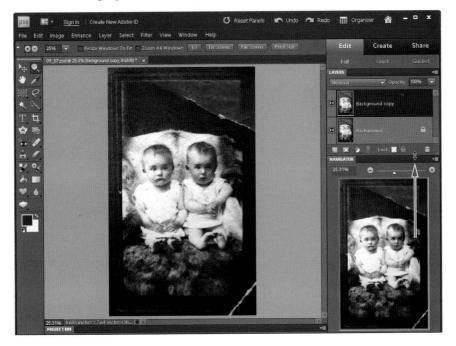

You could also work with your panels floating, but as you'll need to move around the image at high magnification this arrangement might be the most convenient.

Using the Clone Stamp tool to fill in missing areas

The first thing you'll do is to eliminate the creases using the Clone Stamp tool. The Clone Stamp tool paints with information sampled from another part of the image, which is perfect for both covering unwanted objects and replacing missing detail, as you'll be doing for the worn areas along the creases.

Using the Clone Stamp feels very much like using the Spot Healing Brush in content-aware mode—except that you get to specify precisely which part of the image will be sampled as you paint.

1 With the help of the Navigator panel or the Zoom tool, zoom in on the crease in the lower right corner.

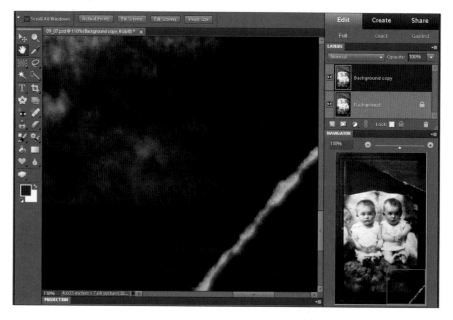

2 Select the Clone Stamp tool (🖌), which is grouped with the Pattern Stamp tool in the toolbox.

3 Click the small white triangle at the far left of the tool options bar and choose Reset Tool from the menu.

The Reset Tool command reinstates the default values for the Clone Stamp tool: Size: 21 px, Mode: Normal, Opacity: 100%, with the Aligned option activated.

4 In the tool options bar, open the Brush Picker. Choose Basic Brushes from the Brushes menu, and then select a hard mechanical brush with a diameter of 48 pixels. You can leave the other tool options at their default settings.

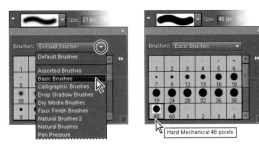

5 Move the Clone Stamp tool to the left of the crease at the bottom of the picture. Hold down the Alt / Option key and click to set the source point—the area to be sampled. Centering the source on a horizontal line makes it easier to align the brush for cloning. The tool duplicates the pixels from this point in your image as you paint elsewhere.

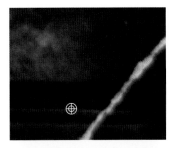

6 Position the brush over the damaged area so that it is aligned horizontally with the source reference point. Click and drag to the right over the crease to copy the source image over the damaged area. As you drag, cross-hairs appear, indicating the source—that is, the area that the Clone Stamp tool is sampling.

7 To repair the upper part of the crease, set the source position in the area above the crease and drag downwards. This will help you blend the repair with the vertical edges of the photograph's mount.

8 Continue to drag the brush over the creased, damaged area, resetting the source position as necessary, until the repair is complete.

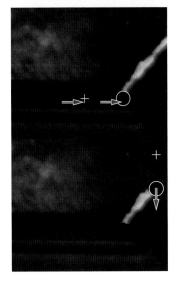

Note: If necessary, Alt-click / Option-click a different part of the image to establish a new sample source for the Clone Stamp tool.

The cross-hairs follow the movement of the brush. With the Aligned option activated in the tool options bar, the cross-hairs maintain the same position relative to the brush that was established when you made the first brush stroke. When the Aligned option is disabled, the cross-hairs return to their original position at the beginning of each new stroke, regardless of where it is made.

9 Now you can smooth out the fold across the upper right corner. The fold is quite severe; there is a significant difference in the background tones on either side of it, as well as surface damage and wrinkling. For this relatively complex operation the Healing Brush tool ( ) is the best choice.

10 When you're done, choose File > Save to save your changes.

Using the Selection Brush tool

The next step in restoring this photo is to use the Dust & Scratches filter to remove the stray spots and scuffed edges from the scanned image. This filter smooths the pixels by blurring the image just slightly, which is fine for the background, but the children should be kept as detailed and sharp as possible. To do that, you'll need to make a selection to isolate our subjects from the background.

1 Activate the Selection Brush tool ( ), which is grouped with the Quick Selection tool in the toolbox. Be careful not to choose one of the painting brush tools by mistake.

Although the Quick Selection tool can be faster than the Selection Brush, it automatically expands a selection based on similarities in color and texture—for this grainy black and white image the Selection Brush will give you far more control.

2 In the tool options bar, select a round brush shape and set the brush size to about 60 px (pixels). Leave the other options at the default values: Mode should be set to Selection and Hardness should be set to 100%.

3 Drag the Selection Brush around the edges of the photograph first, and then work your way inward. Decrease or increase the brush size as needed, using the left and right bracket keys ([,]) on your keyboard, as you paint the selection to include everything but the children. Don't worry if some of your strokes overlap on the babies; you'll learn how to refine the selection in the next exercise.

4 Choose Select > Save Selection. Type **Backdrop** as the name of the saved selection and click OK to close the Save Selection dialog box.

Painting with the Selection Brush tool is a very intuitive way to create a complex selection. In images like this one, where there are no distinct color blocks, few sharp boundaries between pictured items and few crisp geometric shapes, the Selection Brush tool is especially useful.

Another advantage of the Selection Brush tool is that it is very forgiving. You can hold down the Alt / Option key as you paint to remove an area from a selection. Alternatively, you can use the Selection Brush in Mask mode—another intuitive and natural-feeling way to refine the selection—as you'll do in the next exercise.

What is a mask?

A mask is simply the opposite of a selection. A selection is a defined area that you can modify; everything outside the selection is unaffected by the changes you make. A mask protects an area from changes, just like the solid areas of a stencil or the masking tape you'd put on window glass at home before you paint the frame.

Another difference between a mask and a selection is the way Photoshop Elements presents them visually. You're familiar with the flashing black and white dashed outline that indicates a selection marquee. A mask appears as a colored, semi-transparent overlay on the image. You can change the color and opacity of the mask overlay to make sure it contrasts with the image you're working on, or to see more of the detail hidden beneath it. The overlay color and opacity settings are accessible in the tool options bar when the Selection Brush tool is set to operate in Mask mode.

Refining a saved selection

As you progress through this book, you're gathering lots of experience with saving selections. In this procedure, you'll amend the selection you saved in the previous exercise and replace it with an improved version.

1   Make sure that your Backdrop selection is still active in the image window. If it's not still active, choose Select > Load Selection, choose the saved selection, and then click OK.

2   Make sure the Selection Brush tool (🖌) is still selected in the toolbox.

3   In the tool options bar, select Mask from the brush Mode menu. You can see the mask as a semi-transparent colored overlay on the un-selected—or protected—areas of the image. In this mode, the Selection Brush tool paints a mask rather than a selection.

4   Examine the image, looking for unmasked areas with details that should be protected (places where the Selection Brush strokes overlapped onto the children) and parts of the backdrop that are masked and should not be.

Use the Navigator panel slider or the Zoom tool (🔍) to adjust your view of the image, as necessary.

5 Reduce the brush size for the Selection Brush to about 30 pixels, and then paint out any areas that you want to mask. If you over-paint onto the background area, press the Alt / Option key as you paint to erase part of the mask.

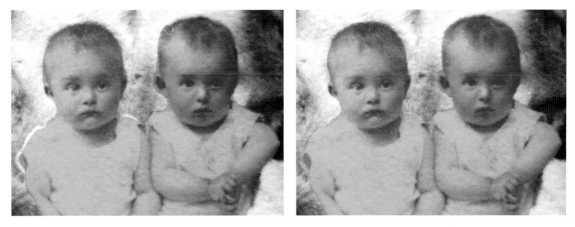

6 Switch between Selection and Mask modes, making corrections until you're satisfied that all the details you want to preserve are masked.

7 Choose Select > Save Selection. In the Save Selection dialog box, choose Backdrop from the Selection menu. Under Operation, activate the option Replace Selection, and thenclick OK.

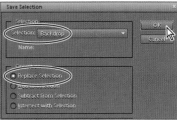

8 While the Selection Brush tool is still active, make sure that the Selection mode, not the Mask mode, is active in the tool options bar. Keep the selection active for the next procedure.

Creating a layer mask

You've just learned about the concept of masking as a method for editing a selection. In this section we'll look at a more permanent kind of mask.

You could use your selection (even in a later session, now that you've saved it) to temporarily isolate part of an image layer for editing—or protect the rest of the image from modification, depending on which way you look at it.

A layer mask serves the same purpose, but is both more convenient and more versatile. Unlike a saved selection, a layer mask doesn't need to be loaded—it can be permanently linked to a particular layer in an image. so that any modification made to that layer will be applied only to those areas not protected by the layer mask. The parts of the layer protected by the layer mask are hidden from view when it's blended with the other layers in your image.

Like the selection mask you worked with in the previous exercise, layer masks can be edited by painting and erasing. You can add to or subtract from the layer mask without affecting the image pixels on the layer to which it is attached.

1   If the Backdrop selection is not still active in the image window from the previous exercise, choose Select > Load Selection, choose your saved selection, and then click OK.

2   Make sure the layer Background copy is still selected, and then click the Add Layer Mask button () at the bottom of the Layers panel.

Your active selection in the image window is converted to a layer mask on the currently selected layer. A mask thumbnail appears on the background copy layer.

The white frame around the layer mask thumbnail indicates that the mask is currently selected—any change you make right now will modify the mask, not the image pixels on this layer. To edit the image instead, you would first need to click the image thumbnail.

3   Alt-click / Option-click the layer mask thumbnail to make the mask visible in the image window. With the mask selected, as it is now, you can edit it in the image window using painting and selection tools—or even the Text tool. Alt-click / Option-click the layer mask thumbnail again to hide the mask in the image window.

Changes made to a masked layer will be applied at full strength through the white parts of the mask; black areas in a layer mask represent the parts of your image that are completely protected.

A gray area will allow a modification to be applied at a strength equivalent to the percentage of white present; a layer mask containing a simple gradient from white to black can be a great way to fade one image into another.

4   Shift+Alt-click / Shift+Option-click the layer mask thumbnail to make the mask visible in the image window as a semi-transparent overlay. You can change the color and opacity of the mask overlay by right-clicking / Control-clicking the layer mask thumbnail and choosing Mask Options from the context menu. Shift+Alt-click / Shift+Option-click the layer mask thumbnail again to hide the layer mask overlay.

5   Click the eye icon beside the image thumbnail on the original Background layer to make the layer temporarily invisible. You can see that the protected areas of the masked layer are actually hidden from view.

While this layer mask is active, any change made to the underlying layer will be visible only in the figures of the babies; any change you make to the masked layer will be applied only the backdrop around them.

6   Right-click / Control-click the layer mask thumbnail and choose Disable Layer Mask from the context menu. The mask thumbnail is marked with a red X. In the image window, you can see that the image pixels on this layer have not been permanently modified by the layer mask.

If you keep the layer mask linked to the Background copy layer as it is now, it will remain editable—even in a later work session. You can switch the mask on or off, as you just did, and you can even use it to modify an active selection in the image window by choosing from the commands in the context menu.

For the purposes of this exercise however, we've already refined our selection, and we have no other reason to keep the mask active.

7   Right-click / Control-click the layer mask thumbnail and choose Apply Layer Mask from the context menu.

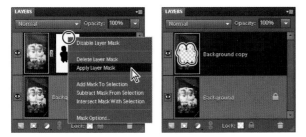

The layer mask can no longer be edited; it has been permanently merged with the Background copy layer. The babies are no longer simply hidden—they have been permanently deleted from the image on this layer; the checkerboard pattern in the layer thumbnail indicates that they have been replaced by an area of transparency.

8   Click the box at the left of the image thumbnail on the original Background layer to make the layer visible once more.

Filtering flaws out of the backdrop area

Now that you've applied the layer mask to your working layer to isolate the twins from their surroundings, you're ready to use a filter that will soften the backdrop of the image, effectively hiding any tiny scratches and dust specks.

1   Make sure that the Background copy layer is still selected in the Layers panel.

2   Choose Filter > Noise > Dust & Scratches.

3 In the Dust & Scratches dialog box, make sure that Preview is selected, and then set the Radius to 6 pixels and the Threshold to 10 levels. Move the dialog box so that you can see most of the image window.

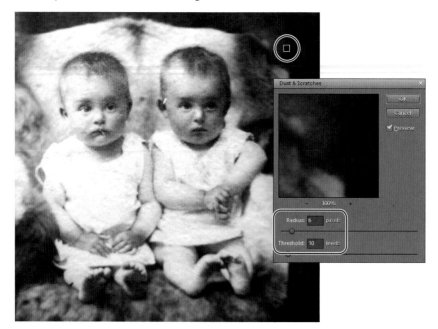

4 Examine the results in the image window and in the the Dust & Scratches dialog box preview. To change the image area visible in the magnified preview, drag in the preview or click with the square cursor in the image window. The scuffed edges of the image have been softened and the flecks of dust and tiny scratches have been eliminated.

5 Click OK to close the Dust & Scratches dialog box.

6 Choose File > Save to save your work.

Adding definition with the Smart Brush

Being a selection tool and an adjustment tool in one, the Smart Brush provides a quick and easy way to apply an adjustment to just part of a photo. Unfortunately, like the Quick Selection tool, the Smart Brush makes its selection based on similarities in color and texture in an image, which makes it a little difficult to use on an image such as our example. However, you've already spent time creating an accurate selection with the Selection Brush and, as you've seen, you can use that selection to create a mask that will effectively hide any effect from the Smart brush that extends outside the area you intend to adjust.

1 In the Layers panel, right-click / Control-click the original Background layer and choose Duplicate Layer from the context menu. In the Duplicate Layer dialog box, click OK to accept the default name: Background copy 2. Drag the new layer to the top position in the Layers panel, above the Background copy layer.

2   Select the Smart Brush tool (✎) in the toolbox. The floating Smart Paint panel appears. If the panel does not appear, you can open it by clicking the colored thumbnail in the tool options bar. Drag the Smart Paint panel aside so that you can see the two babies in the image window. From the categories menu at the top of the Smart Paint panel, choose Lighting, and then select Darker from the list of Smart Paint adjustments.

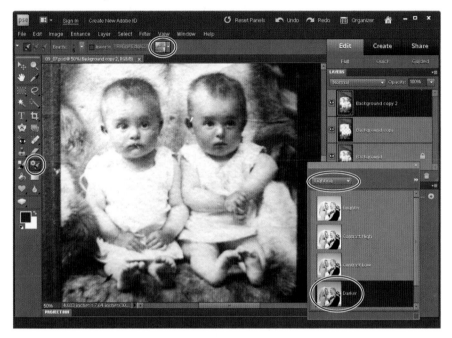

3   In the tool options bar, open the Brush Picker and set the brush Diameter to 30 pixels, and the Hardness to 75%.

4   Make sure the layer Background copy 2 is selected in the Layers panel. With the Smart Brush, paint over the face of the baby on the left and over the arms and legs of both babies. Don't worry about the selection spilling over onto the background, but try to exclude the babies' clothes. Hold down the Alt / Option key as you paint to subtract from the Smart Brush selection.

5   Choose Select > Deselect Layers to make the adjustment inactive.

6 From the categories menu at the top of the Smart Paint panel, choose Portrait, and then select Details from the list of Smart Paint adjustments.

7 With the Smart Brush, paint completely over both babies and their clothes. This time you can be even more casual with your brushwork; don't worry at all if the effect spills over onto the background—you'll tidy it up in a moment.

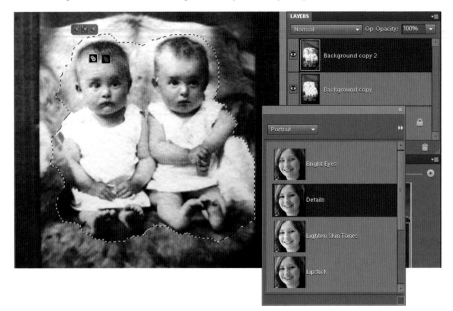

8 Choose Select > Deselect Layers to make the new adjustment inactive; then, close the floating Smart Paint adjustments panel.

Merging layers

You'll now merge the two new Smart Brush adjustment layers with the layer Background copy 2 below them.

1 Ctrl-click / Command-click to select the top three layers in the Layers panel: Details 1, Darker 1, and Background copy 2.

2 Choose Layer > Merge Layers. The three selected layers are merged into one. The new merged layer takes its name from the layer that was on top in the stacking order: Details 1. The Smart Brush adjustments are no longer live; they can no longer be edited.

3 Make sure the new merged layer is still active in the Layers panel and choose Select > Load Selection.

4 In the Load Selection dialog box, choose the saved selection Backdrop from the Selection menu. Activate the Invert option, and then click OK.

5 Click the Add Layer Mask button ( ) at the bottom of the Layers panel. Right-click / Control-click the new layer mask thumbnail on the Details 1 layer and choose Apply Layer Mask from the context menu.

6 To assess the effects of your Smart Brush adjustments, toggle the visibility of the layer Details 1 by clicking the eye icon beside its thumbnail in the Layers panel.

7 In the Layers panel, Ctrl-click / Command-click to select the top two layers: Details 1 and Background copy.

8 Choose Layer > Merge Layers. The two selected layers are merged into one. The new merged layer takes its name from the layer that was on top in the stacking order: Details 1.

Finishing up the project

Compared to the original condition of the photograph, the image is already vastly improved, but it needs just a few finishing touches before you save your work.

1 Use the Zoom and Hand tools—or the Navigator panel—to examine the entire image, looking for dark or light flecks created by dust on the negative or the ravages of time, especially in the dark areas of the photograph.

2 In the toolbox, select the Blur tool ( ) and type **40 px** as the brush Size in the tool options bar.

3 Click or drag the tool over any dust spots you find, to blend them into the surrounding area.

4   Use the Clone Stamp tool to remove the pink smudge from the dress of the baby on the right and the Healing Brush to remove the black mark on the calf of the child on the left and the white mark on the ear of the other baby.

5   Choose File > Save, and then close the file.

Original   Retouched

Congratulations, you've finished this lesson on recomposing, repairing and retouching images. You've explored a variety of techniques for fixing visual flaws in your photos, from straightening an image to smoothing wrinkles from skin. You sampled one area of an image to repair another with both the Clone Stamp and the Healing Brush and worked with selections and masks. You learned how to reset a tool to its default settings and worked more with layers and the Smart Brush. You also learned how to crop an image from the inside, rearranging its composition and altering its proportions without trimming away important elements.

Take a moment to review the lesson by reading through the review on the next page before you move on to chapter 10, "Working with Text."

Review questions

1   What is the purpose of the brushes and erasers that appear in the tool options bar when you select the Recompose tool?

2   How can you quickly undo a whole series of edit steps at once?

3   What are the similarities and differences between the Healing Brush tool and the Spot Healing Brush tool for retouching photos?

4   Why was it necessary to make a selection before applying the Dust & Scratches filter to restore our damaged photograph?

5   What is the difference between a selection and a mask?

Review answers

1   Use the green Mark For Protection brush to define areas in the image that you want protected from a scaling operation. Use the red Mark For Removal brush to define any areas that you want removed from the image; the Recompose tool will cut those areas before compressing others. Each of the Recompose brushes has its associated eraser.

2   The Undo History panel lists every action performed on the file in chronological order To restore the file to an earlier state, select an earlier action—higher in the list—in the Undo History panel. If you change your mind before making further changes to the file, you can still restore the image to a later state by selecting a step lower in the list.

3   Both healing tools blend pixels from one part of an image into another. Although the Spot Healing Brush tool enables you to remove blemishes quicker than is possible with the Healing Brush, the Healing Brush can be customized, and enables you to specify the source reference area, giving you more control.

4   The Dust & Scratches filter smooths out pixels in an image by blurring them slightly, effectively putting detail slightly out of focus. It was necessary to create a selection so that only the background was blurred, preserving sharpness and detail in the subjects.

5   A mask is simply the opposite of a selection. A selection is an active area to which adjustments can be applied; everything outside the selection is unaffected by any changes that are made. A mask protects an area from changes.

10 WORKING WITH TEXT

Lesson overview

Adding text messages to your photos is another way to make your images and compositions even more memorable and personal.

Whether you want to add straightforward classic typography, or use effects, masks, and transparencies to turn your text into a striking design element in its own right, Photoshop Elements has all the right tools to make the job easy.

In this lesson you'll learn the skills and techniques you need to work with text in Photoshop Elements:

- Working with the canvas

- Adding a border to an image

- Formatting and editing text

- Overlaying text on an image

- Applying effects and Layer Styles

- Hiding, revealing, merging, and deleting layers

- Copying a text layer from one image to another

- Working with multiple image windows

- Warping text

- Creating a type mask

 You'll probably need between one and two hours to complete this lesson.

Photoshop Elements provides you with the tools you'll need to add crisp, flexible, and editable type to your pictures. Whether you want classic typography or wild effects and wacky colors, it's all possible in Photoshop Elements. Apply effects and layer styles to make your text really stand out or blend it into your image using transparency. Create a type mask and fill your text with any image you can imagine.

Getting started

Before you start working on the exercises in this lesson, make sure that you have installed the software on your computer from the application CD (see the Photoshop Elements 9 documentation) and that you have correctly copied the Lessons folder from the CD in the back of this book onto your computer's hard disk. (See "Copying the Classroom in a Book files" on page 2.)

This lesson assumes that you are already familiar with the main features of the Photoshop Elements workspace. Should you need to brush up on the basic concepts review "Getting Started" and "A Quick Tour of Photoshop Elements" at the start of this book, or refer to Photoshop Elements Help.

Each of the projects in this lesson builds on skills learned in the previous exercises.

1 Start Photoshop Elements and click the Organize button in the Welcome screen. Check the name of the currently loaded catalog displayed in the lower left corner of the Organizer workspace. If your CIB Catalog is not already loaded, choose File > Catalog and select it from the list in the Catalog Manager.

2 Choose File > Get Photos And Video > From Files And Folders. In the Get Photos And Videos From Files And Folders dialog box, locate and open your Lessons folder. Select the Lesson10 folder, disable any automatic processing option that is currently active, and then click Get Media. In the Import Attached Keyword Tags dialog box, click Select All, and then click OK.

3 Click the Show All button in the Find bar. If you don't see filenames below the thumbnails in the Media Browser, choose View > Show File Names.

Placing text on an image

The first project involves creating a text layer, and then formatting and arranging text on a photograph. You'll also add a border and a greeting to the photo so it can be printed as a card or even mounted in a picture frame.

Using a text search to find a file

If you've worked through the previous lessons, you're already familiar with locating files by their keyword tags. The image files for this lesson are tagged "Lesson 10" but all of them also have descriptive names, which will make it easy to find just the pictures required for each exercise rather than all the files in your Lesson10 folder.

With such a relatively small number of sample images in your Lessons folder these methods may seem like overkill, but as your photo library grows you'll appreciate having as many options as possible to help find the file you want quickly and easily.

1   Type the letters **sis** in the Text Search box, at the left of the bar above the Media Browser.

2   The Media Browser displays a single image: 4sisters.jpg—a photograph of four young girls on vacation in Europe. Select the image in the Media Browser.

3   Click the small arrow on the Fix tab above the Task Pane and choose Full Photo Edit from the menu.

Note: For detailed information on using the text search feature in the Organizer, see the section "Using a text search to find photos" on page 100 in Lesson 3.

Working with the image canvas

You can think of the canvas as the equivalent of the paper on which a photo is printed.

While you're working with a digital photo, image data may temporarily lie outside the canvas space, but it will be clipped to the boundary of the canvas as soon as the image is flattened. To extend our limited analogy just a little further, think of the layer data as the image projected by a photographic enlarger in the darkroom. Although the projected image may be offset or enlarged so that it falls outside the borders of the paper, the data still exists; you can continue to work with it right up until the moment that the photographic paper is exposed.

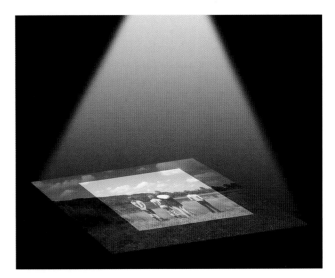

Adding a border to a photo

By default, the canvas is the same size as the image; if you increase the size of the image file, the canvas is enlarged automatically. You can also enlarge the canvas independently from the image size; the result is just as if you printed a photo at the same size on a larger sheet of paper.

In this exercise you'll do just that—enlarge the canvas without increasing the size of the image—effectively adding a border around the photo. By default, the extended canvas, and therefore the border, takes on the Background color as set in the color swatches at the bottom of the toolbox.

You'll create the border in two stages in order to make it asymmetrical.

1   If the photo has opened in a floating image window, click the Arrange button at the top of the workspace, and then click the Consolidate All button at the upper left of the Arrange menu.

2   Drag the Layers panel out of the Panels Bin by its header bar, and then hide the Panels Bin by un-checking its name in the Window menu. Hide the Project Bin by double-clicking its header bar.

3 If you don't see a reasonable amount of blank canvas surrounding the image, choose View > Zoom Out or press Ctrl+- (minus) / Command+– (minus).

4 Choose Image > Resize > Canvas Size. Move the Canvas Size dialog box, if necessary, so that you can see at least the left half of the image.

5 Set the Canvas Size dialog box as shown in the illustration:

- Activate the Relative option.

- Choose Inches from the units menus and type a value of **1.2** for both the Width and Height of the border.

- Leave the Anchor control at the default centered setting.

6 Click the small color swatch beside the Canvas Extension Color menu.

7 A color picker appears and the pointer becomes an eye-dropper cursor when you move it over the image. Sample a rich moss green from one of the brighter areas on the second girl's top. If you can't pick up exactly the color you want with the eye-dropper, try dragging the circular indicator in the large color field in the color picker, or type new values for Hue (H), Saturation (S), and Brightness (B). The Brightness value should not be above about 45% or the color will compete with both the photo and the text you'll place in the next exercise.

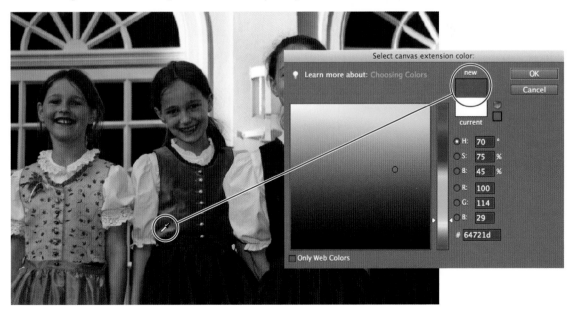

8 Click OK to close the Color Picker and again to close the Canvas Size dialog box. The new colored border appears around the photo in the image window.

9 Now you'll extend the border below the image to create a space for the text message. Choose Image > Resize > Canvas Size.

10 In the Canvas Size dialog box, confirm that the Relative check box is still activated. Leave the Width value at **0** and set the Height to **2 inches**. In the Anchor control diagram, click the center square in the top row. Leave the Canvas Extension Color setting unchanged and click OK.

Canvas Size

Learn more about: Canvas Size   OK   Cancel

Current Size: 4.27M
Width: 20.833 inches
Height: 13.833 inches

New Size: 4.91M
Width: 0   inches
Height: 2   inches
☑ Relative
Anchor:

Canvas extension color: Other...

11 If you can't see all of the border framing the image, double-click the Hand tool or choose View > Fit On Screen.

Adding a quick border

When precision isn't an issue, you can quickly add a border to an image by using the Crop tool, rather than increasing the size of the canvas.

1 Zoom out far enough so that you can see some of the blank art-board surrounding the image in the edit window.

2 Use the crop tool to drag a cropping rectangle right around the image.

3 Drag the corner handles of the crop marquee outside the image area onto the art-board to define the size and shape of border that you wish to create.

4 When you're satisfied, click the Commit button in the lower right corner of the image. The canvas expands to fill the cropping rectangle, taking on the background color set in the color swatch at the bottom of the toolbox.

Adding a text layer

With the Type tools you can place editable type anywhere on your image.

1 In the toolbox, select the Horizontal Type tool (**T**).

2 Set up the tool options bar as shown in the illustration below. Choose Myriad Pro from the Font Family menu and Bold from the Font Style menu. In the Font Size text box, type **80** pt and then press Enter / Return in your keyboard. Choose Center Text (▤) from the paragraph alignment options. Click the small white triangle beside the color swatch—not the swatch itself—and select white as the text color.

● **Note:** Photoshop Elements includes several variants of the Type tool. Throughout the remainder of this lesson, the term Type tool will always refer to the Horizontal Type tool, which is the default variant.

3 Click inside the extended border area below the photo to set the text input cursor, and then type **GREETINGS FROM BAVARIA!** in uppercase. Click the Commit button (✔) in the tool options bar to accept the text. Don't worry about the positioning of the text—you'll adjust that later.

In the Layers panel the image now has two layers: a locked Background layer containing the image and a text layer containing your greeting. Most of the text layer is transparent, so only the text itself interrupts your view of the Background layer.

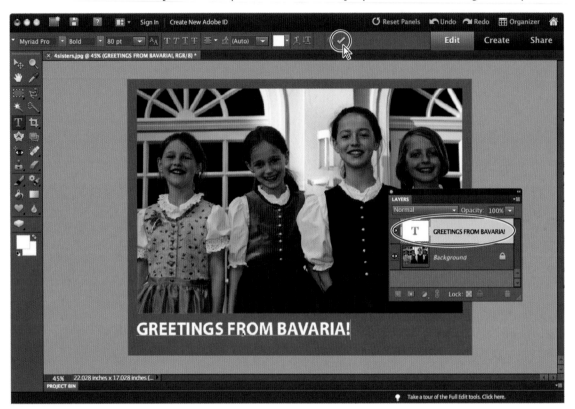

When you use the Type tool, Photoshop Elements automatically creates a new text layer in your image. The type you enter remains active on the text layer, just like type in a word processing document—you can edit its content, scale it, reposition it, or change its color at any time.

4 Make sure the text layer is still selected in the Layers panel, and then select the Move tool (▶₊) in the toolbox.

5 Place the cursor inside the text box and drag to position it so that the message is aligned with the left edge of the photo, and roughly the same distance from the lower edge of the border as it is from the left edge.

6 With the move tool, drag the handle on the upper right corner of the text box to scale the text so that the right side is aligned with the right edge of the photo.

▶ **Tip:** Don't press the Enter or Return keys on the main part of your keyboard to accept text changes. When you have active text in your file, these keys add a line break in the text. Click the Commit button in the tool options bar to accept the text or press the Enter key in the numeric keypad section of your keyboard.

You don't need to hold down the Shift key as you drag; the text will be scaled proportionally by default.

7   If necessary, drag the text to adjust its position or use the arrow keys on your keyboard to nudge it into place; then click Commit button (✔) on the text object bounding box.

Editing a text layer

Adding vector-based text is a nondestructive process; your original image is not overwritten by the text. If you save your file in native Photoshop (PSD) format with layers enabled, you can reopen it and still move, edit, or delete the text layer without affecting the image.

Using the Type tool is much like typing in a word processing application. If you want to edit the message, select the text and type over it. To change the typeface, font style, size or text color, select the characters you want to change and adjust the settings in the tool options bar accordingly.

1   If necessary, choose View > Zoom In to enlarge the image until you can comfortably read the text you added in the previous exercise.

2   Confirm that the text layer GREETINGS FROM BAVARIA! is still selected in the Layers panel and select the Type tool again.

Now you'll change the text color for just part of the message.

Tip: If you need to correct any typing errors or make other changes to text, remember that using the Type tool is like working in a word processing application. Click once to place the insertion point within the text. Use the arrow keys to move the text cursor forward or back. Drag to select multiple characters. Type to add text or to overwrite selected characters. Press the Backspace or Delete key to erase characters. Click the Commit button in the tool options bar to accept any changes.

3   Swipe to select just the word "GREETINGS" or simply double-click the word, and then click the Text Color swatch in the tool options bar to open the Color Picker. Sample the color from the sunlit yellow wall in the background.

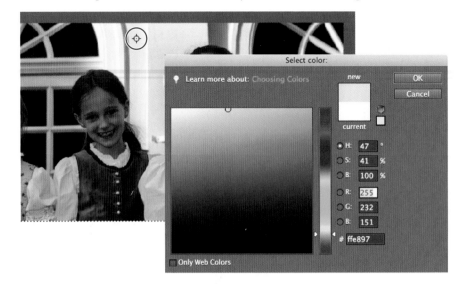

4   Click the radio button beside the Saturation (S) value in the Color Picker to activate the Saturation controls. The sampled color is a little weak for the background green, so you can use the slider to increase the Saturation to 60%, and then click OK.

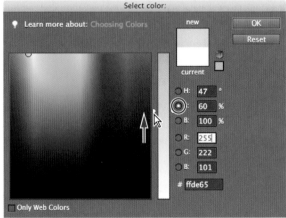

5   Click the Commit button (✓) in the tool options bar.

6   Swipe to select the exclamation mark (!) at the end of the message, and then click the Text Color swatch in the tool options bar to open the Color Picker. With the eyedropper cursor, sample the color from the word "GREETINGS."

7   Click OK, and then click the Commit button in the tool options bar.

GREETINGS **FROM BAVARIA!**

Saving a work file with layers

You can save your work file complete with layers so you can return to edit it later. As long as you save your work in the right format and enable layers, your text and adjustment layers remain "live" and editable.

1   Choose File > Save.

2   In the Save As dialog box, navigate to your My CIB Work folder and choose Photoshop (PSD) as the file format. Under Save Options, confirm that the option Layers is activated. Activate the option Include In The Organizer and disable Save In Version Set With Original.

3   Name the new file **4sisters_card_work**, and then click Save.

4   If the Photoshop Elements Format Options dialog box appears, keep Maximize Compatibility selected and click OK.

5   Choose File > Close.

Bravo, you've finished your first text project. In this section, you've formatted and edited text, and worked with a text layer. You've also created a photo border by increasing the canvas size without enlarging the image itself and gained experience with using the color picker.

Distinguishing between pixel-based and vector graphics

Computer graphics can be divided into two types: pixel-based images (otherwise called bit-mapped, or raster images), which are primarily created by cameras and scanners, and vector images—graphics constructed with drawing programs.

Pixel-based images such as photos are made up of pixels that you can detect when you zoom in. To produce a medium quality print of a photo, you need to make sure that the file is at least 250 ppi (pixels per inch). For viewing on screen, 72 ppi is fine.

Vector images consist of artwork formed from paths, like a technical line drawing. Vectors may form the outlines of an illustration, a logo, or type. The big advantage of vector images over pixel-based images is that they can be enlarged or reduced by any factor without losing detail. Live type on a text layer has this advantage.

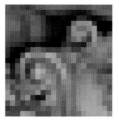

Pixel-based image   Vector type   Rasterized type

Overlaying text on an image

In the last exercise, you preserved the layering of your work file by saving in a file format that supports layers. This gives you the flexibility to make changes to the images, text, and effects even after the file has been saved, without needing to rebuild the image from the beginning or modify the original. Your layers have kept the text and effects separate from the image itself.

In this project, you'll do what many professional photographers and studios sometimes do to protect proprietary images: stamp a copyright notice over the photos. You'll apply a style to a text layer so that it appears as if the type is set in clear glass overlaid on the images.

Creating a new document for the text

Your first task for this project is to prepare the text in its own file.

1 If you're not already in the Editor in Full Edit mode from the previous exercise, switch to it now by clicking the arrow on the Fix tab above the Task Pane and choosing Full Photo Edit.

2 In the Editor, either choose Window > Reset Panels or click the Reset Panels button (![icon]) at the top of the workspace.

3 Choose File > New > Blank File. In the New dialog box, name the file **Overlay**. From the units menu to the right of the Width text box, choose Pixels. Type **600** for both the Width and Height values.

4 Set the file Resolution to **72** pixels/inch, the Color Mode to RGB Color, and the Background Contents to Transparent; then, click OK.

The image window should show only a checkerboard pattern, representing the background transparency you specified when you created the file. This pattern indicates 100% transparency; the layer will act like a pane of clear glass onto which you can place text or graphics.

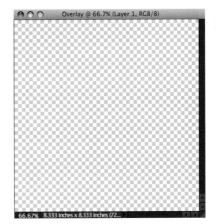

If you don't see the checkerboard pattern, close the new file without saving, and then repeat the last two steps, being careful to select Transparent from the Background Contents menu.

If you still don't see a checkerboard pattern, check your preferences. Choose Preferences > Transparency from the Edit menu on Windows / Photoshop Elements menu on Mac OS. From the Grid Size menu, choose any of the options other than None, and then click OK to close the Preferences dialog box.

5 Select the Type tool (T), and then set up the tool options bar as shown in the illustration below. Choose Arial from the Font Family menu, and Bold from the Font Style menu. Type **120** pt in the Font Size box; then, press Enter / Return. Choose Center Text (⊟) from the paragraph alignment options. Click the triangle beside the color swatch—not the swatch itself—and choose black as the text color. Make sure that Leading (to the left of the color swatch) is set to Auto.

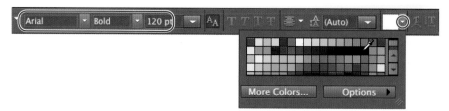

6 Click near the center of the image window and type **copyright** ; then press Enter / Return and type **2011**. Click the green Commit button (✓) in the tool options bar to accept the text you typed.

● **Note:** You can scale or reshape the text by dragging the handles on the bounding box with the Move tool. Because Photoshop Elements treats text as vector shapes, the letter shapes remain smooth even if you enlarge the text. If you tried this with bit-mapped text, you'd see jagged, stair-step edges in the enlarged text.

7 Select the Move tool (►₊) in the toolbox and click one of the corner handles of the text bounding box. In the tool options bar, make sure that the option Constrain Proportions is activated, and then type 85% in either the Width (W) or Height (H) text box.

8 With the Move tool still selected, move the pointer outside a corner of the text bounding box. When the pointer changes to the curved double-arrow rotate cursor, drag the text counter-clockwise to rotate it around its center by 45°. Hold down the Shift key as you drag to constrain the rotation to 15° increments.

9 Drag the text to the lower right of the square image as shown in the illustration below, and then click the Commit button at the edge of the bounding box.

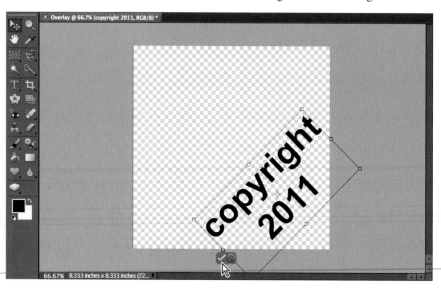

Applying a Layer Style to a text layer

Next, you'll apply an effect to your text by adding a Layer Style. Layer Styles are preset combinations of several adjustments that can be applied to your text layer in one easy action. Photoshop Elements gives you a wide variety of choices, from bevels and drop shadows to imaginative chrome and neon effects.

1 Make sure the text layer is still selected. At the top of the Effects panel in the Panel Bin, click the Layer Styles button (🖳), and then open the menu to the right to see the available effects categories. For this exercise, you'll use one of the effects from the Wow Plastic category.

2 In the top row of the Effects panel, select the Wow-Plastic Clear effect and click Apply. You could also apply the effect to the selected text layer by double-clicking the swatch, or simply dragging it directly onto your text.

When you apply a Layer Style to a text layer, both the text and the effect remain editable. You could go back and edit the text without affecting the layer style, or edit, replace, or remove the effect without affecting your ability to edit the text.

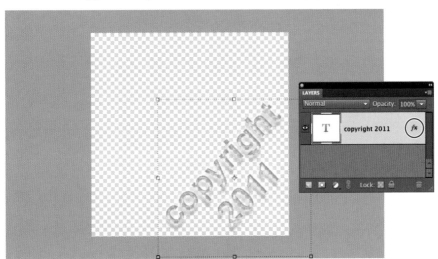

In the Layers panel, a layer to which a layer style effect has been applied can be identified by the *fx* icon. Double-clicking the *fx* icon will open the Style Settings dialog box, where you can modify each of the preset components that contribute to that effect.

3 Choose File > Save and save the file to your My CIB Work folder in Photoshop (PSD) format, making sure you activate the Layers option. Make sure that the file will be included in the Organizer, but not in a Version Set; then, click Save. If the Photoshop Elements Format Options dialog box appears, keep Maximize Compatibility selected, and then click OK, keeping the file open.

4 Choose Preferences > General from the Edit / Photoshop Elements menu. Activate Allow Floating Documents In Full Edit Mode, and then click OK.

Locating the lesson files

Now that you've prepared the copyright text, you'll place it onto a series of images. Once again, you can use a text search to find the files you want.

1 Switch to the Organizer by clicking the Organizer button (⬛) at the top right of the Editor work-space, leaving your Overlay file open.

2 In the Organizer, click the Show All button in the Find bar, and then type the word **paint** in the Text Search box above the Media Browser.

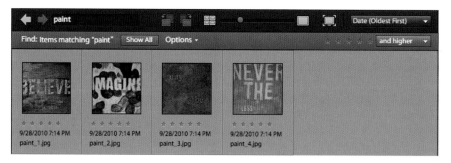

3 The Media Browser displays four images: paint_1.jpg to paint_4.jpg: photographs of paintings. Select all four images, and then click the small arrow on the Fix tab above the Task Pane and choose Full Photo Edit.

Adding the same text to multiple images

A great advantage of having your text on its own layer is that it can be copied from one image to another, complete with any layer style that has been applied.

1 Make sure you have the Project Bin open. Collapse the grouped Effects and Content panels by double-clicking the group's header bar.

2 Click the Arrange button (⬛) at the top of the workspace and choose the last of the "5 Up" layouts—the second layout in the last row.

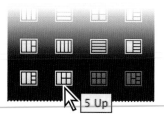

3 Click the name tab of any of the paintings to make it the active window. Press Ctrl+– (minus sign) / Command+– (minus sign) repeatedly to zoom out until you can see the entire image. Choose Window > Images > Match Zoom. The view in all of the open image windows is matched to the active image.

4 Watch the Layers panel as you double-click each of the thumbnail images in the Project Bin in turn; each has a single layer named "Background."

5 Make Overlay.psd the active image; then hold down the Shift key and drag the text layer from the Layers panel onto the image paint_1.jpg.

● **Note:** Holding down the Shift key as you drag a text layer to another file ensures that the text will appear in the same position in the target file as it occupies in the source.

6 To make the new text layer more transparent, reduce its opacity to 45%, either by typing **45** into the Opacity value box, or by dragging the slider to the left.

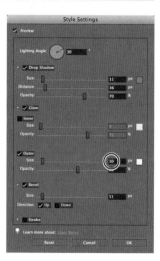

7 Make sure that the image paint_1.jpg is still the active file. In the Layers panel, double-click the *fx* icon on the text layer.

8 Under Glow in the Style Settings dialog box, change the size of the Outer Glow from 22 pixels to 10 pixels. Click OK to close the Style Settings dialog box.

9 Hold down the Shift key and drag the text layer with its refined layer style from the image paint_1.jpg onto the other three images.

10 The text message is more visible on the files paint_3.jpg and paint_4.jpg. In both these cases, you can decrease the opacity of the text layer to 35%.

Working with layer blending modes

1 Experiment with the text layer's opacity for the image paint_2.jpg. This file is far more problematic; an opacity value high enough to make the whole copyright message visible produces too strong an effect over the lighter areas. You'll need to apply a different technique.

2 Increase the layer opacity to 100%, and then choose Layer > Simplify Layer. Note the change in the Layers panel: the text layer thumbnail has been replaced by a standard image thumbnail with large areas of transparency and the *fx* icon has disappeared.

The text and its layer style have been merged into a bit-mapped image. While the text was still "live" it was resolution independent—but if you enlarged the content of the layer now you would see jagged, pixelated edges.

You can no longer edit the message with the Text tool, and the layer style can no longer be modified; however, simplifying the layer has made it possible to change its blending mode.

3 In the Layers panel, set the blending mode for the copyright 2011 layer to Hard Light. Even at 100% opacity, the effect is still a little vague. Set the Opacity value to 65%, and then choose Layer > Duplicate Layer. Voilà—130%!

4 Choose File > Close All. If you wish, you can save your efforts to your My CIB Work folder. If you do save the files, be sure to activate the Layers option for the Photoshop (PSD) format so that the layers in the files are preserved.

Done! In this project, you've created a new document to set up and store a live text layer, applied a Layer Style from the Effects panel, and copied layers between image files. You've also gained a little more experience with blending modes.

About type

A font is a collection of characters—letters, numerals, punctuation marks, and symbols—in a particular typeface, which share design characteristics such as size, weight, and style. A typeface family is a collection of similar fonts designed to be used together. One example is the Myriad typeface family, which is a collection of fonts in a number of styles including Regular, Bold, Italic, Condensed and other variations. Other typeface families might consist of different font style variations.

Font family	
Myriad Pro	Times New Roman
Font style	
Regular, **Bold**, *Italic*, Condensed	Regular, **Bold**, *Italic*

Traditionally, font sizes are measured in points, but can also be specified in millimeters or inches, as with large lettering on signs, for example. The most common formats for computer fonts are Type 1 PostScript, TrueType, and OpenType.

Each font conveys a feeling or mood. Some are playful or amusing, some are serious and businesslike, while others might convey an impression of elegance and sophistication. To get a feel for which typeface best suits your project, it's a good idea to try out several fonts. One way to find out more about type is to go to www.adobe.com/type. Adobe Type offers more than 2,200 fonts from the world's leading type designers, which you can browse by categories such as style, use, theme, classification, and designer. This will make it easy to find the perfect font for any assignment. You can even type in your sample copy and compare different fonts.

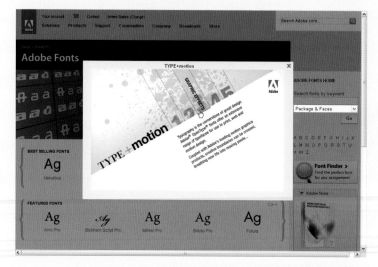

Using Layer styles and distortions

In this exercise you'll have more fun with text. You'll distort text and apply effects, all the while keeping the text layer live and editable.

Locating the lesson image

1 If you're still in the Editor from the last exercise, switch to the Organizer now by clicking the Organizer button (⊞) at the top right of the Editor workspace.

2 In the Organizer, click the Show All button in the Find bar, and then type the word **any** in the Text Search box at the left of the bar above the Media Browser.

The Media Browser displays a single image: anything.jpg, a cropped photograph of raindrops on a car window.

3 Click to select the image anything.jpg in the Media Browser, and then choose Edit > Edit With Photoshop Elements.

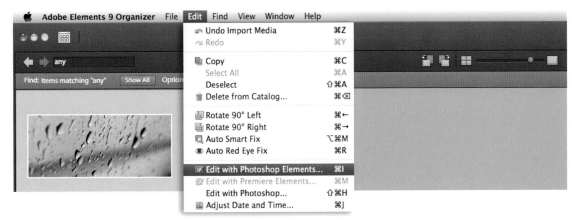

Adding a layer style

In the first exercise, you'll place some text, and then add a layer style that will give the letters a three-dimensional look to integrate them with the background image.

1   In the Editor, either choose Window > Reset Panels or click the Reset Panels button ( ) at the top of the workspace.

2   Choose Window > Images > Consolidate All To Tabs. Alternatively, drag the title bar of the image window to the top of the Edit pane and release the mouse button when the image dims and a blue line appears around the Edit pane.

3   Select the Type tool ( ) from the toolbox, and then set up the tool options bar as shown in the illustration below:

  •   From the Font Family menu, choose a bold sans-serif style such as Impact (as an alternative, you could choose Arial Black).

  •   Type **220** pt in the Font Size box; then, press Enter / Return.

  •   Choose Center Text ( ) from the paragraph alignment options.

  •   Click the triangle beside the color swatch (not the swatch itself) and choose Pastel Green Cyan for the text color.

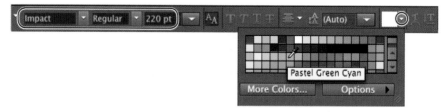

4   Using the Horizontal Type tool, click a little below the center of the image and type the word **anything** in lower case.

5   Click the Commit button ( ) in the tool options bar to accept the text.

6   Choose the Move tool ( ) in the toolbox and drag the text to center it as shown in the illustration below.

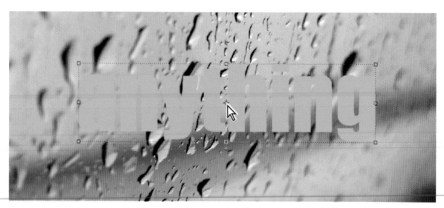

7 In the Effects panel, click the Layer Styles button (), and then choose the category Glass Buttons from the effects categories menu to the right. Double-click the fourth effect in the third row: Translucent Glass.

The Translucent Glass style, like all the Effects panel presets, is made up of a combination of image adjustments that are all applied to the image at once. The effect, in this case a Layer Style, remains "live" and editable. You can change the settings for each of the component adjustments to fine-tune the layer style.

8 In the Layers panel, double-click the *fx* icon on the text layer to open the Style Settings dialog box. Set the style controls as you see in the illustration below:

- Drag the Lighting Angle wheel or type in the text box to set an angle of **–30°**.

- Click the Inner Glow color swatch to open the color picker. Type a value of **0** in the text boxes for Hue (H), Saturation (S), and Brightness (B); then, click OK to close the color picker.

- Set the Size for the Inner Glow to **25 px**, and the Opacity to **100%**.

- Set the Bevel Size to **22 px**.

- Click OK to close the Style Settings.

9 In the Layers panel, change the opacity of the text layer to **65%**, either by typing the new value directly into the text box or by dragging the Opacity slider.

10 Choose File > Save As. Save the new file in Photoshop (PSD) format to your My CIB Work folder, making sure the Layers option is activated so that you can edit the type even after the file has been closed. Include the image in the Organizer, but not in a Version Set. Type the name **anything_text**, and then click Save.

Warping text

It's easy to stretch and skew text into unusual shapes using the Photoshop Elements Warp Text effects; the hard part is to avoid *over*using them!

1 Make sure the Type tool is active, and then click anywhere on the text "anything" in the image window.

It's not necessary to highlight the text because warp effects are automatically applied to the entire text layer.

2 In the tool options bar, click the Create Warped Text button (🍎) to open the Warp Text dialog box. Choose the Wave effect from the Style menu.

3 The Warp Text dialog offers a number of controls for changing the way the effect is applied. For this exercise you need only make one adjustment. Use the slider to set the Bend value to **−50**%, reversing the direction of the wave curve, and then click OK to close the Warp Text dialog box.

In the Layers panel, the text layer thumbnail now displays a Warped Text icon.

4 The text layer is still editable. To check this out, first click the text layer; then, double-click the text with the Type tool and type the word **interesting** over it.

5 Choose File > Save.

Simplifying layers

Many of the layer blending modes will not work for a layer with a live layer style. Various other editing operations are not possible for a live text layer. For example, although you can apply the Free Transform and Skew commands from the Image > Transform menu, the Distort and Perspective commands in that menu are dimmed. Painting tools and Enhance menu commands are also disabled for live text.

Before you can perform some of these operations, you must first simplify the text; for others you'll need to simplify the layer style as well. When you simplify vector text it is converted to a bitmap image that cannot be edited with the Text tool.

> ▶ **Tip:** If you need to refresh your understanding of vector and bit-mapped graphics, please review the notes on page 322.

If you simplify the text together with its layer style, they are merged into a single bit-mapped layer and can no longer be modified separately.

When you want to experiment with any of these techniques, it's a good idea to use a copy of the text layer; that way, you'll be able to preserve your text and layer style settings in editable form.

1   In the Layers panel, make sure the text layer is still selected. Click the Options menu icon at the right of the panel's header bar to open the Layers panel Options menu. Choose Duplicate Layer. Click OK to accept the default name, "interesting copy."

2   Click the eye icon to the left of the original text layer to make the layer invisible in the image window.

3   Right-click / Control-click the *fx* icon on the "interesting copy" layer and choose Simplify Layer from the context menu.

The text layer thumbnail is replaced by a standard image thumbnail and the *fx* icon has disappeared. The text and its layer style have been merged into a bit-mapped image. Like the layer style, the 65% opacity setting has been applied permanently; although the text still appears partially transparent you can see that the layer opacity value is now 100%. In other words, the simplified layer is partially transparent even at its maximum opacity setting.

You can also invoke the Simplify Layer command from the Layer Menu. This will produce the same result that you observed in step 3.

4   Choose Edit > Undo Simplify Layer.

5   Right-click / Control-click the layer "interesting copy," avoiding both the *fx* icon and the layer thumbnail. Choose Simplify Layer from the context menu.

The text layer thumbnail is replaced by a standard image thumbnail, but this time the layer has retained the *fx* icon; the layer style is still live. Note that the simplified layer has also retained its opacity value of 65%.

Working with simplified text

Although the text is no longer live, the simplified layer can be edited just like any other image.

You should be careful, however, with any modification involving scaling. Unlike vector graphics, bit-mapped images are not resolution-independent; over-enlargement will result in a jagged, pixelated appearance.

In this exercise you'll add some finishing touches that will make your stylized text appear more convincingly part of the background image.

1   Make sure the simplified layer is still selected in the Layers panel; then, choose Image > Transform > Perspective.

2 Drag the handle at the lower left corner of the bounding box downwards, about half of the distance to the bottom edge of the image.

3 Drag the handle at the lower right corner of the bounding box a slightly shorter distance upwards.

4 Use the arrow keys on your keyboard to re-center the text, and then click the Commit button ( ) to accept the changes.

5 Select the Rectangular Marquee Tool and drag a selection marquee to surround the left third of the image. Hold down the Shift key and drag another marquee to add to the right third of the image to the selection.

6 Choose Select > Feather. In the Feather Selection dialog box, type a value of **50** pixels for the Feather Radius, and then click OK.

7 Choose Filter > Blur > Gaussian Blur. In the Gaussian Blur dialog box, set the blur radius to **2** pixels, and then click OK.

8 Choose Select > Deselect, or press Control+D / Command+D.

9 In the Layers panel, change the blending mode for the layer "interesting copy" to Soft Light, and increase the layer's opacity to **80%**.

The simplified text is now matched more closely to the tone, perspective, and focal depth of the background image.

10 Choose File > Save.

Working around transparency in a layer

Next, you'll use a painting tool to create a different look for the simplified text.

In preparation, you'll lock the transparent pixels on the layer, which will enable you to paint on the filled areas in the layer without the need to make a selection or be careful about painting over the edges.

1 Right-click / Control-click the layer "interesting copy" and choose Duplicate Layer from the context menu. Click OK in the Duplicate Layer dialog box to accept the default name for the new layer. Hide the layer "interesting copy" by clicking the eye icon beside the layer thumbnail.

2 Select the Pattern Stamp tool, which is grouped with the Clone Stamp tool. Set the tool options as shown below: brush Size: 100 px, brush Mode: Normal, Opacity: 100%. Click the Pattern swatch and choose the first pattern, Bubbles.

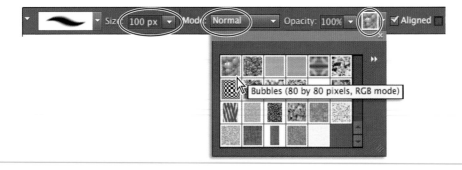

3   Make sure that the layer "interesting copy 2" is
    still active, and then click the Lock Transparent
    Pixels button at the bottom of the Layers panel
    to prevent changes being made to the transpar-
    ent areas of the simplified layer. A lock icon
    appears on the layer "interesting copy 2."

4   Right-click / Control-click the fx icon on the layer "interesting copy 2" and
    choose Clear Layer Style from the context menu. Change the layer blending
    mode to Normal, and increase the opacity to **100%**.

5   Make sure that the Pattern Stamp tool is still selected in the toolbox; then, paint
    over the text in the image window. The pattern is applied only to the simplified
    text; the locked transparent pixels remain unaffected.

Hiding, revealing, and deleting layers

Toggling the visibility of layers by clicking the eye icons in the Layers panel is a
great way to assess different design solutions within one file.

1   Click the eye icon beside the thumbnail for the layer "interesting copy 2" to hide
    the layer. The eye icon is hidden also, leaving an empty box to indicate that the
    layer is not visible. Note that although the layer is selected, the Blending Mode
    and Opacity options are dimmed and unavailable; you can't edit a hidden layer.

2   In the Layers panel, click the empty box to the left of the text layer "interesting."
    The eye icon reappears and your live, warped text with its translucent glass
    effect is once more visible in the image window.

You can now delete the layer with the bubbles pattern, leaving just the Background
layer with the original image, the live text layer, and your refined simplified layer.
Deleting layers that you no longer need reduces the size of your image file.

Tip: To delete more than one layer at once, Ctrl-click / Command-click to select the layers you wish to delete and right-click / Control-click any of them. You can also delete selected layers by choosing Layer > Delete Layer, or by simply dragging them to the Trash icon at the bottom of the Layers panel.

3   To delete the layer "interesting copy 2," right-click / Control-click the layer and choose Delete Layer from the context menu. Click Yes to confirm the deletion.

4   Select the original text layer, "interesting." Right-click / Control-click the layer and choose Clear Layer Style from the context menu. Alternatively, choose the same command from the Layer menu or the Layers panel Options menu.

The type in the text layer no longer has the three-dimensional translucent glass look, but it's still warped.

5   Select the Type tool. Drag across the text in the image window to select it, and then click the Create Warped Text button (⊥) in the tool option bar to open the Warp Text dialog box. Choose None from the Style menu, and then click OK to close the Warp Text dialog box.

6   Hide the layer "interesting" and reveal the layer "interesting copy;" then, choose File > Save and close the file.

In this project, you've applied a Layer Style to live text; then, warped it and painted it with little blue bubbles. You should be ashamed of yourself! You've also gained a lot more experience in working with layers. You learned how to protect transparent pixels on a layer, how to edit and clear layer styles and warp effects, and how to hide, reveal or delete a layer.

Working with paragraph type

With point type, or headline type, each line of type is independent—the line expands or shrinks as you edit it, but it doesn't automatically wrap to the next line. Point type (the name derives from the fact that it is preceded by a single anchor point) is perfect for small blocks of text like headlines, logos, and headings for Web pages. Probably most of the text you add to your images will be of this type.

If you work with larger blocks of type and you want your text to reflow and wrap automatically, it's best to use the paragraph type mode. By clicking and dragging with the type tool you'll create a text bounding box on your image. The bounding box can be easily resized to fit your paragraph text perfectly.

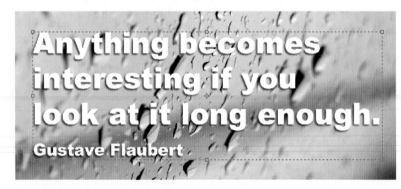

Creating a type mask

You can have a lot of fun with the Type Mask tool. Photoshop Elements offers two variants—one for horizontal type and the other for vertical type. The Type Mask tool turns text outlines into a mask through which an underlying image is visible.

Locating the lesson image

1 If you're still in the Editor from the last exercise, switch to the Organizer now by clicking the Organizer button (▦) at the top right of the Editor workspace.

2 In the Organizer, click the Show All button in the Find bar, and then type the word **run** in the Text Search box, at the left of the bar above the Media Browser.

3 The Media Browser displays a single image: runners.jpg, a photo of competitors in a marathon. Click to select the image in the Media Browser; then, click the arrow on the Fix tab above the Task Pane and choose Full Photo Edit.

Working with the Type Mask tool

The Type Mask tool (🔳) enables you to fill letter shapes with parts of an image. This can create a much more interesting graphic effect than plain text filled with a solid color.

1 In the Editor, either choose Window > Reset Panels or click the Reset Panels button (🔄) at the top of the workspace.

2 Choose Window > Images > Consolidate All To Tabs. Alternatively, drag the title bar of the image window to the top of the Edit pane and release the mouse button when the image dims and a blue line appears around the Edit pane.

3   Drag the Layers and Effects panels out of the Panels Bin by their name tabs and position them at the bottom of the workspace where they won't block your view of the image. Hide the Panels Bin by un-checking its name in the Window menu, and then double-click the Hand tool or choose View > Fit On Screen.

4   Select the Horizontal Type Mask tool (𝕋) which you'll find grouped with the other type tools in the tool box.

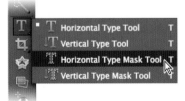

5   Set up the text attributes in the tool options bar:

- Choose a font from the Font Family menu. We chose Mercurius CT Std, Black Italic, but if you don't have that font, choose any typeface that's blocky enough to let plenty of the image show through the letter forms.

- Type a new value of **950** pt for the font Size (you may need to adjust that for a different font).

- Choose Center Text (▤) from the paragraph alignment options.

- You don't need to worry about a color for the text; the type will be filled with detail from our marathon image.

6 Click at a horizontally centered point low in the image and type **RUN!**

7 Hold down the Ctrl / Command key on your keyboard; a bounding box surrounds the text in the image window. Drag inside the bounding box to reposition the type mask.

8 If you wish to resize the text, hold down the Ctrl / Command key and drag a corner handle of the bounding box. The operation is automatically constrained so that the text is scaled proportionally. Alternatively, you can double-click the text with the Type Mask tool to select it, and then type a new font size in the tool options bar.

9 When you're satisfied with the result, click the green Commit button in the tool options bar. The outline of the text becomes an active selection. If you're not happy with the placement of the selection, use the arrow keys on your keyboard to nudge it into place.

10 Choose Edit > Copy, and then Edit > Paste. In the Layers panel, you can see that the cutout type image has been placed onto a new layer, surrounded by transparency.

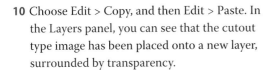

11 Hide the Background layer by clicking the eye icon beside the layer thumbnail.

Adding impact to a type mask

The text is no longer live—the mask was converted to a selection outline, so it can no longer be edited with a text tool; however, you can still apply a layer style or an effect to enhance it or make it more prominent.

1 If necessary, select Layer 1 in the Layers panel to make it the active layer.

2 Select the Move tool (🕂) and drag the cut-out type to center it in the image window; then, press the up arrow and right arrow keys eight times each.

3 Expand the Effects panel, if necessary, and click the Layer Styles button (▤). Choose the effects category Drop Shadows from the menu.

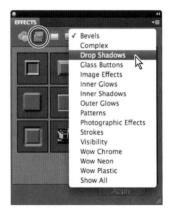

4 In the Drop Shadows panel, double-click the drop-shadow effect named High: the third effect swatch in the first row.

5 In the Layers panel, select the Background Layer; then, choose Image > Rotate > Flip Layer Horizontal. Click OK to confirm the conversion of the background, and then click OK to accept the default name.

6 Choose Enhance > Adjust Color > Adjust Hue/Saturation. In the Hue/Saturation dialog box, reduce the Saturation value to –60 and increase the Lightness to +60; then, click OK.

7 In the Layers panel, select the layer with the cut-out type; then, double-click the *fx* icon. In the Style Settings dialog box, set the Lighting Angle to 45°. Increase the Drop Shadow Size to 40 px, the Distance to 50 px, and the Opacity to 80%; then, click OK.

8 Choose File > Save As. In the Save As dialog box, choose Photoshop (PSD) as the file format, enable layers, and save the file to your My CIB Work folder. Make sure that the new file will be included in the Organizer, but not in a Version Set; then, name the file **runners_mask** and click Save. Close the file.

Congratulations! You've completed another lesson. You've learned how to format and edit text, and how to work with a text layer. You've created a photo border by working with the document canvas, used the Effects panel to apply Layer Styles, warped and painted text, and created a text mask. You learned about locking transparent pixels on a layer and how to edit and clear layer styles and text effects. You also learned how to hide, reveal and delete a layer. Take a few moments to work through the lesson review on the next page before you move on.

Review questions

1 What is the advantage of having your text on a separate layer?

2 How do you hide a layer without removing it?

3 In the Layers panel, what do the lock buttons do and how do they work?

4 What's the difference between point type and paragraph type?

Review answers

1 Because the text remains separate from the image, Photoshop Elements text layers remain "live"—text can be edited in later work sessions, just as it can in a word processing application.

2 You can hide a layer by clicking the eye icon to the left of the layer's name in the Layers panel. To make the layer visible again, click the empty box where the eye icon should be to restore it.

3 Lock buttons prevent changes to a layer. The Lock All button, which looks like a padlock, locks all the pixels on the selected layer so that the layer is protected from changes. Blending and Opacity options become unavailable. The Lock Transparent Pixels button, which looks like a checkerboard, locks only the transparent pixels on a layer. To remove a lock, select the locked layer and click the active lock icon to toggle it off. (This does not work for the Background layer, which can be unlocked only by renaming and converting it into an ordinary layer.)

4 Point type is ideal for headlines, logos and other small blocks of text where each line is independent and does not wrap to the next line. Paragraph text is used where you want larger amounts of text to wrap automatically to the next line. The size of the paragraph text bounding box can be easily changed to fit the text perfectly to your design.

11

COMBINING MULTIPLE IMAGES

Lesson overview

Although you can do a lot to improve a photo with tonal adjustments, color corrections and retouching, sometimes the best way to produce the perfect image is simply to fake it!

Photoshop Elements delivers powerful tools that will enable you to do just that by combining multiple images. Merge ordinary scenic photos into stunning panoramas that truly recapture the feel of the location or combine a series of shots to produce the perfect group photo where everybody is smiling and there are no closed eyes. Deal with difficult lighting conditions by blending differently exposed pictures.

In this lesson you'll learn some of the tricks you'll need for combining multiple images to create that perfect shot that you didn't actually get:

- Merging multiple photos into a panorama
- Assembling the perfect group shot
- Removing unwanted elements
- Blending differently exposed photographs
- Combining images using layers
- Resizing and repositioning selections
- Creating a gradient clipping mask
- Defringing a selection

You'll probably need between one and two hours to complete this lesson.

If you're ready to go beyond fixing pictures in conventional ways, this lesson is for you. Why settle for that scenic photo that just doesn't capture the way it really looked? Or that group portrait where Dad's looking away and Mom's eyes are closed? Combine images to produce the perfect shot. Merge photos to make a stunning panorama, remove obstructions from the view, and even get little Jimmy to stop making faces.

Getting started

Before you start working on the exercises in this lesson, make sure that you have installed the software on your computer from the application CD (see the Photoshop Elements 9 documentation) and that you have correctly copied the Lessons folder from the CD in the back of this book onto your computer's hard disk. (See "Copying the Classroom in a Book files" on page 2.)

This lesson assumes that you are already familiar with the main features of the Photoshop Elements workspace. Should you need to brush up on the basic concepts review "Getting Started" and "A Quick Tour of Photoshop Elements" at the start of this book, or refer to Photoshop Elements Help.

While you're working on the projects in this lesson, you'll use sample images from the CIB Catalog that you created in the "Getting Started" section at the beginning of this book:

1 Start Photoshop Elements and click the Organize button in the Welcome screen. Check the name of the currently loaded catalog displayed in the lower left corner of the Organizer workspace. If your CIB Catalog is not already loaded, choose File > Catalog and select it from the list in the Catalog Manager.

2 Choose File > Get Photos And Video > From Files And Folders. In the Get Photos And Videos From Files And Folders dialog box, locate and open your Lessons folder.

3 Select the Lesson11 folder. Disable the option Get Photos From Subfolders and any automatic processing option that is currently active, and then click Get Media. In the Import Attached Keyword Tags dialog box, click Select All, and then click OK.

4 Click the Show All button in the Find bar. In the Keyword Tags panel, expand the Imported Keyword Tags category, and then click the find box beside the Lesson 11 tag to isolate the images for the projects in this lesson.

5 If you don't see filenames below the thumbnails in the Media Browser, choose View > Show File Names.

Merging photos into a panorama

The images you'll use for this first exercise are four slightly overlapping photos of the German city of Dresden, taken from across the river Elbe. The lens used for these shots did not have a wide enough angle to capture the entire scene—a common problem for many of us when taking photos at a scenic location. These photos provide an ideal opportunity to create a panorama; in the following exercises you'll learn how to have Photoshop Elements do most of the work for you.

Although it is possible to start the Photomerge Panorama process from the Organizer, we'll switch to the Editor first, to set up the workspace.

1 In the Organizer, Ctrl-click / Command-click to select all four pictures of the Dresden skyline (11_01a.jpg through 11_01d.jpg) in the Media Browser, and then right-click / Control-click any of the selected thumbnails and choose Edit With Photoshop Elements from the context menu.

2 In the Editor, either choose Window > Reset Panels or click the Reset Panels button (⟳) at the top of the workspace. Drag the Layers panel out of the Panels Bin by its header bar, and then hide the Panels Bin by un-checking its name in the Window menu. Drag the lower right corner of the Layers panel to make it large enough to show four layers; then, position the panel at the lower left corner of the workspace.

3 Choose Window > Images > Consolidate All To Tabs, or click the Arrange button (⊞) at the top of the workspace, and then click the Consolidate All button at the upper left of the Arrange menu.

4 Choose File > New > Photomerge Panorama to open the Photomerge dialog box.

Setting up the Photomerge Panorama options

In the Photomerge dialog box you have the option to select individual source files or the entire contents of a specified folder, and a choice of layout methods that will affect the way the source images will be stitched together to create your panorama.

Photomerge Panorama layout options

Auto   Analyzes the source images and applies either a Perspective or Cylindrical layout, depending on which produces a better photomerge.

Perspective   Creates a consistent composition by designating one of the source images (by default, the middle image—or images, in this case) as a reference. The other images are then repositioned, stretched, or skewed as necessary, so that overlapping content is matched.

Cylindrical   Reduces the "bow-tie" distortion that can occur with the Perspective layout by displaying individual images as on an unfolded cylinder. Overlapping content is still matched. The reference image is placed at the center. This is best suited for creating wide panoramas.

Spherical   Aligns and transforms images as if mapped to the inside of a sphere. This is particularly effective for a set of images that cover 360 degrees, but can also produce great results in other cases. For our sample images, there is noticeable distortion in the horizontal line of the river-bank.

Collage   Aligns images and matches overlapping content by rotating and scaling the source photos.

Reposition   Aligns the images and matches overlapping content without scaling, skewing, or stretching any of the source photos. In our example, there has been a problem with matching the construction crane at the junction of the two photos on the right. You can often fix this kind of problem very easily with the Clone Stamp tool or the Spot Healing Brush.

Interactive Layout   A message will appear on screen when Photoshop Elements can't align photos automatically. This may happen when Photomerge can't identify specific detail to match, often in photos without man-made structures. You can then choose the Interactive Layout option to open the Photomerge dialog box where you'll find the tools you need to position the source images manually.

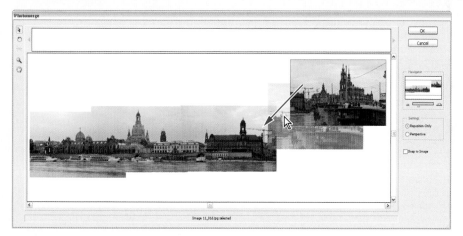

1 Under Layout, select Cylindrical.

2 Under Source Files in the Photomerge dialog box, select Files from the Use menu, and then click the Add Open Files button. The four images that you opened in the Editor appear in the source files list.

Tip: To add more files to the selection, click Browse. To remove a photo from the source list, select the file, and then click Remove. To add all the photos from a specific folder on your hard disk as source images for a panorama, select Folder from the Use menu, and then click Browse.

Note: If the Blend Images Together option is disabled, a simple rectangular blend is applied. You may prefer this if you intend to retouch the layer blending masks manually.

3 Make sure that the Blend Images Together option is activated below the source files list. This option calculates the optimal borders between overlapping photos, and also color-matches the images. Click OK.

4 Watch the Layers panel while Photoshop Elements creates a new file for the panorama, and places each source image on its own layer. Photomerge calculates the overlapping areas, adds a blending mask to each image layer accordingly, and then color-matches adjacent images as it blends the seams. When the Clean Edges dialog box appears, drag it aside so that you can see the edges of all the source images, and the checker-board transparency around them.

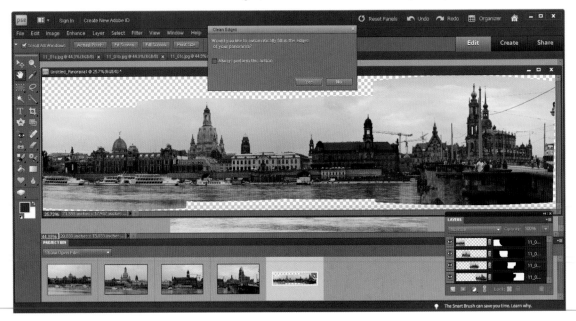

You can see that cropping away the transparency would interrupt the skyline and spoil the image. Photoshop Elements 9 can help you solve this problem, by using content-aware healing to fill the missing areas.

5   In the Clean Edges dialog box, click Yes. Photoshop Elements does a great job, although there are just a few areas in the image where the content-aware healing process has produced unwelcome artefacts.

6   Press Ctrl+Z / Command+Z. This will not undo the healing operation—only the last step in the process, the de-selection of the area that was filled. Use the Zoom and Hand tools to examine the extended image in detail; the re-instated selection will help you to look in the right places to spot the anomalies. When you're done, press Ctrl+D / Command+D, or choose Select > Deselect.

7   Use a few strokes with the Spot Healing Brush or the Clone Stamp to remove the unwelcome artefacts.

▶ **Tip:** If necessary, refer to "Removing unwanted objects from images" and "Using the Clone Stamp tool to fill in missing areas" in Lesson 9.

8   Choose File > Save. Name the file **Dresden_Panorama** and save it to your My CIB Work folder in Photoshop (PSD) format. Make sure that you enable layers, and include the file in the Organizer; then, click Save.

Now let's have a closer look at how well Photoshop Elements matched the overlapping areas between the source images. Depending on your source files, you may at times notice small problem areas—edge artifacts along the line where the images are blended. In these cases you can either try a different layout option for the photomerge operation, or retouch the layer blending masks manually.

9   In the Layers panel, click the eye icon (👁) beside the top layer (Layer 1, the panorama extended by the content-aware fill) to hide it. Use the Zoom tool and resize and scroll the image window, if necessary, to focus on the right half of the panorama. Hold down Alt+Shift / Option+Shift and click the layer mask thumbnail on the bottom layer.

In the edit window, the mask associated with this layer appears as a semi-transparent overlay, enabling you to see which part of the image in the lower layer has contributed to the panorama. The unused portion is hidden by the layer mask.

10 Click the image thumbnail for the bottom layer; then, Alt-click / Option-click the layer mask thumbnail.

The layer mask is displayed in opaque black and white; black represents masked portions of the layer and white represents areas that have contributed to the blend.

▶ **Tip:** If you were unhappy with any portion of the seam between images, you could alternate between these two views of the layer mask to adjust the blend by painting (or erasing) directly onto the mask. If you do this with a panorama extended by content-aware fill, you'll need to erase the corresponding area of the top layer, creating a "window" so that your changes to lower layers are visible.

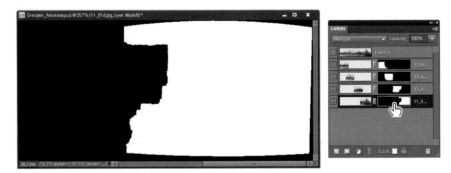

11 Use the same technique to inspect the blended seams between the other source layers. When you're done, make the top layer visible once more, choose File > Save, and then choose File > Close all. Stay in the Editor for the next exercise.

Creating a Photomerge Panorama interactively

The automatic layout options in the Photomerge dialog box usually do a good job, but if you need manual control over the way source images are combined to create a panorama, choose the Interactive Layout option in the Photomerge dialog box.

1 In Full Edit mode in the Editor, choose File > New > Photomerge Panorama.

2 In the Photomerge dialog box, select Folder from the Use menu, and then click Browse. In the Choose (A) Folder dialog box, navigate to your Lesson11 folder. Inside the Lesson11 folder, select the folder Panorama_2 and click OK / Choose.

3 Choose Interactive Layout from the Layout options. Make sure the option Blend Images Together is activated, and then click OK.

4 Explore the tools and controls in the Photomerge dialog box:

   • Use the Zoom tool (🔍) or the Navigator controls to zoom in or out of the image. Drag the red rectangle in the Navigator to shift the view in the zoomed image.

   • Switch between the Reposition Only and Perspective settings.

   • With the Perspective option activated, you can click any source image in the Photomerge workspace with the Set Vanishing Point tool (🔧) to set the vanishing point in that image as the reference around which the other images will be composed.

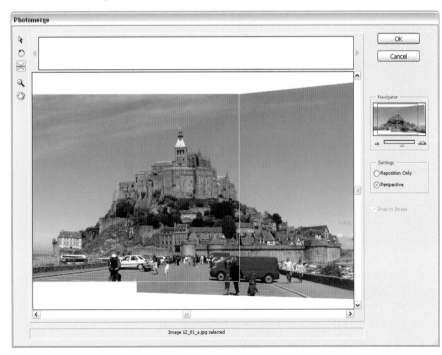

Note: If the composition can't be assembled automatically, a message will appear on screen. You can then assemble the panorama manually in the Photomerge dialog box by dragging images from the photo bin into the work area, and arranging them as you wish.

- Use the Select Image tool (![icon]) to select any of the photos in the work area; then drag the selected photo or use the arrow keys on the keyboard to reposition it as desired.

- To remove a photo from the composition (if you are using more than two source images), drag it from the work area into the photo bin above. To add an image to the composition, drag it from the photo bin into the work area.

- Use the Rotate Image tool (![icon]) to rotate a selected photo.

5 When you're satisfied with the result, click OK. The Photomerge dialog box closes, and Photoshop Elements goes to work. You'll see windows open and close as you wait for Photoshop Elements to create the panorama.

6 In the Clean Edges dialog box, click Yes. Photomerge Elements fills the areas outside the two source images using content-aware healing. For the sky, the result is very good, but—as might be expected—Photomerge has been unable to deal with the cyclist at the lower left. The image will need to be cropped.

Vanishing point

The vanishing point in an image is the point at which receding parallel lines seem to meet when seen in perspective. For example, as a road stretches out ahead of you, it appears to grow narrower with distance, until it has almost no width at the horizon. This is the vanishing point.

You can change the perspective of the Photomerge Panorama composition by specifying a different image to be used as reference for the vanishing point.

Select Perspective under Settings in the Photomerge dialog box, and then click an image with the Vanishing Point tool. Photoshop Elements analyzes the image and composes the Photomerge Panorama in reference to the vanishing point in that image.

Cropping the merged image

Now you'll use the Crop tool to trim the very few unsuccessfully extended areas from the image.

1   Choose View > Fit On Screen, and then choose Image > Crop. Drag the handles of the cropping rectangle to make it as large as possible without including the blur below the cyclist or any dark artefact you may see at the upper left; then, click the Commit button in the lower right corner of the cropping rectangle.

Note: The Crop tool removes those parts of an image that fall outside the adjustable cropping rectangle. Cropping can be very useful for changing the visual focus of a photo. When you crop an image, the resolution remains unchanged.

2   Choose File > Save. Name save the merged image **Panorama_2**, to be saved to your My CIB Work folder in Photoshop format with Layers activated. Make sure that the file will be included in the Organizer. Click Save, and then close the file.

Tip: Saving your file in Photoshop format enables you to preserve the layers, so that you can always return to adjust them if necessary. If you save in JPEG format the image will be flattened and layer information will be lost.

Creating a composite group shot

Shooting the perfect group photo is a difficult task, especially if you have a large family of squirmy kids. Fortunately, Photoshop Elements offers a solution: a powerful photo blending tool called Photomerge Group Shot. The next exercise will show you how multiple photos can be blended together into one with amazing precision.

Working with Photomerge Group Shot

No longer do you need to put up with family photos where someone has their eyes closed, someone else has looked away at the wrong moment, and you-know-who has just made an even odder facial expression than usual. Photomerge Group Shot lets you merge the best parts of several images into the perfect group photo.

Typically, you would use the Photomerge Group Shot feature to create a merged image from a series of very similar source images such as you might capture with your camera's burst mode, as was the case with the photos in this illustration.

For this exercise however, you'll work with just three distinctly different images to make it easier for you to learn the technique.

1 If you're still in the Editor from the last exercise, switch to the Organizer now by clicking the Organizer button (▦) at the top right of the Editor workspace.

2 In the Keyword Tags panel, click the Find box beside the Lesson 11 tag to isolate the sample files for this lesson, and then Ctrl-click / Command-click to select the images 11_02a.jpg, 11_02b.jpg and 11_02c.jpg.

3 Choose File > New > Photomerge Group Shot.

4 Photoshop Elements has automatically designated the first image as the source image. To replace it, click the second thumbnail in the Project Bin (11_02b.jpg). Drag the first thumbnail (11_02a.jpg) from the Project Bin and drop it into the Final image pane on the right.

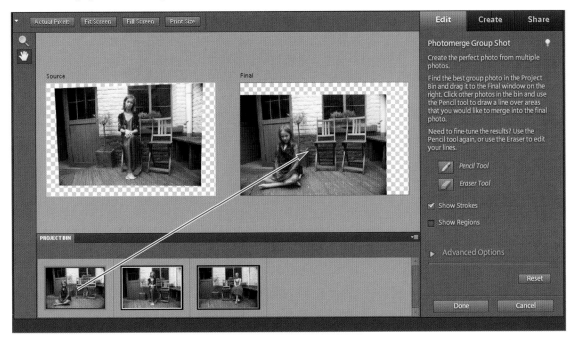

If you were composing a group shot from a series of similar photos, you would make the best image in the series the Final image, and then use each of the other photos as sources for those elements you would like to replace.

We chose the image 11_02a.jpg as the Final (target) image because it includes more of the wooden decking than the other photos. As the girl in the photo is sitting further forward than the girls on the chairs, it's preferable that we retain the decking around her rather than try to blend it to either of the other photos.

5 Use the Zoom and Hand tools to magnify and position the image so you can see all of the girl in the Source pane and at least part of the girl in the Final image.

6 In the Photomerge Group Shot panel at the right of the workspace, select the Pencil tool (✏). Make sure that the Show Strokes option is activated, and the Show Regions option is not.

With the Pencil tool you can quickly mark any area or object in the Source image that you wish to copy to the Final image; Photoshop Elements will do all the selecting, copying, pasting, and aligning for you!

7 With the Pencil tool (), draw one stroke in the Source image, from the top of the girl's head to the hem of her dress, as shown in the illustration below. Allow the edges of your stroke to just slightly overlap the window and wall behind the girl's head. Extend the end of the stroke just far enough onto the wooden decking to pick up the shadow of the light-colored fabric.

When you release the mouse button, Photoshop Elements merges the girl from the Source image into the Final image—including the shadow below her skirts!

Seeing the magic of this tool in action will probably cause you some healthy mistrust whenever you come across an unlikely photo in the future.

Click with the Pencil tool to add any part of the subject that was not copied from the source. Use the Eraser tool ( ) to delete part of a stroke drawn with the Pencil tool; the area copied to the Final image will be adjusted accordingly.

Sometimes it can be a little tricky to make the perfect selection—especially when you're working with a more complex source image than our example. You may find you are copying more of the source image than you want.

If you've switched several times between the Pencil and Eraser tools and you still can't get the selection right, click the Reset button below the Photomerge Group Shot controls and start again. Try modifying the shape that you're drawing with the Pencil tool, reducing the brush size, changing the direction of the stroke, or making shorter strokes.

8 Double-click the green framed image (11_02c.jpg) in the Project Bin to make it the Source image. Use the Zoom and Hand tools to move the Source image in its frame so you can see all of the girl in the pink dress; then, use the Pencil tool to add her to the Final image. Be sure to include the shadow below her left foot.

9 Double-click the Hand tool so that you can see the areas that are still missing from the Final image. With the Pencil tool, drag a line through the right side of the Source image as shown in the illustration below.

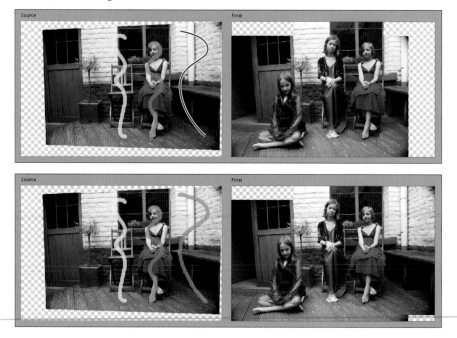

10 In the Project Bin, click the thumbnail with the yellow border to make it the source image once more; then, drag with the Pencil tool through the upper left corner of the image in the Source pane.

11 To see which part of each of the three source images was used for the merged composition, first click the Fit Screen button above the Edit pane so that you can see the entire image, and then activate the Show Regions option in the Photomerge Group Shot panel. The regions in the Final image are color coded to correspond to the borders of the thumbnails in the Project Bin.

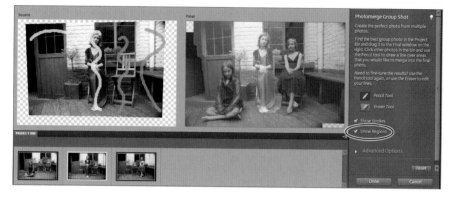

12 Select the Hand tool; then click the Actual Pixels button above the edit pane, or zoom in even closer, and use the Hand tool to position the image at a boundary between colored regions in the Final image.

13 Toggle Show Regions off and on while you look for imperfections along the region boundaries in the merged image. If necessary, use the Pencil and Eraser tools to add to or subtract from the portions of the source images that are being merged to the Final image. When you're satisfied with the result, click Done.

14 The merged image needs to be cropped slightly. Choose Image > Crop to place a cropping rectangle on the image, and then drag the handles of the cropping rectangle to trim off the empty corners of the photo.

15 Click the Commit button at the bottom right of the cropping rectangle; then, choose File > Save and save the merged image to your My CIB Work folder as **11_02_Composite**, in Photoshop (PSD) format. Make sure that the Layers option is activated and that the new file will be included in the Organizer. Click Save, and then choose File > Close All.

▶ Tip: The Photomerge Faces feature works similarly to the Photomerge Group Shot tool, except that it's specialized for working with faces. You can have a lot of fun merging different faces into one. Try merging parts of a picture of your own face with one of your spouse to predict the possible appearance of future offspring. Choose File > New > Photomerge Faces, or click the Faces button in the Photomerge panel In Guided Edit mode to create your own Frankenface.

Removing unwelcome intruders

The Photomerge Scene Cleaner helps you improve a photo by removing passing cars, tourists, and other unwanted elements. The Scene Cleaner works best when you have several shots of the same scene, so that you can combine the unobstructed areas from each source picture to produce a photograph free of traffic and tourists.

Using the Scene Cleaner

When you're sightseeing, it's a great idea to deliberately take a few extra shots of any busy scene so that later you can use the Photomerge Scene Cleaner to put together an uncluttered image.

It's not necessary to use a tripod; as long as your photos were shot from roughly the same viewpoint, Photoshop Elements will align the static content in the images automatically. An easy way to capture a series of images that will perform well with the Scene Cleaner is to stand in one position, frame up your shot, and then shoot several sequences using your camera's burst mode. Once you've imported them into Photoshop Elements, you can review your photos and choose the least cluttered shot from each burst.

You can use up to ten images in a single Scene Cleaner operation; the more source images, the more chance that you'll produce a perfect result. In this exercise, you'll do the best you can with just three photos.

1   If you're still in the Editor from the last exercise, switch to the Organizer now by clicking the Organizer button (▦) at the top right of the Editor workspace.

2   If necessary, isolate the sample photos for this lesson by clicking the Find box beside the Lesson 11 tag, which is listed under Imported Keyword Tags in the Keyword Tags panel.

3   In the Media Browser, Ctrl-click / Command-click or drag a marquee to select the images 11_03a.jpg, 11_03b.jpg and 11_03c.jpg: three photos of an old Russian submarine.

4   Choose File > New > Photomerge Scene Cleaner.

The selected images open in Full Edit mode, where Photoshop Elements analyzes and aligns the images before opening the Scene Cleaner.

5   By default, the first image in the Photo Bin, 11_03a.jpg (framed in blue), has been loaded as the Source image. Drag the image framed in green, 11_03c.jpg, from the Project Bin to the Final pane. This is the image you will clean: the base image for your composite.

6   Zoom in and use the Hand tool to position the images so that you can see the lower right corner. If necessary, scroll down in the Photomerge Scene Cleaner panel at the right, so that you can see the tools at the bottom.

7   Select the Pencil tool (✐) in the Photomerge Scene Cleaner panel; then, drag a line through the family in the foreground of the Final image. For the purposes of this demonstration, try to replicate the line you see in the illustration below.

When you release the mouse button, information is copied from the Source image to replace the area that you marked in the Final pane.

8 Move the pointer away from the Final image; you may see a blurry blending artefact in the lower right corner. Use the Zoom tool to focus on the problem area. This time, you'll use the Pencil tool in the Source image, which includes more of the pavement in the foreground than does the Final image. With the Pencil tool, draw a short line into the lower right corner of the Source Image.

9 Double-click the Hand tool to see the all of both images. Select the Pencil tool again and drag a line along the lower edge of the Source image. Hold down the Shift key as you drag with the Pencil tool to constrain the line to the horizontal.

The pavement in the foreground of the Source image is copied to the Final pane. The result is good, but now we have a problem in the lower left corner of the blended image.

10 Still working in the Source image, extend the left-hand end of your most recent line upwards, about half-way to the woman's feet. The corner is improved, but there's a small area of the artefact left behind where we ended the stroke.

11 In the Project Bin, click the photo with the yellow border to switch it into the Source pane. Click once in the Source image with the pencil tool, at the left edge of the image, and just above the blue line. There is a tiny improvement, but this image does not extend far enough to the left to be of more use.

12 Working with only these three images, there's not a lot more we can do for the photo. If you can't see all of the Final image, double-click the Hand tool; then, activate the Show Regions option in the Photomerge Scene Cleaner panel, to see which part of each source image contributed to the blended result.

13 Click Done, and then choose View > Fit On Screen. Choose Image > Crop and drag the corner handles of the cropping rectangle to maximize the image while avoiding the areas that are empty or stretched. When you're satisfied, click the Commit button in the corner of the bounding box.

14 Choose File > Save. Name the file **11_03_Depopulated** and save it to your My CIB Work folder, in Photoshop (PSD) format. Activate Layers and make sure the file will be included in the Organizer. Click Save, and then close all four files.

Blending differently exposed photos

There are many common situations where we (or our cameras in automatic mode) are forced to choose between properly exposing the foreground or the background.

Interior shots often feature overexposed window views where the scene outside is washed-out or lost completely. Subjects posing in front of a brightly lit scene or backlit by a window are often underexposed, and therefore appear dull and dark. A person posing in front of a city skyline at night is another classic example of this kind of exposure problem; we need to use a flash to make the most of our subject in the foreground, but the background is better exposed without it.

Photomerge Exposure provides a great new way to deal with photos captured in difficult lighting conditions, enabling you to combine the best-lit areas from two or more images to make the perfect shot.

1   If you're still in the Editor from the last exercise, switch to the Organizer now by clicking the Organizer button (⊞) at the top right of the Editor workspace.

2   In the Organizer, click the Find box beside the Lesson 11 tag in the Keyword Tags panel, if necessary, to isolate the images for this lesson.

3   Ctrl-click / Command-click to select the images 11_04a.jpg and 11_04b.jpg, two different exposures of the same stained-glass window.

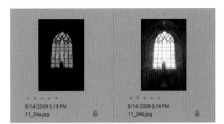

4   Click the arrow on the Fix tab above the Task Pane and choose Full Photo Edit.

Using the Photomerge Exposure tool

When you're faced with difficult lighting conditions, you can simply take two or more photos at different exposure settings and let the Photomerge Exposure tool align them and blend them together.

Photoshop Elements can detect whether the images you've chosen to blend with the Photomerge Exposure tool were taken with the exposure bracketing feature on your camera, or with and without flash.

The Photomerge Exposure tool has two working modes; it will default to Automatic mode for exposure-bracketed shots, or open in Manual mode for a set of photos captured with and without flash.

Merging exposures automatically

For this exercise you'll work with two interior shots of a stained-glass window captured with exposure bracketing.

One shot has been correctly exposed to capture the dimly lit interior, but the window appears "burnt out" so that all color and detail have been lost. The other photo is exposed perfectly to capture the glowing colors in the stained glass, but has failed to register any detail in the church walls and vaulted ceiling.

1 Ctrl-click / Command-click to select both photos in the Photo Bin, and then choose File > New > Photomerge Exposure. Wait while Photoshop Elements aligns the content in the source photos and creates the composite image.

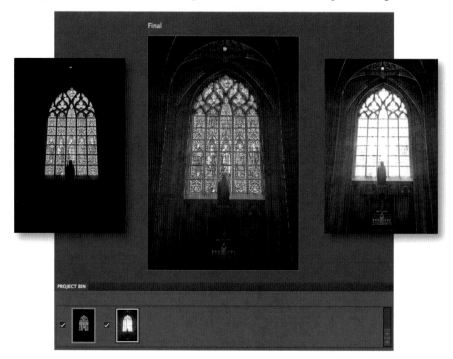

Photomerge Exposure has defaulted to Automatic mode for these exposure bracketed shots, and has successfully combined the differently exposed areas to produce an image that looks like what we actually saw but couldn't capture in a single shot.

2 Use the Zoom and Hand tools to inspect the merged image.

Adjusting the automatically merged image

Even in Automatic mode, Photomerge Exposure provides you with controls to fine-tune the way the source images are combined.

1 If necessary, click the Fit Screen button above the Edit pane or double-click the Hand tool so that you can see the entire image.

2 To increase the contrast in the blended image, drag the Shadows slider in the Photomerge Exposure panel to the left to set a Shadows value of –50.

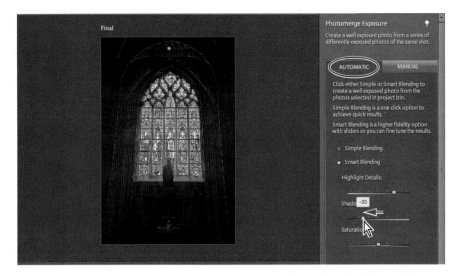

3 Use the Zoom tool to zoom in on the stained-glass window. Increase the Highlight Details value to 100 and the Saturation value to 10.

4 Click Done, and then wait while the merged image file is generated.

5 Choose File > Save. Name the file **11_04_Leadlight** and save it to your My CIB Work folder, in the default Photoshop (PSD) format with the Layers option activated. You know the drill.

6 Choose File > Close All.

Merging exposures manually

Photomerge Exposure does a great job of merging your exposure bracketed shots automatically, producing good results in Automatic mode for most backlit situations. When Photoshop Elements detects shots taken with Flash / No Flash, Photomerge Exposure defaults to Manual mode.

Select two or more images in the Photo Bin, and then choose File > New > Photomerge Exposure. Depending on your photos, Photomerge Exposure may open in Manual or Automatic mode.

You can easily switch modes by clicking the Manual and Automatic tabs in the Photomerge Exposure panel.

On the Manual tab you'll find basic instructions together with the Selection (Pencil) tool—for identifying the areas you wish to copy from the Foreground (source) image—and the Eraser tool for modifying your selection.

There are also controls for showing or hiding Selection tool strokes and the color-coded regions indicating the areas being contributed to the blend by each source image.

Activating the Edge Blending option will smooth the edges between merged regions and the Transparency slider lets you fine tune the way each source photo is blended into the final composite image.

For more detail on using the Photomerge Exposure feature, please refer to Photoshop Elements Help.

Combining multiple photographs in one file

In this project, you'll use layers to combine three photos into one—yet another way to use the power of Photoshop Elements to produce that great image that you never actually captured.

You'll apply a clipping mask to one image in order to blend it smoothly into the background picture; then, you'll add a selection from another photo and learn how to remove the colored fringe that is often visible surrounding such a selection.

Your final work file will retain the original pixel information from all three source images, so you can go back and make adjustments to any of them—or even rearrange the whole composition—at any time.

1   If you're still in the Editor from the last exercise, switch to the Organizer now by clicking the Organizer button (▦) at the top right of the Editor workspace.

2   In the Organizer, click the Find box beside the Lesson 11 tag in the Keyword Tags panel, if necessary, to isolate the images for this lesson.

3   Ctrl-click / Command-click to select the images 11_05b.jpg and 11_05c.jpg, a scenic view of an alpine valley and photo of a sunlit para-glider.

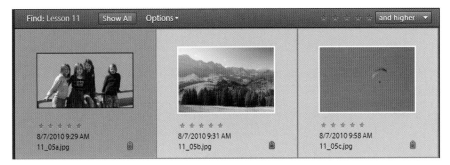

4   Click the arrow on the Fix tab above the Task Pane and choose Full Photo Edit.

Arranging the image layers

In the first exercise, you'll place these two images on separate layers to create a composite background to which you'll add foreground figures later.

1   Click the Arrange button (▤) at the top of the workspace and choose the layout at the right of the top row, Tile All Horizontally.

2 Click the title tab of the image 11_05c.jpg (the para-glider) to make it the active window. Select the Move tool (🖑) and hold down the Shift key as you drag the para-glider onto the alpine view. Release the mouse button, and then the Shift key. Holding the Shift key as you drag a layer to another file ensures that the image appears in the same position in the target file as it occupies in the source.

3 Close the image 11_05c.jpg (the one you just copied from) and double-click the Hand tool or choose View > Fit On Screen.

4 In the Layers panel, select Layer 1 (the para-glider) to make it the active layer. Choose Image > Resize > Scale. In the tool options bar, make sure Constrain Proportions is activated, and then type **50%** in the W (width) field. Click the Commit button in the lower right corner of the bounding box.

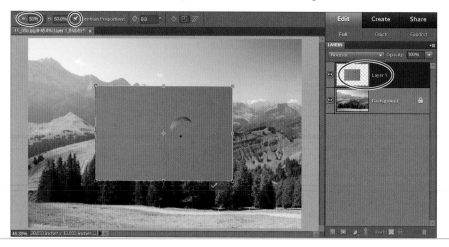

5 With the Move tool, drag the para-glider on Layer 1 right into the upper right corner of the image; then, drag the lower left handle of the bounding box upwards and to the right to reduce the size of the image further. As you drag in the image window, keep your eye on the width (W) and height (H) values in the tool options bar; stop when the width and height reach 80%.

6 Click the Commit button on the bounding box to accept the changes.

Creating a gradient layer mask

A layer mask allows only part of the image on a layer to show and hides the rest by making it transparent. Layers lower in the stacking order will be visible through the transparent areas in the masked layer.

In the next steps you'll create a gradient that fades from fully opaque to fully transparent, and then use this gradient to create a mask with a soft edge. This will make it easy to blend the images together without a visible edge.

1 With Layer 1 selected as the active layer, click the Add Layer Mask button (⬜) at the bottom of the Layers panel to add a new, blank layer mask.

2 In the toolbox, select the Gradient tool (▨); then, click the Default Foreground And Background Colors button beside the foreground and background color swatches, or press the D key on your keyboard.

3 In the tool options bar, click the Radial Gradient (◉) button, the second in the row of gradient type options, and then click the Edit button to the left.

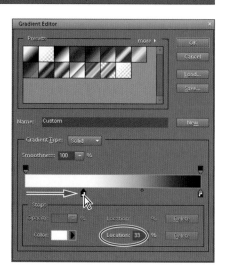

4 In the Gradient Editor dialog box, drag the left-hand marker below the black and white gradient strip to the right. As you drag the marker, keep an eye on the Location value below the gradient strip; stop dragging when the value reaches 33%. Click OK to close the Gradient Editor.

5 Make sure that Layer 1 is still selected in the Layers panel. Starting from a point between the parachute and the parachutist, drag a line upwards with the Gradient tool. Release the mouse button when you reach the top of the image.

6 To see the layer mask displayed in the image window as a semi-transparent overlay, hold down the Shift button, and then Alt-click / Option-click the layer mask thumbnail on Layer 1.

As you can see, the central area of the mask is completely clear; the soft edge created by the gradient you painted begins well away from the para-glider. This is a result of the modification that you made in the Gradient Editor dialog box in step 4.

7 Review step 4 on the facing page. You moved the left color stop marker to a location 33% of the distance from the start to the end of the gradient strip. By doing this, you set the gradient so that the transition from foreground color to background color began one-third of the way along the line you dragged with the Gradient tool in step 6. Had you not made this adjustment to the gradient, the fade would have begun at the point you first clicked, and the para-glider would have been partially masked.

8 Hold down the Shift button, and then Alt-click / Option-click the layer mask thumbnail once more to hide the overlay.

Although your gradient mask blends the image on Layer 1 very smoothly into the layer beneath it, it's obvious that the color in our para-glider image will need to be adjusted.

Matching the colors of blended images

Every color-matching problem will have its own solution, but this exercise should at least give you an idea of what kinds of things you can try.

In this case you'll use a blending mode together with several different adjustments to both color and lighting.

1 In the Layers panel, click the layer thumbnail on Layer 1; then, use the menu at the top of the panel to change the blending mode to Hard Light. Leave the opacity set to 100%.

2   Choose Enhance > Adjust Lighting > Levels. In the Levels dialog box, drag the gray slider beneath the center of the tone graph to the left slightly, or type in the text box, to set a new midtone value of **1.2**; then, click OK.

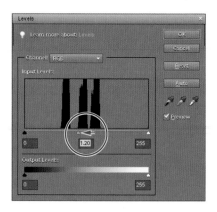

3   Choose Enhance > Adjust Color > Adjust Hue/Saturation. In the Hue/Saturation dialog box, use the menu above the sliders to switch from the Master channel to the Cyans channel. Set the Saturation value for the Cyans channel to **−90**. Switch to the Blues channel and set the Saturation to **−50**; then click OK.

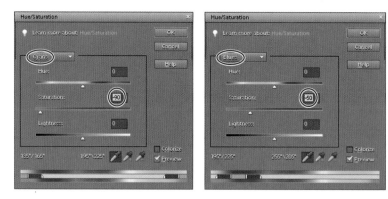

4   Choose Enhance > Adjust Lighting > Brightness/Contrast. Reduce the value for Brightness to **−10**; then, click OK.

As you can see in the before and after illustration to the right, this combination of adjustments has not only matched the colors in the blended images, but has also dimmed the para-glider slightly, helping it to fit in better with the hazy aerial perspective in the background image.

5   Choose File > Save As. Save the file to your work folder, in Photoshop format with Layers enabled. Make sure the file will be included in the Organizer, but not in a Version Set. Name the new file **11_05_Composite**, and then click Save. Keep the blended image open for the next exercise.

Cleaning up selection edges with the Defringe command

Defringing removes the annoying halo of color that often surrounds a selection copied and pasted from one image to another. In this exercise you'll add a foreground image of four sisters, so that they appear to be overlooking our alpine valley. To do this, you'll select and delete the background from the photo of the girls and use the Defringe feature to blend the selection halo into the background.

1   Choose View > Fit On Screen; then, choose File > Open. Navigate to and open your Lesson11 folder. Select the file 11_05a.jpg, and then click Open.

2   With the image 11_05a.jpg selected as the active window in the Edit pane, choose Select > All. Choose Edit > Copy, and then File > Close. In the Layers panel, make sure that Layer 1, the top layer of your composite image, is still selected; then, choose Edit > Paste. The image of the four sisters is placed on a new layer named Layer 2, right above the layer that was selected.

3   With the new selected in the Layers panel, select the Move tool (⤲) and drag the photo of the girls to the lower left corner of the image.

4   Choose Image > Resize > Scale. Make sure that Constrain Proportions is activated in the tool options bar, and then drag the upper right handle of the bounding box upwards and to the right, until the wooden rail extends just a little outside the right border of the image. Click the Commit button near the lower right corner of the bounding box to accept the change. Press the left arrow key twice to nudge the content of Layer 2 just a fraction to the left.

5 Select the Magic Wand tool (✦). In the tool options bar, set the Tolerance to **25**, activate Anti-alias, and disable Contiguous and Sample All Layers. Click on the pink-colored background of the Layer 2 image with the Magic Wand tool. If necessary, hold down the Shift key and click to select any un-selected pink areas in the background.

6 Zoom in on the faces of the three girls on the right. Small areas in the sun-lit skin of all three faces have become selected. Pick up the Lasso tool (✎); then, hold down the Alt / Option key and drag around the selected areas in the faces to subtract them from the selection. Zoom in on the right hand of the girl on the left, and then both hands of the girl on the right. Use the same technique to clear the selected areas. Check the pink sweater at the girl's right hip.

7 Press the Delete key to delete the pink background, and then press Ctrl+D / Command+D, or choose Select > Deselect to clear the selection.

8 Zoom in to the edge of the left hand and lower arm of the girl in the purple sweater. A pinkish fringe or halo is clearly visible here.

9 Choose Enhance > Adjust Color > Defringe Layer. In the Defringe dialog box, enter **5** pixels for the width and click OK. Most of the fringe is eliminated.

10 Double-click the Hand tool in the toolbox, or choose View > Fit On Screen to see the whole image in the edit window.

11 Select the Magic Wand tool (✦). In the tool options bar once more, and click anywhere in the cleared area surrounding the girls. Choose Select > Modify > Border and set a border width of 4 pixels; then, click OK.

12 Choose Filter > Blur > Blur More, and then repeat the command to soften the harder edges of the pasted image. Press Ctrl+D / Command+D, or choose Select > Deselect to clear the selection.

13 Choose File > Save, and then close the document.

Congratulations, you've completed the last exercise in this lesson. You've learned how to create a stunning composite panorama, how to merge multiple photos into the perfect group shot, how to remove obstructions from a view, and how to compose several photos into a single image by arranging layers and using a gradient to define a layer mask. You've also gained some experience with solving difficult lighting problems by combining shots taken at different exposures.

Take a moment to work through the lesson review on the next page before you move on to the next chapter, "Advanced Editing Techniques."

Review questions

1 In the Photomerge dialog box, which tools can be used to fine-tune a panorama created from multiple images, and how do they work?

2 What does the Photomerge Group Shot tool do?

3 Why is it that sometimes when you think you're finished with a transformation in Photoshop Elements you cannot select another tool or perform other actions?

4 Why does Photomerge Exposure open sometimes in Automatic mode and at others in Manual mode?

5 What is a fringe and how can you remove it?

Review answers

1 The Select Image tool is used to select a specific image from within the merged panorama. This tool can also be used to drag an image so that it lines up more closely with the other images in the panorama. The Rotate Image tool is used to rotate merged images so that their content aligns seamlessly. The Set Vanishing Point tool is used to specify the vanishing point for the perspective in the panorama. Setting the vanishing point in a different photo changes the point around which the other photos will be stretched and skewed to match the perspective.

2 With the Photomerge Group Shot tool you can pick and choose the best parts of several pictures taken successively, and merge them together to form one perfect picture.

3 Photoshop Elements is waiting for you to confirm the transformation by clicking the Commit button, or by double-clicking inside the transformation boundary.

4 Photomerge Exposure detects whether your source photos were taken with exposure bracketing or with and without flash and defaults to Automatic or Manual mode accordingly. Manual mode works better for source files taken with flash/no flash.

5 A fringe is the annoying halo of color that often surrounds a selection pasted into another image. When the copied area is pasted onto another background color, or the selected background is deleted, pixels of the original background color show around the edges of your selection. The Defringe Layer command (Enhance > Adjust Color > Defringe Layer) blends the halo away so you won't see an artificial-looking edge.

12 ADVANCED EDITING TECHNIQUES

Lesson overview

In this final chapter you'll learn some advanced editing concepts and try some of the innovative tools that Adobe Photoshop Elements delivers to help you improve the quality and clarity of your images.

Discover the benefits of working with raw image files and how the power and simplicity of the Camera Raw plug-in makes it easy for you to achieve professional-looking results with your color corrections and tonal adjustments. Save your raw files in the versatile DNG format and take advantage of Camera Raw's non-destructive editing.

Enjoy the creative possibilities of combining and calibrating multiple filters, creating your own special effects to turn your photos into art.

This lesson will introduce some essential concepts and skills for making the most of your photos:

- Working with raw images
- Converting files to DNG format
- Using the histogram to assess a photo
- Improving the quality of highlights and shadows
- Resizing and sharpening an image
- Creating custom effects in the filter gallery
- Using the Cookie Cutter tool

 You'll probably need between one and two hours to complete this lesson.

Discover the advantages of working with raw images in the Camera Raw window, where the easy-to-use controls make it simple to correct and adjust your photos like a professional. Learn how to use the Histogram panel to help you understand what a less-than-perfect picture needs and to give you visual feedback on the solutions you apply. Finally, have some fun putting together your own filter effects.

Getting started

Note: This lesson
builds on the skills and
concepts covered in
the earlier chapters and
assumes that you are
already familiar with
the main features of the
Photoshop Elements
workspace. Should you
need to brush up on
the basic concepts, see
Lesson 1, "A Quick Tour
of Photoshop Elements"
or refer to Photoshop
Elements Help.

Before you start working on the exercises in this lesson, make sure that you
have installed the software on your computer from the application CD (see the
Photoshop Elements 9 documentation) and that you have correctly copied the
Lessons folder from the CD in the back of this book onto your computer's hard
disk. (See "Copying the Classroom in a Book files" on page 2.)

Improving a camera raw image

In this first exercise you'll be working with a raw image from a Nikon camera as
you explore the correction and adjustment controls in the Camera Raw window.

1 Open Photoshop Elements and click the Organize button in the Welcome
   screen. In the Organizer, check the name of the currently loaded catalog in the
   lower left corner of the workspace. If your CIB Catalog is not already loaded,
   choose File > Catalog and select it from the list in the Catalog Manager.

2 Choose File > Get Photos And Video > From Files And Folders. In the Get
   Photos And Videos From Files And Folders dialog box, locate and select your
   Lesson12 folder. Disable any automatic processing option that is currently
   active, and then click Get Media. In the Import Attached Keyword Tags dialog
   box, click Select All, and then click OK.

3 In the Organizer, click the Show All button
   in the Find bar. Type the word **climb** in
   the Text Search box, at the left of the bar
   above the Media Browser.

4 The test search returns a single image:
   12_01_CliffClimb.NEF—a photo of a
   seaside cliff in Normandy, France.
   Right-click / Control-click the thumbnail
   in the Media Browser and choose Edit
   With Photoshop Elements.

Photoshop Elements opens the image in the Camera Raw window.

Working with camera raw images

The moment you open a camera raw file for the first time, the Camera Raw plug-in
creates what is sometimes referred to as a *sidecar file* in the same folder as the
image file. The sidecar file takes the name of the camera raw file, with the extension
".xmp." Any modification that you make to the raw photograph is written to the
XMP (Extensible Metadata Platform) file, rather than to the image file itself.

1 Use the Windows System Tray (XP), the Notification Area (Vista), or the Dock on Mac OS to switch back to the Elements Organizer.

2 Make sure that the image of the cliff is selected in the Media Browser; then, click the Display button () at the upper right of the workspace and choose Folder Location from the menu. In the Folders panel at the left of the Media Browser, right-click / Control-click the Lesson12 folder and choose Reveal In Explorer / Reveal In Finder.

3 A Windows Explorer / Finder window opens to show the contents of your Lesson12 folder. The new XMP sidecar file, 12_01_CliffClimb.XMP is listed beside the NEF image file. Return to Adobe Photoshop Elements (the Editor).

Getting to know the Camera Raw window

1 In the Camera Raw window, make sure that the Preview checkbox above the image window is activated.

On the right side of the Camera Raw window is a control panel with three tabs: Basic, Detail, and Camera Calibration. For this set of exercises you'll work with the Basic tab—the default—which presents controls for making adjustments that are not possible with the standard editing tools in Photoshop Elements.

What is a raw image?

Raw files are referred to as such because, unlike many of the more common image file formats that you may recognize, such as JPEG or GIF, they are unprocessed by the digital camera or image scanner. In other words, a raw file contains all the unprocessed image data captured for every pixel by the camera's sensors, without any software instructions about how that data is to be interpreted and displayed as an image on any particular device.

A limited but basically effective analogy or model for understanding the distinction is the difference between sending a film off for automatic processing by a commercial machine and using your own darkroom where you can control everything from the development of the negative to the way the image is exposed and printed onto paper.

The benefits of working with a raw image

Raw images are high-quality image files that contain the maximum amount of original image data in a relatively small file size. Though larger than a compressed image such as a JPEG file, a raw image contains more data than a TIFF image and uses less space.

Many types of image processing result in loss of data, effectively degrading the quality of the image. If a camera produces compressed files for instance, some data deemed superfluous is discarded. If a camera maps the whole range of captured image data to a defined color space, the spread of the image data can be narrowed. Processes such as sharpening and white balance correction will also alter the original captured data.

Whether you are an amateur photographer or a professional, it can be difficult to understand all the process settings on your digital camera and just what they mean in terms of data loss and image degradation. One solution is to use the camera's raw setting. Raw images are derived directly from the camera's sensors, prior to any camera data processing. Not all digital cameras have the capability to capture raw images, but many of the newer and more advanced cameras do offer this option.

Capturing your photos in a raw format means you have more flexibility when it comes to producing the image you want. Many of the camera settings such as sharpening, white balance, levels, and color adjustments can be undone when you're working with your image in Photoshop Elements. For instance, automatic adjustments to exposure can be undone and recalculated based on the raw data.

Another advantage is that, with 12 bits of data per pixel, it's possible to extract shadow and highlight detail from a raw image that would have been lost in the 8 bits/channel JPEG or TIFF formats.

Raw files provide an archival image format, much like a digital negative. In much the same way that you could produce a range of vastly different prints from the same film negative in a darkroom, you can reprocess a raw file repeatedly to achieve whatever results you want. Photoshop Elements doesn't save your changes to the original raw file; rather, it saves the settings you used to process it.

Note: Raw filenames have different extensions, depending on the camera used to capture the image. Examples are Canon's CRW and CR2, Epson's ERF, Fuji's RAF, Kodak's KDE and DER, Minolta's MRW, Olympus' ORF, Pentax's PTX and PEF, Panasonic's RAW, and the various flavors of Nikon's NEF.

2   In the bar above the image window, hold the pointer over each of the tools in turn to see a tooltip with the name of the tool and the respective keyboard shortcut. Click on the Crop tool and hold the mouse button down to see a menu of cropping ratio options. Click the Toggle Full Screen Mode button at the right of the tool bar to switch to full screen mode.

When you open a camera raw photo, Photoshop Elements reads information in the image file to ascertain which model of camera created it and applies the appropriate preset camera settings profile to the image data.

3   Click the menu icon at the right of the Basic tab's header bar to see the choices available from the control panel Options menu. You can apply the same settings that you used for the last image you worked with, save your own settings as the new default for the camera that captured this image, or have Photoshop Elements revert to the default Camera Raw profile for your camera by choosing Reset Camera Raw Defaults.

4   Switch to the Detail tab to see the controls for sharpening an image and reducing the digital artefacts known as noise.

5   Try a few of the zoom levels listed in the menu at the lower left of the image window. Use a magnification of 100% or higher when working with the controls on the Detail tab. For now, choose Fit In View and switch back to the Basic tab.

Workflow overview for raw images

To make use of the raw image editing capabilities in Photoshop Elements, you'll first need to set your camera to save images in its own raw format.

After processing a raw file in the Camera Raw window, you can then open the adjusted image in Photoshop Elements, where you can work with it just as you would with any other photo. When you're done, you can save the results in any format supported by Photoshop Elements.

Photoshop Elements can open only raw files from supported cameras. To see an up-to-date list of the currently supported camera models and file formats, visit the Adobe website or search in Community Help.

Note: The RAW plug-in, used to open raw files from a digital camera, is updated over time as new cameras are added to the list of those supported. You can check for updates and download the latest version of the plug-in at www.adobe.com.

Adjusting the white balance

The Camera Raw white balance presets can be helpful when you need to rectify a color cast caused by incorrect camera settings or poor lighting conditions. If your camera was not correctly set up to deal with overcast conditions, for example, you could correct your image by choosing the Cloudy preset from the White Balance menu. Other presets help you to compensate for the deficient color balance caused by different types of artificial lighting. Incandescent lighting typically causes an orange-yellow color cast; fluorescent lighting is notorious for a dull greenish tint.

The As Shot setting reads the embedded metadata that records the camera settings when the image was captured, while the Auto setting recalculates the white balance based on an analysis of the image data.

1   Experiment with some of the presets available in the White Balance menu. Switch the setting back and forth to compare the Auto, Cloudy, and Tungsten preset to the default As Shot setting. In the following pages you'll discover why the appropriate white balance is so important to the overall look of the image.

As Shot

Auto

Cloudy

Tungsten

2   For now, choose As Shot from the White Balance presets menu.

For many photos, the right white balance preset will produce satisfactory results, either used "as is," or as a starting point for manual adjustment. When none of the presets seems to take your image in the right direction, you can use the White Balance tool () to sample a color from the photo to be used as a neutral reference in relation to which Camera Raw will recalculate the white balance.

The ideal sample for this purpose is a light to medium gray that is neither discernibly warm or cool in tone. In some images it can be difficult to identify such a color; in the absence of a definitive visual reference you may sometimes rely on what you know about the photo—that it was taken on a cloudy day, for example, or under fluorescent lighting.

Our lesson photo could be such a difficult case; the large area of stone can almost be considered as monochromatic and the small area of sky is pale and overexposed, so it's hard to judge visually just which way the white balance should be shifted.

Fortunately, however, the girl in the photo provides us with a reliable reference, because we happen to know that her sweater should be a neutral gray.

3 Zoom into the image by choosing 100% from the Zoom Level menu in the lower left corner of the preview window, or by double-clicking the zoom tool.

4 Select the Hand tool (🖐) from the tool bar and drag the image upwards and to the left in the preview window until you can see the girl climbing the cliff face.

5 Select the White Balance tool (🖋), right beside the Hand tool in the tool bar.

6 Sample a medium gray from the shadow that runs diagonally across the girl's back. If you see little effect, click a slightly different point.

The White Balance is now set to Custom and the image has become warmer. The color of the algae at the base of the cliff is a more life-like, vibrant green and the skin on the girl's legs looks more natural, having lost the original blue-gray cast.

7 Zoom out by choosing Fit In View from the Zoom Level menu in the lower left corner of the preview window.

8 Use the White Balance menu to alternate between your custom settings and the As Shot preset, noting the change in the preview window, as well as any differences in the Temperature and Tint settings.

9 Repeat step 8 for each of the other white balance presets, comparing the position of the sliders and look of the image to your custom adjustment. When you're done, return the white balance to your custom setting.

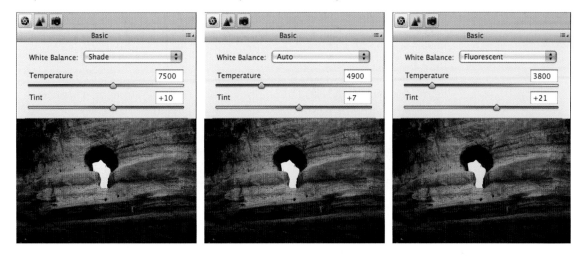

Camera Raw white balance settings

A digital camera records the white balance at the time of exposure as metadata, which you can see when you open the file in the Camera Raw dialog box. This setting usually yields the correct color temperature. You can adjust it if the white balance is not quite right. The Basic tab in the Photoshop Camera Raw dialog box includes three controls for correcting a color cast in your image:

White Balance Balances color in the image to reflect the lighting conditions under which the photo was taken. A white balance preset may produce satisfactory results as is, or you may want to customize the Temperature and Tint settings.

Temperature Fine-tunes the white balance to a custom color temperature. Move the slider to the left to correct a photo taken in light of a lower color temperature; the plug-in makes the image colors bluer to compensate for the lower color temperature of yellowish ambient light. Move the slider to the right to correct a photo taken in light of higher color temperature; the plug-in makes the image colors warmer to compensate for the higher color temperature of bluish ambient light.

Tint Fine-tunes the white balance to compensate for a green or magenta tint. Move the slider to the left to add green to the photo; move it to the right to add magenta.

To adjust the white balance quickly, click an area in the preview image that should be a neutral gray or white with the White Balance tool. The Temperature and Tint sliders automatically adjust to make the selected color as close to neutral as possible. If you're using a white area to set the white balance, choose a highlight area that contains significant white detail rather than a specular highlight.

—From Photoshop Elements Help

Working with the Temperature and Tint settings

The White Balance tool can accurately remove any color cast or tint from an image but you may still want to tweak the Temperature and Tint settings. Depending on the subject matter and the effect you wish to achieve, you might actually want a slight, controlled color tint. In this instance, the color temperature seems fine, but you can fine-tune the green/magenta balance of the image using the Tint control.

1 If you don't see the entire image in the Camera Raw preview zoom out by double-clicking the Hand tool or by choosing Fit In View from the Zoom Level menu in the lower left corner of the preview window.

2 Test the Temperature slider in the Basic tab by dragging it from one end of its range to the other. You'll see that the colors of the image become cooler or warmer as you move the slider. In this case, the corrected temperature of the image seemed fine but this slider could help you on other occasions—for toning down the overly warm tones resulting from tungsten lighting, for example.

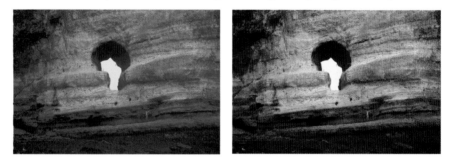

3 Reset the Temperature control to the corrected value of 5150 either by dragging the slider or typing the value **5150** into the Temperature text box.

4 Experiment with the extremes of the Tint slider. The custom Tint value was +5. Increase the setting to +12 with the slider or type **+12** in the Tint text box.

▶ **Tip:** As well as helping to correct color and improve the tonal range, the white balance settings can also be used creatively to achieve dramatic atmospheric effects.

Using the tone controls on a raw image

The settings for tonal adjustments are located below the White Balance controls on the Basic tab. In this exercise, you'll use these controls to correct exposure, check highlights and shadows, and adjust brightness, contrast, and saturation. Before you adjust any of the settings, you should understand what each of the controls does:

Exposure adjusts the lightness or darkness of an image. Underexposed images are too dark and look dull and murky; overexposed images are too light and look washed out. Use the Exposure control to lighten an underexposed image or correct the faded look of an overexposed image.

Recovery attempts to recover details from burned-out highlights. The Recovery control can reconstruct some detail in areas where one or two color channels have been clipped to white. Clipping occurs when a pixel's color values are higher or lower than the range that can be represented in the image; over-bright values are clipped to output white, and over-dark values are clipped to output black.

Fill Light recovers details from shadows, without brightening blacks. The Fill Light control does something close to the inverse of the Recovery control, reconstructing detail in areas where one or two of the color channels have been clipped to black.

Blacks specifies which input levels are mapped to black in the final image. Raising the Blacks value expands the areas that are mapped to black.

Brightness adjusts the brightness of the image, much as the Exposure slider does. However, instead of clipping the image in the highlights (areas that are completely white, with no detail) or shadows (areas that are completely black, with no detail), Brightness compresses the highlights and expands the shadows when you move the slider to the right. In general, it's best to use the Brightness slider to adjust the overall brightness after you have set the white and black clipping points with the Exposure and Blacks sliders.

Contrast is the amount of difference in brightness between light and dark areas of an image. The Contrast control determines the number of shades in the image, and has the most noticeable effect in the midtones. An image without enough contrast can appear flat or washed out. Use the Contrast slider to adjust the midtone contrast after setting the Exposure, Blacks, and Brightness values.

Clarity sharpens the definition of edges in the image. This process helps restore detail and sharpness that tonal adjustments may reduce.

Vibrance adjusts the saturation so that clipping is minimized as colors approach full saturation, acting on all lower saturated colors but having less impact on higher saturated colors. Vibrance also prevents skin tones from becoming oversaturated.

Saturation is the purity, or strength, of a color. A fully saturated color contains no gray. The Saturation control makes colors more vivid (containing less black or white) or more muted (containing more black or white).

First you'll adjust the Exposure setting, checking for clipping in the brighter areas.

1 Hold down the Alt / Option key as you drag the Exposure slider slowly to the right. Watch the preview in the image window to see which parts of the image will be forced towards white as the highlights are clipped as a result of this adjustment. Set the Exposure to +2.00. You can clearly see the clipping indicated at the right end of the graphed curve in the histogram.

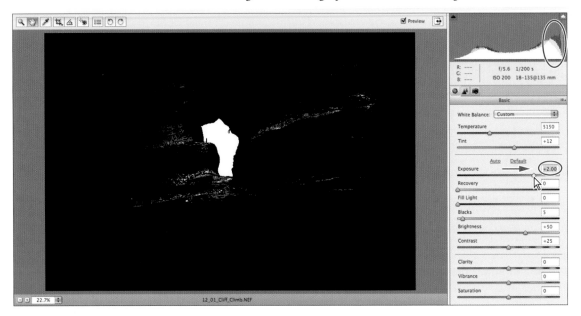

2 Keep holding the mouse button down on the slider control, but release the Alt / Option key to see the effect of the excessive exposure adjustment on the image. Press and release the Alt / Option key several times to see the correlation between the highlights clipping preview and the over-exposed image. Continue to switch between these 2 views as you drag the slider left to set a value of +0.8.

In the histogram, the main body of the distribution curve has moved left—most of the clipping has been resolved. The small spikes in the curve that are still clipped at the right end of the graph represent the small area of sky in the image.

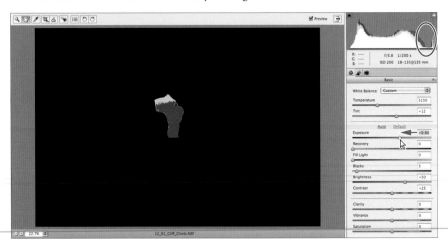

3   Press and release the Alt / Option as you drag the Recovery slider to 15. The clipping is completely corrected, as you can see in both the clipping preview and the histogram. We don't really expect to find any pure white in this image, so—without changing the Recovery setting—you can reduce the Exposure to +0.65, noting the effect on the image and the movement in the histogram curve.

4   Hold down the Alt / Option key and drag the Blacks slider to the right to a value of 20. Areas that appear in the clipping preview will be forced to a solid black. Switch between the clipping preview and the image to assess the effect.

5   Watch the clipping preview as you drag the slider slowly to the left until only the deepest shadows register as black. We set the Blacks value to 7.

6   Click the Brightness slider, and then press the up arrow on the keyboard to increase the value to +60.

7   Click the Contrast slider; then, press the up arrow key on the keyboard to increase the value to +30.

8   Choose a magnification level of 100% from the Zoom menu at the lower left of the image window. Use the Hand tool to center your view on the girl; then, drag both the Clarity and Vibrance sliders to +50. Double-click the Hand tool to see the entire image. The adjustments to Clarity and Vibrance have brought out a lot of the color detail in the stone.

9   Click the Preview checkbox at the right of the tool bar repeatedly to compare the adjusted photo to the raw image.

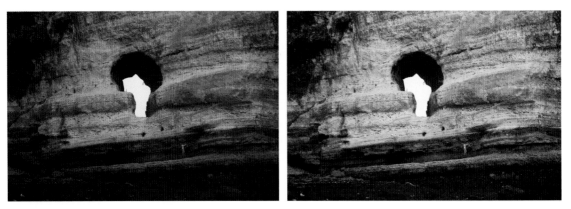

This image was actually shot in a very unusual and difficult conditions: shooting into the deep shade of the cliffs, late in the afternoon, with intense backlighting from the window of bright but overcast sky.

The photo looked flat, dull, a little indistinct, and far too dark. It now shows a broader range of detail and is more vivid; the color is warmer and the tones are much closer to what we would expect of weathered sandstone and tide-line algae. Compare the horizontal ledges and the interior of the key-hole arch; the impression of depth and dimension in the photo has been enhanced considerably. The figure of the climber being more noticeable, even the sense of scale has been heightened.

Your work in the Camera Raw window is done, but if you wished, you could edit the image further in Photoshop Elements. What this photo needs now is some selective editing to add color and perhaps even cloud detail to the window of sky: an easy job using selection techniques that you've already explored in the Editor.

Remember that everything you've done to this image in the Camera Raw window has been recorded only in the XMP sidecar file, not written to the original image. This is one advantage of working with raw images—the original image data remains absolutely intact. Your adjustments are applied only when you output a copy of the enhanced image in another file format.

Saving the image

By saving this file in the DNG format you can retain all the flexibility of the camera raw file—you can come back and reprocess it to achieve a different effect any time you want. Photoshop Elements doesn't save your changes to the original raw file—it simply creates a separate record of all your adjustments and settings; the original image data remains intact.

About the DNG format

Raw file formats are becoming common in digital photography. However, each camera manufacturer has its own proprietary raw format. The result is that not every raw file can be read or edited by software other than that provided with the camera. This may make it difficult to use some of these images in the future, as the manufacturers might not support every format indefinitely.

To help alleviate these problems, Photoshop Elements gives you the option to save raw images in in the DNG format, a publicly available archival format for raw files generated by digital cameras. The DNG format provides an open standard for files created by different camera models, and helps to ensure that you'll still be able to access your files in the future.

1   To convert and save the image, click the Save Image button at the lower left of the Camera Raw dialog box.

2   Under Destination in the Save Options dialog box, click Select Folder. In the Select Destination Folder dialog box, navigate to and open your Lessons folder; then click to highlight your My CIB Work folder and click Select.

3   Under File Naming, leave Document Name selected in the menu on the left. Click the menu on the right and select 1 Digit Serial Number. This will add the number 1 to the end of the file name.

4   Click Save. The file, together with all your current settings, will be saved in DNG format, which you can reprocess repeatedly without losing the original data.

5   Click the Open Image button in the right lower corner of the Camera Raw dialog box. Your image will open in a regular image window in Photoshop Elements.

6   Choose File > Save. Navigate to your My CIB Work folder, name the file 12_01_CliffClimb_Work, and choose the Photoshop format. Make sure that the new file will be included in the Organizer, but not in a Version Set.

7   Click Save, and then choose File > Close.

You've now experienced some of the advantages of using a camera raw format. Even though this format gives you more control and allows you to edit your image in a non-destructive way, a lot of professionals choose not to use raw images. Raw files are usually considerably bigger than high-quality JPEGs and take much longer to be saved in your camera—quite a disadvantage for action shots or when you're taking a lot of pictures.

About histograms

In the previous exercise, you referred to the histogram in the Camera Raw window as you learned about clipping in highlights and shadows.

In this part of the lesson, you'll learn how to use the Histogram panel in Full Edit mode—both as a guide to help you understand an image's deficiencies, and also as a source of dynamic feedback as you make changes to improve its quality.

In the following exercises, you'll work on an image that was shot in poor lighting and also has a slight magenta cast. This is quite a common problem—many digital cameras introduce a slight color cast into images.

Using the histogram

A histogram is a graph that maps the spread of tonal values present in an image, indicating how much tonal detail an image contains, from the shadows at the left end of the curve, through the midtones, to the highlights at the right of the curve. The histogram can help you to recognize where corrections need to be made, and then to assess how effective an adjustment will be, even as you set it up.

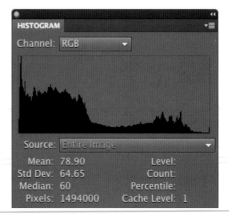

In the histogram below it's very apparent that there is not a good spread of tonal information in this image. The curve is weighted heavily towards the shadows at the left and deficient in the midtones. You can see clearly that the image is overly dark, and has a flat, dullish appearance, lacking in midtone contrast.

Excessive tonal adjustment can degrade image information, causing posterization, or color-banding. The histogram in the illustration below reveals that the image has already lost tonal detail in certain ranges; there are gaps, bands, and anomalous spikes in the curve. Any further adjustment will only degrade the image more.

Understanding highlights and shadows

In the next part of this lesson, you'll adjust the highlights and shadows and make additional tonal corrections to this photo while keeping an eye on the Histogram.

1 Make sure you are in Full Edit mode. Choose File > Open, navigate to your Lesson12 folder, select the file 12_02.psd and click Open.

2 Choose File > Save As. Name the image **12_02_Work** and save it to your My CIB Work folder in Photoshop (PSD) format, with the usual option settings.

3 If the Histogram panel is not already visible, choose Window > Histogram. From the Channel menu at the top of the Histogram panel, choose RGB.

4 In order to watch the effects of your adjustments more closely, you can drag the Histogram panel out of the Panel bin and position it beside the image.

The histogram shows that there is a lack of data in the midtone range for this image: it needs more pixels with values in the midtones and less clustered in the shadows at the left end of the distribution curve. You can adjust the tonal range of this photo in the Levels dialog box, which includes its own histogram curve.

Adjusting levels

1 Choose Enhance > Adjust Lighting > Levels. In the Levels dialog box, make sure that the Preview is option is activated.

You'll use the shadows, midtone, and highlights sliders (left, middle, and right respectively) below the histogram graph in the Levels panel as well as the Set Black Point, Set Gray Point, and Set White Point eyedroppers (left, middle, and right respectively).

Although the midtones are the range most in need of adjustment in this image, it's important to get the highlights and shadows right first. We'll try two slightly different methods for setting the white and black points in the image—both making use of the controls in the Levels dialog box.

2   In the Levels dialog box, hold down the Alt / Option key as you drag the highlights slider to the left to a value of 235—just inside the right-hand end of the tonal curve. The clipping preview shows you where the brightest parts of the image are: principally in the cloud reflections on the water.

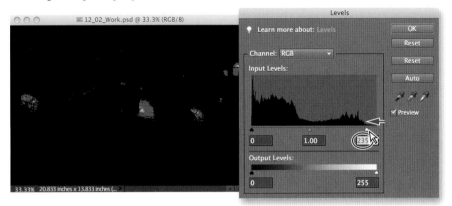

3   Watch the histogram as you release first the Alt / Option key, and then the mouse button. The curve in the histogram shifts—possibly a bit far—to the right. You can see that the right-hand end of the curve has become truncated. Move the highlights slider in the Levels dialog box to a value of 240. The curve in the histogram is adjusted accordingly.

4   In the Levels dialog box, click Reset and we'll try another method for adjusting the highlights. Select the Set White Point Eyedropper tool and watch the histogram as you click in the brightest of the reflections on the water. The white line in the histogram indicates the shape of the curve prior to this adjustment. The result is very similar to the previous method, but it won't be as easy to fine-tune any clipping at the right end of the curve. Now you'll correct the shadows.

Tip: If your image has an easily identified neutral grey, neither too warm nor cool, you can quickly remove a color cast using the Set White Point Eyedropper.

5 Hold down the Alt / Option key and drag the shadow slider to a value of 4. The area below the girl's right ear shows as a dark patch in the clipping preview. Watch the histogram as you release the mouse button and the Alt / Option key.

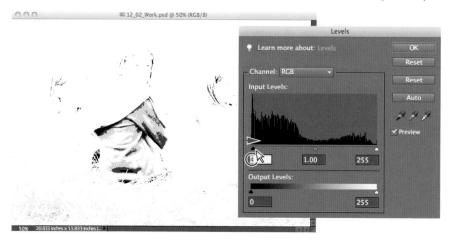

6 In the Levels controls, drag the midtone slider (the gray triangle below the center of the graph) to the left to set the midtone value to 1.35.

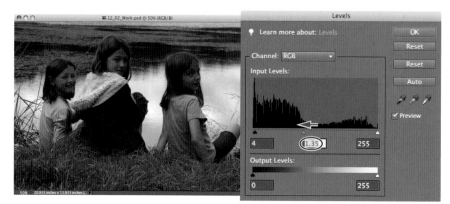

▶ **Tip:** Don't worry about the yellow alert icon in the Histogram panel; you'll deal with that in a moment.

7 Notice the change in the Histogram. Compare the original data (displayed in white) to the data for the corrections that you have made (displayed in black). The fullest part of the curve has shifted right into the midtones and the highlights are better represented.

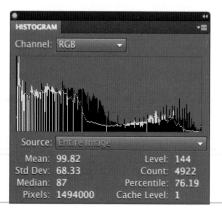

The changes have caused some gaps and banding in the distribution curve.

Where possible, you should try to avoid modifications that create large gaps in the histogram; even if the image still looks fine on screen, large gaps may indicate a loss of image data that will be apparent as color banding when the photo is printed.

8 Click OK to close the Levels dialog box. In the Histogram panel, click the yellow alert icon to refresh the histogram display with new, rather than cached data.

9 Select Edit > Undo Levels, or press Ctrl+Z / Command+Z to see how the image looked prior to redistributing the tonal values. Choose Edit > Redo Levels, or Press Ctrl+Y / Command+Y to reinstate your corrections. Leave this image open for the next part of this lesson.

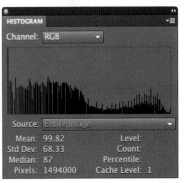

About Unsharp Mask

Now you can add some crispness to the image, which will make it look much better when printed. Using the sharpening tools correctly can improve an image's clarity and impact significantly.

In this exercise you'll use the Unsharp Mask. How can something be *un*sharp and yet sharpen an image? The term unsharp mask has it roots in the print industry: the technique was implemented by making an out-of-focus negative film—the unsharp mask—and then printing the original negative sandwiched with this unsharp mask. This produced a halo around object edges—optically giving them more definition.

If you're planning to resize an image, do so *before* you apply the Unsharp mask; if it's scaled with the image, the halo effect can appear as an obvious artefact.

1   With the file 12_02_Work.psd still open in the Full Edit mode, choose Image > Resize > Image Size.

This image needs to be made smaller, but with a higher resolution (pixels per inch).

Resolution refers to the fineness of detail you can see in an image, measured in pixels per inch (ppi): the more pixels per inch, the greater the resolution. Generally, the higher the resolution of your image, the better the printed result.

2   If necessary, disable the Resample Image check box at the bottom of the dialog box, and then type **300** in the Resolution text field. Notice that the width and height values adjust. This method increases the resolution of the image without the loss of information that results from resampling to fit smaller dimensions at the same density of pixels per inch.

3   Now, activate the Resample Image option, to reduce the height and width of the image without affecting the resolution. Click OK.

4   Choose File > Save. Keep the file open for the next part of this lesson.

Applying the Unsharp Mask filter

Before you apply any filter in Photoshop Elements, it's best to set the zoom level to 100%; viewing the image at full size makes it easier to spot unsightly artefacts.

Tip: To temporarily disable the preview in the Unsharp Mask dialog box, hold the mouse button down on the preview pane.

1   With the file 12_02_Work.psd still open in Full Edit mode, double-click the Zoom tool, or choose View > Actual Pixels. Use the Hand tool to center your view on the face of the girl on the right.

2   Choose Enhance > Unsharp Mask. The amount of unsharp masking you apply will be determined by the subject matter. A portrait shot, such as this image, should be softer than an image of an automobile or a city skyline. The range of the Amount setting extends from 1 to 500, with 500 being the sharpest.

3   Drag the the image in the Unsharp Mask preview to focus on the face of the girl on the right. Drag the Amount slider or type **100** in the Amount text field. Set the sharpening Radius to **1.5** pixels.

4   Increase the Threshold just slightly to **2** levels. Threshold is a key control in this dialog box, as it tells the filter what not to sharpen. In this case the value 2 means that a pixel will not be sharpened if it falls within 2 shades of the pixel beside it (on a scale of 255).

5   Click OK. Choose File > Save, and then File > Close.

Without sharpening.

Unsharp mask applied.

As you've seen, the Unsharp Mask filter can't mysteriously correct the focus of your image. It only gives the impression of crispness by increasing the contrast between adjacent pixels. As a rule of thumb, the Unsharp Mask filter should be applied to an image only once, as a final step in your processing. If you use Unsharp Mask too much, you'll run the risk of over sharpening your image producing artifacts that will give it a flaky, grainy look.

Tip: To sharpen a photo automatically, choose Enhance > Auto Sharpen. If you want more control over the process, choose Adjust Sharpness from the Enhance menu.

Using the filter gallery

Note: Not all filters are available from the Filter Gallery—some are available only individually as Filter menu commands. The Filter Gallery does not include the effects and layer styles that you'll find in the Effects panel.

You can have a lot of fun experimenting with filter effects in the Filter Gallery, where you can apply multiple filters to your image and tweak the way they work together, effectively creating new custom effects. Each filter has its own sliders and settings, giving you a great deal of control over the effect on your photo. The possibilities are endless—it's up to you! Have a look at "About Filters" in Photoshop Elements Help to find out more about the different filters.

You can achieve even more creative and sophisticated results by applying different Filter gallery configurations to multiple duplicate layers of the same image, and then blending the layers using partial transparency, blending modes, and masks.

Both of the examples in the illustration below were created using such a combination of techniques. Both examples were composed from multiple layers and both make use of layer masks so that adjacent areas can be treated differently.

For this exercise, we'll keep it simple, exploring the possibilities for using the Filter Gallery on a single image layer.

1 If you're still in the Editor from the last exercise, switch to the Organizer now by clicking the Organizer button (⊞) at the top right of the Editor workspace.

2 In the Organizer, click the Find box beside the Lesson 12 tag in the Keyword Tags panel, if necessary, to isolate the images for this lesson.

3 Select the image 12_03.jpg in the Media Browser; then, click the small arrow on the Fix tab above the Task Pane and choose Full Photo Edit.

Creating effects with filters

Many filters use the foreground and background colors currently active in the toolbar to create effects, so you should take a moment to set them now.

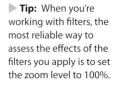

1 Click the Default Foreground And Background Colors button beside the color swatches at the bottom of the toolbox. This resets the default colors: black in the foreground and white in the background.

2 Choose File > Save As. Navigate to your My CIB Work folder, name the file 12_03_Work, choose the Photoshop (PSD) format, and then click Save.

3 Choose Filter > Filter Gallery. If necessary, use the menu in the lower left corner of the Filter Gallery window to set the magnification level to 100%.

4 When you move the pointer over the image in the preview pane, the cursor changes into the hand tool (✋). If you can't see the entire photo, drag the image in the preview pane so that you can see at least three of the girls' faces. If you don't see the center pane listing filter categories, click the button with the blue arrow, to the left of the OK and Cancel buttons.

▶ **Tip:** When you're working with filters, the most reliable way to assess the effects of the filters you apply is to set the zoom level to 100%.

5 In the center pane, expand the Brush Strokes category by clicking the arrow to the left of the category name, and then choose the Spatter filter. Experiment with the entire range of the control sliders. You can see the effect of the filter in the preview pane. Set both the Spray Radius and Smoothness to **10**.

6 Collapse the Brush Strokes category. Click the New Effect layer button () at the lower right of the Filter Gallery dialog box, expand the Artistic filters category, and choose the Watercolor filter. The Spatter and Watercolor filters are applied simultaneously.

7 Experiment with the full range of the sliders, and then set the Brush Detail to **8**, Shadow Intensity to **0**, and Texture to **2**. Collapse the Artistic filters category.

8 Click the New Effect Layer button () again. Expand the Distort category and choose the Diffuse Glow filter. Experiment with the sliders; then set the Graininess value to **5**, Glow Amount to **3**, and Clear Amount to **10**.

9 Click the New Effect Layer button at the bottom of the right-hand pane once more. Expand the Texture category and choose the Texturizer filter. Choose Canvas from the Texture menu; then, set the Scaling value to **200%** and the Relief to **5**. From the Light menu, choose Top Right.

10 Click OK. Wait while Photoshop Elements applies your multiple filter, and then choose Enhance > Adjust Color > Adjust Hue/Saturation. In the Hue/Saturation dialog box, set the Saturation value to **+30** and the Lightness to **–5**. Click OK.

11 Choose File > Save, and then close the file.

Experimenting with filters in the gallery

The possibilities are endless for combining different filters at varied settings.

1 Still in the Editor, choose File > Open and reopen the image 12_03.jpg.

2 Choose Filter > Filter Gallery. Be careful to choose the second listing for Filter Gallery in the Filter menu—the first listing simply applies the previous settings without opening the Filter Gallery dialog box. The Filter Gallery opens with your previous filters, and all their settings, exactly as you left them.

3 Experiment with different combinations of two or more of the four filters that you've already applied, turning the others off and on one at a time by clicking the eye icon to the left of each filter name.

4 The stacking order of the filters in the list will alter the way they interact, though this may be more noticeable with some filters than others. Experiment by dragging the filters to rearrange their order. Try deleting some of your filters and adding more, and then experiment more with the order.

5 There's no need to apply the changes to the image; click Cancel to close the Filter Gallery dialog box, keeping the file open for the next exercise.

Using the Cookie Cutter tool

The Cookie Cutter tool enables you to crop an image with your choice of an extensive library of Cookie Cutter shapes. In this exercise, you'll crop the image with a heart-shaped cutter.

1 Select the Cookie Cutter tool from the toolbox.

2 Click the Shapes menu in the tool options bar to view the default selection of shapes. The name of each shape appears as a tool tip when you move the pointer over its swatch. Click to select the shape named Heart Card; then, press the Esc key on your keyboard to close the Shapes picker.

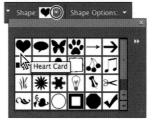

▶ **Tip:** There are many more cutout shapes available; click the double arrow in the upper right corner of the shapes panel to see a menu of over 20 different categories.

3 From the Shape Options menu in the tool options bar, choose Unconstrained and activate the From Center option.

4 Starting between the faces of the two girls on the right, drag in the image to create the cutter shape. Hold the Shift key as you drag to scale the shape proportionally. You can use the handles on the bounding box to resize or reshape the cutter, and drag inside the bounding box to reposition it.

5   Cancel the cropping operation, by clicking the Cancel button at the lower right of the Cookie Cutter bounding box, or by pressing the Esc key. Keep the file open for the next exercise.

Cookie Cutter Shape Options

Unconstrained Draws the shape to any size or proportion you'd like.

Defined Proportions Keeps the height and width of the cropping shape in proportion.

Defined Size Crops the photo to the exact size of the shape you choose.

Fixed Size Lets you specify exact measurements for the finished shape.

From Center Draws the shape from the center.

Enter a value for **Feather** to soften the edges of the finished shape.

Note: Feathering softens the edges of the cropped image so that the edges fade out and blend in with the background.

—From Adobe Photoshop Elements Help

Creating your own cutter

If you can't find a Cookie Cutter shape that suits your photo, don't worry—it's easy enough to create your own.

1   Right-click / Control-click the image's single layer, the Background layer, and choose Duplicate Layer from the context menu. In the Duplicate Layer dialog box, click OK to accept the default layer name.

2   With the new Background copy layer selected in the Layers panel, click the Add Layer Mask button () at the bottom of the panel.

3 Click the eye icon beside the Background layer to hide it from view.

4 Click the new Layer Mask thumbnail on the Background copy layer to make it active for editing, and then choose Edit > Fill Layer. Under Contents in the Fill Layer dialog box, choose Black from the Use menu; then, click OK.

In the image window, you see only the checkerboard pattern that indicates layer transparency; the Background layer is currently invisible, and the black fill in the layer mask hides the image on the Background copy layer completely.

5 Click the box to the left of the Background layer thumbnail to reinstate the eye icon and make the layer visible again. Hold down the Shift key; then, Alt-click / Option-click the layer mask thumbnail to see the mask displayed as a semi-transparent overlay in the image window.

6 Press the E key to select the Eraser tool. In the tool options bar, choose Brush from the Mode menu and make sure that the Opacity is set to 100%.

7 Open the Brush Picker and choose Thick Heavy Brushes from the Brushes menu. The name of each brush appears in a tooltip when you hold the pointer over the swatch. Select the second brush in the set—the Rough Flat Bristle brush: then, press the Esc key to close the Brush Picker. Press the right bracket key (]) repeatedly to increase the brush size to 300 pixels.

8 With the Eraser tool, scribble a rough line in the image window to quickly clear the red overlay from the faces of all four girls.

9 Hold down Shift+Alt / Shift+Option and click the layer mask thumbnail to hide the mask overlay; then, hide the Background layer.

10 As you can see, the Rough Flat Bristle brush is partly transparent. In the image window, make another short stroke or two over each girl's face.

▶ **Tip:** When you wish to make a hard-edged mask, you can use any of the mechanical selection tools (either the Rectangular or Elliptical Marquee tool, or the Polygonal Lasso tool) rather than a brush or an eraser.

That's all there is to it! By using a layer mask in this way, you've effectively created your own ragged-edged cookie-cutter shape.

11 Choose File > Save As. Save the file to your work folder in Photoshop format with layers enabled. Make sure the file will be included in the Organizer without being saved in a Version Set. Name the new file **12_03_BrushMask**, and then click Save. Close the file.

Congratulations, you've finished this lesson on advanced editing in Photoshop Elements. You discovered how to take advantage of the Camera Raw plug-in and learned to correct images using the Histogram panel as both a diagnostic tool and a dynamic feedback reference. You also found out how to create custom effects using the Filter Gallery, had a little fun with the Cookie Cutter tool, and gained more experience with layer masks. Take a minute or two now to brush up on your new skills by reading through the lesson review on the facing page.

Learning more

You've picked up some great tricks and techniques—but this book is just a start. You can learn even more by using the Photoshop Elements Help system, which is integrated with the application. Don't forget to look for tutorials, tips, and expert advice in the Inspiration Browser and on the Adobe website, www.adobe.com.

Review questions

1 What is a camera raw image, and what are some of its advantages?

2 What are the different methods for adjusting the white balance in the Camera Raw window?

3 How do you use the Levels controls to correct highlights and shadows?

4 What is the Cookie Cutter tool used for?

Review answers

1 A raw file is one that is unprocessed by a digital camera, though not all cameras create raw files. One of the advantages of raw images is the flexibility of having detailed control over settings that are usually pre-applied by the camera. Image quality is another plus—because raw formats have 12 bits of available data, it's possible to extract shadow and highlight detail that would have been lost in an 8 bits/channel JPEG or TIFF file. Finally, raw files provide an archival image format, much like a digital negative: you can reprocess the file whenever you want to produce different results, while your original image data remains unchanged.

2 In the Camera Raw window you can set the white balance in an image automatically by using the White Balance eyedropper. Clicking on a neutral color with the White Balance eyedropper automatically adjusts the Temperature and Tint sliders. Alternatively, you can choose a preset from the White Balance menu. The options include corrections based on a range of common lighting conditions. It's also possible to correct the white balance manually with the Temperature and Tint sliders.

3 In the Levels dialog box, you can adjust the shadows and highlights in your image by using either the slider controls below the Levels histogram, or the Set Black Point and Set White Point eyedroppers. You can hold down the Alt / Option key as you drag a slider to see a clipping preview, which gives you visual feedback on the location of the darkest and lightest areas of your image. With the Set Black Point and Set White Point eyedroppers you can click directly in the image to define the white and black points, or double-click the eyedroppers to call up the color picker where you can define the values precisely.

4 The Cookie Cutter tool is used to crop an image into a variety of shapes. Use the default shapes set, or select a shape from an extensive library.

INDEX

A

Add Missing Person button, 65
Adjust Color Curves command, 264
adjust lighting, 269
adjustment layers, 255, 273
    applying to a limited area, 256
Adobe Photo Downloader
    options, 73
    Windows, 24
Adobe Photoshop Elements
    Installing, 2
Adobe Photoshop Services, 169
Adobe TV, 5
album online, sharing, 168
albums, 90
    creating, 90
    icon, 168
Artwork library, 115
ASF, 78
auto adjustments, 194
Auto-Analysis, 68
Auto Color, 187, 207, 249
Auto Contrast, 187, 207, 249
auto-fixing, 187, 207, 249
Auto Levels, 187, 207, 249
automatically fixing red eyes, 40
Automatically Suggest Photo Stacks
    dialog box, 88
automatic correction, 196, 208
Auto Smart Fix, 85
AVI, 78

B

background
    adding, 141

backing up and synchronizing, 169
    checking status, 173
    multiple computers, 174
    setting options, 172
Back To Previous View button, 49, 50,
    52, 91
balance, 256
Basic tab, 389
batch processing, 187, 206
Before & After view, 195, 223
black and white
    converting to, 232
Black And White - High Contrast tool,
    216
Blacks adjustment, 397
blemishes, removing, 284, 309
blending modes, 254, 266
    Multiply, 267
    Normal, 286
    Overlay, 267
    Screen, 254
Blue Sky tool, 216
Blur tool, 289, 307
border
    quick, 317
brightness, 269, 397, 400
Brightness/Contrast dialog box, 255, 269
brush size, 228

C

calendar, 12, 49
calibration, 243
camera, importing from
    Windows, 24
camera raw. *See* raw images

canvas
    working with, 313
Canvas Size dialog box, 315, 316
capturing frames from video, 78
card reader, 24, 43, 73
cast (color), removing, 396
catalog
    about, 3
    creating, 9, 34, 110
    reconnecting missing files, 113
categories
    applying and editing, 55
    converting, 58
    creating, 55
    hierarchy, 58
    sub-categories, 55
choosing files
    in the Organizer, 17
Clarity, 397
Clarity slider, 400
clipping, 397, 406
clipping layer, 375
Clone Stamp tool, 284, 296
color, 195, 196
Color Cast Eyedropper tool, 190, 191
color cast, removing, 190, 396
color correction, 208
color management, 242
    Allow Me To Choose setting, 243
    Always Optimize For Computer Screens
        setting, 243
    Always Optimize For Printing setting,
        243
    No Color Management setting, 242
    setting up, 242
Color Replacement tool, 236
Color Settings dialog box, 242
combining multiple images, 371
Commit button, 122, 124, 125, 131, 196
Community Help, 4
comparing, 214
Complete view, 99
composites, 360
contact sheets, 151
Content palette, 116
contrast, 196, 269, 397, 400

Convert To Black And White
    dialog box, 232
Cookie Cutter tool, 415
    shape options, 416
Copy, 261
copying
    Classroom in a Book files, 2
    Lessons files from the CD, 2
correcting images, 257
Create Category dialog box, 61
Create panel, 12
Create Warped Text button, 334, 340
cropping, 357
Crop To Fit option, 155
Crop tool, 278, 279, 281, 359

D

Daily Note, 51
Darken Highlights slider, 268
Date View button, 49
defringing, 381
digital video, 8, 30, 78
Display button, 15
distortions, 331
Divide Scanned Photos, 83
DNG, 401
drag-and-drop, 36
drop shadows, 344
Dust & Scratches, 303, 309

E

Edit Keyword Tag dialog box, 57, 58
Edit Keyword Tag Icon dialog box, 57, 58
Editor, 8, 30, 69, 78, 161, 175
    workspace, 18
effects
    applying, 144, 325
Elliptical Marquee tool, 245
e-mail, 22
    stacks, 87
E-mail Attachments button, 22
embossing effect, 325
enhance, 270
Enhance menu, 203

exporting, 174

exposure, 397, 398

    fixing problems, 246

F

faded image, fixing, 266

fading, 268

Fill Light, 397

Fill Page With First Photo option, 154

Film Strip, 15

Filter Gallery, 410

filters, 303

    Unsharp Mask, 409

find bar, 95

finding files, 58, 59

    by visual similarity, 102

    using a text search, 100

    using details and metadata, 98

Find this photo in the Photo Browser
    button, 50

Fit Screen button, 260

fixing color, 208

Fix tab, 12

flatten, 175

flaws, 303

floating document windows
    enabling, 19

Folder Location View, 96

Folders to Watch list, 46

fonts, 330

Frankenface, 366

Full Edit workspace, 18

Full Sceen View, 17

    editing in, 182

    organizing images in, 60

G

general fixes, 195

getting photos, 10

Grab Frame button, 78

gradient clipping path, 377

gradient layer, 377

Gradient tool, 378

graphics
    adding, 144

gray level, 270

guided activities, 192

Guided Edit
    creative projects, 192

    using for editing, 189

Guided Edit workspace, 18

H

Hand tool, 214, 393

Hardness, 298

Healing Brush tool, 284, 286, 288, 298

Heart Card, 415

Help
    navigating, 28

    searching, 28

    using, 28

Hidden tag, 54

Hide Hidden Files command, 101

hiding files, 100

highlights, 404

Histogram panel, 404

histograms, about, 402

Horizontal Type tool, 317

Hot-linked tips, 29

I

Image Size, 408

importing files
    advanced options, 73

    by searching, 42

    frames from video, 78

    from a camera or card reader, 24, 43

    from a scanner, 82, 83

    from files and folders, 10, 38

    from PDF document, 80

    from specific locations, 38

    using drag and drop, 35

    using watched folder, 45

importing images
    from the Mac OS Finder, 37

individual prints, 157

Input Levels box, 270

Inspiration Browser, 26, 161
intensity, 262
International Color Consortium (ICC), 242
Internet Explorer, 175
Items pane, 165

J

JPEG, 175

K

Keyword Tag Cloud, 62
Keyword Tag Hierarchy button, 63
keyword tags
    about, 14
    converting, 58
    creating and applying, 56
    finding faces, 64
    importing, 38
    organizing, 14
    searching by, 62
    working with, 52

L

layer blending modes
    working with, 328
layers
    arranging, 375
    clipping mask, 375
    copying, 254
    flattening, 175
    hiding and revealing, 339
    locking, 235
    masking, 356
    merging, 306
    working with, 143
Layers panel, 260, 319
Layers Panel Options, 260
Layers Panel Options dialog box, 260
layer styles, 144, 325, 331, 332
layout options
    photomerge panorama, 352
levels, 404
    adjusting, 269

Levels dialog box, 256, 404
Lighten Shadows slider, 268
lighting, 195, 255
    adjust using Guided Edit, 191
    auto fix, 196
Lighting panel, 268
locking layers, 235

M

Mac OS Finder
    dragging files from, 37
Magic Wand tool, 244, 382, 383
Map View, 103
Mark As Hidden command, 101
mask, 300
media, 6
Media Browser, 12, 14
merged images, 359, 366
merging layers, 306
metadata, 95
    finding files using, 98
    support for audio and video files, 98
Midtone Contrast slider, 268
midtones, 405
Minimize button, 36, 113
missing file icon, 113
MLV, 78
monitor calibration, 243
Move tool, 318, 376
MPEG, 78
MPG, 78
multiple images, combining, 375
Multitouch support, 20

N

Navigator panel, 288, 289, 300
neutral tones, 405
new document
    creating, 323
New Layer button, 285
noise, 303

O

online album
    adding photos, 166
    creating, 165
    icon, 167, 168, 172
online sharing service, 169
opacity, 267
Opacity slider, 267
OpenType fonts, 330
operators, 100
ordering prints, 170
Organizer, 8–10, 30–31
    editing photos in, 180
    viewing thumbnails, 46
    workspaces, 12
Organize tab, 12
organizing images, 8, 30, 84
Out Of Bounds
    guided edit, 192
overexposed images, 397
    correcting, 265
overlay, 267

P

Panel bin, 21
panels
    floating, 21
    working with, 21–22
panorama, 350
    layout options, 352
paragraph alignment options, 317, 324
paragraph type, 340
paste, 261
Pattern Stamp tool, 338
People Recognition
    about, 64
perspective
    changing, 358
photo books, 128
    adding graphics, 134
    adding text, 135
    changing image order, 128
photo collages, 138
    adding backgrounds, 141

photo downloader
    Advanced dialog box, 44, 74
    Standard dialog box, 43
Photographic Effects
    guided edits, 192
Photo Mail button, 163
Photomerge Exposure tool, 371
    merging exposures automatically, 372
    merging exposures manually, 374
Photomerge Faces tool, 366
Photomerge Group Shot tool, 360
Photomerge Panorama tool, 357, 361
Photomerge Scene Cleaner tool, 367
Photoshop.com
    creating account, 26, 161
Photoshop Express, 171
Photoshop (PSD) format, 265
picture frame, 312
Picture Package, 154
pixel-based graphics, 322
point type, 340
posterization, 403
PostScript, 330
prerequisites, 1
previewing, 270
printing, 151
Print Photos dialog box, 154
Print Preview, 158
    fine-tuning composition before printing, 157
Process Multiple Files dialog box, 187, 206, 248
profile, 242
Properties - Keyword Tags panel, 56, 61
Properties - Metadata panel, 99

Q

Quick Edit mode, 18, 195
Quick Edit panel, 17, 182
Quick Fix
    adjustment previews, 196
    using for editing, 194
Quick Organize panel, 17, 60
Quick Selection tool, 230, 257

R

ratings, assigning, 53
raw images
    about, 390
    adjusting, 388
    benefits, 390
    white balance settings, 395
    workflow overview, 391
Recompose tool, 280–283
    Mark For Protection brush, 281
    Mark For Removal brush, 282
Recovery, 397
Rectangular Marquee tool, 245
red eye, 40, 223, 224
    automatic fix, 40
Red Eye Removal tool, 216, 224, 244
reducing file size, 23
renaming files, 188, 207, 249
Replace Color dialog box, 236
replacing color, 236
resetting tools, 296
resizing an image, 408
resolution, 157
RGB, 243
Rotate Image tool, 358
rotating, 44

S

sampled source, 286
saturation, 397
Save For Web, 175
Scan dialog box, 83
Scene Cleaner tool, 367
Screen, 254
Search button, 42
Select A Frame menu, 155
Select Image tool, 358
Selection Brush tool, 228, 257, 298
selections
    creating, 257
    inverse, 231
    loading, 226
    making, 226
    saving, 230
Select Printer menu, 154

semi-transparent, 300
Set White Point Eyedropper tool, 405
shadow and highlight, 195, 268, 406
shadows, 404
Shadows/Highlights dialog box, 268
Shapes menu, 415
Share panel, 12, 22
sharing photos in e-mail, 22
sharing service, 169
sharpening, 187, 196, 207, 249, 409
Shutterfly, 159
Side By Side View, 15, 16
size and quality, 23
skin tones, 211, 215
slide shows, 52, 170
smart albums, 93
Smart Brush pins, 201
Smart Brush tool, 197, 304
smart fix, 195, 216
smart paint adjustments, 198, 201, 305
Smart Tags, 68
Spot Healing Brush tool, 284, 289
spots, removing, 285
stacks
    combining, 87
    creating, 86
    e-mailing, 87
star rating, 54
Start People Recognition button, 66
Straighten tool, 277

T

Task Pane, 12
Temperature setting, 395–396
text
    adding to multiple images, 326
    centering, 317, 324
    color, 317
    correcting, 320
    creating type mask, 341
    drop shadows, 344
    formatting, 317
    overlaying on images, 322
    paragraph type, 340
    placing on images, 312

point type, 340
scaling or reshaping, 324
warping, 334
text layer, 319
Text Search box, Organizer, 100, 313, 326, 388
Threshold, 409
thumbnails, 38
timeline, 95
tint, 395–396
Tint controls, 396
Tint slider, 396
tone controls, 397
touch up tools, 216
transparent, 377
TrueType fonts, 330
Type 1 PostScript fonts, 330
typefaces, 330
Type tool, 332

U

underexposed images, 397
brightening, 250
correcting with blending modes, 261
Unsharp Mask, 408
untagged, 95
Using Photo Mail, 163

V

Vanishing Point tool, 358
vector graphics, 322
Version sets, 84
Vibrance, 397
video, acquiring frames, 78
visibility, 101

W

warping text, 334
Warp Text dialog box, 334, 340
watched folders, 45
Web browsers, 175
Welcome screen, 34, 110
white balance, 397

adjusting, 392
settings, 395
Whiten Teeth tool, 216
Windows Explorer
dragging files from, 36
WMV, 78
work files, 61
workspaces
Editor, 18
Organizer, 12
wrinkles and spots removal, 285

Z

Zoom All Windows, 271
Zoom tool, 271, 300

Production Notes

The *Adobe Photoshop Elements 9 Classroom in a Book* was created electronically using Adobe InDesign CS3. Art was produced using Adobe InDesign, Adobe Illustrator, and Adobe Photoshop.

References to company names in the lessons are for demonstration purposes only and are not intended to refer to any actual organization or person.

Team credits

The following individuals contributed to the development of this edition of the *Adobe Photoshop Elements 9 Classroom in a Book*:

Project coordinators, technical writers: John Evans & Katrin Straub

Production: Manneken Pis Productions (www.manneken.be)

Copyediting & Proofreading: John Evans & Katrin Straub

Designer: Katrin Straub

Special thanks to Torsten Buck, Ross Evans, Connie Jeung-Mills, Petra Laux, Rémy Level, Berenice Seitz and Philipp Meyer, David Van Ness, and Christine Yarrow.

Typefaces used

Adobe Myriad Pro and Adobe Warnock Pro are used throughout the lessons. For more information about OpenType and Adobe fonts, visit www.adobe.com/type/opentype/.

Photo Credits

Photographic images and illustrations supplied by Torsten Buck, Han Buck, John Evans, Yanin Jotisuta, Rémy Level, Katrin Straub, Meena Wongpornpakdee, and Adobe Systems Incorporated. Photos are for use only with the lessons in the book.

Contributors

John Evans has worked in computer graphics and design for more than 20 years, initially as a graphic designer, and then since 1993 as a multimedia author, software interface designer, and technical writer. His multimedia and digital illustration work associated with Japanese type attracted an award from Apple Computer Australia. His other projects range from music education software for children to interface design for innovative Japanese font design software. As a technical writer his work includes software design specifications, user manuals, and copy editing for *Adobe Photoshop Elements 7 Classroom in a Book*, *Adobe Photoshop Lightroom 2 Classroom in a Book*, and *Adobe Creative Suite 4 Classroom in a Book*. More recently he has authored *Adobe Photoshop Elements 8 Classroom in a Book* and *Adobe Photoshop Lightroom 3 Classroom in a Book*.

Katrin Straub is an artist, a graphic designer, and author. Her award-winning print, painting, and multimedia work has been exhibited worldwide. With more than 15 years experience in design, Katrin has worked as Design Director for companies such as Landor Associates and Fontworks in the United States, Hong Kong, and Japan. Her work includes packaging, promotional campaigns, multimedia, website design, and internationally recognized corporate and retail identities. She holds degrees from the FH Augsburg, ISIA Urbino, and The New School University in New York. Katrin has authored many books, from the *Adobe Creative Suite Idea Kit* to Classroom in a Book titles for Adobe Photoshop Lightroom 2, Adobe Creative Suite 4, Adobe Soundbooth, and several versions of *Adobe Photoshop Elements Classroom in a Book* and *Adobe Premiere Elements Classroom in a Book*.

Tao Buck and her sisters have been volunteering as photomodels for the last five editions of the Photoshop Elements Classroom in a Book. When she is not riding her unicycle, Tao wants to become a top model or at least as famous as Audrey Hepburn.

Zoë Buck loves to juggle with numbers, play chess, do gymnastics, and at this very moment is considering becoming a biologist.

Han Buck would like to become a rock singer, an architect, a painter (actually, she is one already), or else "work from home and do nothing like her parents."

Mia Buck strives to become a ballerina and great pianist (although she does not believe in practicing).

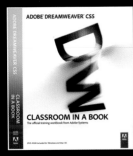

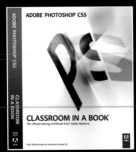

Sound Off!

Visit us at **www.osborne.com/bookregistration** and let us know what you thought of this book. While you're online you'll have the opportunity to register for newsletters and special offers from McGraw-Hill/Osborne.

We want to hear from you!

Sneak Peek

Visit us today at **www.betabooks.com** and see what's coming from McGraw-Hill/Osborne tomorrow!

Based on the successful software paradigm, Bet@Books™ allows computing professionals to view partial and sometimes complete text versions of selected titles online. Bet@Books™ viewing is free, invites comments and feedback, and allows you to "test drive" books in progress on the subjects that interest you the most.

Is your Web site keeping you awake all night?

We can help.

Doing business on the Internet can give you sleepless nights. That's why you need software that works seamlessly with your organization, and an implementation partner trained and equipped to handle change.

At Melonfire, we create customized business applications designed to let you work faster and more efficiently. Applications secure and robust enough to handle the demands of your business, yet flexible enough to quickly adapt to new needs and technologies. So you can go to bed every night without worrying about tomorrow. Sweet dreams.